Mastering Joomla! 1.5 Extension and Framework Development

The Professional's Guide to Programming Joomla!

James Kennard

BIRMINGHAM - MUMBAI

Mastering Joomla! 1.5 Extension and Framework Development

The Professional's Guide to Programming Joomla!

First published: November 2007

Production Reference: 2131107

Published by Packt Publishing Ltd.
32 Lincoln Road
Olton
Birmingham, B27 6PA, UK.

ISBN 978-1-847192-82-0

www.packtpub.com

Cover Image by Vinayak Chittar (vinayak.chittar@gmail.com)

Credits

Author

James Kennard

Reviewers

Joseph L. LeBlanc

Riccardo Tacconi

Toby Patterson

Senior Acquisition Editor

Douglas Paterson

Development Editor

Rashmi Phadnis

Technical Editors

Adil Rizwan Ahmed

Ved Prakash Jha

Editorial Manager

Dipali Chittar

Project Manager

Abhijeet Deobhakta

Indexer

Hemangini Bari

Proofreader

Chris Smith

Production Coordinator

Manjiri Nadkarni

Cover Designer

Shantanu Zagade

About the Author

James Kennard is a computer programmer with a particular interest in web-based services. His interests in Joomla! started as a result of an internal assignment at work when he was tasked with identifying suitable web systems to host a number of intranet and Internet applications.

James currently maintains one open-source Joomla! component, which has been translated into over fifteen languages. Examples of his work can be found on his personal website: www.webamoeba.co.uk.

About the Reviewers

Joseph L. LeBlanc started with computers at a very young age. His independent education gave him the flexibility to experiment and learn computer science. Joseph holds a bachelor's degree in Management Information Systems from the Oral Roberts University.

Joseph is currently a freelance Joomla! extension developer. He released a popular component tutorial in May 2004, then later authored the book *Learning Joomla! 1.5 Extension Development: Creating Modules, Components, and Plugins with PHP*. Work samples and open-source extensions are available at www.jlleblanc.com. In addition to freelancing, he is a board member of the DC PHP Conference. He has also worked as a programmer for a web communications firm in Washington, DC.

Riccardo Tacconi works for an Italian company as a system administrator and web developer using PHP, MySQL, and Oracle. He is an MCP and studies IT part-time at the British Open University. His main interests are web development, Windows and Linux administration, Robotics, and Java software development (JMF, motion detection, CV, and distributed systems).

He loves Linux and he is a proud member of the local Linux User Group: GROLUG. He tries to innovate ways to substitute Windows-based technologies with Linux and open-source alternatives.

Toby Patterson is a private consultant and member of the Joomla! Development Workgroup. His company, Green Mountain Information Technology and Consulting, specializes in integrating data into websites using their Joomla! extensions, Database Query and Logos Query Manager. Recently Toby worked in Romania and Thailand helping non-profit organizations in creating web applications. He currently lives in Bangkok, Thailand.

Table of Contents

Preface	**1**
Chapter 1: Introduction to Joomla!	**7**
Overview	7
History	8
Requirements	9
Extension Types and Their Uses	9
Components	10
Modules	10
Plugins	10
Languages	11
Templates	11
Tools	11
Extension Manager	12
JED and JoomlaCode.org	12
Development Tools	13
J!Code	14
J!Dump	14
Summary	16
Chapter 2: Getting Started	**17**
The Application and Document	17
Request to Response	18
The Process	18
URI Structure	22
Directory Structure	24
Libraries	26
A Quick Lesson in Classes	27
Inheriting from JObject	28

Working with the Request	**29**
The Factory	**30**
The Session	**31**
Predefined Constants	**32**
Multilingual Support	**34**
UTF-8 String Handling	34
Coding Standards	**36**
phpDocumentor	37
Summary	**39**
Chapter 3: The Database	**41**
The Core Database	**41**
Extending the Database	**42**
Table Prefix	42
Schema Conventions	42
Common Fields	42
Schema Example	44
Dealing with Multilingual Requirements	45
Querying the Database	**46**
Writing Queries	46
Getting Results	47
loadResult( ) : string	48
loadResultArray(numinarray : int=0) : array	48
loadAssoc( ) : array	48
loadAssocList(key : string='') : array	49
loadObject( ) : stdClass	49
loadObjectList(key : string='') : array	50
loadRow( ) : array	50
loadRowList(key : int) : array	51
Using ADOdb	51
JTable	**52**
CRUD	54
Manipulating Common Fields	58
Publishing	59
Hits	59
Checking Out	59
Ordering	60
Parameter Fields	61
Date Fields	62
Summary	**63**
Chapter 4: Component Design	**65**
Setting up a Sandbox	**65**
The Structure	**67**

The MVC	**68**
Building a Model	70
Building a View	75
Building a Controller	78
Building an MVC Component	82
Rendering Other Document Types	**87**
Feed	87
PDF	90
Raw	91
Dealing with Component Configuration	**93**
Elements and Parameters	**95**
Extending JElement	96
Using Custom JElement Classes	98
Help Files	**99**
Routing	**100**
Packaging	**102**
XML Manifest File	103
SQL Install and Uninstall Files and Queries	110
Install and Uninstall Files	111
Summary	**113**
Chapter 5: Module Design	**115**
Setting Up a Sandbox	**115**
First Steps	**116**
Standalone Modules	117
Modules and Components Working Together	118
Frontend and Backend Module Display Positions	119
Module Settings (Parameters)	**120**
Helpers	**121**
Layouts (Templates)	**124**
Media	126
Translating	**126**
Packaging	**127**
XML Manifest File	127
Summary	**131**
Chapter 6: Plugin Design	**133**
Setting Up a Sandbox	**134**
Events	**136**
Listeners	**138**
Registering Listeners	138
Handling Events	138

Plugin Groups	**141**
Authentication	142
Content	144
Editors	146
Editors-xtd	148
Search	151
System	152
User	152
XML-RPC	155
Loading Plugins	**155**
Using Plugins as Libraries (in Lieu of Library Extensions)	**156**
Translating Plugins	**159**
Dealing with Plugin Settings (Parameters)	**160**
Packaging	**161**
XML Manifest File	162
File Naming Conflicts	165
Summary	**165**
Chapter 7: Extension Design	**167**
Supporting Classes	**167**
Helpers	**168**
Using and Building getInstance() Methods	**169**
Using the Registry	**174**
Saving and Loading Registry Values	175
The User	**177**
User Parameters	178
The Session	**184**
The Browser	**185**
Assets	**189**
Summary	**190**
Chapter 8: Rendering Output	**193**
The joomla.html Library	**193**
Behavior	196
Email	200
Grid	200
Image	203
List	204
Menu	208
Select	209
Building Component HTML Layouts (Templates)	**212**
Iterative Templates	213

Component Backend	**214**
Admin Form	215
Toolbar	216
Sub-Menu	222
Itemized Data	**224**
Pagination	224
Ordering	228
Filtering and Searching	231
Summary	**241**
Chapter 9: Customizing the Page	**243**
Application Message Queue	**243**
Redirects	**245**
Component XML Metadata Files and Menu Parameters	248
Using Menu Item Parameters	**257**
Modifying the Document	**258**
Page Title	259
Pathway/Breadcrumb	259
JavaScript	261
CSS	262
Metadata	263
Custom Header Tags	263
Translating	**264**
Translating Text	264
Defining Translations	265
Debugging Translations	267
Using JavaScript Effects	**268**
JPane	268
Tooltips	269
Fx.Slide	271
Summary	**275**
Chapter 10: APIs and Web Services	**277**
XML	**277**
Parsing	278
Editing	282
Saving	283
AJAX	**284**
Response	284
Request	286
LDAP	**290**
Email	**294**

File Transfer Protocol	**297**
Web Services	**299**
Building a Web Service (XML-RPC Plugin)	**301**
Summary	**309**
Chapter 11: Error Handling and Security	**311**
Errors, Warnings, and Notices	**312**
Return Values	313
Customizing Error Handling	314
Dealing with CGI Request Data	**315**
Preprocessing CGI Data	315
Escaping and Encoding Data	317
Escaping and Quoting Database Data	318
Encode XHTML Data	319
Regular Expressions	320
Patterns	320
Matching	322
Replacing	323
Access Control	**323**
Menu Item Access Control	325
Extension Access Control	325
Attacks	**327**
How to Avoid Common Attacks	328
Using the Session Token	328
Code Injection	329
XSS (Cross Site Scripting)	331
File System Snooping	332
Dealing with Attacks	332
Log Out and Block	333
Attack Logging	335
Notify the Site Administrator	336
Summary	**337**
Chapter 12: Utilities and Useful Classes	**339**
Dates	**340**
File System	**345**
Paths	345
Folders	347
Files	351
Archives	354
Arrays	**355**
Trees	**359**
Log Files	**361**
Summary	**364**

Appendix   **365**

Classes   **365**

JObject   366
  Properties   366
  Constructors   366
  Methods   367
JUser   368
  Properties   368
  Constructors   369
  Methods   369
JModel   372
  Properties   372
  Constructors   372
  Methods   372
JView   374
  Properties   375
  Constructors   375
  Methods   375
JController   378
  Properties   379
  Constructors   379
  Methods   379
JTable   383
  Properties   383
  Constructors   383
  Methods   384
JError   388
  Methods   388
JDocument   393
  Properties   393
  Constructors   393
  Methods   394
JApplication   398
  Properties   398
  Constructors   399
  Methods   399
JURI   407
  Properties   407
  Constructors   407
  Methods   407
JLanguage   411
  Properties   411
  Constructors   411
  Methods   412
JLanguageHelper   416
  Methods   416

JText	417
Methods	417
JElement	417
Properties	418
Constructors	418
Methods	418
JParameter	419
Properties	419
Constructors	419
Methods	420
JCache	422
Properties	422
Constructors	423
Methods	423
JMail	424
Constructors	425
Methods	425
JMailHelper	427
Methods	427
JFactory	428
Methods	428
JRegistry	431
Properties	431
Constructors	431
Methods	431
JSession	434
Properties	434
Constructors	434
Methods	435
JRoute	438
Methods	438
JMenu	438
Properties	438
Constructors	439
Methods	439
JPathway	441
Properties	441
Methods	441
JDatabase	442
Properties	442
Constructors	443
Methods	443
Parameters (Core JElements)	**452**
Configuration	**455**
Index	**459**

Preface

This book will guide you through the complexities of implementing components, modules, and plugins in Joomla! 1.5. It provides useful reference material that explains many of the advanced design features and classes available in Joomla! 1.5.

Joomla! is one of the world's top open-source content management systems. The main sources of the PHP MySQL application's success are its comprehensive extension libraries, which extend Joomla! far beyond content management, and its very active forums where one can easily tap into the knowledge of other Joomla! users, administrators, and developers.

The architecture of the latest version of Joomla! differs in many ways from previous versions. Resultantly backward-compatibility with some extensions has been broken; the race is on for developers to update their skills in order to rectify the problems and start building new extensions. Perhaps the most important of the changes is the reorganization and classification of files and classes. This change encourages but does not force developers to use the Joomla! libraries consistently between extensions.

What This Book Covers

Chapter 1 deals with the history of Joomla! and gives an overview of the technology in general.

Chapter 2 covers the process from request to response and also talks about directory and URI structure along with a brief description of libraries. It also introduces a number of common classes, variables, and constants that are used frequently when creating Joomla! extensions.

Chapter 3 deals with the database. It talks about extending the database, conventions for the database schema, and common fields. Then the focus moves on to storing data common types of data in standard fields and dealing with multilingual requirements. We then cover querying the database and getting results.

Next, the chapter explores how to manipulate common field types. The chapter concludes with a brief description of the JTable. The JTable is used to display and edit regular two-dimensional tables of cells. The JTable has many facilities that make it possible to customize its rendering and editing but provides defaults for these features so that simple tables can be set up easily.

Chapter 4 is about designing components. It starts with the structure and a basic design of a component using the MVC design pattern. Then we learn configuring the component and its various elements and parameters. The chapter finishes by discussing component packaging and the various install and uninstall files.

Chapter 5 covers designing modules. It explains standalone modules, module settings, frontend and backend modules, and modules and components working together. Then we talk about using templates and packaging the modules.

Chapter 6 deals with designing plugins. It initially deals with listeners/observers and then the various plugin groups like authentication, content editors, search, and others. Then comes loading, translating, and using plugins as libraries. Finally it deals with, plugin settings and how to package plugins.

Chapter 7 is all about designing extensions. Here, we start with helper classes then cover building and using `getInstance()` methods. Then we cover the registry along with saving and loading registry values. Towards the end of the chapter, we explain the User, Session, Browser and the assets.

Chapter 8 explains ways to render output and how to maintain consistency throughout. It starts with the `joomla.html` library and then continues to describe how to build component HTML layouts. Then it discusses how to output the backend of a component. The chapter ends with the details of itemized data and pagination.

Chapter 9 deals with customizing the page. We cover things like modifying the document and translating, along with a brief explanation of using JavaScript effects from the mootools library, which is included in Joomla!.

Chapter 10 explores some of the Joomla! APIs, specifically in relation to web services. We also discuss some of the more common web services and take a more in-depth look at the Yahoo! Search API. The chapter finishes by describing how we can create our own web services using plugins.

Chapter 11 provides an introduction to handling and throwing errors, warnings, and notices. Further, it talks about building secure Joomla! extensions. It also describes a number of common mistakes made when coding with Joomla! and explains how to avoid them.

Chapter 12 explains various utilities and useful classes like dates, arrays, tree structures, and others.

The *Appendix* details the more common Joomla! classes. It also provides information on how to handle the ever-useful JParameter object. The appendix ends with a description of the Joomla! settings in relation to the registry/config.

What You Need for This Book

To use this book effectively you need access to a Joomla! 1.5 installation. In order to run Joomla! 1.5 you need the following software: PHP 4.3 or higher (4.4.3 or greater is recommended), MySQL 3.23 or higher and Apache 1.3 or higher or an equivalent webserver.

Conventions

In this book, you will find a number of styles of text that distinguish between different kinds of information. Here are some examples of these styles, and an explanation of their meaning.

There are two styles for code. Code words in text are shown as follows: "When we populate the $oldValue variable using the getValue() method we supply a second parameter."

A block of code will be set as follows:

```
$user =& JFactory::getUser();
if ($user->guest)
{
    // user is a guest (is not logged in)
}
```

New terms and **important words** are introduced in a bold-type font. Words that you see on the screen, in menus or dialog boxes for example, appear in our text like this: "In the **System** tab we must set **Debug Language** to **Yes**".

 Warnings or important notes appear in a box like this.

 Tips and tricks appear like this.

Reader Feedback

Feedback from our readers is always welcome. Let us know what you think about this book, what you liked or may have disliked. Reader feedback is important for us to develop titles that you really get the most out of.

To send us general feedback, simply drop an email to feedback@packtpub.com, making sure to mention the book title in the subject of your message.

If there is a book that you need and would like to see us publish, please send us a note in the **SUGGEST A TITLE** form on www.packtpub.com or email suggest@packtpub.com.

If there is a topic that you have expertise in and you are interested in either writing or contributing to a book, see our author guide on www.packtpub.com/authors.

Customer Support

Now that you are the proud owner of a Packt book, we have a number of things to help you to get the most from your purchase.

Downloading the Example Code for the Book

Visit http://www.packtpub.com/support, and select this book from the list of titles to download any example code or extra resources for this book. The files available for download will then be displayed.

 The downloadable files contain instructions on how to use them.

Errata

Although we have taken every care to ensure the accuracy of our contents, mistakes do happen. If you find a mistake in one of our books—maybe a mistake in text or code—we would be grateful if you would report this to us. By doing this you can save other readers from frustration, and help to improve subsequent versions of this book. If you find any errata, report them by visiting http://www.packtpub.com/support, selecting your book, clicking on the **Submit Errata** link, and entering the details of your errata. Once your errata are verified, your submission will be accepted and the errata added to the list of existing errata. The existing errata can be viewed by selecting your title from http://www.packtpub.com/support.

Questions

You can contact us at questions@packtpub.com if you are having a problem with some aspect of the book, and we will do our best to address it.

1
Introduction to Joomla!

This book is intended for use as a reference book for existing Joomla! developers. It focuses on the Joomla! framework and how to utilize it to enhance and standardize extensions.

Overview

Joomla! is a modular and extensible PHP MySQL CMS (Content Management System). Joomla! is an open-source project, which is released under version 2 of the GPL license. Joomla! has fast become one of the most popular open-source CMS, as is proved by its numerous awards and massive online community.

One of the things that has made Joomla! so popular is the large number of freely and commercially available extensions, which enable users to do far more than simply manage content. This list details some common functions that extensions perform:

- Banner Ads & Affiliates
- Calendars
- Communication (Chat Rooms, Forums, Guest Books, Mailing Lists, Newsletters)
- Content & News (Blogs, eCards, News)
- Documentation (Downloads, FAQs, Wikis)
- eCommerce (Auctions, Shopping Carts)
- Forms
- Gallery & Multimedia
- Intranet & Groupware
- Search & Indexing

History

Rice Studios, formerly Miro, created a closed-source CMS called 'Mambo' in the year 2000. One year later, Mambo was re-licensed under two separate licenses, one of which was open source. The open-source version became known as 'Mambo Site Server'.

In 2002 Mambo Site Server was re-branded 'Mambo Open Source' (Also referred to as MamboOS or MOS) in an attempt to differentiate the commercial and open-source flavors of Mambo. All rights to Mambo Open Source were officially released into the open-source community in 2003.

Mambo Open Source was extremely successful and won a large number of prestigious open-source awards.

In 2005 the commercial version of Mambo was re-branded as 'Jango'. Rice Studios, at that time still Miro, also chose to form the Mambo Foundation, a non-profit organization. The intention was to create a body that would help protect the principles of Mambo and provide a more structured working methodology.

The creation of the Mambo Foundation created a rift in the Mambo Open Source community. The creation of the Mambo Foundation was seen by many as an attempt by Rice Studios to gain control of the Mambo Open Source project.

Not long after the Mambo Foundation was created, a group, consisting mainly of the Mambo Open Source core developers, publicly announced that they intended to abandon Mambo Open Source. The group formed a non-profit organization called 'Open Source Matters'.

Open Source Matters created the Joomla! project, a guaranteed 100% open-source GPL project. The first release of Joomla! (Joomla! 1.0) was very similar to the then current release of Mambo, the majority of extensions at the time being compatible with both.

Restraints within Joomla! 1.0 led to a complete re-think of how Joomla! should be constructed. After a long development period, and two beta releases, Joomla! 1.5 was released in mid 2007.

Joomla! 1.5 is extensively different to Joomla! 1.0 and Mambo. Joomla! 1.5 introduces many new classes and implements a comprehensive framework. These changes have lead to reduced compatibility between Joomla! and Mambo.

The most notable change, for most third-party extension developers, is the introduction of the **MVC (Model View Controller)** design pattern in components. These changes now mean that all third-party developers tend to develop for Joomla! or Mambo, but not both.

Requirements

To use Joomla! and develop new extensions there are a number of basic requirements. This list details the minimum requirements:

- MySQL 3.23 available at `http://www.mysql.com`
- PHP 4.3 available at `http://www.php.net`
- A web server (if using Apache, minimum version is 1.13.19, which is available at `http://www.apache.org`)

 Precise version requirements may differ depending upon the exact version of Joomla! that is being used.

An easy way to quickly obtain and install all of these is to use **XAMPP** (X, Apache, MySQL, PHP, and Perl). This project packages all of the necessary pieces of software required to run Joomla! in one installation package. XAMPP is available for the Linux, Mac, Solaris, and Windows operating systems. To learn more about XAMPP please refer to `http://www.apachefriends.org/xampp.html`.

Another easy way to get started with Joomla! is to use **JSAS** (Joomla! Stand Alone Server). JSAS enables us to quickly set up multiple Joomla! installations on a Windows-based system. To learn more about JSAS please refer to `http://jsas.joomlasolutions.com`.

Joomla! itself is relatively easy to set up and, if necessary, an administration and installation guide can be found on the official Joomla! help site: `http://help.joomla.org`.

 Whenever we are developing extensions for Joomla! it is always good practice to test the extensions on multiple systems. Extensions should preferably be tested on Windows and Linux systems and tested using PHP 4 and PHP 5.

Extension Types and Their Uses

A Joomla! extension is anything that extends Joomla!'s functionality beyond the core. There are three main types of extension: **components**, **modules**, and **plugins**.

There are also **languages** and **templates**, but these are solely designed to modify page output, irrespective of the data being displayed. Although we will discuss the use of translation files and templates, we will not explicitly cover these two extension types in this book.

Tools, sometimes referred to as extensions, are essentially any type of extension that does not fall into the extension type categories just described. We will not be discussing how to create tools in this book.

Extensions are distributed in archive files, which include an XML manifest file that describes the extension. It is from the manifest file that Joomla! is able to determine what type the extension is, what it is called, what files are included, and what installation procedures are required.

Components

Components are undoubtedly the most fundamental Joomla! extensions. Whenever Joomla! is invoked a component is always called upon. Unlike other extensions, output created by a component is displayed in the main content area. Since components are the most fundamental extension, they are also generally the most complex.

One component of which all Joomla! administrators will be aware, is the content component. This component is used to display articles, content categories, and content sections.

In addition to outputting component data as part of an XHTML page, we can output component data as Feeds, PDF, and RAW documents.

Many components tend to include, and sometimes require, additional extensions in order for them to behave as expected. When we create our own components it is generally good practice to add 'hooks' in our code, which will enable other extensions to easily enhance our component beyond its base functionality.

Modules

Modules are used to display small pieces of content, usually to the left, right, top or bottom of a rendered page. There are a number of core modules with which we will be instantly familiar, for example the menu modules.

Plugins

There are various types of plugin, each of which can be used differently; however, most plugins are event driven. Plugins can attach listener functions and classes to specific events that Joomla! can throw using the global event dispatcher.

This table describes the different core plugin types:

Plugin Type	Description
authentication	Authenticate users during the login process
content	Process content items before they are displayed
editors	WYSIWYG editors that can be used to edit content
editors-xtd	Editor extensions (normally additional editor buttons)
search	Search data when using the search component
system	System event listeners
user	Process a user when actions are performed
xmlrpc	Create XML-RPC responses

In addition to the core plugin types we can define our own types. Many components use their own plugins for dealing with their own events.

Languages

Joomla! has multilingual support, which enables us to present Joomla! in many different languages. Language extensions include files that define translated strings for different parts of Joomla!.

We will discuss how to create language files and how to use translations in Chapter 2 and Chapter 9.

Templates

We use templates to modify the general appearance of Joomla!. There are two types of template extension: site templates and admin templates.

Most Joomla! sites use bespoke site templates to modify the appearance of the frontend (what the end-user sees). Admin templates modify the appearance of the backend (what the administrators see); these templates are less common.

There are many websites that offer free and commercial Joomla! templates, all of which are easy to locate using a search engine.

Tools

Tools, although referred to as extensions, are very different to components, modules, and plugins. The term 'tools' is used to describe any other type extension that can be used in conjunction with Joomla!.

Tools are not installed to Joomla!; they are generally standalone scripts or applications, which may, or may not, require their own form of installation.

A good example of a Joomla! tool is **JSAS** (Joomla! Stand Alone Server). JSAS provides an easy way to set up Joomla! installations on a Windows-based system. To learn more about JSAS please refer to `http://jsas.joomlasolutions.com`.

Extension Manager

Joomla! uses the extension manager to manage extensions that are currently installed and to install new extensions. When we install new extensions we use the same installation mechanism irrespective of the extension type. Joomla! automatically identifies the type of extension during the extension installation phase.

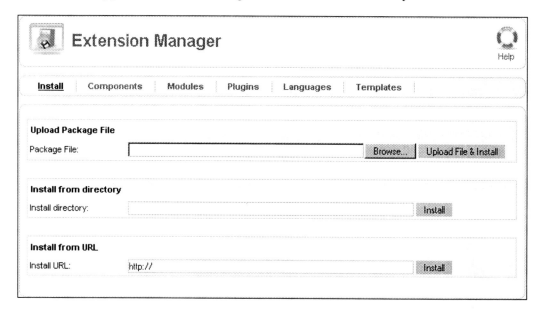

JED and JoomlaCode.org

JED (Joomla! Extension Directory) is an official part of Joomla! and is maintained by the 'Sites and Infrastructure' working group. The directory categorizes details of third-party Joomla! extensions on which users are allowed to post reviews and ratings.

Details of extensions that are listed in JED are submitted and maintained by the extension owner or developer. A listed extension can include a category, name, description, homepage, image, license, version, download link, demonstration link, developers name, email address, and Joomla! version compatibility information.

JED is the normal place where administrators look for extensions for their Joomla! installation. Before we create new extensions it is good practice to investigate any similar existing extensions; JED is the perfect place to begin. If we intend to make an extension publicly available JED is one of the best places to advertise an extension.

Another invaluable resource is the developers' forge: `http://www.joomlacode.org`. This official site is used to host open-source Joomla! projects. It provides third-party open-source Joomla! developers with free access to useful project development tools. This list details some of the tools with which JoomlaCode.org provides us:

- Document Manager
- Forums
- FRS (File Release System)
- Mail Lists
- News
- SVN (Subversion)
- Tasks
- Tracker
- Wiki

If we intend to create an open-source Joomla! project, it is advisable to consider using JoomlaCode.org to host the project, even if we do not intend to use all of the features it provides.

Development Tools

There are numerous development tools available, which we can use to develop Joomla! extensions. Most of these tools are not specific to Joomla!, but are PHP tools.

When we come to choose an editor for modifying PHP source files, it is important that we ensure that the editor supports UTF-8 character encoding.

There are two development tools built especially for Joomla!. They are J!Code and J!Dump.

J!Code

A recent addition to the Joomla! developers toolkit is J!Code. Based on EasyEclipse and PHPEclipse, J!Code is an **IDE** (Integrated Development Environment) designed specifically for developing Joomla! extensions.

J!Code is currently in the early stages of development and has yet to release a stable version.

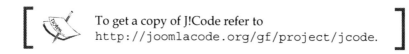

To get a copy of J!Code refer to
http://joomlacode.org/gf/project/jcode.

J!Dump

J!Dump allows us to output variables during development. The output is displayed in a configurable pop-up window and describes data types, and object properties and methods.

J!Dump comes as two separate extensions: a component, which we use to configure the functionality of J!Dump, and a system plugin, which defines functions that we use to 'dump' data to the J!Dump popup. Both extensions are required in order for J!Dump to function correctly.

To use J!Dump the plugin must be published. If it is not, when we attempt to use the J!Dump functions we will encounter fatal errors.

The most important function in J!Dump is the dump() function. We can pass a variable to this function and it will be displayed in the popup. This example demonstrates how we use the dump() function:

```
// create example object
$object = new JObject();
$object->set('name', 'example');

// dump object to popup
dump($object, 'Example Object');
```

Using this will create a popup, which looks like this:

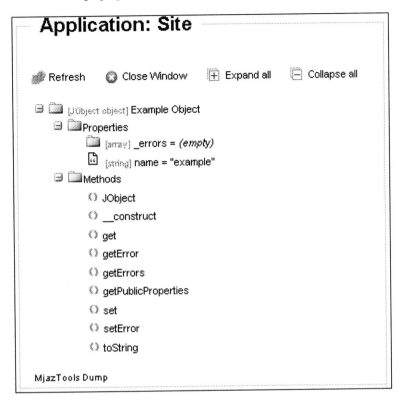

Other functions we can use include `dumpMessage()`, `dumpSysinfo()`, `dumpTemplate()`, and `dumpTrace()`.

To get a copy of J!Dump refer to
`http://joomlacode.org/gf/project/jdump`.

Summary

One of the most pleasurable things about working with Joomla! is the encouragement of openness and friendliness amongst the members of the Joomla! community. It is, without a doubt, the community that is driving the Joomla! project. The name 'Joomla!' is derived from the Swahili word 'Jumla', meaning 'all together'. The Joomla! community lend a true sense of jumla to the project.

In this chapter we have seen that there are essentially six types of extension: **components, modules, plugins, languages, templates**, and **tools**. As we have seen, each type has a very specific use. We have lightly discussed the way in which extensions of different types can be dependant upon one another.

Whilst we did not dwell on development tools, we have investigated the two most prominent tools, J!Code and J!Dump. Even experienced PHP developers should investigate other/new development tools.

2
Getting Started

This chapter explains some of the fundamental concepts behind Joomla!. It describes the process from request to response. We touch lightly on some of the coding aspects and explain how to use some of the more common Joomla! elements.

The Application and Document

The application is a global object used to process a request. The two application classes that we are interested in are **JSite** and **JAdministrator**. Joomla! uses JSite and JAdministrator to process frontend and backend requests respectively. Application classes extend the abstract base class JApplication; much of the functionality of JSite and JAdministrator is the same.

The document is a global object used to buffer a response. There are a number of different documents: **HTML**, **PDF**, **RAW**, **feed,** and **error**. The HTML document uses the site templates and renders an XHTML page. The PDF document renders content in as a PDF file. The RAW document enables components to output RAW data with no extra formatting. The feed document is used to render news feeds. The error document renders the error templates.

When we output data in our extensions, it is added to the document. This enables us to modify the output before sending it; for example, we can add a link to a JavaScript file in the document header at almost any point during the application lifetime.

The application object is always stored in the $mainframe variable. The application object is a global variable, which can be accessed from within functions and methods by declaring $mainframe global:

```
/**
 * Pass-through method to check for admin application.
 *
 * @access public
 * @return boolean True if application is JAdministrator
 */
function isAdmin()
{
    global $mainframe;
    return $mainframe->isAdmin();
}
```

Unlike the application, to access the global document object we use the static JFactory::getInstance() method:

```
$document =& JFactory::getDocument();
```

 Note that we use the =& assignment operator to retrieve the document. This ensures that we get a reference to the global document object and that we do not create a copy of the object.

Request to Response

Frontend and backend requests are placed with the root index.php and administrator/index.php entry points respectively. When we create extensions for Joomla!, we must never create any new entry points. By using the normal entry points, we are guaranteeing that we are not circumventing any security or other important procedures.

The Process

To help describe the way in which the frontend entry points process a request, we use a series of flow charts. The processes involving the backend are very similar.

The first flow chart describes the overall process at a high level in seven generic steps. The following six flow charts describe the first six of these generic steps in detail. We do not look at the seventh step in detail because it is relatively simple and the framework handles it entirely.

Receive Frontend Request	**Load Core**	**Build Application**
Overall process as handled by `index.php`	Loads required framework and application class	Builds the application JSite object

Initialize Application

Prepares the application

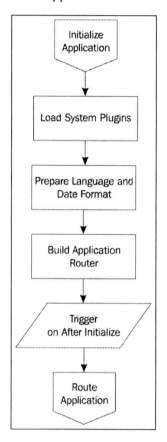

Route Application

Determines application route

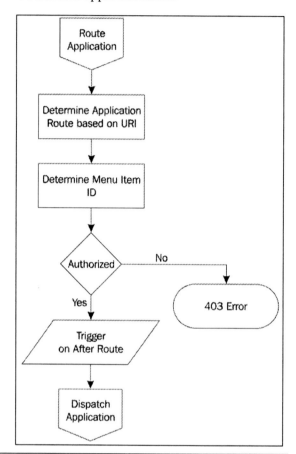

Dispatch Application

Executes the determined route through
a component

Render Application

Renders the application (exact rendering
process depends on the document type)

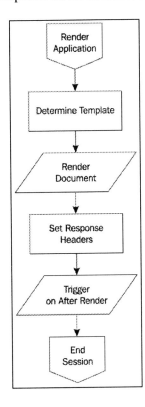

Dispatch Application column:

Dispatch Application

→ Determine Component

→ Build Breadcrumb

→ Type is HTML
  - Yes → Build HTML Head
  - No ↓

→ Set Document Title and Description

→ Component Enabled and Exists
  - No → 404 Error
  - Yes → Load Language Files

→ Execute Component

→ Trigger on After Dispatch

→ Render Application

Render Application column:

Render Application

→ Determine Template

→ Render Document

→ Set Response Headers

→ Trigger on After Render

→ End Session

URI Structure

During Joomla! installation, we send **URIs** (Uniform Resource Indicators) packed full of useful query data. Before we delve into data and its uses, the following diagram will describe the different parts of a URI:

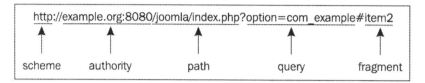

The query element is the part of the URI from which we retrieve the data. Query data is composed of a series of key-value pairs each separated by an ampersand.

The first query value we will look at is `option`. This value determines the component being requested. Component names are always prefixed with `com_`. In this example, we access the component named `example`:

```
http://www.example.org/joomla/index.php?option=com_example
```

The menus are the primary means by which users navigate the Joomla! interface. Menus consist of a number of menu items, each of which defines a link to a component (internal) or a URI (external). We can also modify menu items by changing parameters specific to the chosen component, and assigning templates to them.

A unique ID identifies every menu item. The ID enables us to invoke a component without using the query `option` value. Instead, we can use the `Itemid` query value. This value also serves a secondary purpose; when the menu item ID is known, the menu item can be highlighted and any submenu items are displayed (depending on the exact setup of the installation). In this example, we invoke menu item `1`:

```
http://www.example.org/joomla/index.php?Itemid=1
```

Some components can output data in different formats. If we want to output data in a different format, we can use the query value `format`. This will only work if the component we are accessing supports the specified format. In this example, we invoke component `example` and request the data in `feed` format:

```
http://www.example.org/joomla/index.php?option=com_example&format=feed
```

Another common query value is `task`, which is used to determine the task the component will perform. When we create our own components, it is advantageous to use them. The reason behind this is that these components are partially implemented in the framework that we will be using. In this example, we request the component `example` and invoke the task `view`:

```
http://www.example.org/joomla/index.php?option=com_example&task=view
```

When we build our own URIs, we need to make sure that we do not conflict with any of the core query values. Doing so could result in unexpected behavior. The following is a list of some of the main core query values:

- format
- hidemainmenu (backend only)
- Itemid
- layout
- limit
- limitstart
- no_html
- option
- start
- task
- tmpl
- tp
- vars
- view

When we output URIs, we must use the static `JRoute::_()` method. Using this means that we do not have to keep track of the menu item ID. The following example shows how we use the method:

```
echo JRoute::_('index.php?option=com_example&task=view');
```

If we are using this method from within a component and are linking to the current component, we do not need to specify `option`. Note that we do not encode the ampersand, as per the XHTML standard; this is because JRoute will handle this for us.

There is another advantage of using the static `JRoute::_()` method. Joomla! supports **SEO (Search Engine Optimization)**. If enabled, the `JRoute::_()` method will automatically convert addresses into SEO addresses. For example, the previous piece of code might produce:

```
http://example.org/joomla/index.php/component/com_example
```

 Always use the static `JRoute::_()` method to output URIs.

Directory Structure

Developing for Joomla! requires an understanding of the overall directory structure. The following tree diagram describes the different folders and their purposes within an installation:

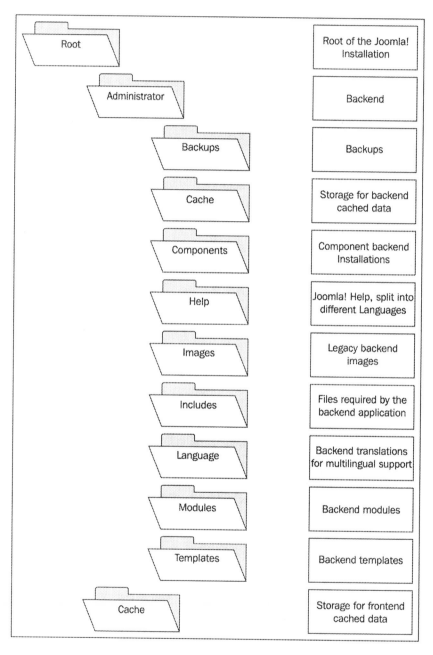

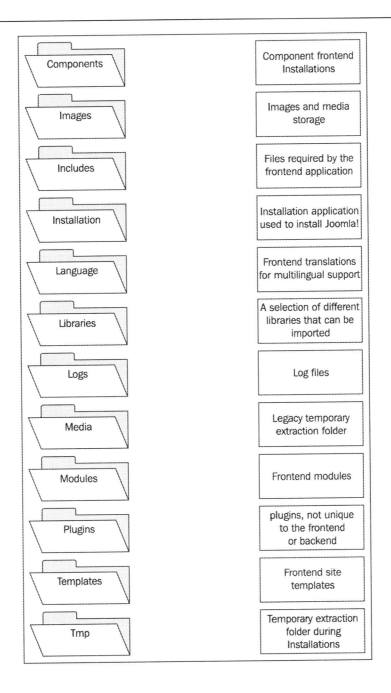

Libraries

Joomla! includes a selection of useful libraries, including its own library — `joomla`. To import a library we use the `jimport()` function. In this example we import the `joomla.filesystem.file` library, which is specifically for handling files:

```
jimport('joomla.filesystem.file');
```

When we import a library, we have the option of importing the entire library or just a small part of it. The previous example imports the `/libraries/joomla/filesystem/file.php` file. If we want, we can import all of the files in the filesystem directory. To do this we need to use the asterisk wildcard:

```
jimport('joomla.filesystem.*');
```

 Joomla! does not currently support library extensions. Future developments might include the ability to upload custom libraries and to implement dependencies.

The following table details the base libraries that are included in Joomla!:

Library	Description	License
archive	tar file management class (`www.phpconcept.net`).	PHP License 3
bitfolge	Feed and vCard utilities (`www.bitfolge.de`).	GNU LGPL
domit	DOM (Document Object Model) XML Parser (`www.phpclasses.org/browse/package/1468.html`).	GNU LGPL
geshi	Generic Syntax Highlighter (`qbnz.com/highlighter`).	GNU GPL
joomla	Core Joomla! library.	GNU GPL
openid	Remote login management (`www.openidenabled.com`).	GNU LGPL
pattemplate	Template handling (`www.php-tools.net`).	GNU LGPL
pcl	Archive handling (`www.phpconcept.net`).	GNU GPL
pear	PHP Extension and Application Repository (`pear.php.net`).	Mixed
phpgacl	Generic Access Control (`phpgacl.sourceforge.net`).	GNU LGPL
phpinputfilter	Filter out unwanted PHP / Javascript / HTML tags (`www.phpclasses.org/browse/package/2189.html`).	GNU GPL
phpmailer	Class for sending email using either sendmail, PHP `mail()`, or SMTP (`phpmailer.sourceforge.net`).	GNU LGPL
phputf8	UTF8 and ASCII tools (`phputf8.sourceforge.net`).	Mixed
phpxmlrpc	XML-RPC protocol (`phpxmlrpc.sourceforge.net`).	Special
simplepie	RSS and Atom reader (`simplepie.org`).	GNU LGPL
tcpdf	PDF generator that does not require additional libraries. (`tcpdf.sourceforge.net`).	GNU LGPL

We import these libraries in the same way as the Joomla! library. This example demonstrates how we import the GeSHi class from the geshi library:

```
jimport('geshi.geshi');
```

A Quick Lesson in Classes

Joomla! is designed to run on both PHP 4 and PHP 5 environments. This has an impact on how we build classes and use objects in Joomla!, both of which we will discuss throughout this section. Joomla! has opted to continue using the PHP 4 syntax for reasons of backward compatibility; many webservers are still using PHP 4. As third-party developers, we should follow suit and always build our extensions to be PHP 4 and PHP 5 compatible despite the fact that it may restrict some things.

There are some important things that we need to be aware of, before we start building and using classes. We'll start by looking some naming conventions.

- Class names should start with an uppercase letter.
- All named elements should use the camelCase standard.
- Method names should start with a lowercase letter.
- Non-public elements should start with an underscore.

As only PHP 5 and above support access modifiers, we use a special naming convention to indicate non-public elements. Methods and properties that are non-public are prefixed with an underscore.

We often pass and return objects and arrays by reference. Doing this means that multiple variables can 'point' to the same object or array. Note that in PHP 5 objects are always passed by reference. Methods, functions, and parameters that return and are passed by reference are prefixed with an ampersand. When we use a method or function that returns a reference, we must use the &= assignment operator as the following example demonstrates:

```
function &go()
{
    $instance = new stdClass();
    return $instance;
}

$reference =& go();
```

When we pass objects around we must bear in mind that PHP versions 5 and above handle objects differently. In PHP 5, objects are automatically passed by reference (although technically not the same as references, the effects are essentially the same).

Inheriting from JObject

JObject
_errors: array
<<create>> __construct(): JObect   <<create>> JObject(): JObject   get(property : string,default: mixed = null): mixed   getError(i : int = null,toString : boolean = true) : mixed   getErrors() : int   getPublicProperties(assoc : boolean = false): array   set(property : string,value : mixed = null): mixed   setError(error: mixed) : void   toString() : string

In Joomla! we often come across the class JObject. Many of the classes in Joomla! are subclasses of JObject. This base class provides us with some useful common methods including standard accessors and modifiers and a common error handling mechanism.

To encourage PHP 5 methodology, JObject emulates the PHP 5 constructor allowing us to use the constructor method, __constructor(), in subclasses irrespective of the version of PHP is being used.

When we use inheritance in our classes we should, as a rule, always call the constructor of the parent class. This guarantees that any construction work required by a parent class is executed.

```
/**
 * Some Class which extends JObject
 */
class SomeClass extends JObject
{
    /**
     * Object name
     * @var string
     */
    var $name;

    /**
     * PHP 5 style Constructor
     *
     * @access    protected
     * @param string name
```

```
     */
    function __construct($name)
    {
        $this->name = $name;
        parent::__construct();
    }
}
```

Nearly all Joomla! objects and classes derive from the base class JObject. This class offers several useful methods that all derived classes can use. The `getPublicProperties()` method returns an array of public property names from the object. This is determined at run time and uses the object properties, not the class properties.

The `get()` and `set()` methods are used to get and set properties of the object. If we use `get()` with a nonexistent property, the default value will be returned. If we use `set()` with a nonexistent property, the property will be created. Both of these methods can be used with private properties.

We can keep track of errors that occur in an object using the `getErrors()`, `getError()`, and `setError()` methods. Errors are recorded in the _errors array property. Errors can be strings or JException or Exception objects. JException objects are created when we raise errors; this is explained in detail in Chapter 11.

A full description of the JObject class is available in the *Appendix*.

Working with the Request

Generally when we develop PHP scripts, we work extensively with the request hashes: $_GET, $_POST, $_FILES, $_COOKIE, and $_REQUEST. In Joomla!, instead of directly using these, we use the static JRequest class. We use this because it allows us to process the input at the same time as retrieving it, this decreases the amount of code required and helps improve security.

The request hashes $_GET, $_POST, $_FILES, $_COOKIE, and $_REQUEST are still available, and in cases where we are porting existing applications we need not change the use of these hashes.

The two methods that we use the most are JRequest::setVar() and JRequest::getVar(). As the names suggest, one accesses request-data and the other sets it. In this example, we get the value of id; if id is not set, we return a default value, 0 (the default value is optional).

```
$id = JRequest::getVar('id', 0);
```

The `JRequest::setVar()` method is used to set values in the request hashes. In comparison to the `JRequest::getVar()` method, this method is used relatively infrequently. It is most commonly used to set default values. For example, we might want to set the default task in a component if it is not already selected:

```
JRequest::setVar('task', 'someDefaultTask');
```

A useful trick to guarantee that a variable is set is to use the two methods in conjunction. In this example, if name is not set, we set it to the default value of 'unknown'.

```
JRequest::setVar('name', JRequest::getVar('name', 'unknown'));
```

Some other handy methods in JRequest are `getInt()`, `getFloat()`, `getBool()`, `getWord()`, `getCmd()`, and `getString()`. If we use these methods, we guarantee that the returned value is of a specific type.

 It is important to familiarize yourself with the JRequest methods described above because they are used extensively in Joomla!. In addition, we will use them repeatedly in the code examples presented throughout this book.

There is far more we can achieve using these methods, including preprocessing of data. A more complete explanation is available in Chapter 11.

The Factory

Before we jump into the Joomla! factory, we need to take a quick moment to contemplate the patterns that occur in code. Referred to as *Design Patterns*, commonly occurring patterns within code have been studied for some time and much has been learned from them.

One of the most common patterns with which we will be familiar is the iterator pattern. This pattern describes how we perform one task multiple times using a loop. Joomla! uses numerous Design Patterns, many of which are far more complex than the iterator pattern.

For a complete description of *Design Patterns*, you should consider reading the book *Design Patterns: Elements of Reusable Object-Oriented Software*. This book, originally published in 1994 and written by the *Gang of Four*, is considered the ultimate guide and reference to software *Design Patterns*.

The factory pattern is a *creational pattern* used to build and return objects. The factory pattern is used in cases where different classes, usually derived from an abstract class, are instantiated dependent upon the parameters. Joomla! provides us with the static class JFactory, which implements the factory pattern. This class is important because it allows us to easily access and instantiate global objects.

This example shows how we can access some of the global objects using JFactory.

```
$db =& JFactory::getDBO();
$user =& JFactory::getUser();
$document =& JFactory::getDocument();
```

More information about JFactory can be found in the *Appendix*.

A singleton pattern is used to allow the creation of only a single object of a specific class. This is achieved by making the constructor private or protected and using a static method to instantiate the class. In versions of PHP prior to version 5, we are unable to enforce this restriction.

Many of the Joomla! classes use a pseudo-singleton pattern to allow us to instantiate and access objects. To achieve this, Joomla! often uses a static method called getInstance(); in some cases JFactory acts as a pass through for this method. Classes that implement this method are not always intended to be singleton classes.

We can think of them as being a hierarchy in how we instantiate objects. We should use these methods in order of priority: JFactory method, getInstance() method, normal constructor (new).

> If you're unsure how a specific class implements a getInstance() method, you should check the official API reference at http://api.joomla.org. getInstance() and JFactory methods always return references; always use the =& assignment operator to prevent copying of objects.

In cases where JFactory and a class both provide a method to return an instance of the class, you should generally use the JFactory method in preference. If the class provides a more comprehensive getInstance() method than JFactory, you may want to use the class method to get an instance tailored specifically for your needs.

The Session

Sessions are used in web applications as a means of providing a temporary storage facility for the duration of a client's visit. In PHP, we access this data using the global hash $_SESSION.

Joomla! always provides us with a session, irrespective of whether or not the client user is logged in. In Joomla! instead of accessing the $_SESSION hash, we use the global session object to get and set session data. Session data is stored in namespaces; the default namespace is default. In this example, we retrieve the value of default.example:

```
$session =& JFactory::getSession();
$value = $session->get('example');
```

If we want to retrieve a value from a namespace other than `default`, we must also specify a default value. In this example, we retrieve the value of `myextension.example` with a default value of null:

```
$session =& JFactory::getSession();
$value = $session->get('example', null, 'myextension');
```

Setting values is very similar to retrieving values. In this example, we set the value of `myextension.example` to 1:

```
$session =& JFactory::getSession();
$session->set('example', 1, 'myextension');
```

Sessions store relatively flat data structures; because of this there is a JRegistry object within the session,. The JRegistry class uses a far more sophisticated way of storing data in namespaces. To use this area of the session we use the application method `getUserState()`. A more complete explanation of sessions is available in Chapter 7.

Predefined Constants

There are over 400 constants, many of which are part of the third-party libraries, though we don't need to know them all. One constant with which we will quickly become familiar is `_JEXEC`; this constant is used to ensure that when files are included, they are being included from a valid entry point. You should include the following code, or similar, at the top of your PHP files:

```
defined('_JEXEC') or die('Restricted access');
```

The constants that you will probably use the most relate to paths. The `DS` constant is the character used by the operating system to separate directories; this is normally a backslash (\) or a forward slash (/). This table describes the different path constants; the examples, described within the parentheses, assume that the installation is located in `/joomla` and that we are accessing the installation from the frontend; the actual paths will differ depending on the Joomla! installation:

Name	Description
DS	Directory Separator (/)
JPATH_ADMINISTRATOR	Administrator path (/joomla/administrator)
JPATH_BASE	Path to the entry directory (/joomla)
JPATH_CACHE	Cache path (/joomla/cache)
JPATH_COMPONENT	Component path (/joomla/components/com_example)
JPATH_COMPONENT_ADMINISTRATOR	Component backend path (/joomla/administrator/components/com_example)

Name	Description
JPATH_COMPONENT_SITE	Component frontend path (`/joomla/components/com_example`)
JPATH_CONFIGURATION	Configuration path (`/joomla`)
JPATH_INSTALLATION	Installation path (`/joomla/installation`)
JPATH_LIBRARIES	Libraries path (`/joomla/libraries`)
JPATH_PLUGINS	Plugins path (`/joomla/plugins`)
JPATH_ROOT	Path to the frontend entry directory (`/joomla`)
JPATH_SITE	Path to the public directory (`/joomla`)
JPATH_THEMES	Templates path (`/joomla/templates`)

Four date constants define different date-formats. These formats are designed to be used when displaying dates using the JDate class; a full description of the JDate class is available in Chapter 12. The format values vary depending on the language locale, the default formats are used if they are not defined in the corresponding locale language file (we will discuss multilingual support shortly).

Name	Default Format	Example
DATE_FORMAT_LC	`%A, %d %B %Y`	Sunday, 23 June 1912
DATE_FORMAT_LC2	`%A, %d %B %Y %H:%M`	Sunday, 23 June 1912 00:00
DATE_FORMAT_LC3	`%d %B %Y`	23 June 1912
DATE_FORMAT_LC4	`%d.%m.%y`	23.06.12

A number of constants in Joomla! 1.5 have been deprecated. The following constants are included for legacy compatibility. You should not use these in new extensions. *These constants are only available if the legacy system module is published.*

Deprecated Constant	Description
_ISO	Character set
_VALID_MOS	Use _JEXEC instead
_MOS_MAMBO_INCLUDED	Use _JEXEC instead
_DATE_FORMAT_LC	Use DATE_FORMAT_LC instead
_DATE_FORMAT_LC2	Use DATE_FORMAT_LC2 instead

Multilingual Support

A major strength of Joomla! is its built-in multilingual support. The default language is configured in the Language Manager and can be overridden by a logged in user's preferences.

The static JText class is the standard mechanism used to translate strings. JText has three methods for translating strings, `_()`, `sprintf()`, and `printf()`. The method that you will probably use most is `_()`. This method is the most basic; it translates a string.

In this example, we echo the translation of `Monday` (if a translation cannot be found for the string, the original string is returned):

```
echo JText::_('Monday');
```

The `JText::sprintf()` method is comparable to the PHP `sprintf()` function. We pass one string to translate and any number of extra parameters to insert into the translated string. The extra parameters will not be translated.

In this example, if the translation for `SAVED_ITEMS` is `Saved %d items`, the returned value will be `Saved 3 items`.

```
$value = JText::sprintf('SAVED_ITEMS', 3);
```

Alternatively we can use the `JText::printf()` method. This method is comparable to the PHP function `printf()`. This method returns the length of the resultant string and outputs the translation.

```
$length = JText::printf('SAVED_ITEMS', 3);
```

If we want to create any new translations for our extensions, we can create special INI translation files. A more complete explanation of how to build a translation file is available in Chapter 7.

UTF-8 String Handling

In order for Joomla! to fully support multilingual requirements, Joomla! uses the Unicode character set and **UTF-8 (Unicode Transformation Format-8)** encoding. Unicode is a character set that attempts to include all characters for every common language.

UTF-8 is a lossless encoding of Unicode, which employs a variable character length. This makes it ideal for internet usage because it uses a minimal amount of bandwidth but represents the entire Unicode character set.

When dealing with English characters, UTF-8 uses the same encodings as ASCII and ANSII. This has a purposeful consequence; UTF-8 encoded strings that use these characters appear identical to their ASCII and ANSII alternatives. Applications that are Unicode unaware are therefore able to handle many UTF-8 strings.

One such application that is not Unicode aware is PHP. We therefore have to be careful when manipulating strings. PHP assumes all characters are eight bits (one byte), but because UTF-8 encoded characters can be longer, this can cause corruption of Unicode data.

There is a PHP module, mbstring, which adds support for multi-byte character encodings; unfortunately, not all PHP systems have the mbstring module. In Joomla! we are provided with the static JString class; this class allows us to perform many of the normal string manipulation functions with UTF-8 characters.

This example demonstrates how we can use JString to convert a string to upper case. Note that the method name is identical to the PHP function we would normally use:

```
$string = JString::strtoupper($string);
```

The following table describes the PHP string functions and the corresponding JString methods:

PHP Function	JString method	Description
strpos	strpos	Finds the first occurrence of a string in a string.
substr	substr	Gets a portion of a string.
strtolower	strtolower	Converts a string to lowercase.
strtoupper	strtoupper	Converts a string to uppercase.
strlen	strlen	Counts the length of a string.
str_ireplace	str_ireplace	Substitutes occurrences of a string with another string in a string (case insensitive).
str_split	str_split	Splits a string into an array.
strcasecmp	strcasecmp	Compares strings.
strcspn	strcspn	Gets the length of the string before characters from the other parameters are found.
stristr	stristr	Finds the first occurrence of a string in a string (case insensitive).
strrev	strrev	Reverses a string.
strspn	strspn	Counts the longest segment of a string containing specified characters.
substr_replace	substr_replace	Replaces a defined portion of a string.
ltrim	ltrim	Removes white space from the left of a string.

PHP Function	JString method	Description
rtrim	rtrim	Removes white space from the right of a string.
trim	trim	Removes white space from both ends of a string.
ucfirst	ucfirst	Converts the first character to uppercase.
ucwords	ucwords	Converts the first character of each word to uppercase.
	transcode	Converts a string from one encoding to another. Requires the PHP iconv module.

Coding Standards

Using a standardized format makes code easier to read and allows other developers to edit code more easily. Joomla! uses the PEAR coding standards. A complete guide to the PEAR coding standards is available at http://pear.php.net/manual/en/standards.php.

Here is a break down of the more common rules:

- Indents are four spaces:
  ```
  {
      // four space before me!
  ```
- Control structures have one space between the name and first parenthesis:
  ```
  if (true) {
  ```
- Use curly braces even when they are optional.
- Functions and methods are named using the camelCase standard with a lowercase first character.
- Functions and method declarations have no spaces between the name and first parenthesis. Parameter lists have no spaces at the ends. Parameters are separated by one space: foo($bar0, $bar1, $bar2);
- Optional function and method parameters must be at the end of the parameter list. Optional parameter values, signified by an equals sign, are separated by spaces: function foo($bar0, $bar1, $bar2 = '')
- Use phpDocumentor tags to comment code http://www.phpdoc.org/.
- Use include_once() and require_once() in preference to include() and require().
- Use <?php ?> in preference to all other PHP code block delimiters.

phpDocumentor

phpDocumentor is a documentation tool that allows us to easily create documentation from PHP source code. The documentation is extracted from the source and from special comments within the source; these comments are very similar to those used by JavaDoc.

This example demonstrates how we might document a simple function:

```
/**
 * Adds two integers together
 *
 * @param int $value1 Base value
 * @param int $value2 Value to add
 * @return int Resultant vaue
 */
function addition($value1, $value2)
{
    return ((int)$value1 + (int)$value2)
}
```

The multiline comment denotes a DocBlock, notice that it uses a double asterisk at the start. The first line is a general description of the function, this description can span more than one line. @param and @return are tags.

The @param tag is used to define a parameter in the format (the name is optional):

```
@param type [$name] description
```

The @return tag is used to define the return value in the format:

```
@return type description
```

So our initial example is telling us that the addition() function has two integer parameters named that it will add togther and return the resultant integer value.

When we document complex functions, we might want to provide two descriptions, a long description and a short description. This example demonstrates how we do this:

```
/**
 * Does some complex processing
 *
 * A verbose description of the function that spans more than
 * one line
 *
 * @param int $value1 Base value
```

```
 * @param int $value2 Value to add
 * @return int Resultant vaue
 */
function someComplexFunction($value1, $value2)
{
    // does some complex processing
}
```

Functions are not the only elements that can be documented. Elements that we can document include:

- class methods
- class varaibles
- classes
- define()
- files
- function declarations
- global variables (requires use of the `@global` tag)
- `include()`/`include_once()`
- `require()`/`require_once()`

This list defines some common tags we are likely to encounter:

- `@access private|protected|public`
- `@author name`
- `@param type [$name] description`
- `@return type description`
- `@static`

The DocBlocks are easy to read when they are displayed in code, but, more importantly, we can automatically create documentation from the source code. For more information about using `phpDocumentor` please refer to `http://www.phpdoc.org/`.

Summary

The application embodies the complete process of responding to a request. The document is used to determine the format of the response data and as a buffer to store the response data.

Instead of using the request and session hashes in Joomla!, we use the static `JRequest` class and the global JSession object. The JRoute class enables us to parse and build internal URIs. The JText class is used to translate strings into different languages. Limitations in PHP means we must use JString to handle UTF-8 data; if we do not we run the risk of corrupting data.

Although the coding standards that we use are ultimately up to us, we should consider using the same standards as those implemented by the Joomla! project. If we chose not to use these standards, we should still consider adding doctags to our classes and functions because they can greatly decrease development and debug time.

3
The Database

This chapter details the role of the database in Joomla!. It defines some standard rules we need to abide by. It explains different ways in which we can query the database. It also briefly covers the **ADOdb** emulation that is available for developers wanting to port existing applications.

Joomla! is currently designed to use the MySQL database. However, the architecture does allow for the implementation of other database drivers. There is some uncertainty surrounding the issue of supporting other databases, because of the usage in queries of functions and syntax that are specific to MySQL.

The Core Database

Much of the data we see in Joomla! is stored in the database. A base installation has over thirty tables. Some of these are related to core extensions and others to the inner workings of Joomla!.

There is an official database schema, which describes the tables created during the installation. For more information, please refer to: `http://dev.joomla.org/ component/option,com_jd-wiki/Itemid,31/id,guidelines:database/`.

A tabular description is available at: `http://dev.joomla.org/downloads/ Joomla15_DB-Schema.htm`.

We access the Joomla! database using the global JDatabase object. The JDatabase class is an abstract class, which is extended by different database drivers. There are currently only two database drivers included in the Joomla! core, MySQL and MySQLi. We access the global JDatabase object using JFactory:

```
$db =& JFactory::getDBO();
```

Extending the Database

When we create extensions, we generally want to store data in some form. If we are using the database, it is important to extend it in the correct way. More information on extending the database with components is available in Chapter 4.

Table Prefix

All database tables have a prefix, normally `jos_`, which helps in using a single database for multiple Joomla! installations. When we write SQL queries, to accommodate the variable table prefix, we use a symbolic prefix that is substituted with the actual prefix at run time. Normally the symbolic prefix is `#__`, but we can specify an alternative prefix if we want to.

Schema Conventions

When we create tables for our extensions, we must follow some standard conventions. The most important of these is the name of the table. All tables must use the table prefix and should start with name of the extension. If the table is storing a specific entity, add the plural of the entity name to the end of the table name separated by an underscore. For example, an items table for the extension 'My Extension' would be called `#__myExtension_items`.

Table field names should all be lowercase and use underscore word separators; you should avoid using underscores if they are not necessary. For example, you can name an email address field as `email`. If you had a primary and a secondary email field, you could call them `email` and `email_secondary`; there is no reason to name the primary email address `email_primary`.

If you are using a primary key record ID, you should call the field `id`, make it of type `integer auto_increment`, and disallow `null`. Doing this will allow you to use the Joomla! framework more effectively.

Common Fields

We may use some common fields in our tables. Using these fields will enable us to take advantage of the Joomla! framework. We will discuss how to implement and manipulate these fields, using the JTable class, later in this chapter.

Publishing

We use publishing to determine whether to display data. Joomla! uses a special field called `published`, of type `tinyint(1)`; 0 = not published, 1 = published.

Hits

If we want to keep track of the number of times a record has been viewed, we can use the special field `hits`, of type `integer` and with the default value 0.

Checking Out

To prevent more than one user trying to edit one record at a time we can check out records (a form of software record locking). We use two fields to do this, `checked_out` and `checked_out_time`. `checked_out`, of type `integer`, holds the ID of the user that has checked out the record. `checked_out_time`, of type `datetime`, holds the date and time when the record was checked out. A null date and a user ID of 0 is recorded if the record is not checked out.

Ordering

We often want to allow administrators the ability to choose the order in which items appear. The `ordering` field, of type `integer`, can be used to number records sequentially to determine the order in which they are displayed. This field does not need to be unique and can be used in conjunction with WHERE clauses to form ordering groups.

Parameter Fields

We use a parameter field, a TEXT field normally named `params`, to store additional information about records; this is often used to store data that determines how a record will be displayed. The data held in these fields is encoded as INI strings (which we handle using the JParameter class). Before using a parameter field, we should carefully consider the data we intend to store in the field. Data should only be stored in a parameter field if all of the following criteria are true:

- Not used for sorting records
- Not used in searches
- Only exists for some records
- Not part of a database relationship

Schema Example

Imagine we have an extension called 'My Extension' and an entity called foobar. The name of the table is #__myextension_foobars. This schema describes the table:

Field	Datatype	NOT NULL	AUTO INC	UNSIGNED	DEFAULT
id	INTEGER	✓	✓	✓	NULL
content	TEXT	✓			
checked_out	INTEGER	✓		✓	0
checked_out_time	DATETIME	✓			0000-00-00 00:00:00
params	TEXT	✓			
ordering	INTEGER	✓		✓	0
hits	INTEGER	✓		✓	0
published	TINYINT(1)	✓		✓	0

This table uses all of the common fields and uses an auto-incrementing primary key ID field. When we come to define our own tables we must ensure that we use the correct data types and NOT NULL, AUTO INC, UNSIGNED and DEFAULT values.

The SQL displayed below will create the table described in the above schema:

```
CREATE TABLE '#__myextension_foobars' (
    'id' INTEGER UNSIGNED NOT NULL DEFAULT NULL AUTO_INCREMENT,
    'content' TEXT  NOT NULL DEFAULT '',
    'checked_out' INTEGER UNSIGNED NOT NULL DEFAULT 0,
    'checked_out_time' DATETIME  NOT NULL DEFAULT '0000-00-00
                                        00:00:00',
    'params' TEXT  NOT NULL DEFAULT '',
    'ordering' INTEGER UNSIGNED NOT NULL DEFAULT 0,
    'hits' INTEGER UNSIGNED NOT NULL DEFAULT 0,
    'published' INTEGER UNSIGNED NOT NULL DEFAULT 0,
    PRIMARY KEY('id')
)
CHARACTER SET 'utf8' COLLATE 'utf8_general_ci';
```

Date Fields

We regularly use datetime fields to record the date and time at which an action has taken place. When we use these fields, it is important that we are aware of the effect of time zones. All dates and times should be recorded in UTC+0 (GMT / Z).

When we come to display dates and times we can use the JDate class, described in Chapter 12. The JDate class allows us to easily parse dates, output them in different formats, and apply UTC time-zone offsets.

For more information about time zones, please refer to http://www.timeanddate.com.

 We often use parsers before we display data to make the data safe or to apply formatting to the data. We need to be careful how we store data that is going to be parsed. If the data is ever going to be edited, we must store the data in its RAW state. If the data is going to be edited extremely rarely and if the parsing is reversible, we may want to consider building a 'reverse-parser'. This way we can store the data in its parsed format, eradicating the need for parsing when we view the data and reducing the load on the server. Another option available to us is to store the data in both formats. This way we only have to parse data when we save it.

Dealing with Multilingual Requirements

In the previous chapter we discussed Joomla!s use of the Unicode character set using UTF-8 encoding. Unlike ASCII and ANSII, Unicode is a multi-byte character set; it uses more than eight bits (one byte) per character. When we use UTF-8 encoding, character byte lengths vary.

Unfortunately, MySQL versions prior to 4.1.2 assume that characters are always eight bits (one byte), which poses some problems. To combat the issue when installing extensions we have the ability to define different SQL files for servers, that do and do not support UTF-8.

In MySQL servers that do not support UTF-8, when we create fields, which define a character length, we are actually defining the length in bytes. Therefore, if we try to store UTF-8 characters that are longer than one byte, we may exceed the size of the field. To combat this, we increase the length of fields to try to accommodate UTF-8 strings. For example, a varchar(20) field becomes a varchar(60) field. We triple the size of fields because, although UTF-8 characters can be more than three bytes, the majority of common characters are a maximum of three bytes.

This poses another issue, if we use a varchar(100) field, scaling it up for a MySQL server, which does not support UTF-8, we would have to define it as a varchar(300) field. We cannot do this because varchar fields have a maximum size of 255. The next step is slightly more drastic. We must redefine the field type so as it will accommodate at least three hundred bytes. Therefore, a varchar(100) field becomes a text field.

As an example, the core #__content table includes a field named `title`. For MySQL severs that support UTF-8, the field is defined as:

```
'title' varchar(255) NOT NULL default ''
```

For MySQL severs that do not support UTF-8, the field is defined as:

```
'title' text NOT NULL default ''
```

We should also be aware that using a version of MySQL that does not support UTF-8 would affect the MySQL string handling functions. For example ordering by a string field may yield unexpected results. While we can overcome this using post-processing in our scripts using the JString class, the recommended resolution is to upgrade to the latest version of MySQL.

Querying the Database

When we perform a query, we tell the global JDatabase object the query that we want to execute. We do this using the `setQuery()` method; this does not perform the query.

```
$db =& JFactory::getDBO();
$result = $db->setQuery($query);
```

Once we have set the query we want to perform, we use the `query()` method to execute the query. This is similar to using the PHP function `mysql_query()`. If the query is successful and is a SELECT, SHOW, DESCRIBE, or EXPLAIN query, a resource will be returned. If the query is successful, and is not one of the above query types, `true` will be returned. If the query fails, `false` will be returned.

```
$db =& JFactory::getDBO();
if (!$result = $db->setQuery($query))
{
    // handle failed query
    // use $table->getError() for more information
}
```

Writing Queries

There are some rules we need to be aware of when we build database queries.

- Use the #__ symbolic prefix at the start of all table names.
- Use the `nameQuote()` method to encapsulate named query elements.
- Use the `Quote()` method to encapsulate values.

The symbolic prefix guarantees that we use the correct prefix for the current Joomla! installation; an alternative symbolic prefix to #__ can be used if necessary. `nameQuote()` ensures that named elements are encapsulated in the correct delimiters. `Quote()` ensures that values are encapsulated in the correct delimiters. This example demonstrates the use of all of these rules.

```
$db = JFactory::getDBO();
$query = 'SELECT * FROM '
        .$db->nameQuote('#__test')
        .' WHERE '
        .$db->nameQuote('name')
        .' = '
        .$db->Quote('Some Name');
```

If we were using a MySQL or MySQLi database driver, $query would equal the following:

```
SELECT * FROM 'jos_test' WHERE 'name' = "Some Name";
```

Getting Results

We could use the `query()` method and process the resultant resource. However, it is far easier to use one of the other JDatabase methods, which will get the results from a query in a number of different formats.

To help explain each of the methods we will use a sample table called #__test. The table has two fields, id, an auto-increment primary key, and name, a varchar field. The table below shows the data we will use for demonstration purposes.

id	name
1	Foo
2	Bar

Which methods we choose to use is dependent on three things: the data we want, the format in which we want it, and our personal preference. Much of the Joomla! core prefers methods that return objects.

For the purpose of these examples we won't bother using the `nameQuote()` and `Quote()` methods.

loadResult( ) : string

This method loads value of the first cell in the result set. If we selected all the data from our table, this method would return the ID for the first record, in this example: 1. This is useful when we want to access a single field in a known record. For example, we might want to know the name of record 2:

```
$query = 'SELECT 'name' FROM '#__test' WHERE 'id'=2';
$db =& JFactory::getDBO();
$db->setQuery($query);
echo $db->loadResult();

Bar
```

loadResultArray(numinarray : int=0) : array

This method loads a column. numinarray is used to specify which column to get; the column is identified by its logical position in the result set.

```
$query = 'SELECT 'name' FROM '#__test'';
$db =& JFactory::getDBO();
$db->setQuery($query);
print_r($db->loadResultArray());

Array
(
  [0] => Foo
  [1] => Bar
)
```

loadAssoc( ) : array

This method loads the first record as an associative array using the table column names as array keys. This is useful when we are only dealing with an individual record. If the query returns more than one record, the first record in the result set will be used:

```
$query = 'SELECT * FROM '#__test'';
$db =& JFactory::getDBO();
$db->setQuery($query);
print_r($db->loadAssoc());
Array
(
  [id] => 1
  [name] => Foo
)
```

loadAssocList(key : string=") : array

This method loads an array of associative arrays or an associative array of associative arrays. If we specify the parameter key, the returned array uses the record key as the array key:

```
$query = 'SELECT * FROM '#__test'';
$db =& JFactory::getDBO();
$db->setQuery($query);
print_r($db->loadAssocList());

Array
(
  [0] => Array
    (
      [id] => 1
      [name] => Foo
    )
  [1] => Array
    (
      [id] => 2
      [name] => Bar
    )
)
```

loadObject( ) : stdClass

This method loads the first record as an object using the table column names as property names. This is useful when we are only dealing with an individual record. If the query returns more than one record, the first record in the result set will be used:

```
$query = 'SELECT * FROM '#__test'';
$db =& JFactory::getDBO();
$db->setQuery($query);
print_r($db->loadObject());

stdClass Object
(
  [id] => 1
  [name] => Foo
)
```

loadObjectList(key : string=") : array

This method loads an array of `stdClass` objects or an associative array of `stdClass` objects. If we specify the parameter `key`, the returned array uses the record key as the array key:

```
$query = 'SELECT * FROM '#__test'';
$db =& JFactory::getDBO();
$db->setQuery($query);
print_r($db->loadObjectList());

Array
(
  [0] => stdClass Object
  (
    [id] => 1
    [name] => Foo
  )

  [1] => stdClass Object
  (
    [id] => 2
    [name] => Bar
  )
)
```

loadRow( ) : array

This method loads the first record as an array. This is useful when we are only dealing with an individual record. If the query returns more than one record, the first record in the result set will be used:

```
$query = 'SELECT * FROM '#__test'';
$db =& JFactory::getDBO();
$db->setQuery($query);
print_r($db->loadRow());

Array
(
  [0] => 1
  [1] => Foo
)
```

loadRowList(key : int) : array

This method loads an array of arrays or an associative array of arrays. If we specify the parameter `key`, the returned array uses the record key as the array key. Unlike the other load list methods, `key` is the logical position of the primary key field in the result set:

```
$query = 'SELECT * FROM '#__test';
$db =& JFactory::getDBO();
$db->setQuery($query);
print_r($db->loadRowList(0));
Array
(
  [0] => Array
   (
     [0] => 1
     [1] => Foo
   )

  [1] => Array
   (
     [0] => 2
     [1] => Bar
   )
)
```

Using ADOdb

ADOdb is a PHP database abstraction layer released under the BSD license. ADOdb supports a number of leading database applications. Joomla! does not use ADOdb, but it does emulate some ADOdb functionality in its own database abstraction layer.

We should only use the ADOdb methods if we are porting existing applications that rely on ADOdb or if we are creating extensions that we also want to work as standalone applications using ADOdb.

Joomla! uses the JRecordSet class to emulate the ADOdb ADORecordSet class. The JRecordSet class is not yet complete and does not include all of the ADORecordSet methods. This example shows the basic usage of JRecordSet; $row is an array:

```
$db =& JFactory::getDBO();
$rs = $db->Execute('SELECT * FROM #__test');
while ($row = $rs->FetchRow())
{
    // process $row
}
```

For more information about ADOdb, go to `http://adodb.sourceforge.net/`.

 Although ADOdb emulation is being added to Joomla!, it should be noted that there are currently no plans to integrate ADOdb as the primary means of accessing the Joomla! database.

JTable

Joomla! provides us with the powerful abstract class JTable; with this we can perform many basic functions on table records. For every table that we want to use the JTable class with, we must create a new subclass.

When creating JTable subclasses we must follow some specific conventions. These conventions enable us to integrate our extensions into Joomla! and the Joomla! framework.

Assuming we are building a component, our JTable subclasses should be located in separate files in a folder called `tables` within the component's administrative root. The class name is the table singular entity name prefixed with `Table`. The name of the file is the singular entity name.

We will use the table schema, which we defined earlier in this chapter, for the entity `foobar` in the extension 'My Extension', to demonstrate how we use JTable in conjunction with a database table. *You may want to familiarize yourself with the schema before continuing.*

The class is called `TableFoobar` and is located in the file `JPATH_COMPONENT_ ADMINISTRATOR.DS.'tables'.DS.'foobar.php'`. The first thing we need to do in our class is to define the public properties. The public properties relate directly to the fields and must have exactly the same names. We use these properties as a 'buffer' to store individual records.

The second thing we need to do is to define the constructor. In order to use the `JTable::getInstance()` method, we must override the JTable constructor with a constructor that has a single referenced parameter, the database object.

The third thing we need to do is override the `check()` method. This method is used to validate the buffer contents, returning a Boolean result. If a `check()` fails we use the `setError()` method to set a message that explains the reason why the validation failed.

```
/**
 * #__myextenstion_foobars table handler
 *
 */
class TableFoobar extends JTable
{
    /** @var int Primary key */
    var $id = null;
    /** @var string Content */
    var $content = null;
    /** @var int Checked-out owner */
    var $checked_out = null;
    /** @var string Checked-out time */
    var $checked_out_time = null;
    /** @var string Parameters */
    var $params = null;
    /** @var int Order position */
    var $ordering = null;
    /** @var int Number of views */
    var $hits = null;

    /**
     * Constructor
     *
     * @param database Database object
     */
    function __construct( &$db )
    {
        parent::__construct('#__myextension_foobars', 'id', $db);
    }

    /**
     * Validation
     *
     * @return boolean True if buffer is valid
     */
    function check()
    {
        if(!$this->content)
        {
            $this->setError(JText::_('Your Foobar must contain some
                                                    content'));
            return false;
        }
        return true;
```

```
        }

    }
```

Now that we have created our `TableFoobar` class what do we do with it? Well first of all we need to instantiate a `TableFoobar` object using the static `JTable::getInstance()` method.

```
JTable::addIncludePath(JPATH_COMPONENT_ADMINISTRATOR.DS.'tables');
$table = JTable::getInstance('foobar', 'Table');
```

Note that instead of including the `foobar.php` file, we tell JTable where the containing folder is. When JTable comes to instantiate the `TableFoobar` object, if the class is not defined, it will look in all of the JTable include paths for a file named `foobar.php`.

CRUD

CRUD (Create Read Update Delete) is the name given to the four common data manipulation tasks. We will follow a record through its short 'CRUDy' life. Throughout the CRUD examples `$table` refers to an instance of the `TableFoobar` class and `$id` refers to the ID of the record we are dealing with. In this example, we create a new record; `$table` is an instance of the `TableFoobar` class.

```
$table->reset();
$table->set('content', "Lorem ipsum dolor sit amet");
$table->set('ordering', $table->getNextOrder());
if ($table->check())
{
    if (!$table->store())
    {
        // handle failed store
        // use $table->getError() for an explanation
    }
}
else
{
    // handle failed check
    // use $table->getError() for an explanation
}
```

The `reset()` method ensures that the table buffer is empty. The method returns all of the properties to their default values specified by the class. The `getNextOrder()` method determines the next space in the record ordering. If there are no existing records, this will be 1. In case the `check()` method returns `false`, we should have some handling in place. In most circumstances using a redirect and en-queuing the `check()` error message will suffice.

Let us tidy up our example. Some of the fields have default values defined in the table, so our buffer will not be up to date after the record is created. When we create a new record because the class knows what the table primary key is, the primary key buffer property is automatically updated. After the previous example the buffer for `$table` looks like this:

```
[id] => 1

[content] => Lorem ipsum dolor sit amet

[checked_out] =>

[checked_out_time] =>

[params] =>

[ordering] => 1

[hits] => 0
```

After storing the new record, we can load the record from the database ensuring that the buffer is up to date. This example loads the new record from the table into the buffer.

```
$table->load($table->id);
```

Now the buffer will look like this:

```
[id] => 1

[content] => Lorem ipsum dolor sit amet

[checked_out] => 0

[checked_out_time] => 0000-00-00 00:00:00

[params] =>

[ordering] => 1

[hits] => 0
```

Instead of loading newly added records, we could modify the `TableFoobar` class so that the default values correspond directly to the database table's default values. This way we reduce our overheads and do not have to reload the record.

However, because some of the default values are dependent upon the database, to do this we would have to modify the constructor and override the `reset()` method. For example the `checked_out_time` field default value is `$db->getNullDate()`, and we cannot use this when defining parameters.

The way we updated the table buffer after creating the new record is precisely the same way we would load (read) any existing record. This example shows how we load a record into the buffer:

```
if (!$table->load($id))
{
    // handle unable to load
    // use $table->getError() for an explanation
}
```

Well, we are steaming through this CRUD (not literally). Next up is updating an existing record. There are two ways of updating a record. We can insert the updated data into the buffer and update the record. Alternatively, we can load the record, insert the updated data into the buffer, and update the record. This example shows how we implement the simpler first option:

```
// set values
$table->reset();
$table->setVar('id', $id);
$table->setVar('content', JRequest::getString('content'));
if ($table->check())
{
    if (!$table->store())
    {
        // handle failed update
        // use $table->getError() for an explanation
    }
}
else
{
    // handle invalid input
    // use $table->getError() for an explanation
}
```

Although this works, if it fails, we do not even know whether it is due to an invalid record ID or a more complex problem. There is a quirk we need to be aware of when using the store() method. It only updates the values that are not null; we can force it to update nulls, by passing a true parameter to the store method. The issue with this is we would need to have the record loaded into the buffer so that we do not overwrite anything with null values. This example demonstrates how we can implement this.

```
if ($table->load($id))
{
    // handle failed load
    // use $table->getError() for an explanation
}
```

```
else
{
    $table->setVar('content', JRequest::getString('content'));
    if ($table->check())
    {
        if (!$table->store(true))
        {
            // handle failed update
            // use $table->getError() for an explanation
        }
    }
    else
    {
        // handle invalid input
        // use $table->getError() for an explanation
    }
}
```

The last action that will occur in any record's life is deletion. Deleting a record using JTable subclasses is very easy. This example shows how we delete a record.

```
if (!$table->delete($id))
{
    // handle failed delete
}
```

If we don't pass an ID to the `delete()` method, the ID in the buffer will be used. It is important to bear in mind that if you do pass an ID the buffer ID will be updated.

If we are deleting a record that has relationships with other tables, we can check for dependencies using the `canDelete()` method. The `canDelete()` method has one parameter, a two dimensional array. The inner arrays must contain the keys, `idfield`, `name`, `joinfield`, and `label`. `idfield` is the name of the primary key in the related table. `name` is the name of the related table. `joinfield` is the name of the foreign key in the related table. `label` is the description of the relationship to use in the error message if any dependencies are found.

Imagine that there is another table called #__myextension_children; this table has a primary key called `childid` and a foreign key called `parent`, which is related to the primary key field `id` in #__myextension_foobars. In this example, we verify there are no dependent records in the #__myextension_children table before deleting a record from #__myextension_foobars.

```
$join1 = array('idfield'   => 'childid',
               'name'      => '#__myextension_children',
               'joinfield' => 'parent',
               'label'     => 'Children');
```

```
$joins = array($join1);
if ($table->canDelete($id, $joins))
{
    if (!$table->delete($id))
    {
        // handle failed delete
        // use $table->getError() for an explanation
    }
}
else
{
    // handle dependent records, cannot delete
    // use $table->getError() for an explanation
}
```

We can define more than one join, for example had there been another table called #__myextension_illegitimate_children we could also have defined this in the $joins array.

```
$join1 = array('idfield'   => 'childid',
               'name'      => '#__myextension_children',
               'joinfield' => 'parent',
               'label'     => 'Children');
$join2 = array('idfield'   => 'ichildid',
               'name'      => '#__myextension_illegitimate_children',
               'joinfield' => 'parent',
               'label'     => 'illegitimate Children');
$joins = array($join1, $join2);
```

> The names of primary keys and foreign keys in all of the tables must not be the same as the names of any other fields in any of the other tables. Otherwise, the query will become ambiguous and the method will always return false.

Manipulating Common Fields

Let us rewind a bit, killing off our record in its prime was a little mean after all! Our table includes all of those handy common fields we mentioned earlier and JTable provides us with some useful methods for dealing specifically with those fields. Throughout the Common Fields examples $table refers to an instance of the TableFoobar class and $id refers to the ID of the record we are dealing with.

Publishing

To publish and un-publish data we can use the `publish()` method. This method publishes and un-publishes multiple records at once. If the table includes a `checked_out` field, we can ensure that the record is not checked out or is checked out to the current user. This example publishes a record.

```
$publishIds = array($id);
$user =& JFactory::getUser();
if (!$table->publish($publishIds, 1, $user->get('id')))
{
    // handle unable to publish record
    // use $table->getError() for an explanation
}
```

The first parameter is an array of keys of the records we wish to publish or un-publish. The second parameter is the new published value, 0 = not published, 1 = published; this is optional, by default it is 1. The final parameter, also optional, is used only when the `checked_out` field exists. Only fields that are not checked out or are checked out by the specified user can be updated.

The method returns `true` if the publishing was successful. This is not the same as saying all the specified records have been updated. For example if a specified record is checked out by a different user, the record will not be updated but the method will return `true`.

Hits

To increment the hits field we can use the `hit()` method. In this example we set the buffer record ID and use the `hit()` method.

```
$table->set('id', $id);
$table->hit();
```

Alternatively we can specify the ID when we use the `hit()` method. If we choose to do this, we must remember that the buffer ID will be updated to match the hit ID.

```
$table->hit($id);
```

Checking Out

Before we start checking out records, we first need to check if a record is already checked out. Remember that when a record is checked out we should not allow any other user to modify the record. We can use the `isCheckOutMethod()` to achieve this. In this example, we test to see if any user, other than the current user, has checked out the record:

```
$table->load($id);
$user =& JFactory::getUser();
if ($table->isCheckedOut($user->get('id')))
{
    // handle record is already checked-out
}
```

Once we have determined a record isn't checked out, we can use the checkout() method to check out the record. In this example, we check out the record to the current user; this sets the checked_out field to the user's ID and the checked_out_ time field to the current time.

```
$table->load($id);
$user =& JFactory::getUser();
if (!$table->checkout($user->get('id')))
{
    // handle failed to checkout record
}
```

Now that we have a checked-out record, we need to know how to check it in. To do this we use the checkin() method. This example checks in a record; this will set the checked_out_time field to a null date:

```
$table->load($id);
$user =& JFactory::getUser();
if (!$table->checkin($user->get('id')))
{
    // handle failed to checkin record
}
```

 We should only check records in and out for logged in users. For a more comprehensive check-out system use Joomla!'s access control system explained in Chapter 11.

Ordering

When we want to order items, JTable gives us a number of useful methods. The first one of these we will look at is reorder(). This method looks at each record and moves them up the order chain until any gaps in the order have been removed. In this example, we reorder our table:

```
$table->reorder();
```

Very simple, but for more complicated tables there could be groupings within the records. To deal with this we can provide the reorder() method with a parameter to restrict the records. Imagine that our table also has a field named group; in this example, we reorder the records in group 1:

```
$db =& $table::getDBO();
$where = $db->nameQuote('group').' = 1';
$table->reorder($where);
```

Notice that we get the database object from `$table` not JFactory; this ensures that we are using the correct database driver for the database server that `$table` is using. Although this is not a major issue, as Joomla! begins to support other database drivers, there may be occasions where the database driver being used by a table is different from the global database driver.

You may remember earlier in this chapter we used the `getNextOrder()` method. This method tells us what the next available position is in the order. As with `reorder()`, we have the option of specifying groupings. Imagine that our table also has a field named `group`; in this example, we get the next available position in the records in group 1:

```
$db =& $table::getDBO();
$where = $db->nameQuote('group').' = 1';
$nextPosition = $table->getNextOrder($where);
```

Last of all we can use the `move()` method to move a record up or down one position. In this example, we move a record up the order:

```
$table->load($id);
$table->move(-1);
```

Again, we have the option of specifying groupings. Imagine that our table also has a field named `group`; in this example, we move a record down the order in group 1:

```
$db =& $table::getDBO();
$where = $db->nameQuote('group').' = 1';
$table->load($id);
$table->move(1, $where);
```

Parameter Fields

The JTable class does not provide us with any special methods for dealing with INI parameter fields. The JTable buffer is designed to be populated with the RAW data, as it will be stored in the database.

To handle a parameter field we use the JParameter class. The first thing we need to do is create a new JParameter object and, if we are interrogating an existing record, parse the parameter data.

The JParameter class extends the JRegistry class; the JRegistry class is explained in Chapter 7. This example shows how we can parse INI data using the JParameter class:

```
$params = new JParameter($table->params);
```

Once we have a JParameter object we can access and modify the data in the object using the get() and set() methods:

```
$value = $params->get('someValue');
$params->set('someValue', ++$value);
```

We can return the data to an INI string using the toString() method:

```
$table->params = $params->toString();
```

We can also use the JParameter class in conjunction with an XML metadata file to define the values we might be holding in an INI string. This example shows how we create a new JParameter object and load an XML metadata file; $path is the full path to an XML manifest file:

```
$params = new JParameter('foo=bar', $pathToXML_File);
```

There is a full description explaining how to define an XML metadata file for these purposes in Chapter 4 and the *Appendix*. We can use the render() method to output form elements populated with the parameter values (how these are rendered is defined in the XML file):

```
echo $params->render('params');
```

Date Fields

Different database servers use different date and time formats to store dates and times. It is important that when we come to save dates and times we use the correct format for the database that is being used.

Sadly, there is currently no way to ensure that we are using the format specific to the database being used. Instead we must assume that the database is MySQL based. This means that we must store dates in the format YYYY-MM-DD HH:MM:SS.

The easiest way to do this is to use the JDate class. JDate objects are used to parse and represent date and time values. We use the toMySQL() method to ensure that the value is formatted appropriately:

```
// import JDate class
jimport('joomla.utilities.date');

// get current date and time (unix timestamp)
$myDate = gmdate();
```

```
// create JDate object
$jdate = new JDate($myDate);

// create query using toMySQL()
$query = 'SELECT * FROM #__example WHERE date < '.$jdate->toMySQL();
```

The value that we pass when creating the JDate object can be in the format UNIX timestamp, RFC 2822 / 822, or ISO 8601. A more complete description of JDate is available in Chapter 12.

Summary

We should now be able to successfully create new database table schemas; how we add these tables to the database is explained in more detail in the next chapter, Chapter 4. We can build queries that are ready for use with our specific database driver using the `nameQuote()` and `Quote()` methods. We must remember to use these two methods; if we do not we run the risk of restricting our queries to MySQL databases.

We can extend the abstract JTable class adding an extra element to the data access layer. JTable allows us to perform many common actions on records. Taking advantage of the JTable class can significantly reduce the overheads incurred while programming and it ensures that we use standardized methods to perform actions.

4
Component Design

This chapter explains the concepts behind building Joomla! components and shows you how to build your own components. Components have two main elements, the frontend and the backend.

At the heart of Joomla! components lies the **MVC** (Model-View-Controller) framework. There are many ways in which the MVC design pattern can be implemented; this chapter is specifically interested in Joomla!'s MVC implementation.

Setting up a Sandbox

When we start building a new component, it is imperative that we have a sandbox; somewhere we can test the code. Ideally, we should have more than one system so we can test our components on different server setups.

The quick and easy way to set up a component sandbox is to create the component folders in the frontend and backend. This technique has some major drawbacks, unless we hack the #__components table, and will prevent us from testing all aspects of our code.

A more comprehensive approach is to create a basic installer, which sets up a blank component. The XML displayed can be used to create a blank component called 'My Extension':

```xml
<?xml version="1.0" encoding="utf-8"?>
<!DOCTYPE install SYSTEM "http://dev.joomla.org/xml/1.5/
                                    component-install.dtd">

<install type="component" version="1.5">
    <name>My Extension</name>
    <creationDate>MonthName Year</creationDate>
    <author>Author's Name</author>
    <authorEmail>Author's Email</authorEmail>
```

```
        <authorUrl>Author's Website</authorUrl>
        <copyright>Copyright Notice</copyright>
        <license>Component License Agreement</license>
        <version>Component Version</version>
        <description>Component Description</description>
        <administration>
            <menu>My Extension</menu>
        </administration>
        <install />
        <uninstall />
    </install>
```

To use this create a new XML manifest file, using UTF-8 encoding, and save the code into it. You should update the XML to suit the component you intend to build. We will discuss the role of the XML manifest file in more detail at the end of this chapter.

The component name is used to uniquely identify your component. When you select a name for your component, it is advisable to ensure that the name is not being used by an existing component. The name will also be used in the form `com_parsedname`; this is done automatically by Joomla!. For example, the name 'My Extension' will also be used in the format `com_myextension`.

Once you have built your XML manifest file, create a new archive, which can be ZIP, TAR, GZ, TGZ, GZIP, BZ2, TBZ2, or BZIP2, and add the XML manifest file to it. If you install the archive as a component, you should get a blank component, which you can begin to develop.

To get you started, the frontend for the component will be located at `components/com_myextension`. In this folder, you need to create the root component file called `myextension.php`; this file is executed when the component is invoked from the frontend.

The backend for the component is stored at `administrator/components/com_myextension`. In this folder, you need to create the root admin component file called `admin.myextension.php`; this file is executed when the component is invoked from the backend.

Once you have done this, to access your component from the frontend you will be able to create a new menu item, in the menu manager, which uses your component. To use your component from the backend you can use the link that will now appear in the components menu.

The Structure

Before we are stuck into building an MVC component, we need to understand the folder structure. This diagram shows the structure of a typical MVC component backend folder. The structure of the frontend is essentially the same but without the elements, help, and tables folders.

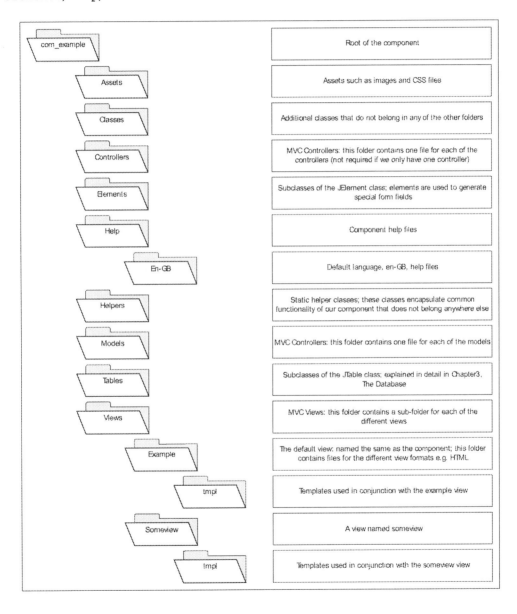

When you create folders in Joomla!, you should include a copy of `index.html` in each. The `index.html` file is a blank HTML file, which prevents users from obtaining a directory listing.

 This folder structure is not compulsory. If we want to use the Joomla! MVC, help (preferences button), and JTable subclasses, we must use the `models`, `views`, `help`, and `tables` folders.

The MVC

A single Joomla! extension often caters for several user types and several interfaces. This diagram describes how two different users might access the same system:

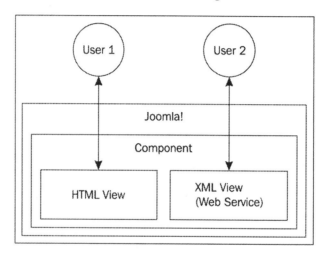

Without the MVC, or a similar solution, we would probably end up duplicating large portions of code when dealing with the HTML and XML views, each of which would contain elements specific to the view. This is extremely inefficient, intensive to maintain, and is likely to result in inconsistencies between views.

The MVC design pattern allows us to create code, that is independent of the interface. This is achieved by separating data access, presentation, and business logic. Separating these out means that we can refactor any part of an MVC-based component without affecting other parts of the component.

There are three parts to the MVC design pattern: the model, view, and controller. The controller and view can both be considered as part of the presentation layer, while the model could be considered as a fusion between the business logic and data-access layers.

There is a similar pattern to the MVC called 3-tier architecture. It is important that we do not confuse the two. 3-tier architecture is more concerned with the data layer; the MVC focuses more on the presentation layer. It is quite likely that we will find ourselves using a combination of the two. For more information about 3-tier architecture, refer to
`http://en.wikipedia.org/wiki/Multitier_architecture`.

Each part of the MVC is represented in Joomla! by an abstract class: JModel, JView, and JController. These classes are located in the `joomla.applictaion.component` library. This diagram shows how the classes relate to one another:

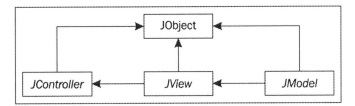

The model is used to handle data. In most cases, the data will be sourced from the database; however, we can use any data source. A single model is designed to work with multiple records; in other words a model does not represent a single record.

The model allows us to modify data; in most cases this is achieved using bespoke methods, which define business processes. The methods that define business logic are essentially defining the behavior of the data.

Models are never aware of controllers or views. It is important to remember this because it often helps us understand better how we are supposed to make the MVC components operate.

The view defines how we present the data. In Joomla!, when we use a view to display HTML we also use layouts (a form of template). This gives us an extra layer of control and enables us to define multiple templates for the same view.

The data that we display in a view originates from one or more models. These models are automatically associated with the view by the controller.

Views never modify data. All modifications to data are completed within the controller.

The controller is the brains behind the operation. Part of the presentation layer, the controller analyses input data and takes the necessary steps to produce the result, presenting the output.

The controller selects the models with which the request is concerned and performs any required data modifications. The controller determines the view to use and associates the models with the view. In some cases, a view will not be required and a redirect will be initiated instead.

The controller executes the action and either redirects the browser or displays data. When displaying data the controller creates a view and optionally associates one or more models with the view

Building a Model

Before we start building a model, we need to determine the name of the model. To make the MVC work as intended, we follow a special naming convention: the component's name, the word Model, the data entity name. The model must be in a file named after the entity and be located in the models folder.

Imagine we are creating a model for the component 'My Extension' and the entity data is called foobar. The model class would be called MyextensionModelFoobar and it would be located in models/foobar.php.

All model classes extend the abstract JModel class. This example shows a very basic implementation of the MyextensionModelFoobar class.

```
// ensure a valid entry point
  defined(_JEXEC) or die('Restricted Access');
// import the JModel class
  jimport('joomla.application.component.model');
/**
 * Foobar Model
 */
class MyextensionModelFoobar extends JModel
{
}
```

I warned you it was basic! Actually, it is so basic it is useless. Before we continue, note that we had to import the joomla.application.component.model library. This guarantees that the JModel class is present.

We use special methods prefixed with the word get to retrieve data from models. Most models only have one of these methods. The next step is to build a get method.

Our example is dealing with the entity foobar, so we'll create a get method, getFoobar(). To ensure that we get the right foobar we need to determine which foobar we are looking for.

We will assume that the ID of the foobar in which we are interested is either the first element in the array `cid` or the value of `id`. We normally use `cid` when we have come from a page with a selection of records and `id` when we have come from a page with one record.

```
/**
 * Foobar Model
 */
class MyextensionModelFoobar extends JModel
{
    /**
     * Foobar ID
     *
     * @var int
     */
    var $_id;

    /**
     * Foobar data
     *
     * @var object
     */
    var $_foobar;

    /**
     * Constructor, builds object and determines the foobar ID
     *
     */
    function __construct()
    {
      parent::__construct();

      // get the cid array from the default request hash
      $cid = JRequest::getVar('cid', false, 'DEFAULT', 'array');
      if($cid)
      {
          $id = $cid[0];
      }
      else
      {
          $id = JRequest::getInt('id', 0);
      }
          $this->setId($id);
    }
```

```
/**
 * Resets the foobar ID and data
 *
 * @param int foobar ID
 */
function setId($id=0)
{
    $this->_id = $id;
    $this->_foobar = null;
}

/**
 * Gets foobar data
 *
 * @return object
 */
function getFoobar()
{
    // if foobar is not already loaded load it now
    if (!$this->_foobar)
    {
        $db =& $this->getDBO();
        $query = "SELECT * FROM ".$db-
        >nameQuote('#__myextension_foobar')
        " WHERE ".$db->nameQuote('id')." = ".$this->_id;
        $db->setQuery($query);
        $this->_foobar = $db->loadObject();
    }
    // return the foobar data
    return $this->_foobar;
}
}
```

Our model is now usable; we can retrieve a record from the table #__myextesnion_ foobar. How we choose to implement get methods is entirely up to us. There are some common techniques used when implementing the get methods, but these should only be used where appropriate.

- Use a property to cache retrieved data:

```
var $_foobar;
```

- Create a private method to load the data:

```
function _loadFoobar()
{
    // Load the data
    if (empty($this->_foobar))
    {
```

```
        $query = $this->_buildQuery();
        $this->_db->setQuery($query);
        $this->_foobar = $this->_db->loadObject();
        return (boolean) $this->_foobar;
    }

      return true;
  }
```

- Create a private method to build a query string:

```
function _buildFoobar()
{
    $db =& $this->getDBO();
    return "SELECT * FROM "
    .$db->nameQuote('#__myextension_foobar')
        " WHERE ".$db->nameQuote('id')      " = "      .$this->_id;
}
```

- Create a private method to build a blank set of data:

```
function initializeFoobar()
{
    if (empty($this->_foobar))
    {
     $foobar = new stdClass;
     $foobar->id = 0;
     $foobar->name = null;
     $this->_foobar =& $foobar;
    }
}
```

Data that we access in a model does not have to come from the database. We can interrogate any data source. Data that we return using the get methods can be of any type. Many of the core components return data in stdClass objects.

As well as accessing data, we use the model to modify data. In this example we implement a save() method; this will act as a pass-through for the JTable class TableFoobar save() method, which we defined in Chapter 3.

```
/**
 * Save a foobar
 *
 * @param mixed object or associative array of data to save
 * @return Boolean true on success
 */
function save($data)
{
```

```
    // get the table
    $table =& $this->getTable('Foobar');
    // save the data
    if (!$table->save($data))
    {
        // an error occurred, update the model error message
        $this->setError($table->getError());
        return false;
    }
    return true;
}
```

In the example we use the `getTable()` method to retrieve an instance of the `TableFoobar` class. We could have used the static `JTable::getInstance()` method but this would have required more effort because it defaults to looking for core JTable subclasses. Core JTable subclasses are prefixed with JTable, non-core tables are prefixed with `Table`.

When we try to save `$data` there are a number of actions that are performed. `$data` is bound to the table, the `check()` method is executed, the data is stored, and the item is checked in. If any of these methods fails then `false` is returned.

Therefore, if the table save method does fail, we copy the error message to the model. This way we can determine what went wrong.

Let's take a look at a method that doesn't use a JTable to modify data. We will implement a `hit()` method, which will increment the value of a foobar's hit counter.

```
/**
 * Increments the hit counter
 *
 */
function hit()
{
    //
    $db =& JFactory::getDBO();
    $db->setQuery('UPDATE '.$db->nameQuote('#__myextension_foobar').'
            .'SET '.$db->nameQuote('hits').' = '.$db-
            >nameQuote('hits').' + 1 '.'WHERE id = '.$this->_id);
    $db->query();
}
```

We could just as easily have used this as a pass-through for the `TableFoobar hit()` method. We can implement many different methods in a model object. How we choose to implement them is entirely up to us.

Building a View

Views are separated by folders; each view has its own folder located in the `views` folder. Within a view's folder we define a different file for each different document type that the view is going to support i.e. feed, HTML, PDF, and RAW. If we are defining a view for the HTML document type, we will also need to create a folder called `tmpl`, which will hold layouts (HTML templates) to render the view.

Before we start building a view class, we need to determine the name of the class. To make the MVC work as intended, we follow a special naming convention: the component's name, the word 'View', and the view name. The view class is stored in a file named `view.documentType.php`.

Imagine we are creating an HTML view for the component 'My Extension' to view the entity foobar. The view class would be called `MyextensionViewFoobar` and it would be located in a file called `view.html.php` in the `views` folder in a subfolder called foobar.

All view classes extend the abstract JView class. This example shows a very basic implementation of the `MyextensionViewFoobar` class:

```
// ensure a valid entry point
   defined(_JEXEC) or die('Restricted Access');

// import the JView class
   jimport('joomla.application.component.view');

/**
 * Foobar View
 */
class MyextensionViewFoobar extends JView
{
}
```

Note that when we build a view we must import the `joomla.application.component.view` library. This guarantees that the JView class is present.

The most important method in any view class is the `display()` method; this method is already defined in the parent class JView. The `display()` method is where all of the workings take place. We interrogate models for data, customize the document, and render the view.

 We never modify data from within the view. Data is only to be modified in the model and controller.

Let us continue modifying our previous example; we will display a Foobar. To do this we need to override the `display()` method, get the necessary data from a `MyextensionModelFoobar` object and render it:

```
/**
 * Foobar View
 */
class MyextensionViewFoobar extends JView
{

    /**
     * Renders the view
     *
     */
    function display()
    {
        // interrogate the model
        $foobar =& $this->get('Foobar');
        $this->assignRef('foobar', $foobar);
        // display the view
        parent::display();
    }

}
```

There is not a big difference here; all we have done is overridden the display method and interrogated the model. Occasionally there are times when we do not need to override the display method. For example if we were outputting static content.

The diagram we looked at earlier, which showed how the three classes—JModel, JView, and JController—relate to one another, describes an aggregate relationship between views and models. That is to say, within a view there can be references to model objects. In our case, there is a reference to a `MyextensionModelFoobar` object.

Going back to our example: the JView `get()` method looks at all the different models with which it is familiar and looks for a method named the same as the first parameter of the `get()` call and prefixed with get. So when we use `$this->get('Foobar')` we are asking the view to find a model with a method called `getFoobar()`, to execute the method, and to return the result.

Slightly confusing is how we ended up with a reference to a `MyextensionModelFoobar` object; because our view is called `MyextensionViewFoobar`, a controller would know that these two classes relate to one another (both are named Foobar). When we use a controller to display a view it automatically attempts to root out a related model and, if it finds one, assigns it to the view. We will explain this in slightly more detail when we cover controllers.

In our case the `getFoobar()` method in the `MyextensionModelFoobar` class returns a `stdClass` object (`stdClass` is a PHP class). Once we have this data, we can assign it to our view ready to be used by our layout (template). We assign data to our view because it makes it very easy to access from within a layout. We need not do this if we are not using layouts to present our view.

There are two ways in which we can assign data to our view: we can use the `assign()` or `assignRef()` method. The two methods are very similar, except that `assignRef()` assigns a reference to the data and `assign()` assigns a copy of the data. For both methods, the first parameter is the name of the data and the second parameter is the data itself.

There is another way in which the `assign()` method can be used, which is similar to a bind function. For more information, refer to the *Appendix.*

As a general rule: when dealing with vectors (objects and arrays) we should use the `assignRef()` method; when dealing with scalars (basic data types) we should use the `assign()` method.

Finally in our overridden `display()` method we call the parent `display()` method. This is what loads and renders the layout, but we do not have a layout. In components, layouts are unique to HTML views.

Layouts are essentially templates; in most cases, there is one template file per layout, which displays a view. Template files are PHP files, which mainly consist of XHTML and use small snippets of PHP to display dynamic data.

In theory, we do not actually need layouts because we can just echo data directly out of the view class. However, layouts enable us to define multiple layouts for the same view, so we can view the same data in a number of different ways.

To create a default layout we create a file called `default.php` in the view's `tmpl` folder. This is the layout that will be used unless otherwise specified. This example shows how we might implement the `default.php` file:

```
<table width="100%" border="0" cellspacing="0" cellpadding="0">
    <tr>
        <th>Name</th>
        <td><?php echo $this->foobar->name; ?></td>
    </tr>
    <tr>
        <th>Description</th>
        <td><?php echo $this->foobar->description; ?></td>
    </tr>
</table>
```

We access foobar using $this->foobar. We can do this because we used the assignRef() method to assign this data to the view. This example assumes that the entity Foobar has the attributes name and description.

A more complete description of how to build and use layouts is available in Chapter 8.

Building a Controller

We can use controllers in many different ways. The MVC design pattern might insinuate that we only need one controller; in reality, it can be very useful to implement multiple controllers, one controller per entity.

Controllers extend the abstract JController class, which we import from the joomla. application.component.controller library. It can be useful to add an extra layer of inheritance with an additional abstract controller class; this makes particular sense if we are using multiple controllers, which use common methods.

Controllers use tasks, string names, to identify what we want to do. Within the controller, there is a task map, which is used to map task names to methods. When we instantiate a new controller, the task map is automatically populated with task and method names.

If we had a JController subclass with three methods, foo(), bar(), and _baz(), our task map would look like this:

Task	Method
foo	foo()
bar	bar()

Notice that the _baz() method is missing; this is because _baz() is a private method, which is denoted by the underscore at the start of the name. The task map uses a many-to-one relationship: we can define many tasks for one method. To add additional entries to the task map we can use the registerTask() method. More information about this method is available in the *Appendix*.

Within JController there is a special method called execute(). This method is used to execute a task. For example, if we wanted to execute the task foo, we would use the following:

```
$controller->execute('foo');
```

Assuming $controller is using the task map we spoke of earlier, the controller will execute the foo() method.

When the execute() method is performed the controller will also perform an authorization check. For more information about how to define permissions, refer to Chapter 11.

Unlike models and views there are is no specific naming convention to which we must adhere when we define a controller class. The core controllers tend to use the format: component name, the word 'Controller', and optionally the entity name.

For example, we might choose to name our controller MyextensionControllerFoobar. We will assume we only have the one entity, so we will name our example controller MyextensionController.

Controllers are normally located in a folder called controllers, or, if there is only one controller, it is in the root of the component in a file called controller.php.

 Wherever you choose to locate your controllers, you will have to import them manually.

To use the abstract JController class we must import the joomla.application. component.controller library; this guarantees that the JController class is available to be extended. This example defines a controller called MyextensionController:

```
// Check to ensure this file is included in Joomla!
   defined('_JEXEC') or die('Restricted Access');
   jimport('joomla.application.component.controller');
/**
 * MyExtension Controller
 *
 */
class MyextensionController extends JController
{
}
```

There are many methods within the JController class, which we can override. The most commonly overridden method is display(). This method instantiates a view object, attaches a model to the view and initiates the view.

There are two important request variables, which are used by the display() method to determine what it does. The view request determines which view to instantiate. The layout argument determines which layout to use if the document type is HTML.

This might sound as if it does everything we need. However, there is a common reason for overloading the `display()` method. We might want to increment a hit counter associated with an entity. In this example, we do just that:

```
/**
 * MyExtension Controller
 *
 */
class MyextensionController extends JController
{
    /**
     * Display
     *
     */
    function display()
    {
        // get the Foobar model and increment the counter
        $modelFoobar =& $this->getModel('Foobar');
        $modelFoobar->hit();
        // display foobar
        parent::display();
    }
}
```

 Note that to obtain the `MyextensionModelFoobar` object we use the `getModel()` method and supply it with the name of the model.

There are a great many different tasks that we might want our controller to be able to handle. This table identifies the common task and method names we use to identify tasks (we are not limited to these; we can use others if we want to):

Task/Method	Description
add	Create a new item.
apply	Apply changes to an item and return to the edit view.
archive	Archive an item. Most components do not implement archiving: for an example of a component that does, you can study the core content component.
assign	Assign an item to something.
cancel	Cancel the current task.
default	Make an item the default item.
publish	Publish an item.

Task/Method	Description
remove	Delete an item.
save	Save an item and return to a list of items.
unarchive	Un-archive an item.
unpublish	Un-publish an item.

Imagine we want the controller to be able to deal with a save task. To do this we need to implement a method that will deal with the task. For the sake of simplicity we will name the method save(). This is an example of how we might implement the method.

```
/**
 * Save a Foobar and redirect
 *
 */
function save()
{
    // get the data to be saved ($_POST hash)
    $data = JRequest::get('POST');

    // get the model
    $model = $this->getModel('Foobar');
    // bind the array to the model and save it.
    if ($model->save($data))
    {
        $message = JText::_('Foobar Saved');
    }
    else
    {
        $message = JText::_('Foobar Save Failed');
        $message .= ' ['.$model->getError().']';
    }
    $this->setRedirect('index.php?option=com_foobar', $message);
}
```

This method is relatively generic, which makes the method very resilient to changes in the component. Making methods relatively generic makes future development easier and reduces the impact of changes.

We get a copy of the $_POST hash; this assumes that the data will always be submitted via a POST request. We proceed to get an instance of the relevant model and attempt to save the data.

Using $_POST might look like a security issue, but because of the way in which the save() method is implemented in JModel (using the JTable bind() method), only the values that we require will be used.

We don't need to check in the record because the save() method in the model automatically does this for us.

Finally, we set up a redirect; this will be used to redirect the browser to a new location. This does not immediately redirect the browser, it just sets the redirect URI for when we execute the controller's redirect() method.

Notice that we don't call the parent display() method. This is because we want to separate out each task. We could have next decided to display a view, but this would mean that a refresh of the page would execute the save method a second time!

 The use of redirects is considered unnecessary by some developers, who believe that we should instead invoke other controllers and controller methods. However, many of the core Joomla! components use redirects.

Building an MVC Component

Knowing how to build each element of an MVC component is only the beginning. We need to know how to put all of this into practice! Planning your component is crucial because so many of the MVC elements are interdependent.

The best place to start is identifying the entities that your component deals with. An easy way to do this is to create an **ERD** (Entity Relationship Diagram). If you are not familiar with ERDs there are plenty of online resources available.

The next step is to build a database schema. When you do this, you must take into consideration all of the aspects covered in Chapter 3. Remember to make use of the common fields and to use the naming conventions.

To ensure you gain the best performance from your database, normalize your tables to at least 2NF (2nd normal form). If you are not familiar with database normalization, there is a good tutorial available on the official MySQL developer zone website: http://dev.mysql.com/tech-resources/articles/intro-to-normalization.html.

Once you have done this, you should have a good basis on which to start building your component. The best place to start is with the controllers. How you choose to design your controllers normally depends on the complexity of your component and the number of entities you are dealing with.

For each major entity, you should identify the tasks associated with each. You can use the table in the previous section, which identified common task and method names to help identify tasks.

We have seen how to build models, views, and controllers but we have yet to see how we actually use them. To get started we need to create a PHP file named after the component in the component's frontend folder and we need to create a PHP file named after the component and prefixed with `admin.` in the component's backend folder.

These files are executed when the component is invoked via the frontend and backend respectively. This example shows how we might implement one of these files:

```
// Check to ensure this file is included in Joomla!
   defined('_JEXEC') or die('Restricted Access');

// get the controller
   require_once(JPATH_COMPONENT.DS.'controller.php');

// instantiate and execute the controller
   $controller = new MyextensionController();
   $controller->execute(JRequest::getCmd('task', 'display'));

// redirect
   $controller->redirect();
```

You will often find that these files are relatively simple. In the above example we get the controller class file, instantiate a new controller, execute the task, and redirect the browser. The `redirect()` method will only redirect the browser if a redirect URI has been set; use `setRedirect()` to set a redirect URI and, optionally, a message.

We can do far more with these files if we wish, but often we do not need to; generally, it is better to keep the processing encapsulated in controllers.

It is common practice to use multiple controllers, one for each entity. These are generally stored in a folder called `controllers` in files named after the entity. Each controller class is named after the entity and prefixed with `MyextensionController`.

When we use multiple controllers, we generally use the URI query request value c to determine the controller to instantiate. This demonstrates how we can deal with multiple controllers:

```
// Check to ensure this file is included in Joomla!
defined('_JEXEC') or die('Restricted Access');

// get the base controller
require_once(JPATH_COMPONENT.DS.'controller.php');
```

```
// get controller
if ($c = JRequest::getCmd('c', 'DefaultEntity'))
{
    // determine path
    $path = JPATH_COMPONENT.DS.'controllers'.DS.$c.'.php';
    jimport('joomla.filesystem.file');
    if (JFile::exists($path))
    {
        // controller exists, get it!
        require_once($path);
    }
    else
    {
        // controller does not exist
        JError::raiseError('500', JText::_('Unknown controller'));
    }
}
// instantiate and execute the controller
    $c = 'MyextensionController'.$c;
    $controller = new $c();
    $controller->execute(JRequest::getCmd('task', 'display'));
// redirect
    $controller->redirect();
```

An alternative method is to encapsulate this within another layer of inheritance. For example we could create the controller class MyextensionController and add a getInstance() method to it that will return an object of the desired subclass. This example demonstrates how we might implement such a method:

```
/**
 * Gets a reference to a subclass of the controller.
 *
 * @static
 * @param string entity name
 * @param string controller prefix
 * @return MyextensionController extension controller
 */
function &getInstance($entity, $prefix='MyExtensionController')
{
    // use a static array to store controller instances
    static $instances;
    if (!$instances)
    {
        $instances = array();
    }
    // determine subclass name
    $class = $prefix.ucfirst($entity);
```

```
    // check if we already instantiated this controller
if (!isset($instances[$class]))
{
    // check if we need to find the controller class
    if (!class_exists( $class ))
    {
        jimport('joomla.filesystem.file');
        $path = JPATH_COMPONENT.DS.'controllers',
                    strtolower($entity).'.php';

        // search for the file in the controllers path
        if (JFile::exists($path)
        {
            // include the class file
            require_once $path;

            if (!class_exists( $class ))
            {
                // class file does not include the class
                return JError::raiseWarning('SOME_ERROR',
                        JText::_('Invalid controller'));
            }
        }
        else
        {
            // class file not found
            return JError::raiseWarning('SOME_ERROR',
            JText::_('Unknown controller'));
        }
    }

    // create controller instance
    $instances[$class] = new $class();
}

    // return a reference to the controller
    return $instances[$class];
}
```

We can now alter the component root file to use the `getInstance()` method:

```
// Check to ensure this file is included in Joomla!
    defined('_JEXEC') or die('Restricted Access');
// get the base controller
    require_once(JPATH_COMPONENT.DS.'controller.php');
    $c = JRequest::getCmd('c', 'DefaultEntity')
    $controller = MyextensionController::getInstance($c);
    $controller->execute(JRequest::getCmd('task', 'display'));
// redirect
    $controller->redirect();
```

This list details some important things to consider when designing and building controllers:

- If you have one major entity, you should consider building one controller.
- If you have a number of entities, you should consider using a separate controller for each.
- To manage multiple controllers, it can be useful to create another controller, which instantiates the controllers and siphons tasks to them.
- If you have a number of similar entities, you should consider building an abstract controller, which implements common tasks.

Up to this point, we have hardly mentioned the back and frontends in relation to the MVC. The way in which the MVC library is constructed leads us to using separate controllers, views, and models for the front and back ends.

Since we will generally be using the same data in the front and backend, we might want to use some of the same MVC elements in the frontend and backend. If you do choose to do this, it is normal to define the common MVC elements in the backend.

To access models and views located in the backend from the frontend we can manually tell Joomla! about additional paths to look in. It is relatively unlikely that you would want to use the same view in the front and back-end. If you do want to do this, you should carefully consider your reasons.

This is an example of an overridden controller constructor method. It tells the controller that there are other places to look for models and views.

```
/**
 * Constructor
 *
 */
function __construct()
{
    // execute parent's constructor
    parent::__construct();
    // use the same models as the back-end
    $path = JPATH_COMPONENT_ADMINISTRATOR.DS.'models';
    $this->addModelPath($path);
    // use the same views as the back-end
    $path = JPATH_COMPONENT_ADMINISTRATOR.DS.'views'
    $this->addViewPath($path);
}
```

If we use this, the controller will look for models and views in the component's backend folders, as well as the default frontend folders. In this example, the frontend models and views will take precedence. If we wanted the admin paths to take precedence, all we would need to do is move the `parent::__construct()` call to the end of the overridden constructor method.

Rendering Other Document Types

We mentioned earlier that you can create a view for the document types, feed, HTML, PDF, and RAW. We have already briefly explained how to implement views for the HTML document type. This section describes how to create feed, PDF, and RAW views.

Every view, created in the `views` folder as a separate folder, can support any number of the document types. This table shows the naming convention we use for each.

Document Type	File Name	Description
Feed	`View.feed.php`	Renders an RSS 2.0 or Atom feed.
HTML	`view.html.php`	Renders a `text/html` view using the site template.
PDF	`view.pdf.php`	Renders an `application/pdf` document.
RAW	`view.raw.php`	Renders any other type of document; defaults to `text/html`, but we can modify this.

There is a fifth document type, error. We cannot create views within our components for this document type. The error document renders using a template from the site template or core error templates.

To request a page as a different document type, we use the request value format. For example to request the component My Extension in feed format, we might use this URI:

```
http://www.example.org/joomla/index.php?option=com_
myextension&format=feed
```

The four document types might sound restricting. However, the RAW document type has a clever trick up its sleeve. When Joomla! encounters a unknown format, it uses the RAW document. This means that we can specify bespoke formats. We will discuss this in more detail in a moment.

Feed

Before you choose to create a feed view you should consider whether the data is worthy of a feed. The data in question should be itemized and it should be likely to change on a regular basis.

Joomla! supports **RSS** 2.0 (Really Simple Syndication) and **Atom** (Atom Syndication Format) feeds; which is being used makes no difference as to how we build a feed view class.

We use the JFeedItem class to build feed items and add them to the document. JFeedItem objects include properties that relate to the corresponding RSS and Atom tags. The properties marked with a dash are not used by the corresponding feed format.

Property	Required by RSS	Required by Atom	Description
Author			Author's name
authorEmail	-	-	Author's email address, not currently supported by Joomla!
Category		-	Category of item
Comments		-	URI to comments about the item
Date		-	Date on which the item was created (UNIX timestamp)
Description			Description of the item
Enclosure			JFeedEnclosure object; describes an external source, for example a video file
Guid		-	Item ID, must be unique
Link			URI
pubDate			Date on which the item was published
Source	-	-	3rd party source name, not currently supported by Joomla!
Title			Name

For more information about how these tags work in RSS please refer to http://www.rssboard.org/rss-specification. For more information about how these tags work in Atom please refer to http://tools.ietf.org/html/rfc4287.

This example shows how we can build a feed; this would be located in a display() method in a view class that deals with feeds.

```
// set the basic link
$document =& JFactory::getDocument();
$document->setLink(JRoute::_('index.php?option=com_myextension'));

// get the items to add to the feed
$db =& JFactory::getDBO();
$query = 'SELECT * FROM #__myextension WHERE published = 1';
$db->setQuery($query);
$rows = $db->loadObjectList();

foreach ($rows as $row)
```

```
{
    // create a new feed item
    $item = new JFeedItem();

    // assign values to the item
    $item->author = $row->author;
    $item->category = $row->category;
    $item->comments = JRoute::_(JURI::base().'index.php?option=
                        com_myextension&view=comments&id='.$row->id);
    $item->date = date('r', strtotime($row->date));
    $item->description = $row->description;
    $item->guid = $row->id;
    $item->link = JRoute::_(JURI::base().'index.php?option=
                        com_myextension &id='.$row->id);
    $item->pubDate = date();
    $item->title = $row->title;

    $enclosure = new JFeedEnclosure();
    $enclosure->url = JRoute::_(JURI::base().'index.php?option=com_
                    myextension &view=video&format=raw&id='.$row->id);
    // size in bytes of file
    $enclosure->length = $row->length
    $enclosure->type = 'video/mpeg';

    $item->enclosure = $enclosure;

    // add item to the feed
    $document->addItem($item);
}
```

If a view is available in HTML and feed formats, you might want to add a link in the HTML view to the feed view. We can use the HTML link tag to define an alternative way of viewing data. This example shows how we can add such a tag to the HTML header. This code should be located in the view class's `display()` method.

```
// build links
$feed = 'index.php?option=com_myextension&format=feed';
$rss = array(
            'type' => 'application/rss+xml',
            'title' => 'My Extension RSS Feed'
        );
$atom = array(
            'type' => 'application/atom+xml',
            'title' => 'My Extension Atom Feed'
        );
```

```
// add the links
$document =& JFactory::getDocument();
$document->addHeadLink(JRoute::_($feed.'&type=rss'), 'alternate',
                                       'rel', $rss);
$document->addHeadLink(JRoute::_($feed.'&type=atom'), 'alternate',
                                        'rel', $atom);
```

To use this you will need to modify `$feed` to point to the correct location for your component.

PDF

Views that support the PDF document type build the data to be rendered in PDF format in HTML. Joomla! uses the TCPDF library to convert that HTML into a PDF document. Not all HTML tags are supported. Only the following tags will affect the layout of the document; all other tags will be removed.

- h1, h2, h3, h4, h5, h6
- b, u, i, strong, and em, sup, sub, small
- a
- img
- p, br, and hr
- font
- blockquote
- ul, ol
- table, td, th, and tr

As well as setting the PDF document content, we can modify the application/ generator, file name, metadata/keywords, subject, and title. This example shows how we can modify all of these. This should be done within the view class's `display()` method.

```
$document =& JFactory::getDocument();
$document->setName('Some Name');
$document->setTitle('Some Title');
$document->setDescription('Some Description');
$document->setMetaData('keywords', 'Some Keywords');
$document->setGenerator('Some Generator');
```

This screenshot depicts the properties of the resultant PDF document:

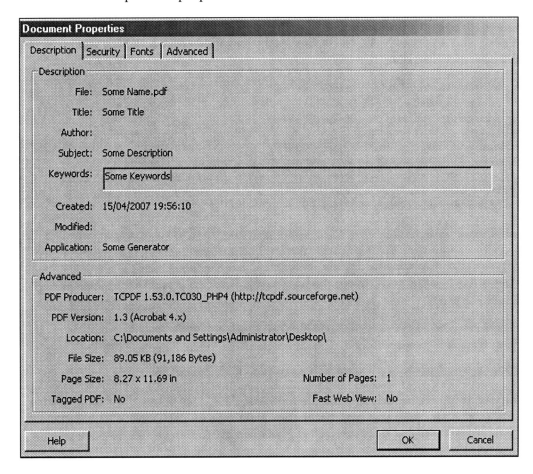

To add content to the document all we need to do is output the data as we would normally.

RAW

The RAW document type allows us to do anything we want to the document. Any document we want to return that is not HTML, PDF, or a feed, is RAW. For example if we wanted to output data in XML format, we could use the RAW document.

There are three important methods to output a document exactly as we want. By default RAW documents have a MIME type (Internet Media Type) of text/html; to change the MIME type we can use the setMimeEncoding() method.

```
$document =& JFactory::getDocument();
$document->setMimeEncoding('text/xml');
```

If we are outputting a document in which the content has been modified at a set date, we may want to set the document modified date. We can use the `setModifiedDate()` method to do this. In this example you would need to replace `time()` with an appropriate UNIX timestamp to suit the date to which you are trying to set the modified date:

```
$document =& JFactory::getDocument();
$date = gmdate('D, d M Y H:i:s', time()).' GMT';
$document->setModifiedDate($date);
```

Normally we serve all Joomla! responses using UTF-8 encoding. If you want to use a different character encoding you can use the `setCharset()` method:

```
$document =& JFactory::getDocument();
$document->setCharset('iso-8859-1');
```

Imagine we want to create an XML response using the RAW document. First, let us choose a name for the document format. The name must not be the same as any of the existing formats and although we could use the name 'raw', it is not very descriptive. Instead, we will use the name xml. This URI demonstrates how we would use this:

```
http://www.example.org/joomla/index.php?option=com_
myextension&format=xml
```

When we do this, the document will be of type JDocumentRaw.

The next thing we need to do is create the view class. This name of the file includes the format name, note that we use the format name 'xml', not 'raw'. For example, the file might be named `myview.xml.php`. This example demonstrates how we might construct the view class:

```
class MyextensionViewMyview extends JView
{
    function display($tpl = null)
    {
        // modify the MIME type
        $document =& JFactory::getDocument();
        $document->setMimeEncoding('text/xml');

        // add XML header
        echo '<?xml version="1.0" encoding="UTF-8" ?>';

        // prepare some data
        $xml = new JSimpleXMLElement('element');
        $xml->setData('This is an xml format document');
```

```
        // output the data in XML format
        echo $xml->toString();
    }
}
```

This will output a very basic XML document with one XML element:

```
<?xml version="1.0" encoding="UTF-8" ?>
<element>This is an xml format document</element>
```

The great thing about this is it enables us to create many formats for one view.

Dealing with Component Configuration

The chances are that a component that we are building is going to need some configuration options. Every component can store default parameters about itself.

A relationship exists between menu items and the component configuration. The configuration edited from within the component defines the default configuration. When we create a new menu item, we can modify the component configuration specifically for the menu item. This enables us to override the default configuration on a per-menu-item basis.

To define component parameters we must create an XML metadata file, called `config.xml`, in the root of our component in the backend. The file contains a root element `config`, and nested within this is a `params` tag. In this tag, we define different parameters, each in its own `param` tag.

This example defines two parameters, a title and a description (a complete description of the different parameters and their XML definition is available in the *Appendix*):

```
<?xml version="1.0" encoding="utf-8"?>
  <config>
    <params>
        <param name="title" type="text" default="My Title"
               label="Title" description="Title of page" size="30" />
        <param name="description" type="textarea" default=""
               label="Description" rows="5" cols="50" description=
                        "Description to display at top of page." />
    </params>
  </config>
```

Once we have created the XML file, the next step is to use the file to allow an administrator to edit the component parameters. Joomla! provides us with an easy way of doing this.

In the backend, components have a customizable menu bar. There is a special button we can add to this menu bar, called preferences, which is used to enable editing of a component's parameters. A complete description of the menu bar is available in Chapter 8.

This example shows how we add the button. We use two parameters to define the name of the component and the height of the preferences box. Adding buttons to the administration toolbar is explained in detail in Chapter 8.

```
JMenuBar::preferences('com_myextension', '200');
```

When an administrator uses this button, they will be presented with a preferences box. The first parameter determines which component's parameters we want to modify. The second parameter determines the height of this box. This screenshot depicts the preferences box displayed for com_myextension using the XML file we described earlier:

Now that we can define and edit parameters for a component, we need to know how to access these parameters from within the frontend of our component. To achieve this we use the application getPageParameters() method:

```
$params =& $mainframe->getPageParameters('com_myextension');
```

The great thing about this method is that it will automatically override any of the component's default configuration with the menu item's configuration. If it did not, we would have to merge the two manually.

The returned object is of type JParameter. This class deals specifically with XML metadata files, which define parameters. To get a value from the component parameters we use the get() method:

```
$title = $params->get('title');
```

We can use this snippet of code anywhere in our component. Many of the core components retrieve component parameters in models, views, and controllers.

Elements and Parameters

We have mentioned using parameters in the component configuration file; there are many other instances where we can use the `param` tag, for example defining module parameters. When we use the `param` tag in XML files, we are defining data items. As part of this we use the XML to produce rendered forms. JElement is the abstract class subclasses of which can be used to render each of the parameters.

JElement subclasses are used in conjunction with a single `param` tag and render a form input tag based upon it. There are a number of predefined parameter types (JElements) that we can use:

- category
- editors
- filelist
- folderlist
- helpsites
- hidden
- imagelist
- languages
- list
- menu
- menuitem
- password
- radio
- section
- spacer
- sql
- text
- textarea
- timzones

A full description of each of these is available in the *Appendix*.

Before we move on, it is important that we understand a bit more about JElement. In Chapter 3, we talked about the use of the parameter fields in databases. Theses fields are INI strings, which we can use in conjunction with the JParameter class.

The JParameter class handles these strings and uses XML definitions, like the ones we have discussed in this chapter, to help comprehend the data. As part of JParameter we can render the INI string using an XML definition. It is at this point that JElement kicks in.

A JElement subclass always overrides the `fetchElement()` method. This method is what renders a single form input element. Because JParameter deals with INI strings, a JElement form element can only return a single value. For example, we cannot define a JElement subclass that renders a select list that allows multiple options to be selected.

Extending JElement

Before we create a new JElement subclass, we should carefully consider if we need to. If the data is coming from the database, we should always think about using the `sql` element; this is a very generic element, which allows us to create a select list based on a database query.

When we create new JElement subclasses, we must follow some specific naming conventions. JElement subclasses are named after the element type and prefixed with the word JElement. The class is stored in a separate file named after the element type. The file is in the `elements` folder in the component's administrative root.

Imagine we want to create a new element type, menus. The class would be called JElementMenus and be located in the file `menus.php`. The class needs to extend the core JElement class; we do not need to import the `joomla.html.parameter.element` library because the JParameter class does this atomically when it loads JElements.

In order to build the class, we need to decide on the XML we are going to use to define a JElementMenus parameter. This element is very similar to the `lists` element so we may as well use a similar structure. This example demonstrates the XML we are going to use:

```
<param name="name" type="menus" label="Menus" description=
                   "A Grouped List" default="1" class="Some CSS">
    <group>Group 1
        <option value="1">Value 1</option>
        <option value="2">Value 2</option>
        <option value="3">Value 3</option>
    </group>
    <group>Group 2
        <option value="4">Value 4</option>
        <option value="5">Value 5</option>
    </group>
</param>
```

We use nested `group` tags to group the different options together. The option tags are identical to those used by JElementList. For a complete description of menu select lists, please refer to `http://www.w3schools.com/tags/tag_optgroup.asp`.

To build the JElementMenus class, there are two things we should always do when defining JElement subclasses: override the `fetchElement()` method and set the `_name` property.

To implement our `fetchElement()` method we will use the static `JHTMLSelect` class; this class is used to build select lists and menu select lists. There are two methods that we need to be aware of: `JHTMLSelect::option()` and `JHTMLSelect::genericList()`.

`JHTMLSelect::option()` returns an object that represents a list option. `JHTMLSelect::genericList()` returns a rendered HTML string of a form select tag based on an array of objects and a few additional parameters.

This example shows how we can implement the JElementMenus class:

```
/**
 * Renders a Menus Selection List
 *
 */
class JElementMenus extends JElement
{
    /**
     * Element type
     *
     * @access    protected
     * @var       string
     */
    var    $_name = 'Menus';
    /**
     * Gets an HTML rendered string of the element
     *
     * @param string Name of the form element
     * @param string Value
     * @param JSimpleXMLElement XML node in which the element is
     *                                                  defined
     * @param string Control set name, normally params
     */
    function fetchElement($name, $value, &$node, $control_name)
    {
        // get the CSS Style from the XML node class attribute
        $class = $node->attributes('class') ? 'class="'.$node->
                attributes('class').'"' : 'class="inputbox"';
```

```
            // prepare an array for the options
            $groups = array();
            foreach ($node->children() as $group)
            {
                // create new Group, <OPTGROUP> signifies a group
                $text = $group->data();
                $groups[] = JHTMLSelect::option('<OPTGROUP>',
                                               JText::_($text));
                        foreach ($group->children() as $option)
                {
                    // add an option to the group
                    $val = $option->attributes('value');
                    $text = $option->data();
                    $groups[] = JHTMLSelect::option($val,
                                        JText::_($text));
                }

                // end the group
                $groups[] = JHTMLSelect::option('</OPTGROUP>');
            }
            // create the HTML list and return it (this sorts out the
            //                                   selected option for us)
            return JHTMLSelect::genericList($groups,
        ''.$control_name.'['.$name.']', $class, 'value', 'text', $value,
                                            $control_name.$name);
        }
    }
```

Using Custom JElement Classes

To use our JElementMenus class we need to do more than add a `param` tag of type 'menus' to our XML file. We need to tell Joomla! where it can find the JElementMenus class. To do this we use the `addpath` attribute.

Building on our previous example of a component `config.xml` file, this XML defines another parameter, using the menus type JElement (assuming that the JElementMenus class is located in the `administrator/components/com_myextension/elements` folder):

```xml
<?xml version="1.0" encoding="utf-8"?>
    <config>
    <params addpath="/administrator/
    components/com_myextension/elements">
    <param name="title" type="text" default="My Title"
    label="Title" description="Title of page" size="30" />
    <param name="description" type="textarea" default=""
```

```
            label="Description" rows="5" cols="50"
            description="Description to display at the top of the page." />
            <param name="menus" type="menus" label="Select Menus"
            description="Test JElementMenus" default="3">
                    <group>Group 1
                        <option value="1">Value 1</option>
                        <option value="2">Value 2</option>
                        <option value="3">Value 3</option>
                    </group>
                    <group>Group 2
                        <option value="4">Value 4</option>
                        <option value="5">Value 5</option>
                    </group>
            </param>
        </params>
    </config>
```

If we attempt to make a menu item using this XML metadata file the Menu Item
Parameters panel will appear like this:

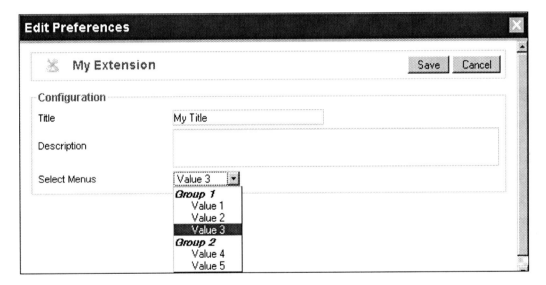

Help Files

The Joomla! core components use special help files, which can be displayed in the
backend using the menu bar button, `help`. In this example, we add a button, which,
if used, will display the contents of the `screen.system.info.html` help file in a
pop-up window.

```
JMenuBar::help('screen.system.info');
```

Core help files are located in the `administrator/help` directory. To support multilingual requirements, the `help` directory contains one folder for each installed language, for example `en-GB`. Located in these folders are the HTML help files.

We can use a similar implementation for our components. We must create a `help` folder in the administration root of our component and add a subfolder for every help language that we support.

Imagine we want to create a generic help file for the component 'My Extension'. In the component's administrative root we need to create a folder called help and in there we need to create a folder called en-GB. Now if we create a file called `help.html` and save it into the `help\en-GB` folder, we can use the administration menubar help button to view it, as this example demonstrates:

```
JMenuBar::help('help', true);
```

By adding the second parameter, we are telling Joomla! to look for help files in the components help folder.

 Help files are stored in XHTML format and the extension must always be .html.

Routing

To make Joomla! respond appropriately to a request the application contains a `JRouter` object. This object determines the direction to take through the application. This is based on URI query values. To make Joomla! URIs friendlier, it can be set up to use **SEF** (Search-Engine Friendly) URIs.

In order to take advantage of SEF URIs, when we render any URI we need to use the `JRoute::_()` method. This method converts normal URIs into SEF URIs; this will only happen if the component we are trying to link to has a router and the SEO options are enabled. In this example we parse the URI `'index.php?option=com_myExtension& category=3&item=6'` into an SEF URI.

```
echo JRoute::_('index.php?option=com_myExtension&
                          category=3&item=6');
```

This is an example of the output we might receive:

`http://example.org/joomla/index.php/component/myExtension/3/6`

The end of the URI, after `index.php`, is called the SEF segments. Each segment is separated by a forward slash.

To create a router for a component we must create a file called `router.php` in the root of the component. In the file we need to define two functions, `BuildRoute()` and `ParseRoute()`, both prefixed with the name of our component. These functions build and parse between a URI query and an array of SEF segments.

The `BuildRoute()` function is used to build an array of SEF segments. The function is passed an associative array of URI query values.

This is an example of the `BuildRoute()` function that we might have been using in the previous example. We must return the array of data segments in the order they will appear in the SEF URI. We must remove any elements from the referenced `$query` associative array parameter; any elements we do not remove will be appended to the end of the URI in query format. For example, if we passed the value `'index.php?option=com_myExtension& category=3&item=6&foo=bar'` to the `JRoute::_()` method, we would get the route:

`http://example.org/joomla/index.php/component/myExtension/3/6?foo=bar`

```
/**
 * Builds route for My Extension.
 *
 * @access public
 * @param array Query associative array
 * @return array SEF URI segments
 */
function myextensionBuildRoute(&$query)
{
    $segments = array();
    if (isset($query['category']))
    {
        $segments[] = $query['category'];
        unset($query['category']);
        if (isset($query['item']))
        {
            $segments[] = $query['item'];
            unset($query['item']);
        }
    }

    return $segments;
}
```

With this function implemented, `JRoute::_()` can build SEF URIs for our component. The next step is to decode SEF URIs. This is an example of the `ParseRoute()` function that we might use to decode the URI:

```
/**
 * Decodes SEF URI segments for My Extension.
 *
 * @access public
 * @param array SEF URI segments array
 * @return array Query associative array
 */
function myextensionParseRoute($segments)
{
    $query = array();

    if (isset($segments[0]))
    {
        $query['category'] = $segments[0];

        if (isset($segments[1]))
        {
            $query['item'] = $segments[1];
        }
    }

    return $query;
}
```

 Note that this is essentially the exact opposite of the `BuildRoute()` function.

Packaging

Components are packaged in archive files. A number of archive formats are supported: `.gz`, `.tar`, `.tar.gz`, and `zip`. There is no specific naming convention for component archive files; however, the following is often used: `com_name-version`. For example, the package for version 1.0.0 of My Extension would be called `com_myextension-1.0.0`.

 When you package a component, ensure you do not include any system files. Mac developers should be especially vigilant and consider using the CleanArchiver utility `http://www.sopht.jp/cleanarchiver/`.

Within the package, as well as the component files, are some special files, which tell Joomla! what to do during installation and un-installation of a component. These include the XML manifest file, an install, uninstall PHP script, and an install and uninstall SQL file.

XML Manifest File

The XML manifest file details everything the installer needs to know about an extension. Any mistakes in the file may result in partial or complete installation failure. XML manifest files should be saved using UTF-8 encoding.

Based on the XML manifest file that we defined at the start of this chapter to create a sandbox, this example demonstrates a large number of the XML manifest file elements that we can use:

```xml
<?xml version="1.0" encoding="utf-8"?>
  <!DOCTYPE install SYSTEM "http://dev.joomla.org/xml/1.5/component-
                                              install.dtd">

  <install type="component" version="1.5">
  <name>My Extension</name>
  <creationDate>MonthName Year</creationDate>
  <author>Author's Name</author>
  <authorEmail>Author's Email</authorEmail>
  <authorUrl>Author's Website</authorUrl>
  <copyright>Copyright Notice</copyright>
  <license>Component License Agreement</license>
  <version>Component Version</version>
  <description>Component Description</description>
  <administration>
    <menu>My Extension</menu>
    <submenu>
      <menu task="view">Items</menu>
      <menu link="option=com_categories&section=com_wfaqs;">
                Categories</menu>
    </submenu>
        <files folder="administration">
        <filename>index.html</filename>
        <filename>admin.myextension.php</filename>
        <filename>install.sql</filename>
        <filename>install.noutf8.sql</filename>
        <filename>uninstall.sql</filename>
    <folder>models</folder>
    <folder>views</folder>
    <folder>controllers</folder>
```

```
        <folder>tables</folder>
        </files>
        <languages folder="administration">
        <language tag="en-GB">en-GB.com_myextension.ini</language>
        <language tag="de-DE">de-DE.com_myextension.ini</language>
        </languages>
        <media destination="com_myextension">
        <filename>logo.jpg</filename>
        <filename>index.html</filename>
        </media>
    </administration>
    <install>
    <sql>
      <file driver="mysql" charset="utf8">install.sql</file>#
      <file driver="mysql" charset="">install.noutf8.sql</file>
    </sql>
    </install>
    <uninstall>
      <sql>
        <file driver="mysql">uninstall.sql</file>
      </sql>
    </uninstall>
    <installfile>install.myextension.php</installfile>
    <uninstallfile>uninstall.myextension.php</uninstallfile>
    <files>
      <filename>index.html</filename>
      <filename>myextension.php</filename>
      <folder>models</folder>
      <folder>views</folder>
      <folder>controllers</folder>
      <folder>tables</folder>
    </files>
    <languages>
      <language tag="en-GB">en-GB.com_myextension.ini</language>
      <language tag="de-DE">de-DE.com_myextension.ini</language>
    </languages>
    <media destination="com_myextension">
      <filename>logo.jpg</filename>
      <filename>index.html</filename>
    </media>
  </install>
```

This is some information regarding this available from the official Joomla! Wiki:
`http://dev.joomla.org/component/option,com_jd-wiki/Itemid,`
`/id,components:xml_installfile/.`

The following table describes the tags you can use in your XML manifest file in detail:

install (Root tag)

There are two different `install` tags. The root tag called install identifies the type of extension and the version Joomla! for which the extension is written.		

Example	`<install type="component" version="1.5">`
	`<!-- sub-tags -->`
	`</install>`	

Attributes	type	Type of extension.
	version	Version of Joomla! the extension is for.
Sub-tags	administration, author, authorEmail, authorUrl, copyright, creationDate, description, files*, install, installfile, languages*, license, media*, name, params, uninstall, uninstallfile, version	

administration

Container for all the component's backend tags. This tag is required even if your component needs no back-end tags.	
Example	`<administration />`
Sub-tags	files, languages, media, menu, submenu

author

Author's name.	
Example	`<author>John Smith</author>`

authorEmail

Author's email address.	
Example	`<authorEmail>johnsmith@example.org</authorEmail>`

authorUrl

Author or component's website address.	
Example	`<authorUrl>http://www.example.org</authorUrl>`

copyright

Copyright notice.	
Example	`<description>Copy me as much as you like!</description>`

description

Component description.	
Example	`<description>Example component description.</description>`

file

SQL file to execute.		
Example	`<query charset="utf8" driver="mysql">install.sql</query>` `<query charset="" driver="mysql">install.noutf8.sql</query>`	
Attributes	charset	UTF-8.
	driver	Database driver name, normally mysql (mysql and mysqli are synonymous in this context).

files

Files and folders that belong in the component's frontend folder. To prevent confusion we normally use the optional 'folder' attribute to make the archive tidier. This tag has two sub-tags, filename and folder, which can be used zero to many times.	
Example	`<files folder="site"><!-- sub-tags --></files>`
Attributes	[folder]	Folder in the archive where the files reside.
Sub-tags	filename, folder

filename

Defines a file we want to copy into the root.	
Example	`<filename>example.php</filename>`

folder

Defines folders we want to copy into the front-end folder; if a folder has subfolders and files we do not have to specify these.	
Example	`<folder>afolder</folder>`

install

Database installation options. Do not confuse this with the root install tag!	
Example	`<install><!-- sub-tags --></install>`
Sub-tags	queries, sql

installfile

File to execute when installing the component. The file can optionally include a function called `com_install()`, returning `true` on success. This is only required if you want to perform additional processing during installation.	
Example	`<installfile>install.php</installfile>`

language

Language tags define a language INI file. The tag includes the attribute `tag`; this is used to identify the language.	
Example	`<language tag="en-GB">en-GB.com_example.ini</language>`
Attributes	tag	Language tag.

languages

Language files. If any of the language files already exist, they will not be overwritten. This tag has one subtag, language. Each language tag defines a language INI file. The language tag must include the attribute tag; this is used to identify the language.		

Example	`<languages folder="languages">`
	   `<!-sub tags -->`
	`</languages>`	

Attributes	[Folder]	Folder in the archive where the files reside.
Sub-tags	language	

license

License agreement.	
Example	`<license>GNU GPL</license>`

media

Media files to be copied to the root Joomla! images folder.		
Example	`<media destination="stories"><!-sub tags --></media>`	
Attributes	[destination]	Destination folder within the Joomla! images folder.
	[folder]	Source folder.
Sub-tags	filename	

menu

Backend menu items.		
Example	`<menu>Menu Name</menu>`	
Attributes	[act]	Optional link parameter.
	[controller]	Optional link parameter.
	[img]	Location of menu item image.
	[layout]	Optional link parameter.
	[link]	URI Link.
	[sub]	Optional link parameter.
	[task]	Optional link parameter.
	[view]	Optional link parameter.

name

Component name.
Example   `<name>example</name>`

param

A parameter. How this tag is used depends upon the type of parameter we are defining; a complete description of these types and their attributes is available in the appendix.
Example   `<param type="text" name="foobar" label="Foobar"/>`

params

Component parameters.	
Example	`<params><!—sub tags --></params>`
Attributes	addPath Directory where custom JElements subclasses can be found.
Sub-tags	param

queries

SQL queries to execute.	
Example	`<queries><!—sub tags --></queries>`
Sub-tags	query

query

SQL queries to execute.	

Example	`<query>CREATE TABLE `#__myextension` (`
	`  `id` int(11) NOT NULL auto_increment,`
	`  `name` varchar(255) NOT NULL default '',`
	`  PRIMARY KEY  (`id`)`
	`) CHARACTER SET `utf8` COLLATE `utf8_general_ci`</query>`

submenu

Backend sub-menu.	
Example	`<submenu><!- sub tags --></submenu>`
Sub-tags	menu

sql

SQL files to execute.	
Example	`<sql><!-- sub tags --></sql>`
Sub-tags	file

uninstall

Database un-installation options. Do not confuse this with the root install tag!	
Example	`<uninstall><!-- sub tags --></uninstall>`
Sub-tags	queries, sql

uninstallfile

File to execute when uninstalling the component. The file can optionally include a function called `com_uninstall()`, returning `true` on success. This is only required if you want to perform additional processing during un-installation.	
Example	`<uninstallfile>uninstall.myextension.php</uninstallfile>`

version

Extension version. Most extensions use three digits in the form `major.minor.patch`; version 1.0.0 normally denotes the first stable release.	
Example	`<version>1.0.0</version>`

SQL Install and Uninstall Files and Queries

Most components have at least one table associated with them. We can use SQL install and uninstall files to create, populate, and remove tables. Normally we create three different SQL files, one for installing on UTF-8-compatible MySQL servers, one for installing on non-UTF-8-compatible MySQL servers, and one uninstall file.

We normally name the SQL installation files `install.extensionname.sql` and `install_backward.extensionname.sql` for UTF-8 and non-UTF-8 servers respectively. We normally name the un-installation SQL file `uninstall.extensionname.sql`. We do not have to use this naming convention.

This is an example of an SQL install file, which creates the table `#__myextension_foobars`, which we defined in the previous chapter:

```
DROP TABLE IF EXISTS `#__myextension_foobars`;
CREATE TABLE `#__myextension_foobars` (
    `id` INTEGER UNSIGNED NOT NULL DEFAULT NULL AUTO_INCREMENT,
    `content` TEXT  NOT NULL DEFAULT '',
    `checked_out` INTEGER UNSIGNED NOT NULL DEFAULT 0,
    `checked_out_time` DATETIME  NOT NULL DEFAULT '0000-00-00
                                                  00:00:00',
    `params` TEXT  NOT NULL DEFAULT '',
    `ordering` INTEGER UNSIGNED NOT NULL DEFAULT 0,
    `hits` INTEGER UNSIGNED NOT NULL DEFAULT 0,
    `published` INTEGER UNSIGNED NOT NULL DEFAULT 0,
    PRIMARY KEY(`id`)
) CHARACTER SET `utf8` COLLATE `utf8_general_ci`;
```

 Note that before we attempt to create the table we first delete it if it exists. This guarantees that we will not encounter a 'table already exists' type error.

We also define the character set and the collation; this ensures that our table is UTF-8-compatible. Obviously, we only do this in the SQL file for UTF-8-compatible MySQL severs. For more information about the differences between UTF-8-compatible and non-UTF-8 compatible MySQL servers, refer to Chapter 3. We only need one uninstall file because it will not be any different whether it is UTF-8 compatible or not. This is an example of the uninstall SQL file:

```
DROP TABLE IF EXISTS `#__some_table`;
```

 You must copy the SQL files into the root of your component's backend as well as defining them in install and uninstall tags.

Alternatively, you can embed the queries inside the XML manifest file in query tags.

```
<queries>
    <query>DROP TABLE IF EXISTS `#__ myextension_foobars`;</query>
    <query>CREATE TABLE `#__myextension_foobars` (
    `id` INTEGER UNSIGNED NOT NULL DEFAULT NULL AUTO_INCREMENT,
    `content` TEXT  NOT NULL DEFAULT '',
    `checked_out` INTEGER UNSIGNED NOT NULL DEFAULT 0,
    `checked_out_time` DATETIME  NOT NULL DEFAULT '0000-00-00
     00:00:00',
    `params` TEXT  NOT NULL DEFAULT '',
    `ordering` INTEGER UNSIGNED NOT NULL DEFAULT 0,
    `hits` INTEGER UNSIGNED NOT NULL DEFAULT 0,
    `published` INTEGER UNSIGNED NOT NULL DEFAULT 0,
    PRIMARY KEY(`id`)
) CHARACTER SET `utf8` COLLATE `utf8_general_ci`;
    </query>
</queries>
```

Install and Uninstall Files

During the install and uninstall phases we can optionally execute install and uninstall files. This allows us to perform additional processing that we may not be able to do using the XML manifest file.

The install file normally includes a function called `com_install()`. This function is used to execute additional processing that we may want/need during installation of our component. If anything fails during the function, we can return Boolean `false`. This will abort the extension installation.

We can also use the install file to output information. This is used for two different purposes: to display some message that explains something about the component and to show the success or failure of any processing.

This example shows how we can use the `com_install()` function. Note that this is executed after the rest of the XML manifest file has been successfully processed.

```
/**
 * Some Component installation script
 *
 * @return boolean false on fail
 */
```

```
function com_install()
{
    $return = true;
    echo '<pre>';
    // do some task
    echo JText::_('Doing Something').': ';
    if (dosomething())
    {
        echo JText::_('Success');
    }
    else
    {
        echo JText::_('Fail');
    }
    echo '</pre>';

    if ($return)
    {
            echo '<p style="text-align: center;">'
            ."\n"
            . JText::_('Thank you for installing Some Component')
            ."\n</p>";
            return true;
    }

    return $return;
}
```

The uninstall file is very similar; the file can include a function called
com_uninstall(). This function is used to execute additional processing that we
may need during un-installation of our component. If anything fails during the
function, we can return Boolean false.

We can also use the uninstall file to output information. This is often used for two
different purposes: to display some message that explains something about the
component and to show the success or failure of any processing in the uninstall file.

Unlike the install file, this function is run before the XML manifest file is processed to
remove the component.

Summary

Components are undoubtedly the most complex extensions, and, as a result, the hardest to implement. Before jumping in head first, it can be a good idea to examine existing components to see how they are constructed. The Web Links component is used as an example because it demonstrates many of the common aspects of a component and does so with a relatively simple and easy-to-understand data structure.

The MVC pattern consists of three parts, the model, view, and controller. Getting to grips with how these interact with one another is fundamental to creating well-formed components.

We investigated the use of the different document formats: feed, HTML, PDF, and RAW. Enabling a component to render the same data in several formats requires very little effort and can make a component far more successful.

Understanding how menu items override the component configuration is imperative when dealing with the component configuration. Administrators also sometimes misunderstand the approach; we should take care to ensure that administrators are aware of the mechanism.

Documentation, especially in open-source extensions, is often over looked. Since Joomla! provides us with an easy way of integrating multilingual documentation in the backend, this short-coming can easily be avoided. It is generally a good idea to create help files with a brief outline while we are still developing components because it helps ensure that when we come to write the complete documentation we do not miss any important information.

More and more administrators are starting to use SEO URIs. This process is not automatic, so to enable SEO URIs in our components we must build a router. We should wait until the ending stages of development before creating a router. It is common for us to change the way in which we handle data during the development phase; creating the router too early may waste valuable time and effort.

Packaging a component is crucial to enable the distribution of the component. When we create the XML manifest file, we should always remember to use UTF-8 encoding and to include the DOCTYPE tag with a link to the Joomla! install component DTD schema.

The install and uninstall PHP scripts are very power tools. Using these to the full potential enables us to create incredibly versatile installers. If there is anything that we want to do during the install or uninstall phase, which we cannot achieve using the XML manifest file, we should add it to the install and uninstall files. It can also be a nice touch to add some generic 'getting started' tips for the administrator to the install file.

5
Module Design

Joomla! modules come in two flavors, frontend and backend. Modules can be standalone or, as is often the case, can work alongside components. In this chapter, we will discuss the following points:

- Setting up a Sandbox
- First Steps
- Module Settings (Parameters)
- Helpers
- Layouts (Templates)
- Translating
- Packaging

Setting Up a Sandbox

When we start building a new module, it is imperative that we have a sandbox, to test our code. Ideally, we should have more than one system so we can test our modules on different server setups.

To set up a sandbox module we can create a basic installer. The XML displayed below can be used to create a blank module called My Extension.

```xml
<?xml version="1.0" encoding="utf-8"?>
    <!DOCTYPE install SYSTEM "http://dev.joomla.org/xml/1.5/
                            module-install.dtd">
    <install version="1.5" type="module" client="site">
    <name>My Extension</name>
    <author>Author's Name</author>
    <authorEmail>Author's Email</authorEmail>
    <authorUrl>Author's Website</authorUrl>
```

```
<creationDate>MonthName Year</creationDate>
<copyright>Copyright Notice</copyright>
<license>Module License Agreement</license>
<version>Module Version</version>
<description>Module Description</description>
<files>
<filename module="mod_myextension">
                mod_myextension.php</filename>
</files>
</install>
```

To use this, create a new XML manifest file, using UTF-8 encoding, and save the above code into it. The name of this file is not important, as long as the extension is .xml. You will need to update the XML to suit the module you intend to build.

The module name can also be used in the form mod_parsedname. For example, the name My Extension would also be used in the format mod_myextension.

Once you have built your XML manifest file, create a new PHP file called mod_myextension.php. This is the file that is invoked when the module is used. If you do not include this file, you will not be able to install the module.

Now create a new archive, which must be .gz, .tar, .tar.gz, or .zip, and add the XML manifest file and PHP file to it. If you install the archive, you will get a blank module ready for you to begin developing.

The module that the above process will install is a frontend module. If we want to create a backend module, we would have to modify the install tag client attribute value from site to administrator.

The module will be located at modules/mod_myextension. If we create a backend module, it will be located at administrator/modules/mod_myextension.

In order to enable and use your module, you will need to use the Module Manager to publish and assign the module to menu items.

First Steps

Now we are ready to start playing with a module. Joomla! allows us a good deal of freedom within modules. The file mod_myextension.php is invoked when the module is used. There are no restrictions as to what we choose to do within this file.

You can output data at any point during the execution of a module. To test this, if you output some data from mod_myextension.php, the data will appear in the module.

Standalone Modules

Standalone modules do not depend on other extensions. These modules tend to require more effort to produce because there is no existing API, other than that which Joomla! provides.

Standalone modules normally use data sources external to Joomla!. If we want to store data within Joomla! we are faced with the problem that modules do not support the execution of custom SQL or other scripts during installation.

There are two good ways in which we can counter this:

- We can use a conditional SQL query when the module is invoked. A consideration, if using this method, is the additional strain that is placed on the database server, especially if you are creating multiple tables. The following example demonstrates how we can achieve this:

```
$db =& JFactory::getDBO();
$query = 'CREATE TABLE IF NOT EXISTS '.$db-
        >nameQuote('#__some_table').' ( '.$db-
        >nameQuote('id').' int(11) NOT NULL auto_increment, '
    .$db->nameQuote('name').' varchar(255) NOT NULL default '', '
        .'PRIMARY KEY  ('.$db->nameQuote('id'). ') '
        .') CHARACTER SET `utf8` COLLATE `utf8_general_ci`';
$db->setQuery($query);
$db->query();
```

- We can use a flag to indicate if the tables have already been created. We can implement a flag in several ways. For example, we could use a blank file or a module configuration option. This example demonstrates how we can use a module configuration option (we will discuss the module configuration options in the next section):

```
if (!$params->get('tablecreated'))
{
    // create the table
    $db =& JFactory::getDBO();
    $query = 'CREATE TABLE IF NOT EXISTS '.$db-
    >nameQuote('#__some_table').' ( '
    $db->nameQuote('id').' int(11) NOT NULL auto_increment, '
    .$db->nameQuote('name').' varchar(255) NOT NULL default '', '
    .'PRIMARY KEY  ('.$db->nameQuote('id'). ') '
    .') CHARACTER SET `utf8` COLLATE `utf8_general_ci`';
    $db->setQuery($query);
    $db->query();

    // set the `tablecreated` flag to true
    $params->set('tablecreated', 1);
}
```

Of course we don't have to use the database to store data. For example, we can use XML files. A full description of using XML in Joomla! is available in Chapter 10.

Modules and Components Working Together

Joomla! does not provide a large API for Modules; it's partly for this reason that generally we create modules in conjunction with components. Modules, which complement components, should take advantage of existing component code. This creates dependencies between the module and the component.

There is currently no formal way of defining dependencies in extensions. We must manually ensure that all dependencies are met. It is important to understand that even if an extension is installed, it may not necessarily work. Extensions can be flagged as disabled; this means that we check if the extension is installed and if it is enabled.

To check that a component is installed, and is enabled, we can use the isEnabled() method in the static JComponentHelper class. This example demonstrates how we can check if some component is installed and enabled:

```
jimport('joomla.application.component.helper');

if (!JComponentHelper::isEnabled('com_somecomponent', true))
{
    JError::raiseError('SOME_ERROR', JText('Module requires the Some
Extension component'));
}
```

Notice that the second parameter we pass to the isEnabled() method is true. This ensures that the method is executed in strict mode. If it is not, components that are not installed will return true.

The way in which the example deals with a missing component is somewhat drastic. A more polite method would be to output a warning message and end processing of the module.

We could achieve this very neatly using a custom module error layout. We will discuss this later in the chapter.

> We can also check that specific plugins and modules are installed and enabled. This works in the same way as described above, except we use the static isEnabled() method in JPluginHelper and JModuleHelper classes.

Frontend and Backend Module Display Positions

For the most part you will probably find yourself building modules.

In the frontend, modules are generally displayed in vertical blocks to the left or right of the page. This list details the available positions; exact positions will depend upon the site template:

- banner
- breadcrumb
- footer
- left
- right
- syndicate
- top
- user1
- user2
- user3
- user4

In the backend, modules are displayed in some very different positions. When creating backend modules we generally have a special position in mind for the module. This list details the available positions; exact positions will depend upon the admin template:

- cpanel
- footer
- header
- icon
- menu
- status
- submenu
- title
- toolbar

We do not specify the position when we create a module; it is up to an administrator where he or she chooses to publish a specific module. Nevertheless, we should always bear in mind the different positions in which a module may end up being published.

Module Settings (Parameters)

An important part of building modules is dealing with module settings. We can define custom parameters for modules in the module XML manifest file. Module parameters fall into two groups, Module Parameters and Advanced Parameters.

There is no difference in the application of Module Parameters and Advanced Parameters; we split them into two groups to help the classification of the parameters, consequently making the administrator's job easier.

As a general rule: Module Parameters are the more basic, although generally more fundamental, of the two. Advanced Parameters pertain to settings that are more complex and are rarely modified.

This example shows how we can add some simple parameters to a module:

```xml
<?xml version="1.0" encoding="utf-8"?>
    <!DOCTYPE install SYSTEM "http://dev.joomla.org/xml/1.5/module-
                             install.dtd">
    <install version="1.5" type="module" client="site">
    <name>My Extension</name>
    <author>Author's Name</author>
    <authorEmail>Author's Email</authorEmail>
    <authorUrl>Author's Website</authorUrl>
    <creationDate>MonthName Year</creationDate>
    <copyright>Copyright Notice</copyright>
    <license>Module License Agreement</license>
    <version>Module Version</version>
    <description>Module Description</description>
    <files>
    <filename module="mod_myextension">mod_myextension.php</filename>
    </files>
    </install>
    <params>
    <param name="aparam" type="text" label="A Parameter"
    description="A description" />
    </params>
    <params group="advanced">
    <param name="anotherparan" type="text" label="Another Parameter"
                description="A description" />
    </params>
    </install>
```

In this instance, we have added the text parameters `aparam` and `anotherparam`. The first is displayed in the Module Parameters category, the second in the Advanced Parameters category, as this screenshot demonstrates:

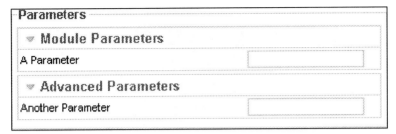

A complete description of the different types of parameters and how to define them in XML is available in the *Appendix.*

Once we have defined all of the module parameters, we can access them in the module using the variable `$params`. This variable is a `JParameter` object; it allows us to retrieve module parameters at run time.

The most important methods we need to be aware of in the `JParameter` class are `def()`, `get()`, and `set()`.

We use `def()` to set a default value for a parameter if no value currently exists for it. This example demonstrates how we would use the method to set a default value of `value` for the parameter `aparam`:

```
$params->def('aparam', 'value');
```

We use `get()` to get the value of a parameter. This example demonstrates how we would use the method to get the value of the parameter `aparam`:

```
$params->get('aparam');
```

We can also pass a second parameter to `get()`, which will be returned if no value already exists for the parameter.

We use `set()` to set a value for a parameter. This example demonstrates how we would use the method to set a value of `value` for the parameter `aparam`:

```
$params->set('aparam', 'value');
```

Helpers

Module helpers are static classes, which we use to encapsulate functions specific to the module. Incorporating the functions in a static class reduces the chance of conflict with other extensions and the core.

We normally name module helper classes using the naming convention: the word mod, the module name, the word Helper. For example, a helper class for the module My Extension would be called `modMyExtensionHelper`.

Module helper classes are normally located in a file called `helper.php` in the root of the module. In this example, we define the class `modMyExtensionHelper` and create a method called `getItems()`:

```
/**
 * My Extension Module Helper
 *
 * @static
 */
class modMyExtensionHelper
{

    /**
     * Gets an array of items
     *
     * @param JParameter Module parameters
     * @return mixed Array of items, false on failure
     */
    function &getItems(&$params)
    {
    $db =& JFactory::getDBO();
    $category = $params->get('category', 0);
    $query = modMyExtensionHelper::_buildQuery($category);
    $db->setQuery($query);
    $instance = $db->loadObjectList();
    return $instance;
    }
    /**
     * Gets an SQL query string
     *
     * @param JParameter Module parameters
     * @return string SQL query
     */
    function _buildQuery($category)
    {
    $db =& JFactory::getDBO();
    return 'SELECT * FROM '.$db->nameQuote('#__some_table').
    ' WHERE '.$db->nameQuote('category').' = '.$category.
    ' AND '.$db->nameQuote('published').' = 1';
    }
}
```

We split the getItems() method into two; this makes the code more readable and aids the logical structure of the class. Notice that the getItems() method returns a reference, which reduces memory overheads when using the method.

We also need to pass a JParameter object to the getItems() method, most likely the module parameters, $params. We then use a parameter named 'category' to determine which records to get from the fictitious database table, #__some_table.

It is common practice to pass the $params object to module helper class methods. If a method is only using one parameter from $params, it is still a good idea to pass the entire object because it will make the addition of any extra parameters easier.

We could have specified $instance as static, only executing the query if it hadn't been executed already. This would only make sense if there were a possibility that the method would be executed more than once. This example shows how we might choose to implement this:

```
/**
 * Gets an array of items
 *
 * @param JParameter Module parameters
 * @return mixed Array of items, false on failure
 */
function &getItems(&$params)
{
    static $instances;
    if (!isset($instances))
    {
        $instances = array();
    }
    $category = $params->get('category', 0);
    if (empty($instances[$category]))
    {
    $db =& JFactory::getDBO();
    $query = modMyExtensionHelper::_buildQuery($category);
    $db->setQuery($query);
    @$instances[$category] = $db->loadObjectList();
    }
    return $instances[$category];
}
```

 Note that we have renamed $instance to $instances and that it is now an array.

This is an example of how we would use the helper we have just defined, and use the `getItems()` method. This assumes we are in the root module file and hence `$params` is available to us.

```
require_once(dirname(__FILE__).DS.'helper.php');
$items =& modMyExtensionHelper::getItems($params);
```

Once we have done this, we could then verify that `$items` is an array. If not, we could raise an error, notice, or warning.

We can use helpers for many different tasks as well as data retrieval. Joomla! encourages, although it does not force, the use of **OO** (Object-Oriented) design. Functionality that we build in helpers is specifically functionality that has no other logical category. Helper classes allow us to stick to OO design without any compromise on the logical design of classes.

Layouts (Templates)

Layouts (templates) are used in modules in much the same way as they are in components. Module layouts allow us to define multiple appearances for data.

Layouts are essentially template files, PHP files, which are mainly XHTML interlaced with snippets of PHP. For a complete explanation of how to build template files please, refer to Chapter 9.

Site templates can override module layouts. To render a module using a layout we use the `getLayoutPath()` method in the static `JModuleHelper` class. This method determines the location of a template file based on two parameters, the parsed module name and the layout name.

In this example we render the default layout (mod_myextension/tmpl/`default.php`) using the `getLayoutPath()` method:

```
require(JModuleHelper::getLayoutPath('mod_myextension'));
```

In this example, we render an alternative layout, aptly named 'alternate' (mod_myextension/tmpl/`alternate.php`):

```
require(JModuleHelper::getLayoutPath('mod_myextension',
                                     'alternate'));
```

If you create alternative module layouts, you can name them the way you want. The name of a layout corresponds directly to the name of a template file. For example, the template file `vert.php` would be the layout vert.

Unlike in components, in modules we do not create XML metadata files to describe each layout. Instead, if we want to allow an administrator to select which layout he or she wants to use, we must add a module parameter and use it accordingly.

This is an example of how we might define a parameter to handle different layouts in the module XML manifest file (*alternatively, we could use a list parameter and manually define each available layout*):

```
<param name="layout" type="filelist" label="Layout"
              description="Style with which to display the module"
              directory="/modules/mod_myextension/tmpl"
              default="default" hide_default="1" hide_none="1"
              stripext="1" filter="\.php$" exclude="^_" />
```

This parameter, named 'layout', generates a list of items based on the template files. It includes PHP files and excludes files with names that start with an underscore. The list of items is displayed without the file extensions, and the values are saved without the file extensions.

Imagine the `tmpl` folder contains the files: `default.php`, `horiz.php`, `index.html`, `vert.php`, and `_item.php`. This is what the parameter would appear like when rendered as a form element:

To use this parameter to render a template we can use the following; note that if the parameter is not defined we use the layout 'default':

```
$layout = $params->get('layout', 'default');
require(JModuleHelper::getLayoutPath('mod_myextension', $layout));
```

We mentioned earlier the possibility of using a bespoke module error layout if anything were to go amiss during the execution of our module. We can use the `JError` class to define an error. Joomla! uses this class to describe errors, and objects of this type are often returned from methods when errors occur.

This example shows how we could use a `JError` object, stored in `$error`, in conjunction with a tailored layout:

```
<p>
    <strong><?php echo $error->code; ?></strong><br />
    <?php echo JText::_($error->message); ?>
</p>
```

If we save this as a layout in the module's `tmpl` folder and call it `_error.php`, we can proceed to use it. We use an underscore at the start of the name because it is an internal template and we don't want it to appear in the selection of layouts. This example shows how we can use the layout in conjunction with a `JError` object:

```
$result = modMyExtensionHelper::someMethod();
if (JError::isError($result))
{
    $params->set('layout', '_error');
    $error =& $result;
}

$layout = $params->get('layout', 'default');
require(JModuleHelper::getLayoutPath('mod_myextension', $layout));
```

Media

If you intend to include any images or other media files with your module, you might want to add the files to the Joomla! root `images` folder. This is the folder that the Joomla! Media Manager uses. You should either add your files to the root of this folder or create a sub-folder.

The way in which the module installer works forces us to go only one folder deep within the `images` folder.

Translating

As part of a module, we can define a set of translations. A full description of how to create language files is available in Chapter 9. When we create module translation files, we must name the file according to a specific naming convention: the language tag, a period, the Joomla! parsed module name. For example, the British English translation file for the module My Extension would be called `en-GB.mod_myextension.php`.

Module translation files are located in the `language` and `administrator/language` folders. If you are creating a frontend module, use the `language` folder. If you are creating a backend module, use the `administrator/language` folder.

By using this specific naming convention, when we use our module, the module's translation file will automatically be loaded. We can, if we so choose, manually load other language files.

If we are creating a module in conjunction with a component, we may want to use a component language file instead of, or in addition to, the module language file. To load a component language file from within a module we can use the global JLanguage object.

This example shows how we would load the My Extension component language file (*you would need to do this before using* JText *to translate any strings*):

```
$language =& JFactory::getLanguage();
$language->load('com_myextension');
```

Packaging

Modules are packaged in archive files. A number of archive formats are supported: .gz, .tar, .tar.gz, and .zip. There is no specific naming convention for module archive files; however, the following is often used: mod_name-version. For example, the package for version 1.0.0 of My Extension would be called mod_myextension-1.0.0.

 When you package a module, ensure you do not include any system files. Apple Mac developers should be especially vigilant and consider using the CleanArchiver utility (http://www.sopht.jp/cleanarchiver/).

Within the package, as well as the module files, there is a special XML manifest file, which describes the module.

Interestingly there is no specific name that we are expected to use for the XML file. When we install a module, Joomla! will interrogate all the XML files it can find in the root of the archive until it finds a file that it believes to be a Joomla! installation XML manifest file.

If you want to use a standard naming convention for your XML manifest file, you should consider using the name of the archive. For example if the module archive is named mod_myextension-1.0.0.zip you might want to call the XML manifest file mod_myextension-1.0.0.xml.

XML Manifest File

The XML manifest file details everything the installer needs to know about an extension. Any mistakes in the file may result in partial or total installation failure. XML manifest files should be saved using UTF-8 encoding. For a base manifest file, you can use the file detailed at the start of this chapter, used to create a sandbox.

The tables below describe the tags you can use in your XML manifest file in detail.

install (Root tag)

The root tag, called 'install', identifies the type of extension and the version Joomla! for which the extension is written.	

Example	`<install type="module" version="1.5">`
	`    <!-- sub-tags -->`
	`</install>`

Attributes	type	Type of extension.
	version	Version of Joomla! the extension is for.

Sub-tags	author, authorEmail, authorUrl, copyright, creationDate, description, files*, languages*, license, media*, name, params, version

author

Author's name.
Example	`<author>John Smith</author>`

authorEmail

Author's email address.
Example	`<authorEmail>johnsmith@example.org</authorEmail>`

authorUrl

Author's or module's website address
Example	`<authorUrl>http://www.example.org</authorUrl>`

copyright

Copyright notice.
Example	`<description>Copy me as much as you like!</description>`

description

Module description.
Example	`<copyright>Example module description.</copyright>`

files

	Files and folders that belong in the module's frontend folder. To prevent confusion we normally use the optional folder attribute to make the archive tidier. This tag has two sub-tags, filename and folder, which can be used zero to many times.	
Example	`<files><!-- sub-tags --></files>`	
Attributes	[folder]	Folder in the archive where the files reside.
Sub-tags	filename, folder	

filename

	Defines a file we want to copy.
Example	`<filename>example.php</filename>`

folder

	Defines folders we want to copy; if a folder has subfolders and files we do not have to specify these.
Example	`<folder>afolder</folder>`

language

	Language tags define a language INI file. The tag includes the attribute tag, which is used to identify the language.	
Example	`<language tag="en-GB">en-GB.com_example.ini</language>`	
Attributes	tag	Language tag.

languages

	Language files. If a language files already exist it will not be overwritten.	

Example	`<languages folder="languages">`
	    `<!—sub tags -->`
	`</languages>`	

Attributes	[Folder]	Folder in the archive where the files reside.
Sub-tags	language	

license

	License agreement.
Example	`<license>GNU GPL</license>`

media

Media files to be copied to the root Joomla! images folder.		
Example	`<media destination="stories"><!-sub tags --></media>`	
Attributes	[destination]	Destination folder within the Joomla! images folder.
Sub-tags	filename	

name

Module name.	
Example	`<name>example</name>`

param

A parameter: How this tag is used depends upon the type of parameter we are defining; a complete description of these types and their attributes is available in the *Appendix*.	
Example	`<param type="text" name="foobar" label="Foobar"/>`

params

Module parameters.		
Example	`<params><!-sub tags --></params>`	
Attributes	addParameterDir	Directory where custom JElements subclasses can be found.
Sub-tags	param	

versionVersion

Extension version: Most extensions use three digits in the form `major.minor.patch`; version 1.0.0 normally denotes the first stable release.	
Example	`<version>1.0.0</version>`

Summary

The two flavors in which modules come, frontend and backend, essentially define two different types of extension. Backend modules are often overlooked because we tend to be less aware of them. We should try to remember that backend modules are very powerful and can greatly enhance the administrative capabilities of components.

Modules are integral to the success of a component. It's not uncommon for one component to include several modules.

The simple nature of modules makes it easy to become sophisticated about them. It's important to remember that because they are used and rendered so frequently, efficient code is essential to good module design.

6

Plugin Design

Plugins enable us to modify system functionality without the need to alter existing code. For example, plugins can be used to alter content before it is displayed, extend search functionality, or implement a custom authentication mechanism. As an example, this chapter shows how to replace a string in an article with an image.

Plugins use the Observer pattern to keep an eye on events. It is by listening to these events that we can modify the system functionality. However, this also means that we are limited to only modifying those parts of the system that raise events.

Plugins represent the listener, and they can define either a listener class or a listener function to handle specific events.

In this chapter, we will cover the following:

- Setting up a Sandbox
- Events
- Listeners
- Plugin Groups
- Loading Plugins
- Using Plugins as libraries (in lieu of library extensions)
- Translating Plugins
- Dealing with Plugin Settings (Parameters)
- Packaging
- File Naming Conflicts

Setting Up a Sandbox

When we start building a new plugin it is imperative that we have a sandbox: somewhere we can test our code. Ideally, we should have more than one system so we can test our plugins on different server setups.

To set up a plugin sandbox we can create a basic installer. The XML displayed below can be used to create a blank plugin called 'Foobar - My Extension'.

```xml
<?xml version="1.0" encoding="utf-8"?>
<!DOCTYPE install SYSTEM
          "http://dev.joomla.org/xml/1.5/plugin-install.dtd">
<install version="1.5" type="plugin" group="foobar">
    <name>Foobar - My Extension</name>
    <author>Author's Name</author>
    <authorEmail>Author's Email</authorEmail>
    <authorUrl>Author's Website</authorUrl>
    <creationDate>MonthName Year</creationDate>
    <copyright>Copyright Notice</copyright>
    <license>Plugin License Agreement</license>
    <version>Plugin Version</version>
    <description>Plugin Description</description>
    <files>
        <filename
            plugin="myextension">myextension.php</filename>
    </files>
    <params/>
</install>
```

To use this, create a new XML manifest file, using UTF-8 encoding, and save the above code into it. You should update the XML to suit the plugin you intend to build.

One of the most important pieces of information in this file is the `group` attribute of the install `tag`. Plugins are organized into logical groups. This list details the core groups:

- authentication
- content
- editors
- editors-xtd
- search
- system
- user
- xmlrpc

We can use other groups as well. For example, the group in our XML is `foobar`.

It may seem slightly obscure, but another piece of important information in the XML is the `filename` tag `plugin` parameter. This parameter identifies the plugin element. The element is a unique identifier used to determine the root plugin file and used as part of the naming convention.

Be careful when you select an element name for your plugin. Only one plugin per group may use any one element name. This table details reserved plugin element names (used by the core):

Group	Reserved element name
authentication	gmail
	joomla
	ldap
	openid
content	emailcloak
	geshi
	loadmodule
	pagebreak
	pagenavigation
	sef
	vote
editors	none
	tinymce
	xstandard
editors-xtd	image
	pagebreak
	readmore
search	categories
	contacts
	content
	newsfeeds
	sections
	weblinks
system	cache
	debug
	legacy

Group	Reserved element name
system	log
	remember
user	joomla
xmlrpc	blogger
	joomla

Once you have built your XML manifest file, create a new PHP file named after the plugin element; this is the file that is invoked when the plugin is loaded. For example, you would have to name the file myextension.php if you were to use the XML displayed above. If you do not include this file, you will not be able to install the plugin.

Now create a new archive, it can be gz, .tar, .tar.gz, or zip, and add the XML manifest file and PHP file to it. If you install the archive, you should get a blank plugin, which you can begin to develop.

Plugins are not stored in separate folders. This is because generally plugins only consist of two files: the XML manifest file and the root plugin file. Installed plugins are located in the root plugins folder in a subfolder named after the plugin group. Our example would be located in the folder plugins/foobar.

In order to use your plugin, you will need to use the Plugin Manager to publish it.

Events

As we have already mentioned, plugins use the Observer pattern to keep an eye on events and handle them. The Observer pattern is a design pattern in a logical function, which is common to programming. This particular pattern allows listeners to attach to a subject. The subject can initiate a notification (essentially an event), which will cause the listeners to react to the event.

The expressions 'listener' and 'observer' are interchangeable, as are 'subject' and 'observable'.

If you are unfamiliar with the Observer pattern, you may want to refer to http://www.phppatterns.com/docs/design/observer_pattern.

When we create plugins, we generally define listeners for specific events.

The application uses a global object called the event dispatcher to dispatch events to registered listeners. The global event dispatcher, a JEventDispatcher object, extends the abstract JObservable class.

In Joomla! a listener can be a class or a function. When we use a class listener, the class should extend the abstract class JPlugin; we extend this class because it implements the methods that are used to attach the listener to a subject.

This diagram illustrates the relationship between the JEventDispatcher class and listeners that extend the JPlugin class:

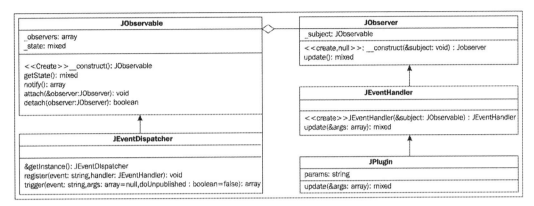

There are several events that are used in the core. In addition to these, we can use our own events. We do not have to define events; we can just use them.

Let's imagine we have a component, which displays information about an entity called Foobar. We might choose to use a custom event called `onPrepareFoobar` to allow listeners to perform any additional processing to the Foobar data before we go ahead and display a Foobar.

To issue an event, we trigger it. There is a method in the application called `triggerEvent()`, which triggers events in the global event dispatcher, notifying the relevant listeners. This is a pass-through method for the JEventDispatcher `trigger()` method.

The `triggerEvent()` method accepts two parameters: the name of the event and an array of arguments to pass to the listener.

Imagine we want to trigger the event `onPrepareFoobar`. This example shows how we can achieve this; it assumes `$foobarData` is an object that represents a Foobar entity. Note that `$mainframe` is the application.

```
$arguments = array(&$foobarData);
$result = $mainframe->triggerEvent('onPrepareFoobar', $arguments);
```

The most important thing to notice here is that we reference and wrap $foobarData in an array. The second parameter must always be an array. This array is dissected, and each element is used as a separate parameter when dispatching an event to a listener.

We purposefully make sure that $foobarData is passed by reference so we can make changes to $foobarData in our listeners.

Once all of the listeners have been updated, the method returns an array of responses. In our example this is recorded in $result. Imagine that all of the onPrepareFoobar listeners return a Boolean value. $result would contain an array of Boolean values.

Listeners

There is one more thing we need to do first. We need to know how to attach listeners to the event dispatcher.

Registering Listeners

When we create a new plugin, if we are using functions, we must inform the application of each function and event. We do this using the application's registerEvent() method. The method accepts two parameters, the name of the event and the name of the handler. This acts as a pass-through method for the global event dispatcher register() method.

Technically the name of the handler can be the name of a class. We rarely need to use the method in that context because when we load a plugin that defines a class, Joomla! automatically registers the class and events.

For example, the core Joomla! search component uses plugins to search for results. The plugin that searches content articles uses the function plgSearchContent() to handle the onSearch event. This is how the function is registered:

```
$mainframe->registerEvent('onSearch', 'plgSearchContent');
```

Handling Events

We mentioned earlier that we could use functions or a class to handle events. We will start by exploring event handling using functions.

Imagine we have a bespoke plugin called My Plugin in the group Foobar and we want to handle an event called onPrepareFoobar.

Before we start building our function we need to name it; generally we use the following naming convention: the word plg, the plugin group, the element name, the event. For example, we might call the function plgFoobarMyPluginPrepareFoobar.

This is an example of a function we could use to handle that event:

```
$mainframe->registerEvent('onPrepareFoobar',
        'plgFoobarMyPluginPrepareFoobar');

/**
 * Makes the name of the foobar uppercase.
 *
 * @param Foobar Reference to a Foobar object
 */
function plgFoobarMyPluginPrepareFoobar(&$foobar)
{
    $foobar->name = strtoupper($foobar->name);
}
```

The most striking part of this function is the parameter. Earlier in this chapter, we described how to trigger an event and we passed an array; each element of that array is passed as a separate parameter to the listeners. In this example we can assume that the one parameter is the Foobar object, which we passed by reference in the triggering events example.

 A single plugin can contain multiple functions for handling multiple events.

If we want to create a listener using a class, we extend the abstract class JPlugin.

Before we start building a listener class, we must determine the name for the class. JPlugin subclasses follow a special naming convention: the word plg, the name of the plugin group, the name of the plugin element. For example, a plugin with the name myplugin in the group foobar might define the JPlugin subclass plgFoobarMyplugin.

This example is designed to handle two events: onPrepareFoobar and onAfterDisplayFoobar:

```
// import the JPlugin class
jimport('joomla.event.plugin');

/**
 * My Plugin event listener
 */
```

```
class plgFoobarMyplugin extends JPlugin
{

    /**
     * handle onPrepareFoobar event
     *
     * @param object Foobar to prepare
     */
    function onPrepareFoobar(&$foobar)
    {
        $foobar->name = JString::strtoupper($foobar->name);
    }

    /**
     * handle onAfterDisplayFoobar event
     *
     * @param object Foobar which is being displayed
     * @return string XHTML to display after the Foobar
     */
    function onAfterDisplayFoobar(&$foobar)
    {
        return '<p>'.JText::_('Foobar Name converted to upper case by
                                My Plugin').'</p>';
    }
}
```

The first thing that should have struck you about this example is that we have not bothered to register any events with the global event dispatcher. The advantage of using classes is we do not need to do this, so long as we follow the strict class naming convention.

 If we do not follow the naming convention, we can register a class in the same way as we register a function, as described earlier in the chapter.

When plugins are imported into Joomla! the global event dispatcher will automatically look for listener classes and register them.

You probably also noticed the names of the two methods are identical to the names of the events they handle. This is essential when creating JPlugin subclasses. As we do not manually register each event to each method, this is the only way in which the event dispatcher can determine which event a method is designed to handle.

The `onAfterDisplayFoobar()` method has one major difference to the other method; it returns a value. You may remember that earlier we mentioned that when an event is triggered we get an array of all the results.

This is an example of how we might choose to handle the results of the
`onAfterDisplayFoobar` event:

```
$arguments = array(&$foobar);
$result = $mainframe->triggerEvent('onAfterDisplayFoobar',
                                          $arguments);

$foobar->onAfterDisplayFoobar = trim(implode("\n", $result));
```

What we are doing is taking all the string values returned by the
`onAfterDisplayFoobar` event handlers and imploding them into one string. This is
then stored in the `onAfterDisplayFoobar` attribute of the `$foobar` object.

We normally do this type of thing in component view classes. A template would
then output the value of the `onAfterDisplayFoobar` parameter after the Foobar
was displayed.

It is important to understand that this event, although the name contains 'After', is
executed before the Foobar is actually outputted, what this is really identifying is that
the 'After' refers to where strings returned from the event handlers will be displayed.

Our event handlers have all been very simple; there are all sorts of other things
we can achieve using plugins. For example, we can modify referenced parameters,
return important data, alter the page title, send an email, or even make a log entry!

When we think of plugins we must think beyond content and think in terms of
events and listeners. The plugin groups, which we will discuss in a moment, will
demonstrate a number of different things we can achieve, which go far beyond
modifying content.

Plugin Groups

Plugins are organized into different groups. Each plugin group is designed to handle
a specific set of events. There are eight core groups:

- authentication
- content
- editors
- editors-xtd
- search
- system
- user
- xmlrpc

Each of these groups performs different functions, we will discuss precisely what they are and how they handle them in a moment.

In addition to the core groups, we can create plugins that belong to other groups. For example, if we created a component named Foobar and we wanted to add plugins specifically for that component we could create a custom plugin group called foobar.

The following sections describe each of the core plugin groups, and creating new plugins for the groups. At the end of each of these sections, we detail the related events.

There are no strict rules regarding which event listeners belong to which group. However using the events in the groups described below will ensure that the plugin is loaded when these events occur.

Authentication

Authentication plugins are used to authenticate a user's login details. Joomla! supports four different authentication methods:

- GMail
- Joomla!
- LDAP
- OpenID

By creating new authentication plugins, we can allow Joomla! to support additional authentication methods. It is common for businesses to run more than one system, each with its own authentication. Joomla! authentication plugins allow us to integrate authentication between systems and reduce system management overheads.

There is only one authentication event, onAuthenticate. This event is used to determine if a user has authentic credentials. To return a result from this event we use the third parameter, a referenced JAuthenticationResponse object.

We set values within the object to signify the status of the authentication. This table describes each of the properties we can set:

Property	Description
birthdate	User's Birthday
country	User's Country
email	User's email address.
error_message	Error message on authentication failure or cancel
fullname	User's Full name

Property	Description
gender	User's gender
language	Language tag
postcode	Postcode or zipcode
status	Status of the authentication
timezone	User's timezone
username	User's username – completed automatically

The status property is used to determine the result of the authentication. This table describes the three different constants we use to define the value of status.

Constant	Description
JAUTHENTICATE_STATUS_CANCEL	Authentication Canceled
JAUTHENTICATE_STATUS_FAILURE	Authentication Failed
JAUTHENTICATE_STATUS_SUCCESS	Authentication Successful

Authentication plugins are stackable. We can use multiple authentication plugins simultaneously. The plugins are used in published order and if any of them sets the status of the JAuthenticationResponse object to JAUTHENTICATE_STATUS_SUCCESS the login is deemed successful and no more authentication plugins are triggered.

The default setup, shown below, places the plugins in the order: Joomla!, LDAP, OpenID, GMail. Only Joomla! authentication is enabled by default.

#		Plugin Name	Published	Order		Access	ID	Type ▲	File
1	☐	Authentication - Joomla	✔	▼	1	Public	1	authentication	joomla
2	☐	Authentication - LDAP	⊗	▲ ▼	2	Public	2	authentication	ldap
3	☐	Authentication - OpenID	⊗	▲ ▼	3	Public	4	authentication	openid
4	☐	Authentication - GMail	⊗	▲	4	Public	3	authentication	gmail

Additional processing can be performed once a login has completed using user plugins. These are discussed later in the chapter.

onAuthenticate

Description	Triggered when a user attempts to log in, this event is used to authenticate user credentials.	
Parameters	username	Username
	password	Password
	response	Referenced JAuthenticationResponse object

Content

The content plugins allow us to modify content items before we display them. The most commonly used content event is onPrepareContent. This event, always the first of all the content events to be triggered, is used to modify the text content.

Let's imagine we want to create a content plugin which will replace all occurrences of ':)' with a small smiley face icon. This is how we could implement this:

```
// no direct access
defined('_JEXEC') or die('Restricted access');

// register the handler
$mainframe->registerEvent('onPrepareContent',
                          'plgContentSmiley');

/**
 * Replaces :) with a smiley icon.
 *
 * @param object Content item
 * @param JParameter Content parameters
 * @param int Page number
 */
function plgContentSmiley(&$row, &$params, $page)
{
    $pattern = '/\:\)/';
    $icon = '<img src="plugins/content/smiley.gif" />';
    $row->text = preg_replace($pattern, $icon, $row->text);
}
```

Notice that we do not return the changes, we modify the referenced $row object. The $row object is the content item; it includes a great many attributes. This table describes the attributes that we are most likely to modify:

Attribute	Description
created	Created date and time in the format 0000-00-00 00:00:00.
modified	Modified date and time in the format 0000-00-00 00:00:00.
text	Body content of the item.
title	Content Item Title.
toc	Table of Contents.

onAfterDisplayContent

Description	Creates an XHTML string, which is displayed directly after the content item.	
Parameters	row	Reference to a content item object.
	params	Reference to a JParameter object, which is loaded with the content item parameters.
	page	Page number.
Returns	XHTML to display directly after the content item.	

onAfterDisplayTitle

Description	Creates an XHTML string, which is displayed directly after the content item title.	
Parameters	row	Reference to a content item object.
	params	Reference to a JParameter object, which is loaded with the content item parameters.
	page	Page number.
Returns	XHTML to display directly after the title of the content item.	

onBeforeDisplayContent

Description	Creates an XHTML string, which is displayed directly before the content item text. For example the 'Content - Rating' plugin.	
Parameters	row	Reference to a content item object.
	params	Reference to a JParameter object, which is loaded with the content item parameters.
	page	Page number.
Returns	XHTML to display directly before the content item text.	

onPrepareContent

Description	Prepares a RAW content item ready for display. If you intend to modify the text of an item, you should use this event.	
Parameters	row	Reference to a content item object. To modify content we must directly edit this object.
	params	Reference to a JParameter object, which is loaded with the content item parameters.
	page	Page number.
Returns	True on success.	

Editors

Probably the most complex of all the core plugins are editors. These plugins are used to render handy client-side `textarea` editors. One of the core editors is TinyMCE (http://tinymce.moxiecode.com/), a separate project in its own right. TinyMCE is a JavaScript-based editor, which allows a user to easily modify data in a `textarea` without the need for any knowledge of XHTML.

This is a screenshot of TinyMCE in action in Joomla!:

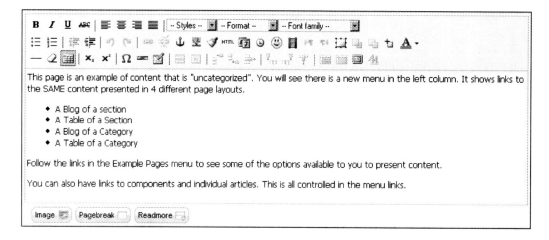

Note that the buttons displayed at the bottom of the editor are not part of the editor. These are created by editors-xtd plugins, explained later in this chapter.

Generally editor plugins are derived from existing JavaScript editors. This is a list of just some of the editors that have already been ported for use with Joomla!:

- ASBRU Web Content Editor
- FCKeditor
- wysiwygPro
- XStandard

Porting an editor for use with Joomla! is no easy task. Intimate understanding of the editor and Joomla! editor plugins is required.

onDisplay

Description	Gets the XHTML field element to use as the form field element.	
Parameters	name	Name of the editor area/form field.
	content	Initial content.
	width	Width of editor in pixels.
	height	Height of editor in pixels.
	col	Width of editor in columns.
	row	Height of editor in rows.
	buttons	Boolean, show/hide extra buttons; see the `onCustomEditorButton` event, part of editors-xtd, explained in the next section.
Returns	XHTML form element for editor.	

onGetContent

Description	Gets some JavaScript, which can be used to get the contents of the editor.	
Parameters	editor	Name of the editor area/form field.
Returns	A JavaScript string that, when executed client-side, will return the contents of the editor. Must end with a semicolon.	

onGetInsertMethod

Description	Gets some JavaScript which defines a function called `jInsertEditorText()`.	
Parameters	name	Name of the editor area/form field.
Returns	A JavaScript string that defines the function `jInsertEditorText(text)`, which, when executed client-side, will insert `text` into the current cursor position in the editor.	

onInit

Description	Initialize the editor. This is only run once irrespective of how many times an editor is rendered.
Returns	An XHTML tag to be added to the head of the document. Normally this will be a script tag containing some JavaScript, which is integral to client-side initialization of the editor.

onSave

Description	Gets some JavaScript, which is used to save the contents of the editor.	
Parameters	editor	Name of the editor area/form field.
Returns	A JavaScript string, which must be executed before a form containing the editor field is submitted. Not all editors will require this.	

onSetContent

Description	Gets some JavaScript, which can be used to set the contents of the editor.	
Parameters	name	Name of the editor area/form field.
	HTML	The new content of the editor.
Returns	A JavaScript string that when executed client-side, will set the contents of the editor to the value of the HTML parameter.	

Editors-xtd

This group is used to extend editor plugins by creating additional buttons for the editors. Unfortunately, the core 'xstandard' editor does not support these plugins. There is only one event associated with this group, onCustomEditorButton.

Since there is only one event associated with the group, we tend to use functions instead of full-blown JPlugin subclasses. This example shows how we can add a button, which adds the smiley ':)' to the editor content.

```
// no direct access
defined('_JEXEC') or die('Restricted access');

$mainframe->registerEvent('onCustomEditorButton',
                          'plgSmileyButton');

/**
 * Smiley button
 *
 * @name string Name of the editor
 * @return array Array of three elements: JavaScript action,
                                Button name, CSS class.
 */
function plgSmileyButton($name)
{
    global $mainframe;

    // get the image base URI
    $doc =& JFactory::getDocument();
    $url = $mainframe->isAdmin() ? $mainframe->getSiteURL() : JURI::
base();
    // get the JavaScript
```

```
$js = "
function insertSmiley()
{
    jInsertEditorText(' :) ');
}
";

$css = "    .button1-left .smiley { background:
            url($url/plugins/editors-xtd/smiley1.gif)
                            100% 0 no-repeat; }";
$css .= "\n    .button2-left .smiley { background:
            url($url/plugins/editors-xtd/smiley2.gif)
                            100% 0 no-repeat; }";
$doc->addStyleDeclaration($css);
$doc->addScriptDeclaration($js);
$button = array("insertSmiley()", JText::_('Smiley'),
                            'smiley');

    return $button;
}
```

Temporarily ignoring the contents of the function, we do two very important things in this code. We define the handler function and we register it with the global event dispatcher.

Moving on to the guts of the `plgSmileyButton()` function, we will start by looking at the `$name` parameter. This parameter is the name of the editor area. It is important we have this so that we can identify which area we are dealing with. Admittedly, we do not use this in our example function, but it is likely that it will be of use at some point.

We build some JavaScript and some CSS. The client will execute the JavaScript when the button is pressed. We define two CSS styles to render the button in different locations.

The `$button` array that we return is an array that describes the button we want the editor to display. The first element is the JavaScript to execute when the button is pressed. The second element is the name of the button. The third element is the name of the CSS style to apply to the button.

This screenshot demonstrates what our button might look like (fourth button):

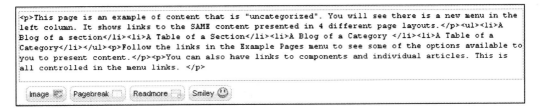

You will also notice that in this example we are using images located in the `editors-xtd` folder. If you are wondering how we achieve this then look no further! The image files would be included in the plugin archive and described in the XML manifest file.

This snippet shows the `files` tag in the XML manifest file:

```
<files>
    <filename plugin="smiley">smiley.php</filename>
    <filename>smiley1.gif</filename>
    <filename>smiley2.gif</filename>
</files>
```

Before we move on, there are some handy methods available to us of which you should be aware. We can interrogate the editor to get some useful JavaScript snippets. This table details the methods to do this:

Method	Description
getContent	JavaScript to get the content of the editor.
save	JavaScript to save the content of the editor. Not all editors use this.
setContent	JavaScript to set the content of the editor.

All of these methods return a JavaScript string. We can use the strings to build scripts that interact with the editor. We use these because most of the editors are JavaScript based, and therefore require bespoke script to perform these functions client-side.

This is an example of how we would use the `getContent()` method to build a script that presents a JavaScript alert that contains the contents of the editor identified by `$name`:

```
// get the editor
$editor =& JFactory::getEditor();

// prepare the JavaScript which will get the value of editor
$getContent = $editor->getContent($name);

// build the JavaScript alert that contains the contents of the editor
$js = 'var content = '.$getContent."\n"
    .'alert(content);';
```

onCustomEditorButton

Description	Build a custom button for an editor.	
Parameters	name	Name of the editor area.
Returns	An array of three elements, the JavaScript to execute when the button is pressed, the name of the button, and the CSS Style.	

Search

We use search plugins to extend the core search component and get search results. There are two events associated with this group, onSearch and onSearchAreas. The purpose of onSearchAreas is a little more obscure.

To help explain, this is a screenshot of the search component:

Search Keyword:		Search

⊙ Any words ○ All words ○ Exact phrase

Ordering: | Newest first | ▾ |

Search Only: ☐ Articles ☐ Weblinks ☐ Contacts ☐ Categories ☐ Sections ☐ Newsfeeds

As part of this, a user has the option as to which areas they want to search. In this case, 'Articles', 'Weblinks', 'Contacts', 'Categories', 'Sections', and 'Newsfeeds'. When we trigger the onSearchAreas event, it is these 'areas' that we expect to be returned.

 A single search plugin can deal with multiple areas.

The onSearch event is more implicit; it is the event that is raised when a search takes place. Listeners to this event should return an array of results. Exactly how you implement this will depend upon what you are searching.

onSearch

Description	Perform a search and return the results.	
Parameters	text	Search string.
	phrase	Search type, 'any', 'all', or 'exact'.
	ordering	Order of the results, 'newest', 'oldest', 'popular', 'alpha' (alphabetical), or 'category'.
	areas	Areas to search (based on onSearchArea).
Returns	An array of results. Each result must be an associative array containing the keys 'title', 'text', 'created', 'href', 'browsernav' (1 = open link in new window), and 'section' (optional).	

onSearchAreas

Description	Gets an array of different areas that can be searched using this plugin. Every search plugin should return at least one area.
Returns	Associative array of different areas to search. The keys are the area values and the values are the labels.

System

There are four important system events. We have mentioned these once before, in Chapter 2 *Getting Started* they occur in a very specific order and occur every time a request is made. This list shows the order in which the four events occur:

- onAfterInitialize
- onAfterRoute
- onAfterDispatch
- onAfterRender

If you look at the diagrams we used to describe the process from request to response in Chapter 2, you will see that each of these events is triggered at a very special point.

onAfterDispatch

Description	Occurs after the application has been dispatched.

onAfterInitialize

Description	Occurs after the application has been initialized.

onAfterRender

Description	Occurs after the application has been rendered, but before the response has been sent.

onAfterRoute

Description	Occurs after the application has been routed.

User

User plugins allow additional processing during user-specific events. This is especially useful when used in conjunction with a component that defines tables that are associated to the core #__users table.

We will take the event onAfterUserStore as an example. This event is triggered after an attempt has been made to store a user's details. This includes new and existing users.

This example shows how we can maintain another table, #__some_table, when a new user is created:

```
$mainframe->registerEvent('onAfterStoreUser',
        'plgUserMaintainSomeTableStoreUser');
```

```
/**
 * Add new rcord to #__some_table when a new user is created
 *
 * @param array User attributes
 * @param boolean True if the user is new
 * @param boolean True if the user was successfully stored
 * @param string Error message
 * @return array Array of three elements: JavaScript action, Button
 *                                        name, CSS class.
 */
function plgUserMaintainSomeTableStoreUser($user, $isnew, $success,
                                           $msg)
{
    // if they are a new user and the store was successful
    if ($isnew && $success)
    {
        // add a record to #__some_table
        $db = JFactory::getDBO();
        $query = 'INSERT INTO '.$db->nameQuote('#__some_table')
                .' SET '.$db->nameQuote('userid').' = '.$user['id'];
        $db->setQuery($query);
        $db->query();
    }
}
```

onBeforeStoreUser

Description	Allows us to modify user data before we save it.	
Parameters	user	Associative array of user details. Includes the same parameters as the user table fields.
	isnew	True if the user is new.

onAfterStoreUser

Description	Allows us to execute code after a user's details have been updated. It's advisable to use this in preference to `onBeforeStoreUser`.	
Parameters	user	Associative array of user details. Includes the same parameters as the user table fields.
	isnew	True if the user is new.
	success	True if store was successful.
	msg	Error message if store failed.

onBeforeDeleteUser

Description	Enables us to perform additional processing before a user is deleted. This is useful for updating non-core tables that are related to the core #__ users table	
Parameters	user	Associative array of user details. Only has the key id, which is the user's ID.

onAfterDeleteUser

Description	Same as `onBeforeDeleteUser`, but occurs after a user has been removed from the #__users table.	
Parameters	user	Associative array of user details. Only has the key id which is the user's ID.
	success	True if the user was successfully deleted.
	msg	Error message if deletion failed.

onLoginFailure

Description	During a failed login this handles an array derived from a JAuthenticationResponse object. See authentication plugins earlier in this chapter.	
Parameters	response	JAuthenticationResponse object as returned from the onAuthenticate event, explained earlier in the chapter.

onLoginUser

Description	During a successful login this handles an array derived from a JAuthenticationResponse object. See authentication plugins earlier in this chapter. This is not used to authenticate a user's login.	
Parameters	user	JAuthenticationResponse object as returned from the onAuthenticate event, explained earlier in the chapter.
	remember	True if the user wants to be 'remembered'.
Returns	Boolean false on failure.	

onLogoutUser

Description	User is attempting to logout. The user plugin 'joomla' destroys the session at this point.	
Parameters	user	Associative array of user details. Only has the keys 'id', which is the user's ID, and 'username', which is the user's username.
Returns	Boolean false of failure.	

XML-RPC

XML-RPC is a way in which systems can call procedures on remote systems via HTTP using XML to encode data. Joomla! includes an XML-RPC server, which we can extend using plugins.

There are essentially two parts to XML-RPC plugins: the event handler for the event `onGetWebServices`, which returns an array of supported web service calls, and a static class or selection of functions that handle remote procedure calls.

For more information about creating XML-RPC plugins, please refer to Chapter 10.

onGetWebServices

Description	Gets an associative array describing the available web service methods.
Returns	An associative array of associative arrays, which define the available XML-RPC web service calls.

Loading Plugins

Before a plugin can respond to an event, the plugin must be loaded. When we normally load plugins we load a group at a time. To do this we use the static `JPluginHelper` class.

This example shows how we would load plugins from the group foobar:

```
JPluginHelper::importPlugin('foobar');
```

It is essential that we import plugins before firing events that relate to them. There is one time when this does not apply; we never need to import 'system' plugins. System plugins are imported irrespective of the request that is being handled. It is, however, unlikely that we would ever need to trigger a system event because Joomla! should handle all system events.

So where and when do we import plugins? Well firstly, it does not matter if we attempt to import the same group of plugins more than once. At what point we choose to import the plugins is entirely up to us. The most common place to import plugins is in a component in a controller.

For example, the search component imports all of the search plugins before it raises any events that are specific to search plugins:

```
JPluginHelper::importPlugin('search');
```

 Note that it is not the responsibility of the plugin to load itself. It is up to the extension that uses the associated plugin group to do this.

In the unlikely event that we want to import a specific plugin, we can do this:

```
JPluginHelper::importPlugin('foobar', 'somePlugin');
```

This example imports the plugin somePlugin, located in the foobar group.

Using Plugins as Libraries (in Lieu of Library Extensions)

We have mentioned the Joomla! library a number of times in the past. Although the library is a powerful part of Joomla!, it is not extensible. There are currently discussions within Joomla! to create library extensions and implement an extension dependency mechanism.

In the meantime, we can use plugins as libraries. Plugins, although not designed for this, are ideally suited to this because they enable us to build up a shared directory structure based on several plugins.

First, we must use a common plugin group for a library; we should think of this as the root library namespace. This XML defines a plugin called 'My Library - Base'.

```xml
<?xml version="1.0" encoding="utf-8"?>
<!DOCTYPE install SYSTEM
                  "http://dev.joomla.org/xml/1.5/plugin-install.dtd">
<install version="1.5" type="plugin" group="mylibrary">
    <name>My Library - Base</name>
    <author>Author's Name</author>
    <authorEmail>Author's Email</authorEmail>
    <authorUrl>Author's Website</authorUrl>
    <creationDate>MonthName Year</creationDate>
    <copyright>Copyright Notice</copyright>
    <license>Plugin License Agreement</license>
    <version>Plugin Version</version>
    <description>Plugin Description</description>
    <files>
        <filename plugin="base">base.php</filename>
        <folder>base</folder>
        <folder>foo</folder>
    </files>
    <params/>
</install>
```

This will create two folders, base and foo, in the plugin folder mylibrary.

Note that we have to include a file with a plugin element, base.php.

To import elements from this pseudo-library we can use the JLoader class. This class is what sits behind the regularly used jimport() function, which we use to import parts of the Joomla! library.

Let's create a function called myimport() to import library elements from the plugin group mylibrary.

```
function myimport($path)
{
    return JLoader::import($path, JPATH_PLUGINS . DS . 'mylibrary');
}
```

A good place to create this function is in the base.php file. So, bearing in mind our folder structure looks something like this:

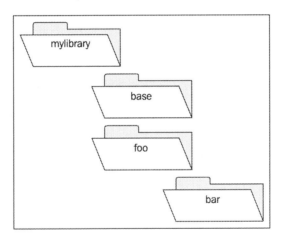

how do we use the myimport() function? This example demonstrates how we would import all of the files in mylibrary/foo/bar:

```
JPluginHelper::importPlugin('mylibrary', 'base');
myimport('foo.bar.*');
```

The first line of the example only needs to be used once. It imports the library plugin, which we defined earlier. Assuming we placed the myimport() function in the base.php file we can now use the function to import a particular part of the pseudo-library.

We should be careful when selecting names for libraries. We should ensure that the names do not conflict with those used in the Joomla! libraries. Otherwise, this could cause problems later. One way to resolve this would be to add an additional layer to library, i.e. we could prefix `somelibrary.` to all `myimport` paths.

We can create additional plugins that belong to the group mylibrary adding additional files to the pseudo-library. This example shows how we might choose to add to this library:

```xml
<?xml version="1.0" encoding="utf-8"?>
<!DOCTYPE install SYSTEM
              "http://dev.joomla.org/xml/1.5/plugin-install.dtd">
<install version="1.5" type="plugin" group="mylibrary">
    <name>My Library - Baz</name>
    <author>Author's Name</author>
    <authorEmail>Author's Email</authorEmail>
    <authorUrl>Author's Website</authorUrl>
    <creationDate>MonthName Year</creationDate>
    <copyright>Copyright Notice</copyright>
    <license>Plugin License Agreement</license>
    <version>Plugin Version</version>
    <description>Plugin Description</description>
    <files>
        <filename plugin="baz">baz.php</filename>
        <folder>baz</folder>
    </files>
    <params/>
</install>
```

Our mylibrary class will now look something like this:

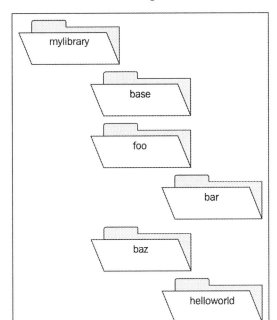

Translating Plugins

As part of a plugin, we can define a set of translations. A full description of how to create language files is available in Chapter 9.

When we create plugin translation files, we must name the file according to a specific naming convention: the language tag, a period, the Joomla! parsed plugin name. For example, the English translation file for the plugin My Extension would be called `en-GB.plg_myextension.ini`.

Plugin translation files are located in the administrator/language folders.

Unlike components and modules, plugin language files are not automatically loaded when a plugin is loaded. To use a plugin language file we must manually load it. We can do this using the static loadLanguage() method in the JPlugin class, as this example demonstrates:

```
JPlugin::loadLanguage('plg_myextension', JPATH_ADMINISTRATOR);
```

Notice that when we load the language file we also tell Joomla! that the file is located in the backend language folder. Plugin language files are always located in the backend. If we do not use this, the language file will only be loaded when we are accessing the backend.

We need to consider where we should include such a piece of code. Adding it at the beginning of a plugin file, although logical, might be loading it unnecessarily because it may not be required. A more appropriate approach might be to load it when a handler method or function is executed.

Dealing with Plugin Settings (Parameters)

To deal with plugin settings we can use the, ever handy, `params` tag in our XML manifest file. This example shows how we can add some simple parameters to a plugin:

```xml
<?xml version="1.0" encoding="utf-8"?>
<!DOCTYPE install SYSTEM "http://dev.joomla.org/xml/1.5/plugin-
                                                  install.dtd">
<install version="1.5" type="plugin" group="foobar">
    <name>Foobar - My Extension</name>
    <author>Author's Name</author>
    <authorEmail>Author's Email</authorEmail>
    <authorUrl>Author's Website</authorUrl>
    <creationDate>MonthName Year</creationDate>
    <copyright>Copyright Notice</copyright>
    <license>Plugin License Agreement</license>
    <version>Plugin Version</version>
    <description>Plugin Description</description>
    <files>
        <filename plugin="elementName">myextension.php</filename>
    </files>
    <params>
        <param name="aparam" type="text" label="A Parameter"
                         description="A description" />
    </params>
</install>
```

In this instance, we have added a text parameter `aparam`. Parameters that we define here are used in the Plugin Manager when we edit a plugin. This screenshot demonstrates how the above parameter would be rendered:

A complete description of the types of parameters and how to define them in XML is available in the *Appendix*.

If we are using a JPlugin subclass, we access the defined parameters via the `params` attribute within the class. The attribute is a JParameter object.

The most important methods we need to be aware of in the JParameter class are `def()`, `get()`, and `set()`.

We use `def()` to set a default value for a parameter if no value currently exists for it. This example demonstrates how we would use the method to set a default value of `value` for the parameter `aparam`:

```
$this->params->def('aparam', 'value');
```

We use `get()` to get the value of a parameter. This example demonstrates how we would use the method to get the value of the parameter `aparam`:

```
$this->params->get('aparam');
```

We can also pass a second parameter to `get()`, a default value, which will be returned if no value already exists for the parameter.

We use `set()` to set a value for a parameter. This example demonstrates how we would use the method to set a value of `value` for the parameter `aparam`:

```
$this->params->set('aparam', 'value');
```

If we are using functions to handle events we must manually get the plugin parameters. To do this we can use the JPluginHelper class. This example demonstrates how we would get the parameters for a plugin called bar, in the group foo:

```
// get an object with all the data about the plugin
$plugin =& JPluginHelper::getPlugin('foo', 'bar');
$params = new JParameter($plugin->params);
```

As a rule, it is easier and more efficient to use a JPlugin subclass if we intend to use parameters with a plugin.

Packaging

Plugins are packaged in archive files. A number of archive formats are supported; `.gz`, `.tar`, `.tar.gz`, and `zip`. There is no specific naming convention for plugin archive files; however, the following is often used: `plg_name-version`. For example, the package for version 1.0.0 of My Extension would be called `plg_myextension-1.0.0`.

When you package a plugin, ensure you do not include any system files. Apple Mac developers should be especially vigilant and consider using the CleanArchiver utility `http://www.sopht.jp/cleanarchiver/`.

Within the package, as well as the plugin files, there is a special XML manifest file, which describes the plugin.

Interestingly there is no specific name that we are expected to use for the XML file. When we install a plugin Joomla! will interrogate all the XML files it can find in the root of the archive until it finds a file that it believes to be a Joomla! installation XML manifest file.

If you want to use a standard naming convention for your XML manifest file, you should consider using the name of the plugin element. For example, if the plugin element is foobar you might want to call the XML manifest file `foobar.xml`.

XML Manifest File

The XML manifest file details everything the installer needs to know about an extension. Any mistakes in the file may result in partial or total installation failure. XML manifest files should be saved using UTF-8 encoding. For a base manifest file, you can use the file detailed at the start of this chapter, to create a sandbox.

The tables below describe the tags you can use in your XML manifest file in detail:

install (Root tag)

The root tag, called install, identifies the type of extension and the version of Joomla! for which the extension is written.		

Example	`<install type="plugin" version="1.5">`
	     `<!-- sub-tags -->`
	 `</install>`	

Attributes	type	Type of extension.
	version	Version of Joomla! the extension is for.
Sub-tags	author, authorEmail, authorUrl, copyright, creationDate, description, files, languages, license, media, name, params, version	

author

Author's name.	
Example	`<author>John Smith</author>`

authorEmail

Author's email address.	
Example	`<authorEmail>johnsmith@example.org</authorEmail>`

authorUrl

Author or component's website address.	
Example	`<authorUrl>http://www.example.org</authorUrl>`

copyright

Copyright notice.	
Example	`<copyright>Copy me as much as you like!</copyright>`

description

Plugin description.	
Example	`<description>Example component description.</description>`

files

Plugin files and folders.	
Example	`<files><!-- sub-tags --></files>`	
Attributes	[folder]	Folder in the archive where the files reside.
Sub-tags	filename, folder	

filename

Defines a file we want to copy.	
Example	`<filename>example.php</filename>`	
Attributes	plugin	Plugin element. Can only be used with one file, the root plugin file.

folder

Defines folders we want to copy; if a folder has subfolders and files we do not have to specify these.	
Example	`<folder>afolder</folder>`

language

Language tags define a language INI file. The tag includes the attribute tag; this is used to identify the language. Language files are copied into the backend languages folder.	
Example	`<language tag="en-GB">en-GB.com_example.ini</language>`	
Attributes	tag	Language tag.

languages

Language files. If any of the language files already exist they will not be overwritten. This tag has one sub tag, language. Each language tag defines a language INI file. The language tag must include the attribute `tag`; this is used to identify the language.		

Example	`<languages folder="languages">`
	    `<!-sub tags -->`
	`</languages>`	

Attributes	[folder]	Folder in the archive where the files reside.
Sub-tags	language	

license

License agreement.	
Example	`<license>GNU GPL</license>`

media

Media files to be copied to the root Joomla! images folder.		
Example	`<media destination="stories"><!-sub tags --></media>`	
Attributes	[destination]	Destination folder within the Joomla! images folder.
Sub-tags	filename	

name

Plugin name.	
Example	`<name>example</name>`

param

A parameter. How this tag is used depends upon the type of parameter we are defining; a complete description of these types and their attributes is available in the appendix.	
Example	`<param type="text" name="foobar" label="Foobar"/>`

params

Plugin parameters.		
Example	`<params><!-sub tags --></params>`	
Attributes	`addParameterDir`	Directory where custom `JElement` subclasses can be found.
Sub-tags	`param`	

version

Extension version. Most extensions use three digits in the form `major.minor.patch`; version 1.0.0 normally denotes the first stable release.	
Example	`<version>1.0.0</version>`

File Naming Conflicts

When we explored the possibility of using plugins as libraries, we saw that plugins of any one group are all stored in the same folder. This can pose a problem if we have two files with the same name in different plugins that are in the same group.

If we attempt to install a plugin that includes a file with the same name as an existing file, the installation will fail. This is a screenshot of the error message received when such incident occurs:

 JInstaller::install: There is already a file called '/joomla/plugins/editors-xtd/smiley1.gif' - Are you trying to install the same CMT twice?

A good way to avoid this is to place any related files in a sub folder. This XML demonstrates how we could achieve this:

```
<files>
    <filename plugin="example">example.php</filename>
    <folder>example</folder>
</files>
```

In instances where there are only two files, for example, the plugin file and an image, it is common to name the image the same as the plugin element:

```
<files>
    <filename plugin="example">example.php</filename>
    <filename>example.gif</filename>
</files>
```

Summary

Joomla! events are occurrences that trigger the event dispatcher to notify the relevant listeners that an event has occurred. Listeners, in plugins, are classes and functions that attach themselves to the global event dispatcher.

We put plugins into groups to increase the efficiency of plugins. The group imports Plugins. Grouping events together means that we only need to import the relevant plugins when we need them. Remember that we are not forced to use the existing groups and that we can define as many new groups as we like.

In lieu of library extensions, we can manipulate plugins to behave like libraries. Plugins can go far beyond the intended use of handling events. If we utilize plugins to our advantage, we can create modular extensions.

7
Extension Design

Over and above the design issues we have discussed in the previous three chapters, there are additional design elements to consider when building extensions. This chapter explains some of the other design elements, common to all extensions, which we have not yet covered.

Supporting Classes

In the last three chapters, we have discussed the creation of subclasses from some of the core classes. In addition to these classes, we may want to define our own unique classes.

The MVC is a very good pattern for creating systems quickly and easily. However, it is not, nor is it intended to be, all encompassing.

Unsurprisingly, many components contain supporting classes. The core component that deals with menus is a prime example. This component defines two additional classes, iLink and iLinkNode. A tree representation of a menu is built using these classes.

When we create classes such as this, it is common practice to place them in a special folder called 'classes'. When creating a component we place this folder in the backend.

Supporting classes can extend existing Joomla! classes, for example the JObject class. They can also be completely unrelated and separate works in their own right.

'PHP Classes', www.phpclasses.org/browse, is a good place to look for existing classes that we can utilize.

 Remember that, although Joomla! provides us with an excellent framework, we should never feel restricted by it. There is nothing to prevent us from building extensions in other ways.

Helpers

Helpers are static classes used to perform common functions. Helpers often complement one other class. For example, the static JToolBarHelper helper class works in conjunction with the JToolBar class.

 There are forty-nine helper classes in the Joomla! core alone.

When building helpers that complement another class, the functions that we place within the helpers must relate to the other class.

Imagine we have a class named SomeItem, which deals with an itemized entity. If each item were to have a category, we might want to be able to get a list of those categories especially for use with the item.

Placing a method to do this in the SomeItem class is questionable because the method is dealing with a different entity. Instead we could create a helper class SomeItemHelper and define a method getCategories() that returns an XHTML drop-down list of categories.

Helpers that do not relate to other classes generally relate to an extension or a library. Many of the core modules define and use a helper class. This diagram illustrates how the helper for the Poll module is constructed:

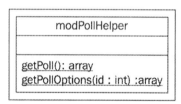

Note that there are some special rules we follow when creating helpers for modules; these are explained in Chapter 5.

This list describes common functions that helpers execute:

- Getting a list (usually an array) of items, often called getList()
- Getting or building a data item
- Getting or building a data structure
- Parsing data
- Rendering data to XHTML, often called render()

When we use helpers in components, we can use the JView loadHelper() method. This method will load a helper, based on the name of the file in which it is located. The method searches predefined locations of helper files. By default, this is the helpers' folder in the root of the component. To add additional paths, use the addHelperPath() method.

Using and Building getInstance() Methods

Many of the core classes in Joomla! use a special method called `getInstance()`. There are various ways to use this method; we will start by looking at using it to implement the singleton pattern.

We restrict the instantiation of a class to one of its own member methods by using the singleton design pattern. This enables us to create only a single instance of the class, hence the name 'singleton'.

To implement a true singleton pattern, the language must support access modifiers. If the language does not, we cannot guarantee that the class will not be instantiated from a different context.

This example shows how we can create a class that, instead of instantiating via the constructor, we instantiate via the `getInstance()` method:

```
/**
 * Demonstrates the singleton pattern in Joomla!
 */
class SomeClass extends JObject
{
    /**
     * Constructor
     *
     * @access private
     * @return  SomeClass New object
     */
    function __construct() { }
    /**
     * Returns a reference to the global SomeClass object
     *
     * @access public
     * @static
     * @return  SomeClass The SomeClass object
     */
    function &getInstance()
    {
```

```
            static $instance;
            if (!$instance)
            {
                  $instance = new SomeClass();
            }
            return $instance;
      }
}
```

Since we are implementing this as a singleton pattern, we need to prevent the instantiation of the object outside of the class. Put simply, the __construct() method needs to be limited to scope of the class. Sadly, we cannot guarantee this in PHP versions prior to 5.

In our example, we use the access doctag, @access, to indicate that the constructor is private. If we were building this class specifically for a PHP 5 or above environment, we would be able to use access modifiers (visibility). For more information about access modifiers, refer to http://php.net/manual/language.oop5.visibility.php.

In the declaration of the getInstance() method we make the method return a reference and we define it as static in the doctags. This means when we use the method we must always use the =& assignment operator, to prevent copying of the returned object, and we must use the method in the static form SomeClass::getInstance().

At the start of the getInstance() method we declare a new static variable. Unlike normal variables, static variables do not die after a function or method has completed. We use the variable as a long-term store to remember the singleton object.

This example demonstrates how we can use this method:

```
$anObject =& SomeClass::getInstance();
$anObject->set('foo', 'bar');
$anotherObject =& SomeClass::getInstance();
echo $anotherObject->get('foo');
```

The two variables, $anObject and $anotherObject, are both pointing to the same object. This means that the example will output bar.

A similar use of the getInstance() method is to only allow instantiation of one object per different constructor parameter. This example demonstrates how we can implement this:

```
/**
 * Demonstrates how to implement getInstance
 */
class SomeClass extends JObject
{
```

```php
/**
 * A private string attribute.
 * @access private
 * @param string
 */
var $_foo = null;

/**
 * Constructor
 *
 * @access private
 * @param string A string
 * @return SomeClass New object
 */
function __construct($foo)
{
    $this->_foo = $foo;
}

/**
 * Returns a reference to a global SomeClass object
 *
 * @access public
 * @static
 * @param string A string
 * @return SomeClass A global SomeClass object
 */
function &getInstance($foo)
{
    static $instances;
    $foo = (string)$foo;

    if (!$instances)
    {
        $instances = array();
    }

    if (!$instance[$foo])
    {
        $instances[$foo] = new SomeClass($foo);
    }

    return $instances[$foo];
}
}
```

This example is extremely similar to the singleton example, except we create a static array to house multiple objects instead of a single object. As with the previous example in the declaration of the `getInstance()` method, we make the method return a reference and we define it as static in the doctags.

An extension of this mechanism is to allow instantiation of subclasses. A good example of this is the core JDocument class that can instantiate JDocumentError, JDocumentFeed, JDocumentHTML, JDocumentPDF, or JDocumentRAW (located at `libraries/joomla/document`).

In this example, we will attempt something similar; assume that the subclasses are located in the root of a component and named with the prefix `SomeClass`:

```
/**
 * Returns a reference to the global SomeClass object
 *
 * @access public
 * @static
 * param string A string
 * @return mixed A SomeClass object, false on failure
 */
function &getInstance($foo)
{
    static $instances;

    // prepare static array
    if (!$instances)
    {
        $instances = array();
    }

    $foo = (string)$foo;
    $class = 'SomeClass'.$foo;
    $file = strtolower($foo).'.php';

    if (empty($instances[$foo]))
    {
        if (!class_exists($class))
        {
            // class does not exists, so we need to find it
            jimport('joomla.filesystem.file');
            if(JFile::exists(JPATH_COMPONENT.DS.$file))
            {
```

```
            // file found, let's include it
            require_once JPATH_COMPONENT.DS.$file;
            if (!class_exists($class))
            {
                // file doesn't contain the class!
                    JError::raiseError(0, 'Class '.$class.'
                                            not found.');
                return false;
            }
        }
        else
        {
            // file where the class should be not found
                JError::raiseError('ERROR_CODE', 'File '.$file.'
                                            not found.' );

            return false;
        }
    }
    $instances[$foo] = new $class();
}

return $instances[$foo];
}
```

Having explained how to implement the getInstance() methods, we need to examine why we would need to. There are three main reasons:

- This makes it easier to keep track of objects. Take the JDatabase object as an example. We can access this object at any time using the static JFactory::getDBO() method. If we were unable to do this, we would need to continually pass the object around or declare it global in every method and function that required it.

- This helps prevent us from duplicating work. For classes that support it, we do not have to continually instantiate a new object of that type every time we need it. This helps reduce the overall work that PHP is required to complete.

- This provides us with a common way of instantiating globally available objects that conforms to standards within the Joomla! core.

Using the Registry

Joomla! provides us with the class JRegistry; this class enables us to store and retrieve data using namespaces. Data stored in a JRegistry object is organized using a hierarchy based on namespaces.

Namespaces are unique hierarchical tree identifiers used to categorize data. Imagine we want to store the number of sightings of animals in an area. We could use the following hierarchy:

```
animal
animal.total
animal.bird
animal.bird.chaffinch
animal.bird.swan
animal.mammal
animal.mammal.badger
animal.mammal.squirrel.red
animal.mammal.squirrel.grey
```

Based on this example, if we wanted to know how many badgers we have sighted, we would retrieve the value using the registry path animal.mammal.badger. If we wanted to know how many mammals we have sighted, we would retrieve the value using the registry path animal.mammal.

 A drawback of using this type of hierarchy is that data items can only be stored in one path. This can be difficult if the location of a data item is ambiguous.

The main purpose of this class in Joomla! is to store global configuration options. There is a global JRegistry object, referred to as the registry or config. We can access this object via JFactory; this example demonstrates how we get a reference to the object:

```
$registry =& JFactory::getConfig();
```

There are two important methods, getValue() and setValue(), which function as accessors and modifiers for registry data. This example demonstrates how we can increment the value foo.bar in the registry using these methods:

```
$registry =& JFactory::getConfig();
$oldValue = $registry->getValue('foo.bar', 0);
$registry->setValue('foo.bar', ++$oldValue);
```

When we populate the $oldValue variable using the getValue() method we supply a second parameter. This is the default value to return if no value currently exists, and this parameter is optional.

The site settings are located in the config namespace within the registry. A table describing the values we expect to be present in the config namespace can be found in the *Appendix*.

Saving and Loading Registry Values

A powerful feature of JRegistry objects is the capacity to save and load data. The class supports two different format types, run-time data and files. Run-time data are arrays and objects. File data can come from files in INI, PHP, and XML format.

In the previous three chapters, we have discussed the handling of extension settings. In addition to those methods, we can use the JRegistry class. This example demonstrates how to load an INI file into the myExtension namespace:

```
$file = JPATH_COMPONENT.DS.'myExtension.ini';
$registry =& JFactory::getConfig();
$registry->loadFile($file, 'INI', 'myExtension');
```

If we make changes to the myExtension namespace, we can save the changes back to our INI file:

```
// import JFile
jimport('joomla.filesyste.file');

// prepare for save
$file = JPATH_COMPONENT.DS.'myExtension.ini';
$registry =& JFactory::getConfig();
$ini = $registry->toString('INI', 'myExtension');

// save INI file
JFile::write($file, $ini);
```

Exporting in XML format is identical except that we substitute all occurrences of INI with XML. Exporting to PHP is slightly different. The site configuration file, configuration.php, is a prime example of using a PHP file to store data.

The PHP format saves values into a class. In the case of the site configuration, the class is called JConfig. We must provide, as a string parameter, the name of the class as which we wish to save the settings when we use the JRegistry toString() method.

This example demonstrates how we would export the settings to a PHP class named
SomeClass:

```
// import JFile
jimport('joomla.filesystem.file');

// prepare for save
$file = JPATH_COMPONENT.DS.'myExtension.php';
$registry =& JFactory::getConfig();
$php = $registry->toString('PHP', 'myExtension',
                          array('class'=>'SomeClass'));

// save PHP file
JFile::write($file, $php);
```

If you choose to use this mechanism to store settings, it is important to consider the
best file format for your settings. PHP and INI formats are restricted to a maximum
depth of zero and one respectively. XML has no depth restrictions.

This might make XML seems like the most suitable; XML, however, is the most
intensive format to parse. Hence, we should use the format that best suits the data
we are storing.

The next three examples demonstrate how we represent the registry tree, which we
defined earlier, in three different formats. Take note of the data loss within the PHP
and INI format examples. This is an example of a PHP string:

```
<?php
class JConfig
{
    var $total = '10';
}
?>
```

This is an example of an INI string:

```
total=10

[bird]
chaffinch=1
swan=2

[mammal]
badger=3
```

This is an example of an XML string:

```
<?xml version="1.0" ?>
<config>
    <group name="bird">
        <entry name="chaffinch">1</entry>

        <entry name="swan">2</entry>
    </group>
    <group name="mammal">
        <entry name="badger">3</entry>
        <group name="squirrel">
            <entry name="red">1</entry>
            <entry name="grey">3</entry>
        </group>
    </group>
    <entry name="total">10</entry>
</config>
```

A complete description of the JRegistry class is available in the *Appendix*.

The User

Many extensions use the currently logged-in user to determine what to display. A user has several attributes in which we might be interested. This table describes each of the attributes:

Attribute	Description
activation	String used to activate new user accounts
Aid	Legacy user group ID
block	True if the user's access is blocked
email	The user's email address
Gid	User group ID
guest	True if the user is a guest (not logged in)
Id	The user's ID, an integer; this is not the same as their username
lastvisitDate	Date and time at which the user last logged in
name	User's name
params	INI string of parameters
password	Hashed password
registerDate	Date and time at which the user account was registered
sendEmail	True if the user wishes to receive system emails
username	User's username
usertype	Name of user group

The browsing user is represented by a JUser object; we can access this object using the getUser() method in the JFactory class. This class has all of the attributes described here. This example demonstrates how we can test if a user has logged in or if the user is a guest:

```
$user =& JFactory::getUser();
if ($user->guest)
{
    // user is a guest (is not logged in)
}
```

User Parameters

The params attribute is special. We design an INI string to store additional parameters about a user. The users.xml file, located in the backend in the root of the user's component, contains the default attributes.

This table details the default parameters defined in the users.xml file:

Parameter	Description
admin_language	Backend language
language	Frontend language
editor	User's editor of choice.
helpsite	User's help site
timezone	Time zone in which the user is located (hours offset from UTC+0)

To access these we use the getParam() and setParam() methods. We could directly access the params attribute but we would then have to parse the data. This example demonstrates how we determine the user's time zone:

```
// get the default time zone from the registry
$registry =& JFactory::getConfig();
$tzdefault = $registry->getValue('config.offset');

// get the user's time zone
$user =& JFactory::getUser();
$tz = $user->getParam('timezone', $tzdefault);
```

Notice that we supply a default value, $tzdefault, which is extracted from the site settings. We use this as the second parameter for getParam(); this parameter is optional.

This example demonstrates how we can modify the value of the user's time zone:

```
$user =& JFactory::getUser();
$user->setParam('timezone', '0');
```

When we perform any modifications to the user's session, unless we save the changes, the modifications will last only until the session expires. User parameters are not used as a temporary store. To store temporary data we should use the session and the user state; we will see both in the next section.

 If we store temporary data in user parameters, we run the risk of saving the data accidently to the user's database record.

A common design issue is the extension of the user beyond their predefined attributes. There are three common ways of dealing with this:

- Add additional fields to the #__users table.
- Create a new table that maintains a one-to-one relationship with the #__users table.
- Use the user's parameters to store additional data.

The first option can cause some major problems. If several extensions choose this method, there is a chance that there will be a naming conflict between fields.

The second option is a good choice if the extra data is searchable, ordered, or used to modify results returned from the queries. To maintain the table successfully, we would have to create a plugin to deal with the events onAfterStoreUser and onAfterDeleteUser, explained in Chapter 6.

The final option is ideal if the extra data is not subject to searches, ordered, or used to restrict query results. We might implement these parameters in one of the three ways:

- Manually edit the parameters using the setParam() method. This is suitable if there are not many parameters or the user never modifies the parameters using a form.
- Use JParameter as the basis to create a form in which users can modify the parameters.
- Allow the user to modify the parameters, via the user's component. To do this, we need to modify the users.xml file (for more information about editing XML, see Chapter 10).

Before we begin, there is something we need to understand. A JUser object essentially has two sets of parameters, a RAW parameters string or array (params) and a JParameter object (_params).

Both of these are loaded from the database when the user's session starts. If we modify either of them, the changes will be present only until the user's session ends. If we want to save the parameters to the database, as is normally the case, we can use the save() method. This will update the parameters based on the RAW parameters alone.

When we use the `setParam()` method only the JParameter object is modified. It is because of this that we must update the RAW `params` attribute before saving. We must take extra care when saving changes to the user's parameters. Poor handling can result in loss of data.

This example demonstrates how we can set the user's `foo` parameter and save the changes to the database:

```
// get the user and add the foo parameter
$user =& JFactory::getUser();
$user->setParam('foo', 'bar');

// update the raw user parameters
$params =& $user->getParameters();
$user->set('params', $params->toString());

// save the changes to the database
if (!$user->save())
{
    JError::raiseError('SOME_ERROR', JText::_('Failed to save
                                            user'));
}
```

Next we will explore parameters that a user can update via a form. We will begin by creating an XML file that defines the extra parameters. We will see the parameters in detail in the *Appendix*. The following XML defines two text parameters, `myparameter` and `myotherparameter`:

```
<?xml version="1.0" encoding="utf-8"?>
<metadata>
    <params>
        <param name="myparameter" type="text" default="example"
          label="My Parameter" description="An example user
          parameter" />
        <param name="myotherparameter" type="text" default="example"
          label="My Other Parameter" description="An example user
          parameter" />
    </params>
</metadata>
```

We can create form elements using this XML and the user's JParameter object. We can get a reference to the JParameter object using the `getParameters()` method:

```
// get the user
$user =& JFactory::getUser();

// get the user's parameters object
$params =& $user->getParameters();
```

Once we have the parameters object, we can load the XML file and render the form elements using the `render()` method, as this example demonstrates:

```
$params->loadSetupFile($pathToXML_File);
echo $params->render('myparams');
```

A form field is created for each parameter, all of which are treated as a form array. The parameter that we provide to the `render()` method is used to name the form array. If we do not provide the parameter, the default name 'params' is used.

Our example will create two text inputs called `myparams[myparameter]` and `myparams[myotherparameter]`. This is a screenshot of how these parameters would appear:

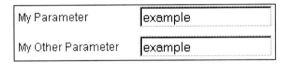

 Alternatively we could use the JParameter `renderToArray()` method that returns an array of arrays that define the different form elements.

Creating a form to deal with extra parameters is only the beginning; we need to process submitted forms. In this example, we retrieve the parameters from the POST array (assuming that the form is submitted using the POST method), add them to the user's existing parameters, rebind them to the user object, and save the changes:

```
// get the user object and the post array.
$user =& JFactory::getUser();
$post = JRequest::get('post');

// get the existing parameters
$params = $user->getParameters();

// add the parameters from the form submission
$params->bind($post['myparams']);

// update and save the user
$user->set('params', $params->toString());
$user->save();
```

The last option we will explore is modifying the `users.xml` file. To do this, we will utilize the JSimpleXML parser. For a complete description of the JSimpleXML parser, please refer to Chapter 10.

The first thing we need to do is get hold of the XML file and parse the contents:

```
// get a parser
$parser =& JFactory::getXMLParser('Simple');

// define the path to the XML file
$pathToXML_File = JPATH_ADMINISTRATOR.DS.'components'.DS.'com_users'.
DS.'users.xml';

// parse the XML
$parser->loadFile($pathToXML_File);
```

In order to add new param tags to the XML, we need to navigate to the params tag:

```
// get the root tag (install)
$document =& $parser->document;

// get the params tag
$params =& $document->params[0];
```

We can now start adding to the XML using the addChild() method to add child param tags, and the addAttribute() method to set the necessary param tag attributes. This example adds the parameters myparameter and myotherparameter, both of which we defined in the previous example:

```
// Add myparameter
$myparameter =& $params->addChild('param');

// modify the myparameter attributes
$myparameter->addAttribute('name', 'myparameter');
$myparameter->addAttribute('type', 'text');
$myparameter->addAttribute('label', 'My Parameter');
$myparameter->addAttribute('description', 'An example user
                           parameter');

// Add myotherparameter
$myotherparameter =& $params->addChild('param');

// modify the myotherparameter attributes
$myotherparameter->addAttribute('name', 'myotherparameter');
$myotherparameter->addAttribute('type', 'text');
$myotherparameter->addAttribute('label', 'My Other Parameter');
$myotherparameter->addAttribute('description', 'An example user
                                parameter');
```

Now that we have made the changes to the XML file, we need to save those changes to the `users.xml` file. We can do this using the JFile class:

```
// create XML string
$xmlString = '<?xml version="1.0" encoding="UTF-8" ?>'."\n";
$xmlString .= $document->toString();

// get the JFile class
jimport('joomla.filesystem.file');

// save the changes
if (!JFile::write($pathToXML_File, $xmlString))
{
    // handle failed file save
}
```

These alterations will enable users to modify `myparameter` and `myotherparameter`, when they use the user's component to modify their details. This screenshot depicts the resultant form with the changes:

If one were to employ this technique, the best place to do so would probably be in a component installation file. It is also important to consider making a backup of the existing file, in case of any unexpected difficulties.

Modifying this file could also lead to problems if the file is ever updated, for example as part of an upgrade. However, it does mean that all of the user's details are editable from one central point.

The Session

When a user accesses Joomla!, a new session is created; this occurs even if the user is not logged in. Instead of accessing the $_SESSION hash, as we do in most PHP applications, we must use the global JSession object.

When we access session data, we provide the value name and, optionally, the namespace. If we do not provide a namespace the default namespace, aptly named, default is assumed. In this example, we retrieve the value of default.example:

```
$session =& JFactory::getSession();
$value = $session->get('example');
```

It is unusual when accessing the session in this way to use anything other than the default namespace. That is why the second parameter in the get() method is not the namespace, but the default value. In this example, we retrieve the value of default. example, returning a value of 1 if the value does not exist:

```
$session =& JFactory::getSession();
$value = $session->get('example', 1);
```

The last parameter is the namespace. This example demonstrates how to retrieve a value from a different namespace (someNamespace):

```
$session =& JFactory::getSession();
$value = $session->get('example', 1, 'someNamespace');
```

In addition to retrieving values, we can also set them. In this example, we set the value of default.example and someNamespace.example:

```
$session =& JFactory::getSession();
$session->set('example', 1);
$session->set('example', 1, 'someNamespace');
```

You might be wondering why we tend to use the default namespace. Due to limitations of the namespace handling within the JSession class, we use a special area of the session known as the 'user-state'.

The user-state is a JRegistry object that is stored in the session. The application accesses this object, which is located in default.registry. There are two application methods that we use, getUserState() and getUserStateFromRequest().

We'll start by exploring getUserState(). This example demonstrates how we can retrieve the value of session.counter, a counter that represents the number of requests a user has made:

```
$mainframe->getUserState('session.counter');
```

Setting user-state values is very similar. This example demonstrates how we can set an alternative template for a user:

```
$mainframe->setUserState('setTemplate', 'someSiteTemplate');
```

The `getUserStateFromRequest()` method is very similar to the `getUserState()` method, except that it checks the request values first. This method is used extensively in Joomla!'s implementation of pagination.

The method has three parameters, the key (a path), the name of the request, and a default value. This example retrieves the value of `com_myextension.list.filter.order`:

```
$order = $mainframe-
    >getUserStateFromRequest('com_myextension.list.filter.order',
                            'filter_order', 'name');
```

The second parameter is especially important. If a request were made in which the query contained `filter_order=owner`, the value returned would be `owner`. It would also update the user-state to equal `owner`.

This method is of particular interest when we want to allow a user to modify their state values. It is for this reason that the `getUserStateFromRequest()` method is used extensively in pagination.

There is not a `setUserStateFromRequest()` method because when we execute the `getUserStateFromRequest()` method the value is updated.

As a final note, Joomla! session data is not always stored in the usual way. Joomla! uses session storage classes to allow alternative methods of data storage. These methods include the database, php-eaccelerator, and php-pecl-apc. We must install php-eaccelerator or php-pecl-apc on the server if we have to use them.

 There is a limitation of database session-storage. The session data size is limited to 65,535 characters. This can cause problems with extensions that require large amounts of session storage space.

The Browser

A useful source of information about the client is the browser. We can use the JBrowser class, located in `joomla.environment.browser`, to investigate the client browser.

Browsers have features that enable them to behave in certain ways. For example, a browser may or may not support JavaScript. We can use the `hasFeature()` method to check for different features.

This example checks for JavaScript support:

```
$browser =& JBrowser::getInstance();
if ($browser->hasFeature('javascript'))
{
    // the browser has JavaScript capabilities
}
```

This is a list of the different features we can check for when using the hasFeature() method:

- accesskey
- cite
- dom
- frames
- hdml
- homepage
- html
- iframes
- images
- java
- javascript
- optgroup
- rte
- tables
- utf
- wml
- xmlhttpreq

Browsers also have quirks (peculiarities of behavior). We can use JBrowser to check for certain quirks in browsers. In this example, we check that the browser is happy to deal with popups:

```
$browser =& JBrowser::getInstance();
if ($browser->hasQuirk('avoid_popup_windows'))
{
    // the browser does not like popups
}
```

Generally, all browsers, except mobile browsers and old browsers, will deal with popups.

This is a list of the different quirks that we can check for using JBrowser:

- avoid_popup_windows
- break_disposition_filename
- break_disposition_header
- broken_multipart_form
- cache_same_url
- cache_ssl_downloads
- double_linebreak_textarea
- empty_file_input_value
- must_cache_forms
- no_filename_spaces
- no_hidden_overflow_tables
- ow_gui_1.3
- png_transparency
- scroll_tds
- scrollbar_in_way
- windowed_controls

Both the quirks and features are hard-coded in Joomla!; they are not retrieved from the browser. This means that JBrowser will not detect popup blockers or other unexpected settings. This is a list of the browsers known to Joomla!:

- AvantGo
- BlackBerry
- Ericsson
- Fresco
- HotJava
- i-Mode
- Konqueror
- Links
- Lynx
- MML
- Motorola
- Mozilla

- MSIE
- Nokia
- Opera
- Palm
- Palmscape
- Up
- WAP
- Xiino

There are a number of handy methods to determine which browser a user is using. This example demonstrates how we would output a formatted string representation of the user's browser:

```
$browser =& JBrowser::getInstance();
$string = ucfirst($browser->getBrowser()).' ';
$string .= $browser->getVersion().' (';
$string .= $browser->getPlatform().')';
```

This is an example of the value of `$string`: `Mozilla 5.0 (win)`.

We will now discuss three additional JBrowser methods that we can use to make our extensions more user friendly and secure.

Imagine we want to prevent robots from viewing an extension. Robots are programs that systematically 'crawl' though a website indexing the content for use in search engines. We can check if a browser is a robot using the `isRobot()` method:

```
$browser =& JBrowser::getInstance();
if ($browser->isRobot())
{
    JError::raiseError('403', JText::_('Robots are disallowed'));
}
```

When we use components, we can choose to modify the MIME type of a response. Before we do this, using JBrowser, we can check that the browser supports the MIME type. This example checks that the browser can handle the MIME type `application/vnd.ms-excel` (an MS Excel file) before displaying a certain link:

```
$browser =& JBrowser::getInstance();
if ($browser->isViewable('application/vnd.ms-excel'))
{
    echo '<a
        href="'.JRoute::_('index.php?option=com_myextension&format=
        raw&application=xls').'">Link to an XLS document</a>';
}
```

Imagine we want to display an image of a padlock if we access the site via **SSL**
(Secure Sockets Layer). We can use the `isSSLConnection()` method:

```
$browser =& JBrowser::getInstance();
if ($browser->isSSLConnection())
{
    echo '<img src="images/padlock.jpg" alt="Secure Connection"
            style="width: 36px; height: 36px;"/>';
}
```

Assets

It is common to want to include additional 'assets' in our extensions. Assets are
normally media, for example image files. This is a list of common files that we can
classify as assets:

- JavaScript
- Image
- Cascading Style Sheet
- Video
- Flash

We deal with asset files in two commom ways.

We can use the `media` tag in our extension XML manifest files to add assets to the
Joomla! Media Manager. This is ideal if we want to allow users the right to modify
the assets.

Within the `media` tag, we must detail each file that we intend to add. Unlike
copying extension files, we cannot define folders that we want to copy into the
Media Manager.

This example demonstrates how we can copy two images, `foo.png` and `bar.jpg`,
from a folder in the extension archive named `assets` into the `stories` folder in the
Media Manager:

```
<media destination="stories" folder="assets">
    <filename>foo.png</filename>
    <filename>bar.jpg</filename>
</media>
```

The `stories` folder is a special folder within the Media Manager. When we edit
content items adding pictures, only files within the `stories` folder can be added
(unless hard-coded).

We can copy files into any folder in the Media Manager using the `media` tag `destination` attribute. If we want to add files to the root of the Media Manager, we need not include the `destination` attribute.

Alternatively, we can create a folder in our extensions called `assets`. Many of the core extensions use this approach. It prevents modification of the assets, and is ideal for any assets that we always require.

When we use this method to add assets to a component, generally we create one `assets` folder and create it in the frontend. Of course, we do not have to do this; where we choose to create such a folder is entirely at the developer's discretion.

Summary

There are restrictions as to what we can do in Joomla!, but there are many ways to achieve the same goal. You should never feel restricted by conventional extension design, but you should always work with Joomla! and take advantage of the facilities with which we are provided.

Building classes that do not relate specifically to part of the Joomla! framework is a common way to extend Joomla! beyond its intended scope. We discussed in a previous chapter the use of plugins in lieu of library extensions. If we want, we can use the same logic, JLoader, to create 'internal' libraries in any extension.

Making extensions easy to build is all part of the logic behind helper classes. These static classes allow us to categorize functionality and increase the code reuse.

Programming patterns are one of the weapons we can use to tackle a problem. Joomla! uses patterns extensively, from the complex MVC to basic iterators. A common pattern found in Joomla! is the use of the `getInstance()` method.

Whenever we have objects that we want to make globally available we should consider implementing a `getInstance()` method in the corresponding class. You can also consider creating a class similar to the core class JFactory to further increase accessibility of global objects.

A JRegistry object handles the site settings and extension settings, stored in INI, XML, and PHP files. We should consider the use of JRegistry before we create any settings files.

The user is a complex entity and how we handle it is very important. We can extend users in various ways. Whichever mechanism we choose, we should always consider creating a 'repair' function to allow administrators to check the database for errors, which may have occurred in relation to any customization of the user made by our extensions.

We must always remember to use the global JSession object to handle sessions. Directly accessing the $_SESSION variable can have some unexpected results.

Modifying our site to suit a browser may seem drastic, but when checking for features and quirks in the browser is as easy as one simple method, it makes sense. Bulletproof extensions always consider the unexpected, and quirks in the browser are just one of those things.

Beyond common code, there is land full of imagery, multimedia, and the occasional unicorn. If we want to give administrators full control over an extension, being able to modify an extension's repository of assets is necessary. Use the installer assets tag to take advantage of the Joomla! Media Manager.

8
Rendering Output

In Joomla!, there are several ways in which we can render output that make our lives easier and force a level of consistency across extensions. In this chapter, we will explore:

- The ever useful `joomla.html` library, which enables us to render output in a common form
- How to build layouts and templates, with particular emphasis on components
- The intricacies of building templates in component backends
- How to deal with itemized data

The joomla.html Library

This part of the library is used to aid in the rendering of XHTML. Integral to this is the static JHTML class. Within this class is a method, `_()`, which we provide with a type and a mixture of additional parameters. This example demonstrates how we use the method to output a tooltip:

```
echo JHTML::_('tooltip', 'content', 'title');
```

There are six basic types. Basic types are identified by a single name. This is a list of the six basic types:

- link
- image
- iframe
- date
- tooltip
- calendar

There are seven grouped types. Grouped types are identified by a group name and a name. This is a list of the seven grouped types:

- behavior
- email
- grid
- image
- list
- menu
- select

Before we start looking at some examples, we need to import the library. We must always do this in order to use the JHTML class:

```
jimport('joomla.html.html');
```

We'll use the basic type link as an example. This example demonstrates how to create a link to the root of a component:

```
echo JHTML::_('link', 'index.php?option=com_somecom', 'Some
                                                Component');
```

The first parameter we provide is the type, in this case link; the following parameters are specific to the link type. We will explain what each of the extra parameters is, for the different types, in a moment.

Next we'll use the type cloak in the email group as an example. This example demonstrates how to create a mailto link without giving away the email address:

```
echo JHTML::_('email.cloak', 'example@example.org');
```

This time the type is prefixed with the group name email and a period. The email. cloak type is used to hide email addresses from spam-bots that crawl websites looking for email addresses. We'll explain how to use this type in more detail later in this section.

There are some types that do not return anything. These types are generally used to add special declarations to the document header. For example the behavior. calendar type adds some JavaScript to the header.

The rest of this section of this chapter describes each of the different types and how to use them. We'll start with the six basic types:

Link		
Gets an XHTML link		
Parameters	url	Link URI
	text	Link text
	[attribs]	An associative array or string of additional attributes to apply to the tag
Returns	Link XHTML string	

Image		
Gets an XHTML image		
Parameters	url	Image URI
	alt	Alternative text if the image is not available
	[attribs]	An associative array or string of additional attributes to apply to the img tag
Returns	Image XHTML string	

Iframe		
Gets an XHTML floating frame (iframe)		
Parameters	url	Frame URI, must be internal
	name	Name of the frame
	[attribs]	An associative array or string of additional attributes to apply to the img tag
	[noFrames]	Message to display if frames are not supported by the browser; default is a null string
Returns	Floating frame XHTML string	

Date		
Takes a date and formats it accordingly. The date should always be UTC. The offset is retrieved from the registry unless a custom offset is provided.		
Parameters	date	Date and time (UTC), supports RFC822, ISO8601, and Unix time stamps
	[format]	Date format; default is DATE_FORMAT_LC
	[offset]	Number of hours offset from UTC
Returns	Date string	

Tooltip		
Gets some XHTML, either an image or a text string, which when displayed in a browser displays a tooltip. In order for this type to work as expected it is necessary to invoke `JHTML::_('behavior.tooltip')`. If we want to modify the appearance of the tooltips, we can redefine the CSS for `.tool-tip`, `.tool-title`, and `.tool-text`.		
Parameters	tooltip	Tooltip content
	[title]	Title of the tooltip
	[image]	Image to use, must be located in includes/js/ThemeOffice
	[text]	Text to use instead of an image
	[href]	Internal link
	[link]	True if link is enabled; default is `true`
Returns	A string or image with a tooltip	

Calendar		
Gets an XHTML form field that can be easily used to select a date		
Parameters	value	Initial date value
	name	Input name
	id	Input ID
	[format]	Format in which to display dates
	[attribs]	Associative array of additional input tag attributes
Returns	XHTML date text form field with an attached JavaScript calendar	

Behavior

These types are special because they deal with JavaScript in order to create client-side behaviors.

We'll use `behavior.modal` as an example. This behavior allows us to display an inline modal window that is populated from a specific URI. A modal window is a window that prevents a user from returning to the originating window until the modal window has been closed. A good example of this is the 'Pagebreak' button used in the article manager when editing an article.

The `behavior.modal` type does not return anything; it prepares the necessary JavaScript. None of the behavior types return data; they are solely intended to import functionality into the document.

This example demonstrates how we can use the `behavior.modal` type to open a modal window that uses `www.example.org` as the source:

```
// prepare the JavaScript parameters
$params = array('size'=>array('x'=>100, 'y'=>100));

// add the JavaScript
JHTML::_('behavior.modal', 'a.mymodal', $params);

// create the modal window link
echo '<a class="mymodal" title="example"
      href="http://www.example.org"  rel="{handler: \'iframe\',
      size: {x: 400, y: 150}}">Example Modal Window</a>';
```

The `a.mymodal` parameter is used to identify the elements to which we want the modal window to attach. In this case, we want to use all `a` tags of class `mymodal`. This parameter is optional; the default selector is `a.modal`.

We use `$params` to specify default settings for modal windows. This list details the keys that we can use in this array to define default values:

- `ajaxOptions`
- `size`
- `onOpen`
- `onClose`
- `onUpdate`
- `onResize`
- `onMove`
- `onShow`
- `onHide`

The link that we create can only be seen as special because of the JavaScript in the `rel` attribute. This JavaScript array is used to determine the exact behavior of the modal window for this link.

We must always specify `handler`; this is used to determine how to parse the input from the link. In most cases, this will be `iframe`, but we can also use `image`, `adopt`, `url`, and `string`.

The `size` parameter is optional; here it is used to override the default specified when we used the `behavior.modal` type to import the JavaScript. The settings have three layers of inheritance:

- The default settings defined in the `modal.js` file
- The settings we define when using the `behavior.modal` type
- The settings we define when creating the link

For information about other parameters, please refer to the `modal.js` file located in the `media/system/js` folder.

This is a screenshot of the resultant modal window when the link is used:

You have reached this web page by typing "example.com", "example.net", or "example.org" into your web browser.

These domain names are reserved for use in documentation and are not available for registration. See RFC 2606, Section 3.

Let's have a look at the several types:

Tooltip		
Adds the necessary JavaScript to enable tooltips, the mootools JavaScript class Tips. To create tooltips we use the basic tooltip type, explain earlier in this chapter.		
Parameters	[selector]	Class suffix; default is `hasTip`
	[params]	Associative array of options. Possible options are: `maxTitleChars`, `timeout`, `showDelay`, `hideDelay`, `className`, `fixed`, `onShow`, and `onHide`

Modal		
Adds JavaScript that enables us to implement modal windows. Modal windows are essentially inline popups that prevent the user from performing actions elsewhere on the page until the modal window has been closed.		
Parameters	[selector]	Selector used to determine which links should use modal windows; default is `a.modal`
	[params]	Associative array of default modal window options

Mootools	
Adds the mootools JavaScript library to the document.	
Parameters	[debug]	Use the uncompressed version of mootools

Caption
Modifies images on the page of class `caption` in such a way that the content of the image tags title attribute appears beneath the image.

Formvalidation
Adds the generic JFormValidator JavaScript class to the document and instantiates an object of this type in `document.formvalidator`. This object can be used to aid the validation of forms.

Switcher
Adds JavaScript that can be used to toggle between hidden and shown page elements. This is specifically used in conjunction with the backend submenu. For example, both the site configuration and system information areas in the backend use this.

Combobox
Adds JavaScript to modify the behavior of text fields (that are of class combobox) so as to add a combo selection. The available selections must be defined in an unordered list with the ID `combobox-idOfTheField`.

Uploader
Adds JavaScript that enables us to create a dynamic file uploading mechanism that allows users to upload a queue of files. For example, the media manager uses this.

Calendar

Adds the necessary JavaScript in order to use the JavaScript `showCalendar()` function to make date selection easier. If we want to use this when a user is not logged in we must add the `joomla.javascript.js` JavaScript file to the document:
 	
`$document =& JFactory::getDocument();`
`$document->addScript('includes/js/joomla.javascript.js');`
 	
Generally, we should use the basic `calendar` type instead.

Keepalive
Adds a special invisible floating frame to the response that is updated regularly in order to maintain a user's session. This is of particular use in pages on which a user is likely to spend a long time creating or editing content.

Email

There is only one email type: `cloak`. Let's see this in detail:

Cloak		
Uses JavaScript to display an encrypted email address in the browser. This prevents the spam-bots, which crawl websites looking for email addresses, from discovering this email address. The form of encryption is very limited and is not a guaranteed way of beating spam-bots.		
Parameters	mail	Email address
	[mailto]	Create mailto link; default is `true`
	[text]	Alternative text to show
	[email]	`text` is an email address; default is `true`
Returns	A JavaScript string used to display an email address	

Grid

The grid types are used for displaying a dataset's item elements in a form in a table in the backend. There are seven grid types, each of which represents handles a common field found used in the database.

Before we begin there are some important things that need to be in place. The form must be called `adminForm`, and it must include two hidden fields, one called `boxchecked` with the default value `0` and one called `task` used to determine which task a controller will execute.

We'll use `grid.id` and `grid.published` as an example. Imagine we have a database table with the primary key `id`, a field called `published`, which we use to determine if an item is visible, and a field called `name`.

We use `grid.published` to display each record's published state.

This example demonstrates how we process each record in a template and output data into a grid/table ($rows is an array of objects representing records from the table):

```php
<?php
$i = 0;
foreach ($rows as $row) :
    $id = JHTML::_('grid.id', ++$i, $row->id);
    $published = JHTML::_('grid.published', $row, $i);
```

```
?>
<tr class="row<?php echo $i%2 ?>">
    <td>';
        <?php echo $id; ?>
    </td>
    <td>
        <?php echo $row->name; ?>
    </td>
    <td align="center">
        <?php echo $published ?>
    </td>
</tr>
<?php
endforeach;
?>
```

If `$rows` were to contain two objects named '**Item 1**' and '**Item 2**', of which only the first object is published, the resulting table would look like this:

Not all of the `grid` types are used for data item elements. The `grid.sort` and `grid.order` types are used to render table column headings. The `grid.state` type is used to display an item state selection box, `All`, `Published`, `Unpublished` and, optionally, `Archived`.

Access		
Gets a text link that describes the access group (legacy group) to which the item is subject. When pressed the access of the item is designed to cycle through the available legacy groups.		
Parameters	row	Referenced object that we are representing. Must contain the attributes `access` and `groupname`.
	i	Physical row number
	[archived]	`-1`, if item is archived
Returns	A text link that describes the access group, which when pressed submits the form with the task `accessregistered`, `accessspecial`, or `accesspublic`	

checkedOut		
Gets a selectable checkbox or displays a small padlock image if the record is locked.		
Parameters	row	Referenced object that we are representing. Must contain the attribute `checked_out` or be a JTable object
	i	Physical row number
	[identifier]	Name of the record primary key; default is `id`
Returns	Checkbox that is a member of a checkbox array; its value is equal to the record ID value. If the row/record is checked out a small padlock image is returned.	

Id		
Gets a selectable checkbox. If `checkedOut` is true, a null string is returned. This is used by most the other `grid` types; it is recommended that all admin grids/tables use this. If the record might be checked out we should consider using `grid.checkedOut` instead.		
Parameters	rowNum	Physical row number
	recId	Record ID
	[CheckedOut]	Record is checked out; default is `false`
	[name]	Name of the checkbox array; default is `cid`
Returns	Checkbox that is a member of a checkbox array; the value is equal to `recId`	

Order		
Outputs an image with an onClick JavaScript to be used at the top of an `order` column. Every data row cell in this column will normally contain a text box called order as this example demonstrates: `<input type="text" name="order[]" size="5" value="<?php echo $row->ordering;?>" class="text_area" style="text-align: center" />`		
Parameters	rows	Array of rows being displayed
	[image]	Admin image name
	[task]	Update order task; default is `saveorder`

Published		
Gets an image that represents a published state. When pressed the image issues a JavaScript event selecting the item, submitting the form with the task `publish` or `unpublish`.		
Parameters	row	Referenced object, which represents a data row/record
	i	Physical row number
	[imgY]	Published image name located in `images`
	[imgX]	Unpublished image name located in `images`
	[prefix]	Task name prefix
Returns	An image used to publish and unpublish an item	

Sort		
Gets a heading for a grid/table column, which when pressed sets the form fields `filter_order` and `filter_order_Dir` to the current column and the preferred direction.		
Parameters	title	Column name
	order	Value with which to populate `filter_order`
	direction	Current direction; `filter_order_Dir` is populated with the opposite, `asc` or `desc`
	selected	The currently selected ordering column; relates to `order`
	[task]	Optional value with which to populate `task`
Returns	A sortable heading for a grid/table column	

State		
Gets a drop-down selection box called `filter_state` with four or five options. Normally used to select the `published`, `unpublished`, or `archived` state. When an option is selected the form is submitted.		
Parameters	[filter_state]	Current state, must be a null string, *, P, U or A; default is *
	[published]	Published (P) name; default is `Published`
	[unpublished]	Unpublished (U) name; default is `Unpublished`
	[archived]	Archived (A) name; default is null which prevents the archived option being displayed
Returns	A drop-down selection box of different states	

Image

We use the image types to enable a form of image overriding. We can check if a template has an image before using a system default image. There are two image types, `image.administrator` and `image.site`.

We will look at `image.site`, in order to demonstrate how it works. This is an example of how to use it with an image named `edit.png`:

```
echo JHTML::_('image.site', 'edit.png');
```

This will output an image tag for the image named `edit.png`. The image will be located in the currently selected template `images` sub-folder. If there isn't an image in that folder named `edit.png`, the image will be located in the folder `/images/M_images`.

We can change these directories using the `$directory` and `$param_directory` parameters.

Administrator		
Get an image tag for a backend image.		
Parameters	file	Name of the image file
	[directory]	Default directory; default is `images`
	[param]	Overriding image file name; intended for use with JParameter
	[param_directory]	Overriding directory; default is `images`
	[alt]	Alternative text
	[name]	Deprecated
	[type]	Get image tag or image location; default is `true` (get image tag)
	[align]	Image-tag alignment attribute value; default is `middle`
Returns	Image tag or image location	

Site		
Get an image tag for a frontend image.		
Parameters	file	Name of the image file
	[directory]	Default directory; default is `images/M_image`
	[param]	Overriding image file name; intended for use with JParameter
	[param_directory]	Overriding directory; default is `images`
	[alt]	Alternative text
	[name]	Deprecated
	[type]	Get image tag or image location; default is `true` (get image tag)
	[align]	Image-tag alignment attribute value; default is `top`
Returns	Image tag or image location	

List

The list types are used for the generation of common selection lists. We'll take a look at the `list.accesslevel` type. This type produces a selection list populated with the legacy groups.

This type is relatively simple; it only requires one parameter, an object that includes the attribute access. This type is intended for use when modifying a single item, so in most cases the parameter will be an object representation of the item.

This code demonstrates how we might use `list.accesslevel`:

```
// get an item
$query = 'SELECT *'
        .' FROM #__sometable'
        .' WHERE id = '.(int)$id;
$db =& JFactory::getDBO();
$db->setQuery($query);
$item = $db->loadObject();


echo JHTML::_('list.accesslevel', $item);
```

Assuming that the selected item has an attribute called `access` and it is 0 (**Public**), the resultant selection list will appear like this:

The list types are generally used to implement a filter when viewing itemized data or, as with `list.accesslevel`, for use when creating or modifying a single item. We discuss how to use the list types to implement a filter later in this chapter.

Accesslevel	
Gets a selection box of the legacy groups. The selected group will be the group identified in the $row attribute, `access`. The resulting form control is named `access`.	
Parameters	row	Object that includes the attribute `access`
Returns	A selection box of the legacy groups	

Category	
Gets a drop-down selection box of different categories related to a specific section. We can use categories outside of the content component in order to maintain categories for a different extension. We do this by specifying a section value equal to that of the extension name, for example com_somecomponent.	

Parameters	name	List name
	section	Section ID or extension name
	[active]	Initially selected category
	[javascript]	String of JavaScript event attributes to add to the category select tag
	[order]	SQL ORDER BY clause; default is ordering
	[size]	Size of the selection box; default is 1
	[sel_cat]	Display a Select a Category option at the top of the category list; default is true
Returns	A selection box of categories in a section	

Genericordering	
Gets an array of options, for use with the select types, of possible positions in an order. Consider using grid.specificordering, if the current position is known.	

Parameters	sql	SQL query to execute; must return the fields text and value
	[chop]	Maximum length of the value of text; default is 30 characters
Returns	Array of different available ordering positions	

Images	
Gets a drop-down list of images available in a directory. The first option in the list is always Select Image. Images must be of type BMP, GIF, JPG, or PNG. By default the list has a JavaScript onChange event associated with it that will update the src attribute of an img tag called imagelib.	

Parameters	name	List name
	[active]	Initially selected option
	[javascript]	JavaScript to include
	[directory]	Images directory; default is images/stories
Returns	Drop-down list populated with image names	

Positions		
Gets a drop-down list of different positions. The positions can contain none, center, left, and right. This is intended to enable the selection of image positions but can be used for other purposes.		
Parameters	name	Name of the drop-down list form control
	[active]	Initially selected position
	[javascript]	String of JavaScript event attributes
	[none]	Show none; default is true
	[center]	Show center; default is true
	[left]	Show left; default is true
	[right]	Show right; default is true
	[id]	Drop-down list ID
Returns	Drop-down list of positions	

Section		
Gets a drop-down list of published sections. The first two options are always Select Section and Uncategorized.		
Parameters	name	Name of the drop-down list form control
	[active]	Initially selected section
	[javascript]	String of JavaScript event attributes
	[order]	SQL ORDER BY clause used when selecting the sections from the #__sections table; default is ordering
Returns	Drop-down list of sections	

Specificordering		
Gets a drop-down list of possible positions in an order. $row is an obect which represents the current item. If $id is false, a hidden field is returned with a textual description. The description is related to creating new items; we use $neworder to suggest that the item will be placed at the start or end of the existing order. The returned control is named ordering.		
Parameters	row	Referenced object with the attribute ordering
	id	If true drop-down list; if false, hidden field
	query	SQL query to execute; must return the fields text and value
	[neworder]	Created at start of order; default is false
Returns	Drop-down list of possible positions in an order	

Users		
Gets a drop-down list of site users. By default this does not include registered users.		
Parameters	name	Name of the drop-down list form control
	active	Initially selected user
	[nouser]	Include No User option; default is false
	[javascript]	String of JavaScript event attributes
	[order]	#__users field to order by; default is name
	[reg]	Exclude registered users; default is true
Returns	Drop-down list of site users	

Menu

The menu types are designed specifically for use with menus. It is unlikely that we should ever need to use any of these because menus are handled for us by Joomla!. However, the menu.treerecurse type may be of interest if we are rendering tree structures.

Linkoptions		
Gets an array of options, for use with select.genericlist, which represents the menu items. We can also add the optional values of All and Unassigned to start of the list.		
Parameters	[all]	Show All; default is false
	[unassigned]	Show Unassigned; default is false
Returns	Array of options	

Ordering		
Gets a drop-down list of menu items from a menu in order to facilitate the modification of menu item ordering. The value of each option is equal to the ordering value of the corresponding menu item. If $id is false, a hidden fields will be returned with a textual description. The description explains that new items will be added to the end of the existing order.		
Parameters	row	An object that represents a menu item
	id	Use dropdown list; default is true
Returns	Drop-down list of menu items from a menu	

Treerecurse		
Builds an array of objects from menu items. Adds the attributes `treename` and `children`. `treename` is the text to display before an item. `children` is number of child menu items.		
Parameters	id	ID of the menu item to build the array
	indent	Current indent
	list	Array of menu items, normally empty
	children	Array of objects representing menu items
	[maxlevel]	Maximum recursive depth; default is `9999`
	[level]	Current recursive level; default is `0`
	[type]	Type of menu item pretext; if `true` pretext is `L`, otherwise pretext is -
Returns	An array of parsed menu items	

Select

The select types are intended to create selection boxes easily. They can be used to create drop-down selection boxes and radio selection buttons.

We'll use `select.genericlist` as an example to create a drop-down selection box with three values. We'll call the drop-down selection box `someoptions` and use the second option as the default.

```
// prepare the options
$options = array();
$options[] = JHTML::_('select.option', '1', 'Option A');
$options[] = JHTML::_('select.option', '2', 'Option B');
$options[] = JHTML::_('select.option', '3', 'Option C');

// render the options
echo JHTML::_('select.genericlist', $options, 'someoptions',
                         null, 'value', 'text', '2');
```

The resultant drop-down selection box will look like this:

Booleanlist		
Gets a pair of Boolean radio options, one with a value of 0, the other with a value of 1.		
Parameters	name	Name of the Boolean inputs
	[attribs]	Additional radio button tag attributes
	[selected]	Initially selected option
	[yes]	True text, default is yes
	[no]	False text, default is no
	[id]	Selection ID
Returns	Pair of Boolean radio options	

Genericlist		
Gets a select list based on an array of options.		
Parameters	arr	An array of associative arrays or objects, normally an array of objects created using select.option
	name	List name
	attribs	Additional list attributes
	[key]	The value key in the associative arrays or objects, normally value
	[text]	The text key in the associative arrays or objects, normally text
	[selected]	Key value of the currently selected option; default is null
	[idtag]	List ID, default is null
	[translate]	Translate text using JText; default is false
Returns	Selectable list of options	

Integerlist		
Gets a selectable list of numbers.		
Parameters	start	Start value
	end	Maximum value
	inc	Increment value, normally 1
	name	List name
	[attribs]	Additional list attributes
	[selected]	Key value of the currently selected option; default is null
	[format]	sprintf() format to apply to the text, for example, Number %d
Returns	Selectable list of numeric options	

Optgroup		
Gets an object that represents an option group.		
Parameters	text	Group name
	[value_name]	Name of the value attribute; default is `value`
	[text_name]	Name of the text attribute; default is `text`
Returns	Object with two attributes—a value and a text name	

Option		
Gets an object that represents a single selectable option.		
Parameters	value	Option value
	[text]	Option name
	[value_name]	Name of the value attribute; default is `value`
	[text_name]	Name of the value attribute; default is `text`
	[disabled]	Option is disabled; default is `false`
Returns	Object with two attributes—a value and a text name	

Options		
Gets an XHTML string of select list options based on the passed array of associative arrays or objects.		
Parameters	arr	An array of associative arrays or objects, normally an array of objects created using `select.option`
	[key]	The value key in the associative arrays or objects, normally `value`
	[text]	The text key in the associative arrays or objects, normally `text`
	[selected]	Key value of the currently selected option; default is `null`
	[translate]	Translate text using JText; default is `false`
Returns	XHTML String of options	

Radiolist		
Gets a radio button selection list.		
Parameters	arr	An array of associative arrays or objects, normally an array of objects created using `select.option`
	name	List name
	[attribs]	Additional list attributes
	[key]	The value key in the associative arrays or objects; default is `value`
	[text]	The text key in the associative arrays or objects; default is `text`
	[selected]	Key value of the currently selected option; default is `null`
	[idtag]	List ID; default is `null`
	[translate]	Translate text, using JText; default is `false`
Returns	Radio button options	

Building Component HTML Layouts (Templates)

When we think of templates we normally envisage site templates detailing precisely what our website is going to look like. In Joomla!, to help separate out the presentation we also have templates within components.

Templates are PHP files that mainly consist of XHTML and include small snippets of PHP to output data. Although there are no strict conventions on the way in which we use our templates, there are some common rules that we normally observe:

- Do not process data
- Use colon and endX in preference of curly braces
- Encapsulate each line of PHP in its own PHP tags
- Keep tag IDs lowercase and use underscore word separators
- Indent for the XHTML, not the PHP

This example shows a very basic template that demonstrates each of the rules:

```
<div id="some_division">
<?php foreach ($this->items as $item) : ?>
    <div id="item_<?php echo $item->id; ?>">
        <?php echo $item->name; ?>
    </div>
<?php endforeach; ?>
</div>
```

Take particular note of the use of the colon to denote the start of the foreach block, and endforeach to denote the end of the block. Using this alternative syntax makes templates easier to read; just imagine hunting for the correct ending curly brace in a large template file!

You almost certainly noticed the use of $this in the example template. Templates are always invoked by a view; when we do this we actually incorporate the template code into the view object's loadTemplate() method.

This means that the variable $this is referring to the view object from which the template was invoked. This is why we attach data to our view; it means that in the template we can access all the data we added to view via $this.

It is generally best to use an existing template in order to build a new template. This ensures that we use the conventions and styles implemented by Joomla! to render our output.

Iterative Templates

We can break down templates into smaller chunks. We can use a separate template to render common or iterative elements; these templates can then be called from other templates.

These sorts of sub-templates are prefixed with the word default_. For example if we had a sub-template to display a form it would be called default_form.php. This example shows what we might have within such a file:

```
<div id="some_division">
  <form action="<?php echo
    JRoute::_('index.php?option=com_myextension&task=submitform');
    ?>" name="someform" id="someform">
  <table width="100%" border="0" cellspacing="0" cellpadding="0">
    <tr>
      <td><label for="name"><?php echo JText::_('Name');
            ?></label></td>
      <td><input name="name" type="text" size="40"
            maxlength="40"></td>
    </tr>
    <tr>
      <td><label for="surname"><?php echo JText::_('Surname');
            ?></label></td>
      <td><input name="surname" type="text" size="40"
            maxlength="40"></td>
    </tr>
    <tr>
```

```
            <td><label for="email"><?php echo JText::_('Email');
                ?></label></td>
            <td><input name="email" type="text" size="40"
                maxlength="40"></td>
        </tr>
    </table>
  </form>
</div>
```

Having created the sub-template how do we use it from within other templates? Well, essentially in the same way in which the first template was invoked. We mentioned earlier the `loadTemnplate()` method; this method loads template files. This example shows how we include the `default_form.php` template in another template file:

```
<!-- Put the form here -->
<?php echo $this->loadTemplate('form'); ?>
```

Notice that we have to echo the output; this is because the `loadTemplate()` method uses PHP output buffering to catch the data that is outputted by the loaded template. Also notice that we do not use the full name of the sub-template; this is because the `loadTemnplate()` method automatically prefixes the string `default_` to the name.

We can take this a step further by restricting the sub-template to just one of the templates. Imagine we have a template in a file called `foobar.php`. If we wanted to make our `default_form.php` file unique to this template, all we need to do is rename it. Instead of prefixing the file name with `default_`, we prefix it with `foobar_`. The great thing about this is we do not need to alter the code.

Component Backend

When we build the backend of a component there are some very important things that we need to be aware of. Components usually take advantage of the toolbar and the submenu.

This is a screenshot of the Banner component:

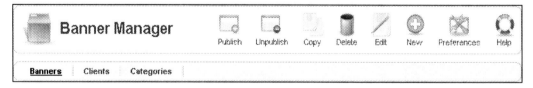

Across the top is the toolbar, and across the bottom is the sub-menu. We'll discuss how to modify these in a moment. First of all we need to be aware of the admin form.

Admin Form

When we create templates for component backends that require a form, we must always name the form `adminForm`. This code demonstrates how we normally define `adminForm` in a template:

```
<form action="<?php echo $this->request_url; ?>" method="post"
                            name="adminForm" id="adminForm">
```

Instead of adding buttons to the form in the usual way we add buttons to the toolbar.

It's normal when creating a form in the backend to also include JavaScript validation. Note that we must never rely on JavaScript validation alone.

This is an example of such a script, which checks a form with two inputs, a text field called `name` and an editor area called `text`:

```
<?php// prepare the editor retrieval JavaScript
$editor =& JFactory::getEditor();
$getText = $editor->getContent('text'); ?>

<script language="javascript" type="text/javascript">
<!--
function submitbutton(pressbutton)
{
    var form = document.adminForm;

    // check we aren't cancelling
    if (pressbutton == 'cancel')
    {
        // no need to validate, we are cancelling
        submitform( pressbutton );
        return;
    }

    // get text
    text = <?php echo $getText; ?>

    // validate
    if (form.name.value == "")
    {
        // no name supplied
        alert( "<?php echo JText::_('You must supply a name',
                                    true); ?>" );
    }
    else if (question == "" && answer == "")
    {
        // no text supplied
```

```
        alert ( "<?php echo JText::_ ( 'You must supply some
                                  text', true ); ?>" );
    }
    else
    {
        // success save the
        <?php echo $editor->save ( 'text' ); ?>
        submitform ( pressbutton );
    }
}
//-->
</script>
```

Most important is our defining of the JavaScript function `submitbutton()`. This function is executed when toolbar buttons are used to submit the form.

The first part of the function checks that the button that has been pressed is not `cancel`. If it is, then the function stops because no validation is required.

We then continue to retrieve the value of `text`. We don't used `form.text.value` to retrieve the value because some editors don't support this. Instead, we use `$editor ->getContent('text')`; this returns a JavaScript string, which when executed gets the value of the editor named `text`.

Once we have done this we proceed to check the values of the two fields. If either of them is empty, we present a JavaScript alert box. When we translate the text to show the alert, we provide a second parameter of `true`. This makes the translated text JavaScript safe.

If no validation problems are encountered we proceed to submit the form. In order to do this, we use a JavaScript function called `submitform()`.

If you require more complex JavaScript form validation, you might want to investigate the use of the `behavior.formvalidation` JHTML type, described briefly earlier in this chapter.

Toolbar

The administration toolbar consists of a title and a number of buttons that, as an administrator, we use to perform actions. The following example shows the toolbar as it appears when we edit an article:

We modify the administrative component toolbar in our view classes using the static JToolBarHelper class. In this example, we add a cancel button to the menu bar and set the title of the menu bar to `FooBar`.

```
JToolBarHelper::title('FooBar');
JToolBarHelper::cancel();
```

There are many different buttons we can add to the menu bar and if we cannot find a suitable button we can define our own. Most of the buttons act like form buttons for the form `adminForm`. For some of the buttons to perform correctly the form must include certain input fields.

The following tables give detail of the buttons that we can add to the toolbar:

addNew(task : string='add', alt : string='New') : void		
Adds an 'add new' button; default task is add.		
Parameters	[task]	Task
	[alt]	Name

addNewX(task : string='add', alt : string='New') : void		
Adds an 'add new' button; default task is add. This method hides the main menu when pressed; the adminForm form must include an input called `hidemainmenu`.		
Parameters	[task]	Task
	[alt]	Name

apply(task : string='apply', alt : string='Apply') : void		
Adds an apply button to the menu bar. The default task is apply.		
Parameters	[task]	Task
	[alt]	Name

archiveList(task : string='archive', alt : string='Archive') : void		
Adds an archive button to the menu bar. The default task is archive. Requires that at least one list item is selected.		
Parameters	[task]	Task
	[alt]	Name

assign(task : string='assign', alt : string='Assign') : void		
Adds an 'assign' button to the menu bar. The default task is assign.		
Parameters	[task]	Task
	[alt]	Name

back(alt : string='Back', href : string='javascript:history.back();') : void		
Adds a 'back' button to the menu bar.		
Parameters	[alt]	Name
	[href]	URI

cancel(task : string='cancel', alt : string='Cancel') : void		
Adds a 'cancel' button to the menu bar.		
Parameters	[task]	Task
	[alt]	Name

custom(task : string='', icon : string='', iconOver : string='', alt : string='', listSelect : boolean=true, x : boolean=false) : void		
Adds a custom button to the menu bar. To use x your form must include an input called `hidemainmenu`.		
Parameters	[task]	Value of the task input
	[icon]	Icon to use
	[iconOver]	Icon to use on mouse over
	[alt]	Name
	[listSelect]	Check if a list item is selected
	[x]	Hide main menu

customX(task : string='', icon : string='', iconOver : string='', alt : string='', listSelect : boolean=true) : void		
Adds a custom button to the menu bar.		
Parameters	[task]	Value of the task input
	[icon]	Icon to use
	[iconOver]	Icon to use on mouse over
	[alt]	Name
	[listSelect]	Check if a list item, `cid[]`, is selected

deleteList(msg : string='', task : string='remove', alt : string='Delete') : void		
Adds a 'delete' button to the menu bar. The default task is `remove`.		
Parameters	[msg]	Delete confirmation message
	[task]	Task
	[alt]	Name

deleteListX(msg : string='', task : string='remove', alt : string='Delete') : void		
Adds a 'delete' button to the menu bar. The default task is remove.		
Parameters	[msg]	Delete confirmation message
	[task]	Task
	[alt]	Name

divider( ) : void
Adds a divider; a vertical line.

editCss(task : string='edit_css', alt : string='Edit CSS') :void		
Adds an 'edit' button to the menu bar. The default task is edit_css.		
Parameters	[task]	Task
	[alt]	Name

editCssX(task : string='edit_css', alt : string='Edit CSS') :void		
Adds an 'edit' button to the menu bar. The default task is edit_css.		
Parameters	[task]	Task
	[alt]	Name

editHtml(task : string='edit_source', alt : string='Edit HTML') : void		
Adds an 'edit' button to the menu bar. The default task is edit_source.		
Parameters	[task]	Task
	[alt]	Name

editHtmlX(task : string='edit_source', alt : string='Edit HTML') : void		
Adds an 'edit' button to the menu bar. The default task is edit_source. Checks the value of the input box checked; if it equals 0, a JavaScript alert message is displayed telling the administrator to make a selection.		
Parameters	[task]	Task
	[alt]	Name

editList(task : string='edit', alt : string='Edit') : void		
Adds an 'edit' button to the menu bar. Requires that at least one list item is selected, cid[].		
Parameters	[task]	Task
	[alt]	Name

editListX(task : string='edit', alt : string='Edit') : void		
	Adds an 'edit' button to the menu bar. Requires that at least one list item is selected, `cid[]`. This method hides the main menu when pressed; the adminForm form must include an input called `hidemainmenu`.	
Parameters	[task]	Task
	[alt]	Name

help(ref : string, com : boolean= false) : void		
	Adds a 'help' button to the menu bar. `$ref` determines the help file to use. `$com` chooses to use a component-specific help file. Component-specific help files are located in the help folder in the administrator component folder.	
Parameters	ref	Help file
	[com]	Use component-specific help files

makeDefault(task : string='default', alt : string='Default') : void		
	Adds a make-default button. The default task is `default`.	
Parameters	[task]	Task
	[alt]	Name

media_manager(directory : string='', alt : string='Upload') : void		
	Adds a button that when pressed allows an administrator to upload a file to the Media Manager.	
Parameters	[directory]	Directory in
	[alt]	Name

preferences(component : string, height : string='150', width : string='570', alt : string='Preferences', path : string = '') : void		
	Adds a 'preferences' button to the menu bar. When pressed a pop-up box appears with the component's preferences as defined by the XML file. If `path` is not specified the default location, `JPATH_COMPONENT_ADMISTRATOR.'config.xml'`, is used.	
Parameters	component	Component name
	[height]	Pop-up box height
	[width]	Pop-up box width
	[alt]	Name
	[path]	Path to the configuration XML file

preview(url : string= ", updateEditors : boolean=false) : void		
Adds a 'preview' button to the menu bar and appends `&task=preview` to the URI.		
Parameters	[url]	URI
	[updateEditors]	Deprecated

publish(task : string='publish', alt : string='Publish') : void		
Adds a 'publish' button to the menu bar.		
Parameters	[task]	Task
	[alt]	Name

publishList(task : string='publish', alt : string='Publish') : void		
Adds a 'publish' button to the menu bar. Requires that at least one list item is selected, `cid[]`.		
Parameters	[task]	Task
	[alt]	Name

save(task : string='save', alt : string='Save') : void		
Adds a 'save' button to the menu bar.		
Parameters	[task]	Task
	[alt]	Name

spacer(width : int=") : void		
Adds a spacer; use width parameter to determine the size of the spacer.		
Parameters	[width]	Spacer width

title(title : string, icon : string='generic.png') : void		
Sets the title and the icon title class of the menu bar.		
Parameters	title	Title
	[icon]	Title class, prepended to `icon-48-`

trash(task : string='remove', alt : string= Trash', check : boolean=true) : void		
Adds a 'trash' button to the menu bar. The default task is `remove`.		
Parameters	[task]	Task
	[alt]	Name
	[check]	Check that an item is selected

unarchiveList(task : string='unarchive', alt : string='Unarchive') : void		
Adds an 'unarchive' button to the menu bar. The default task is unarchive. Requires that at least one list item is selected, cid[].		
Parameters	[task]	Task
	[alt]	Name

unpublish(task : string='unpublish', alt : string='Unpublish') : void		
Adds an 'unpublish' button to the menu bar. The default task is unpublish.		
Parameters	[task]	Task
	[alt]	Name

unpublishList(task : string='unpublish', alt : string='Unpublish') : void		
Adds an 'unpublish' button to the menu bar. The default task is unpublish. Requires that at least one list item is selected, cid[].		
Parameters	[task]	Task
	[alt]	Name

Sub-Menu

The sub-menu appears directly beneath the toolbar. It is automatically populated with the component sub-menu items defined in the component XML manifest file.

If we modify sub-menu items, the automatically generated items will not be included. We can modify entries using the static JSubMenuHelper class. This example adds two options to the sub-menu:

```
// get the current task
$task = JRequest::getCmd('task');

if ($task == 'item1' || $task == 'item2')
{
    // determine selected task
    $selected = ($task == 'item1');

    // prepare links
    $item1 = 'index.php?option=com_myextension&task=item1';
    $item2 = 'index.php?option=com_myextension&task=item2';

    // add sub menu items
    JSubMenuHelper::addEntry(JText::_('Item 1'), $item1,
                $selected);
    JSubMenuHelper::addEntry(JText::_('Item 2'), $item2,
                $selected);
}
```

The `addEntry()` method adds a new item to the sub-menu. Items are added in order of appearance. The first parameter is the name, the second is the link location, and the third is `true` if the item is the current menu item.

This screenshot depicts the given example, in the component **My Extension**, when the selected task is **Item1**:

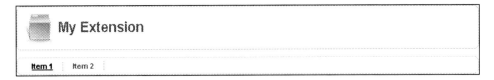

It is common to use this type of code in the root component file if one of the sub-menu options is part of a different component. It's not uncommon for components to use the core categories component to handle categories.

This is an example of a link we might add to the sub-menu if we were using the core categories component to handle categories for the component `com_myextension`:

```
$link = 'index.php?option=com_categories&section=com_myextension';
JSubMenuHelper::addEntry(JText::_('Categories'), $link);
```

There is one more thing that we can do with the sub-menu. We can remove it. This is especially useful with views for which, when a user navigates away without following the correct procedure, an item becomes locked.

If we modify the `hidemainmenu` request value to `1`, the sub-menu will not be displayed. We normally do this in methods in our controllers; a common method in which this would be done is `edit()`. This example demonstrates how:

```
JRequest::setVar('hidemainmenu', 1);
```

There is one other caveat when using this; the main menu will be deactivated. This screenshot depicts the main menu across the top of backend:

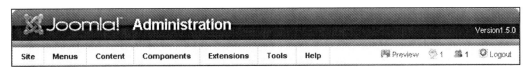

This screenshot depicts the main menu across the top of backend when `hidemainmenu` is enabled; notice that all of the menu items are grayed out:

Itemized Data

Most components handle and display itemized data. Itemized data is data having many instances; most commonly this reflects rows in a database table. When dealing with itemized data there are three areas of functionality that users generally expect:

- Pagination
- Ordering
- Filtering and Searching

In this section we will discuss each of these areas of functionality and how to implement them in the backend of a component.

Pagination

To make large amounts of itemized data easier to understand, we split the data across multiple pages. Joomla! provides us with the JPagination class to help us handle pagination in our extensions.

There are four important attributes associated with the JPagination class:

- `limitstart`: This is the item at which we begin a page, for example the first page will always begin with item `0`.
- `limit`: This is the maximum number of items to display on a page.
- `total`: This is the total number of items across all the pages.
- `_viewall`: This is the option to ignore pagination and display all items.

Before we head into piles of code, let's take the time to examine the listFooter, the footer that is used at the bottom of pagination lists:

The box to the far left describes the maximum number of items to display per page (`limit`). The remaining buttons are used to navigate between pages. The final text defines the current page out of the total number of pages.

The great thing about this footer is we don't have to work very hard to create it! We can use a JPagination object to build it. This not only means that it is easy to implement, but that the pagination footers are consistent throughout Joomla!.

JPagination is used extensively by components in the backend when displaying lists of items. Normally we add a method called `getPagination()` to the model, which deals with the items we are trying to paginate, to get a pagination object. This is an example of such a method:

```
/**
 * Get a pagination object
 *
 * @access public
 * @return JPagination
 */
function getPagination()
{
    if (empty($this->_pagination))
    {
        // import the pagination library
        jimport('joomla.html.pagination');

        // prepare the pagination values
        $total = $this->getTotal();
        $limitstart = $this->getState('limitstart');
        $limit = $this->getState('limit');

        // create the pagination object
        $this->_pagination = new JPagination($total, $limitstart,
                                             $limit);
    }

    return $this->_pagination;
}
```

There are three important aspects to this method. We use the attribute `_pagination` to cache the object. We use the `getTotal()` method to determine the total number of items. We use the `getState()` method to determine the number of results to display.

The `getTotal()` method is a method that we must define in order to use. We don't have to use this name or this mechanism to determine the total number of items. This is an example of how we might implement the `getTotal()` method:

```
/**
 * Get number of items
 *
 * @access public
 * @return integer
 */
function getTotal()
{
```

```
        if (empty($this->_total))
        {
            $query = $this->_buildQuery();
            $this->_total = $this->_getListCount($query);
        }

        return $this->_total;
    }
```

This method uses the private method _buildQuery() to get the query that we use to get the data. This is the same method as the model's getData() method is likely to be using. We then use the private method _getListCount() to count the number of results that will be returned from the query.

 The _getListCount() method is defined in the JModel class.

Moving on to our use of $limit and $limitstart, we use the getState() method. JModel objects store a state object in order to record the state of the model. It is common to use the state variables limit and limitstart to record the list limit and start position.

We set the state variables in the model constructor, as this example demonstrates:

```
/**
 * Constructor
 *
 */
function __construct()
{
    global $mainframe;

    parent::__construct();

    // Get the pagination request variables
    $limit = $mainframe->getUserStateFromRequest('global.list.limit',
            'limit', $mainframe->getCfg('list_limit'));
    $limitstart = $mainframe->getUserStateFromRequest
                    ($option.'limitstart',
                    'limitstart', 0);

    // set the state pagination variables
    $this->setState('limit', $limit);
    $this->setState('limitstart', $limitstart);
}
```

We use the `getUserStateFromRequest()` method to get the `limit` and `limitstart` variables.

We use the user state variable, `global.list.limit`, to determine the limit. This variable is used throughout Joomla! to determine the length of lists. For example, if we were to view the Article Manager and select a limit if 5 items per page, when we move to a different list it will also be limited to 5 items.

If a value is set in the request value limit (part of the listFooter) we use that value. Alternatively we use the previous value, and if that is not set we use the default value defined in the application configuration.

The `limitstart` variable is retrieved from the user state value `$option`, plus `.limitstart`. `$option` is the component name, for example com_content. If we build a component that has multiple lists we should add an extra level to this, normally named after the entity.

If a value is set in the request value `limitstart` (part of the listFooter) we use that value. Alternatively we use the previous value, and if that is not set we use the default value `0`, which will lead us to the first page.

At this stage you might be wondering why we handle this in the constructor and not the `getPagination()` method. As well as using these values for the JPagination object, we also need to use them when getting data from the database.

Assuming we are using a method called `getData()` to retrieve the itemized data, our method might look like this:

```
/**
 * Get itemized data
 *
 * @access public
 * @return array
 */
function getData()
{
    if (empty($this->_data))
    {
        $query = $this->_buildQuery();
        $limitstart = $this->getState('limitstart');
        $limit = $this->getState('limit');
        $this->_data = $this->_getList($query, $limitstart, $limit);
    }

    return $this->_data;
}
```

This method uses the private _buildQuery() method that we discussed earlier. We get the object state variables limit and limitstart and pass them to the _getList() method. The _getList() method is used to get an array of objects from the database based on a query and, optionally, limit and limitstart.

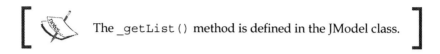 The _getList() method is defined in the JModel class.

The last two parameters will modify the first parameter, a query, in such a way that we only return the desired results. For example if we requested page 1 and were displaying a maximum of 5 items per page, the following would be appended to the query: LIMIT 0, 5.

Ordering

It's generally nice to allow the user to select a column in a table from which they want to be able to order itemized data. In Joomla!; we can use the JHTML grid.sort type to achieve this.

Before we begin we must add two hidden fields to our form of itemized data, filter_order and filter_order_Dir. The first defines the field by which we want to order our data and the latter defines the direction in which we want to order our data, ascending or descending.

At the top of each column in the itemized data table we create a heading using the grid. This is an example of a heading for a name column:

```
<?php echo JHTML::_('grid.sort', 'Name', 'name', $this-
                    >lists['order_Dir'], $this->lists['order']); ?>
```

After grid.sort the parameters are the name that will appear at the top of the column, the sort value, the current order direction, and the current column by which the data is ordered.

We'll concentrate on the last two parameters. Bearing in mind that this code is to be used in a template file, the lists attribute is something that we must have assigned to the JView object in the display() method.

This example demonstrates how we build the `lists` attribute; note that `$option` and `$mainframe` are declared global:

```
// prepare list array
$lists = array();

// get the user state of the order and direction
$filter_order = $mainframe-
            >getUserStateFromRequest($option.'filter_order',
            'filter_order', 'published');
$filter_order_Dir = $mainframe-
            >getUserStateFromRequest($option.'filter_order_Dir',
            'filter_order_Dir', 'ASC');

// set the table order values
$lists['order_Dir'] = $filter_order_Dir;
$lists['order'] = $filter_order;

// add the lists array to the object ready for the layout
$this->assignRef('lists', $lists);
```

We use the application method `getUserStateFromRequest()` to determine the order and the direction, using the paths `$option` plus `filter_order` and `filter_order_Dir` respectively. The default values are `published`, which is the default column by which we will order the data, and `ASC`, the default ordering direction, ascending.

We mentioned earlier that to facilitate the correct usage of JPagination we have to add two hidden fields, `filter_order` and `filter_order_Dir`. These are the fields from which these two `$lists` values are derived.

So now that we have the `lists` attribute sorted we can quickly add those hidden fields to our temple. This example demonstrates how:

```
<input type="hidden" name="filter_order" value="<?php echo
    $this->lists['order']; ?>" />
<input type="hidden" name="filter_order_Dir" value="" />
```

The most important thing to notice here is that we leave the value of the `filter_order_Dir` field empty. This is because the listFooter deals with this for us.

Returning to our column heading there were two other parameters: the text that appears at the top of the column, and the sort value.

The first of these is very straightforward. The second is slightly more ambiguous. It is the value that will be placed in the `filter_order` form field should we choose to order our itemized data by this column.

In order for us to be able to use these headings to their expected effect we need to modify our JModel class to deal with these.

Earlier we spoke about the use of a `_buildQuery()` method to create the query with which we retrieve itemized data. This is an example of such a method:

```
/**
 * Builds a query to get data from #__sometable
 *
 * @return string SQL query
 */
function _buildQuery()
{
    return ' SELECT * ' .
            ' FROM #__sometable ' . $this->_buildQueryOrderBy();
}
```

This method in turn calls a method named `_buildQueryOrderBy()` that builds the ORDER BY clause for the query. Let's imagine that the entity with which we are dealing has three columns: `name`, `published`, and `id`. This is an example of a `_buildQueryOrderBy()` method:

```
/**
 * Builds the ORDER part of a query
 *
 * @return string Part of an SQL query
 */
function _buildQueryOrderBy()
{
    global $mainframe, $option;

    // Array of allowable order fields
    $orders = array('name', 'published', 'id');

    // get the order field and direction
    $filter_order = $mainframe->getUserStateFromRequest(
                    $option.'filter_order',
                    'filter_order', 'published');
    $filter_order_Dir = strtoupper($mainframe->getUserStateFromRequest(
                    $option.'filter_order_Dir',
                    'filter_order_Dir', 'ASC'));

    // validate the order direction, must be ASC or DESC
    if ($filter_order_Dir != 'ASC' && $filter_order_Dir != 'DESC')
    {
        $filter_order_Dir = 'ASC';
```

```
    }

    // if order column is unknown use the default
    if (!in_array($filter_order, $orders))
    {
        $filter_order = 'published';
    }

    // return the ORDER BY clause
    return ' ORDER BY '.$filter_order.' '.$filter_order_Dir;
}
```

As with the view, we retrieve the order column name and direction using the application `getUserStateFromRequest()` method. Since this data is going to be used to interact with the database, we perform some data sanity checks to ensure that the data is safe to use with the database.

Finally, we build the ORDER BY clause and return it. When we deal with entities that have an `ordering` field, we generally build more complex ORDER BY clauses. For example, when we order by ascending `name`, we might want the ORDER BY clause to be ORDER BY name, ordering.

Now that we have done this we can use the table headings to order itemized data. This is a screenshot of such a table:

Notice that the current ordering is name ascending, as denoted by the small arrow to the right of **Name**.

Filtering and Searching

In many respects, the process of filtering and searching itemized data is very similar to ordering itemized data. We'll begin by talking a look at filtering.

This is a screenshot of the filtering and search form controls that appear at the top of the Article Manager:

In this case, there are many filtering options: the section, category, author, and published state. We will start with the easiest—we will look at how to implement a published-state filter.

We can use the `grid.state` type to easily render a published state drop-down selection box. Unlike previous examples, we'll use the type in the JView class's `display()` method. This example demonstrates how we can implement this:

```
// prepare list array
$lists = array();

// get the user-state of the published filter
$filter_state = $mainframe->getUserStateFromRequest(
                $option.'filter_state',
                'filter_state');

// set the table filter values
$lists['state'] = JHTML::_('grid.state', $filter_state);

// add the lists array to the object
$this->assignRef('lists', $lists);
```

We use the application `getUserStateFromRequest()` method to determine the current published state filter value, using the path `$option` plus `filter_state`. The default value is a null string, which indicates that no selection has been made.

Once we have the published state filter value, we use the `grid.state` type to render a drop-down list form control with the available published state properties. This control has some JavaScript associated with it that automatically submits the form when the JavaScript `onChange` event is fired.

A complete description of the `grid.state` type is available earlier in this chapter.

`$lists` is an array because, if we are implementing more than one filter, we can easily add all of these filters to a single attribute within the view, ready for the layout to use. Alternatively, we could use a different view attribute to deal with each filter.

Now that we have a form control we need to display it. We do this in the template, as this example demonstrates:

```
<table>
    <tr>
        <td align="left" width="100%">
        </td>
        <td nowrap="nowrap">
            <?php echo $this->lists['state']; ?>
        </td>
    </tr>
</table>
```

It is normal to use a table with one row and two cells to display filters and search controls. The left-hand cell is used to display the search and the right-hand cell is used to display the filter drop-down selection boxes.

As with most things in Joomla!, there are no strings attached as to how we implement filtering and searching. We don't have to format the filter in this way, and for those of us who prefer a good dose of CSS, it is perfectly acceptable to implement a table-less design.

The next question is: How do we apply a filter? This is far easier than it might sound. When we discussed ordering we described the `_buildQuery()` method in the model. It's back to that method to make some more changes:

```
/**
 * Builds a query to get data from #__sometable
 *
 * @return string SQL query
 */
function _buildQuery()
{
    return ' SELECT * '
        . ' FROM #__sometable '
        . $this->_buildQueryWhere()
        . $this->_buildQueryOrderBy();
}
```

This time we have a call to the `_buildQueryWhere()` method. This method works in much the same way as the `_buildQueryOrderBy()` method except that it returns a WHERE clause instead of an ORDER BY clause.

This example demonstrates how we can implement this method in order to apply the published state filter:

```
/**
 * Builds the WHERE part of a query
 *
 * @return string Part of an SQL query
 */
function _buildQueryWhere()
{
    global $mainframe, $option;

    // get the filter published state value
    $filter_state = $mainframe-
                >getUserStateFromRequest($option.'filter_state',
```

```
                            'filter_state');
        // prepare the WHERE clause
        $where = '';

        // Determine published state
        if ($filter_state == 'P')
        {
            $where = 'published = 1';
        }
        elseif ($filter_state == 'U')
        {
            $where = 'published = 0';
        }


        // return the WHERE clause
        return ($where) ? ' WHERE '.$where : '';
    }
```

The first thing we do is retrieve the published state value from the user state. This will be one of four values: null, P, U, or A. null means 'any'. P and U relate to 'published' and 'unpublished' respectively. A means 'archived'.

Use of the archived published state is unusual. Archived refers to items that are no longer in use and aren't to be modified or viewed in any form. If we want to use archive as a published state, we would have to modify our use of grid.state. This is explained earlier in the chapter.

We then build our WHERE clause and return the result. When we create a method such as this, it is important to remember that any external data we use is sanitized and escaped for use with the database.

This now means that we can implement and use a published state filter. Let's go to the next stage, adding the ability to filter by a category. Unsurprisingly, we start in much the same place, the JView's display method.

This example builds on the previous example and adds a category filter drop-down selection box:

```
// prepare list array
$lists = array();

// get the user state of the published filter
$filter_state = $mainframe->getUserStateFromRequest(
                $option.'filter_state',
                'filter_state');
$filter_catid = $mainframe->getUserStateFromRequest(
```

```
          $option.'filter_catid',
          'filter_catid');

   // set the table filter values
   $lists['state'] = JHTML::_('grid.state', $filter_state);
   $js = 'onchange="document.adminForm.submit();"';
   $lists['catid'] = JHTML::_('list.category', 'filter_catid',
                       'com_myextension', (int)$filter_catid, $js);

   // add the lists array to the object
   $this->assignRef('lists', $lists);
```

This time we also retrieve the current value for `filter_catid`; there are no restrictions on what we call filter form controls, but it is normal to prefix them with `filter_`. Instead of using grid, we use a list type, `list.category`, to render the category filter form control.

Unlike `grid.state`, we must tell `list.category` the name of the control, the extension name (category section), and the current category. Note that we cast the value of `$filter_catid` to an integer for security reasons. Last of all, we include some JavaScript.

This JavaScript forces the `adminForm` form to submit itself, applying the filter immediately. The first entry in the resultant drop-down list is **Select a Category**. We can opt to make our JavaScript slightly more intelligent by not submitting the form if the **Select a Category** option is chosen, as this JavaScript demonstrates:

```
   $js = "onchange=\"if (this.options[selectedIndex].value!='')
           { document.adminForm.submit(); }\"";
```

Now when we build our template, we can add the `lists['catid']` value to the table above the itemized data:

```
   <table>
       <tr>
           <td align="left" width="100%">
           </td>
           <td nowrap="nowrap">
               <?php echo $this->lists['catid']; ?>
               <?php echo $this->lists['state']; ?>
           </td>
       </tr>
   </table>
```

The final stage is to apply the category filter to the itemized data. We do this in much the same way as we modified the results for the published state filter. This example shows how we can modify the JModel _buildQueryWhere() method to incorporate the category.

```php
/**
 * Builds the WHERE part of a query
 *
 * @return string Part of an SQL query
 */
function _buildQueryWhere()
{
    global $mainframe, $option;

    // get the filter values
    $filter_state = $mainframe->getUserStateFromRequest(
                    $option.'filter_state',
                    'filter_state');
    $filter_catid = $mainframe->getUserStateFromRequest(
                    $option.'filter_catid',
                    'filter_catid');

    // prepare the WHERE clause
    $where = array();

    // Determine published state
    if ($filter_state == 'P')
    {
        $where[] = 'published = 1';
    }
    elseif ($filter_state == 'U')
    {
        $where[] = 'published = 0';
    }

    // Determine category ID
    if ($filter_catid = (int)$filter_catid)
    {
        $where[] = 'catid = '.$filter_catid;
    }

    // return the WHERE clause
    return (count($where)) ? ' WHERE '.implode(' AND ', $where) : '';
}
```

To facilitate the easiest way of building the WHERE clause we make $where an array and implode it at the end. Note that we cast $filter_catid to an integer; this ensures the value is safe for use with the database.

Before we move on to explain how to implement a search filter, we will quickly discuss the use of other filters.

So far we have demonstrated how to use grid.state and list.category. There are many other things on which we might want to filter itemized data. Some of these are easily available through the list types, for example list.positions. These are described earlier in the chapter.

If there isn't a suitable list type, we can construct our own filter drop-down selection boxes using the select types. This is an example of how we might construct a custom drop-down selection filter form control (it assumes $js is the same as in the previous examples):

```
// prepare database
$db =& JFactory::getDBO();
$query = 'SELECT value, text' .
         'FROM #__sometable' .
         'ORDER BY ordering';
$db->setQuery($query);

// add first 'select' option
$options = array()
$options[] = JHTML::_('select.option', '0', '- '.JText::_('Select a
"                      Custom Thing').' -');

// append database results
$options = array_merge($options, $db->loadObjectList());

// build form control
$lists['custom'] = JHTML::_('select.genericlist', $options,
                   'filter_custom', 'class="inputbox" size="1" '.$js,
                   'value', 'text', $filter_custom);
```

If we do create custom filter lists such as this, we might want to consider extending JHTML. For example to create a foobar group type we would create a class named JHTMLFoobar in a file named foobar.php. We would then need to use the JHTML::addIncludePath() method to point to the folder where the file is located.

To use the new class we would need to define methods within the class, for example baz(). We would then be able to call baz() using JHTML::_('foobar.baz'). For examples of existing classes we can browse the joomla.html library files.

Next up is searching. This functionality may sound more complex, but in reality it is relatively simple. The first thing we must do to implement a search filter is create the necessary form controls:

```
<table>
    <tr>
        <td align="left" width="100%">
            <?php echo JText::_('Filter'); ?>:
            <input type="text" name="filter_search" id="search"
                    value="<?php echo $this->lists['search'];?>"
                    class="text_area" onchange=
                            "document.adminForm.submit();" />
            <button onclick="this.form.submit();"><?php echo
                    JText::_('Go'); ?></button>
            <button onclick="document.adminForm.
                    filter_search.value='';this.form.submit();">
                    <?php echo JText::_('Reset'); ?></button>
        </td>
        <td nowrap="nowrap">
            <?php echo $this->lists['catid']; ?>
            <?php echo $this->lists['state']; ?>
        </td>
    </tr>
</table>
```

As you can see, this is more complex, displaying the previous filter form controls. We output the text `Filter` and add three form controls—a search text box called `filter_search`, a reset button, and a search button.

The text box is used to allow the user to define the search terms. The search button submits the form. The reset button sets the search text box value to a null string and then submits the form.

We use the `lists['search']`, value to store the value of the current search. To populate this we need to modify the JView display method. This example builds on the previous two examples:

```
// prepare list array
$lists = array();

// get the user state of the published filter
$filter_state = $mainframe->getUserStateFromRequest(
                $option.'filter_state',
                'filter_state');
$filter_catid = $mainframe->getUserStateFromRequest(
                $option.'filter_catid',
```

```
                        'filter_catid');
$filter_search = $mainframe->getUserStateFromRequest(
                        $option.'filter_search',
                        'filter_search');

// set the table filter values
$lists['state'] = JHTML::_('grid.state', $filter_state);
$js = 'onchange="document.adminForm.submit();"';
$lists['catid'] = JHTML::_('list.category', 'filter_catid',
                        'com_myextension', (int)$filter_catid, $js);
$lists['search'] = $filter_search;

// add the lists array to the object
$this->assignRef('lists', $lists);
```

That's it! Now all we need to do is implement the search in the JModel. To do this, we again modify the _buildQueryWhere() method. This example demonstrates how we do it:

```
/**
 * Builds the WHERE part of a query
 *
 * @return string Part of an SQL query
 */
function _buildQueryWhere()
{
    global $mainframe, $option;

    // get the filter values
    $filter_state = $mainframe->getUserStateFromRequest(
                        $option.'filter_state',
                        'filter_state');
    $filter_catid = $mainframe->getUserStateFromRequest(
                        $option.'filter_catid',
                        'filter_catid');
    $filter_search = $mainframe->getUserStateFromRequest(
                        $option.'filter_search',
                        'filter_search');

    // prepare the WHERE clause
    $where = array();

    // Determine published state
    if ($filter_state == 'P')
    {
```

```
        $where[] = 'published = 1';
    }
    else if ($filter_state == 'U')
    {
        $where[] = 'published = 0';
    }

    // Determine category ID
    if ($filter_catid = (int)$filter_catid)
    {
        $where[] = 'catid = '.$filter_catid;
    }

    // Determine search terms
    if ($filter_search = trim($filter_search))
    {
        $filter_search = JString::strtolower($filter_search);
        $db =& $this->_db;
        $filter_search = $db->getEscaped($filter_search);
        $where[] = 'LOWER(name) LIKE "%'.$filter_search.'%"';
    }

    // return the WHERE clause
    return (count($where)) ? ' WHERE '.implode(' AND ', $where) : '';
}
```

This example only searches the `name` field; it's likely that we would actually want to search multiple fields. If this were the case we would need to modify the query appropriately. For example:

```
$where[] = '(LOWER(name) LIKE "%'.$filter_search.'%"'.'
           OR LOWER(text) LIKE "%'.$filter_search.'%")';
```

Notice that we convert the search string to lowercase before commencing. We do this to make the search case-insensitive. We use the JString class to convert the string to lowercase because the normal `strtolower()` function will corrupt some UTF-8 characters.

We use the JDatabase object to escape the search string; this prevents SQL injection and corruption of the query.

Our search facility will now work!

Summary

We have explored the massive joomla.html library that enables us to create standardized XHTML for rendering in our extensions. It's important to explore the library so as to gain as much from it as possible. There are many useful types that can massively reduce our over all development time.

Investigating the use of existing layouts and templates should put us in good stead for creating our own. Remember to take advantage of the predefined CSS styles. This makes it easier for site template developers and ensures that our layouts will not look out of place.

When we create templates in the backend for components there are a number of rules that we should conform to. Using these allows us to create integrated components that adhere to the consistency of the Joomla! interface.

Itemized data requires special attention. If we apply the described functionality, pagination, ordering, filtering, and search, we immediately make our extensions more user-friendly and increase the chances of having successfully created a commercially winning or freely available extension.

9

Customizing the Page

This chapter discusses the following:

- How to modify the document properties to suit the contents of the page
- How to make extensions support the multi-lingual capacities of Joomla!
- How to use some common JavaScript elements to create a more interactive and user-friendly experience

Application Message Queue

You may have noticed that when we raise a notice or a warning, a bar appears across the top of the page containing the notice or warning message. These messages are part of the application message queue.

The **application message queue** is a queue of messages that are rendered the next time the application renders an HTML view. This means that we can enqueue messages in one request but not show them until a later request.

There are three different core types of message: message, notice, and error. This screenshot depicts how each of the different types of application message is rendered:

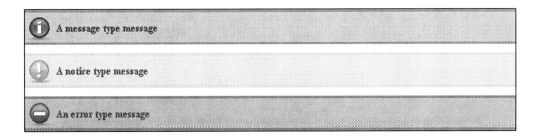

So how do we add a new message to the queue? Well it's quite simple; we use the `enqueueMessage()` method in the application. This example demonstrates how we would add all of the messages shown in the previous screenshot to the message queue:

```
$mainframe->enqueueMessage('A message type message');
$mainframe->enqueueMessage('A notice type message', 'notice');
$mainframe->enqueueMessage('An error type message', 'error');
```

The first parameter is the message that we want to enqueue and the second parameter is the type of message we want to enqueue , which defaults to `message`. It is uncommon to add messages of type `notice` or `error` this way because we usually do that using `JError::raiseNotice()` and `JError::raiseWarning()` respectively.

This means that we will probably ever use only one parameter with the `enqueueMessage()` method. However, it is possible to add messages of other types. This is an example of how we would add a message of type `bespoke`:

```
$mainframe->enqueueMessage('A bespoke type message', 'bespoke');
```

Messages of other types will render in the same format as `message` type messages. Imagine we want to use the `bespoke` message type to render messages but not display them. This could be useful for debugging purposes.

This example demonstrates how we can add a CSS Declaration to the document, using the methods, described earlier in the chapter, to modify the way in which the `bespoke` messages are displayed:

```
$css = '/* Bespoke Error Messages */
#system-message dt.bespoke
{
    display: none;
}

dl#system-message dd.bespoke ul
{
    color: #30A427;
    border-top: 3px solid #94CA8D;
    border-bottom: 3px solid #94CA8D;
    background: #C8DEC7 url(notice-bespoke.png) 4px 4px no-repeat;
}';

$doc =& JFactory::getDocument();
$doc->addStyleDeclaration($css);
```

Now when `bespoke` messages are rendered, they will appear like this:

Redirects

Redirection allows us to redirect the browser to a new location. Joomla! provides us with some easy ways in which to redirect the browser.

Joomla! redirects are implemented using HTTP 301 redirect response codes. In the event that response headers have already been sent, JavaScript will be used to redirect the browser.

The most common time to redirect a browser is after a form has been submitted. There are a number of reasons why we might want to do this:

- This prevents forms from being submitted multiple times when the browser is refreshed.
- We can redirect to different locations dependent upon the submitted data.
- Redirecting to another view reduces the amount of development required for each task in the controller.

Imagine a user submits a form that is used to create a new record in a database table. The first thing we need to do when we receive a request of this type is to validate the form contents. This flow diagram describes the logic that we could implement:

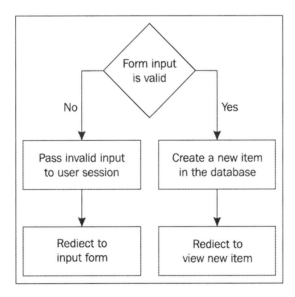

The **No** route passes the invalid input to the session. We do this so that when we redirect the user to the input form we can repopulate the form with the invalid input. If we do not do this the user will have to complete the entire form again.

We may choose to miss out the **Pass invalid input to user session** process, as the core components do. It is normal to include JavaScript to validate forms before they are submitted, and since the majority of users will have JavaScript support, it would be relatively safe to assume that such an occurrence would be very unlikely.

Note that missing out this process is not the same as missing out form validation. We must never depend on JavaScript or other client-side mechanisms for data validation. It is best to start developing forms without the bells and whistles of client-side validation so as to ensure that we properly handle invalid data if the server-side scripts ever need to deal with it.

As a quick aside, a good way to validate form contents is to use a JTable subclass `check()` method.

If we place failed input into the session, we might want to put it in its own namespace. This makes it easier to remove the data later and helps prevent naming conflicts. This example demonstrates how we might add the field value of `myField` to the `myForm` session namespace:

```
// get the session
$session =& JFactory::getSession();

// get the raw value of myField
$myFieldValue = JRequest::getString('myField', '', 'POST',
            JREQUEST_ALLOWRAW);

// add the value to the session namespace myForm
$session->set('myField', $myFieldValue, 'myForm')
```

When we come to display the form we can retrieve the data from the session using the `get()` method. Once we have retrieved the data we must remember to remove the data from the session, otherwise it will be displayed every time we view the form (unless we use another flag as an indicator). We can remove data items from the `myForm` namespace using the `clear()` method:

```
// get the session
$session =& JFactory::getSession();

// Remove the myField
$session->clear('myField', 'myForm');
```

The final thing we do in the **No** route is to redirect the user back to the input form. When we do this, we must add some messages to the application queue to explain to the user why the input has been rejected.

The **Yes** route adds a new record to the database and then redirects the user to the newly created item. As with the **No** route, it is normal to enqueue a message that will say that the new item has been successfully saved, or something to that effect.

There are many scenarios where the use of a redirect is common. This list identifies some of these:

- Canceling editing an existing item
- Copying items
- Creating new items and updating existing items
- Deleting items
- Publishing/unpublishing items
- Updating item ordering

The next question is: How do we redirect? There are essentially two ways in which we can do this. The first is to use the application `redirect()` method.

It is unusual to use this mechanism unless we are developing a component without the use of the Joomla! MVC classes. This example demonstrates how we use the application method:

```
$mainframe->redirect('index.php?option=com_example');
```

This will redirect the user's browser to `index.php?option=com_example`. There are two additional optional parameters that we can provide when using this method. These are used to enqueue a message.

This example redirects us, as per the previous example, and enqueues a `notice` type message that will be displayed after the redirect has successfully completed:

```
$mainframe->redirect('index.php?option=com_example', 'Some Message',
                     'notice');
```

The final parameter, the message type, defaults to `message`.

> The application `redirect()` method immediately enqueues the optional message, redirects the user's browser, and ends the application.

The more common mechanism for implementing redirects is to use the JController `setRedirect()` method. We generally use this from within a controller method that handles a task, but because the method is public we can use it outside of the controller.

This example, assuming we are in a method in a JController subclass, will set the controller redirect to `index.php?option=com_example`:

```
$this->setRedirect('index.php?option=com_example');
```

As with the application `redirect()` method, there are two additional optional parameters that we can provide when using this method. These are used to enqueue a message.

This example sets the controller redirect, as per the previous example, and enqueues a `notice` type message that will be displayed after the redirect has successfully completed:

```
$this->setRedirect('index.php?option=com_example', 'Some Message',
                   'notice');
```

Unlike the application `redirect()` method, this method does not immediately enqueue the optional message, redirect the user's browser, and end the application. To do this we must use the JController `redirect()` method.

It is normal, in components that use redirects, to execute the controller `redirect()` method after the controller has executed a given task. This is normally done in the root component file as this example demonstrates:

```
$controller = new ExampleController();
$controller->execute(JRequest::getCmd('task'));
$controller->redirect();
```

Component XML Metadata Files and Menu Parameters

When we create menu items, if a component has a selection of views and layouts, we can choose which view and which layout we want to use. We can create an XML metadata file for each view and layout. In these files we can describe the view or layout and we can define extra parameters for the menu item specific to the specified layout.

Imagine we have a view named `foobar`, with two layouts: `default.php` and `alternative.php`. The next figure describes the folder structure we would expect to find in the `views` folder (for simplicity, only the files and folders that we are discussing are included in the figure):

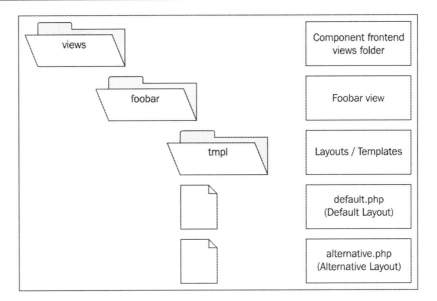

When an administrator creates a link to this view, the options displayed will not give any information beyond the names of the folders and files described above, as this screenshot demonstrates:

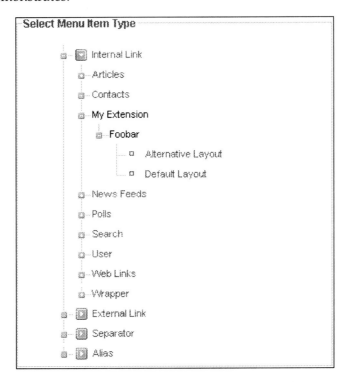

The first element of this list that we will customize is the view name, 'Foobar'. To do this we must create a file in the foobar folder called metadata.xml. This example customizes the name and description of the foobar view:

```xml
<?xml version="1.0" encoding="utf-8"?>
<metadata>
    <view title="My Complete Foobar Title">
        <message>
            <![CDATA[A description of foobar]]>
        </message>
    </view>
</metadata>
```

Now if an administrator were to view the list of menu item types, 'Foobar' would be replaced with the text 'My Complete Foobar Title' as defined in the view tag title attribute. The description, defined in the message tag, is displayed when the mouse cursor is over the view name.

The next task is to customize the definitions of the layouts, default.php and alternative.php.

Layout XML metadata files are located in the tmpl folder and are named the same as the corresponding layout template file. For example, the XML metadata file for default.php would be named default.xml.

So we need to add the files default.xml and alternative.xml to the tmpl folder.

Within a layout XML metadata file, there are two main tags in which we are interested: layout and state. This example shows a basic XML metadata file that defines a name and title for a layout:

```xml
<?xml version="1.0" encoding="utf-8"?>
<metadata>
    <layout title="My Layout">
        <message>
            <![CDATA[Description of my layout.]]>
        </message>
    </layout>
    <state>
        <name>My Layout</name>
        <description>Description of my layout.</description>
    </state>
</metadata>
```

At first this example may seem odd because we appear to be duplicating information in the `layout` and `state` tags. Fear not, there is reason for this madness! The `layout` tag includes information that is displayed in the menu item type list (essentially an overview). The `state` tag includes information that is displayed during the creation of a menu item that uses the layout.

There are occasions when a more detailed description is required when we come to define a menu item. For example, we may want to warn the user that they must fill in a specific menu parameter. We will discuss menu parameters in a moment.

If we used the given XML in the `default.xml` file and we duplicated it in the `alternative.xml` file, renaming the layout, 'My Other Layout', the menu item type list would now appear like this:

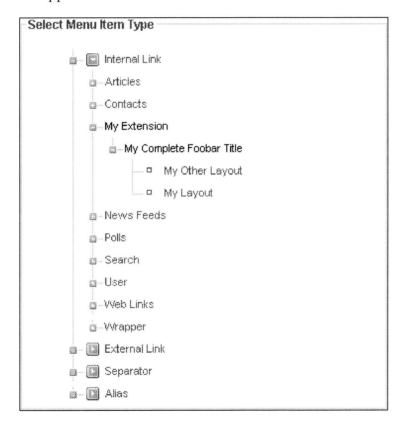

Now that we know how to modify the names and descriptions of views and layouts, we can investigate how to define custom menu parameters.

There are many different types of parameter that we can define. Before you continue, you might want to familiarize yourself with this list of parameter types because we will be using them in the examples (a complete description of these parameters is available in the *Appendix*):

- `category`
- `editors`
- `filelist`
- `folderlist`
- `helpsites`
- `hidden`
- `imagelist`
- `languages`
- `list`
- `menu`
- `menuitem`
- `password`
- `radio`
- `section`
- `spacer`
- `sql`
- `text`
- `textarea`
- `timezones`

Menu parameters can be considered as being grouped into several categories:

- System
- Component
- State
- URL
- Advanced

The system parameters are predefined by Joomla! (held in the `administrator/components/com_menus/models/metadata/component.xml` file). These parameters are used to encourage standardization of some common component parameters. We cannot prevent these parameters from being displayed.

The component parameters are those parameters that are defined in the component's `config.xml` file. Note that changing these parameters when creating a new menu item only affects the menu item, not the entire component. In essence, this is a form of overriding. A full explanation of how to create a component `config.xml` file is available in Chapter 4.

This form of overriding is not always desirable; it is possible to prevent the component parameters from being shown when creating or editing a menu item. To do this we add the attribute `menu` to the root tag (`config`) of the component `config.xml` file and set the value of the attribute to `hide`:

```
<config menu="hide">
```

The remaining parameter groups — State, URL, and Advanced — are defined on a per layout basis in the layout XML metadata files inside the `state` tag. These are the groups in which we are most interested.

The State parameters are located in a tag called `params`. In this example, which builds on the previous `default.xml` example, we add two parameters: a text field named `text_field` and a radio option named `radio_option`:

```
<?xml version="1.0" encoding="utf-8"?>
<metadata>
    <layout title="My Layout">
        <message>
            <![CDATA[Description of my layout.]]>
        </message>
    </layout>
    <state>
        <name>My Layout</name>
        <description>Description of my layout.</description>
        <params>
            <param type="text" name="text_field" label="A Parameter"
                description="Some description of the parameter"
                default="default value"/>
            <param name="radio_option" type="radio" default="1"
                label="Show" description="Show/Hide something">
                <option value="0">Hide</option>
                <option value="1">Show</option>
            </param>
        </params>
    </state>
</metadata>
```

When an administrator creates a new menu item for this layout, they will be presented with these two parameters under the heading 'Parameters — Basic'.

They are not presented under a 'State' heading, because State and URL parameters are consolidated into one section. URL parameters always appear above State parameters.

We define URL parameters in much the same way, only this time we place them in a tag named `url`. The URL parameters are automatically appended to the URI; this means that we can access these parameters using JRequest.

These parameters are of particular use when we are creating a layout that is used to display a single item, which is retrieved using a unique ID. If we use these parameters to define an ID that is retrieved from a table, we should consider using the, often overlooked, `sql` parameter type.

This example builds on the previous example, and adds the URL parameter `id`, which is extracted from the `#__myextension` table:

```xml
<?xml version="1.0" encoding="utf-8"?>
<metadata>
    <layout title="My Layout">
        <message>
            <![CDATA[Description of my layout.]]>
        </message>
    </layout>
    <state>
        <name>My Layout</name>
        <description>Description of my layout.</description>
        <url>
            <param type="sql" name="id" label="Item"
                description="Item to display" query="SELECT id AS
                value, title AS id FROM #__content" />
        </url>
        <params>
            <param type="text" name="text_field" label="A Parameter"
                description="Some description of the parameter"
                default="default value"/>
            <param name="radio_option" type="radio" default="1"
                label="Show" description="Show/Hide something">
                <option value="0">Hide</option>
                <option value="1">Show</option>
            </param>
        </params>
    </state>
</metadata>
```

The query might be slightly confusing if you are not familiar with the `sql` parameter type. The query must return two fields, `value` and `id`. `value` specifies the value of the parameter and `id` specifies the identifier displayed in the drop-down box that is displayed when the parameter is rendered.

 When using the `sql` parameter type, if applicable, remember to include a WHERE clause to only display published or equivalent items.

The Advanced parameters are specifically for defining parameters thath are more complex than the State parameters. These parameters are defined in the `advanced` tag.

This example adds an advanced parameter called `advanced_setting`:

```xml
<?xml version="1.0" encoding="utf-8"?>
<metadata>
    <layout title="My Layout">
        <message>
            <![CDATA[Description of my layout.]]>
        </message>
    </layout>
    <state>
        <name>My Layout</name>
        <description>Description of my layout.</description>
    <url>
        <param type="sql" name="id" label="Item" description="Item to
                display" query="SELECT id AS value, title AS id
                FROM #__content" />
    </url>
        <params>
            <param type="text" name="text_field" label="A Parameter"
                    description="Some description of the
                    parameter" default="default value"/>
            <param name="radio_option" type="radio" default="1"
                    label="Show" description="Show/Hide
                    something">
                <option value="0">Hide</option>
                <option value="1">Show</option>
            </param>
        </params>
        <advanced>
            <param name="advanced_setting" type="radio" default="1"
                    label="Advanced Setting" description="Use
                    Advanced Setting">
                <option value="0">No</option>
```

```
                      <option value="1">Yes</option>
                  </param>
            </advanced>
        </state>
    </metadata>
```

Any Advanced parameters will appear under the 'Parameters Advanced' heading.

The resultant parameters area for this layout will look like this:

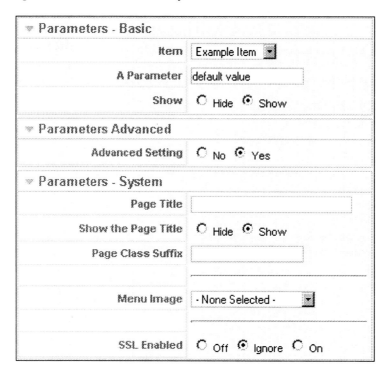

If the extension also specified component parameters, these would be displayed under the heading 'Parameters—Component'.

 All name and description elements from the XML metadata files will be translated into the currently selected locale language.

When we save a menu item, all of the parameters, except URL parameters, are saved to the `params` field in the menu item record. This means that we can end up with naming conflicts between our parameters. We must ensure that we do not name any two parameters the same. This includes not using the predefined System parameter names.

This list details the System parameter names:

- `page_title`
- `show_page_title`
- `pageclass_sfx`
- `menu_image`
- `secure`

Once we have successfully created the necessary XML, we will be able to access the parameters from within our component using a JParameter object. This is described in the next section.

Using Menu Item Parameters

Before we jump in and start using menu item parameters, let us take a moment to consider the overriding effects of the component parameters.

When we save a menu item a second set of component parameters are saved to the menu item. This means that the component parameters are saved as part of the menu item, not the component. The idea is that it allows a component, which can only be installed once, to be linked to from the menu multiple times using different settings.

This raises the question: What is the purpose of the component preferences button in the backend? The preferences button, used to save the component settings, is used to modify the default component settings.

The default settings are used when we create a new menu item as the initial 'Component Parameters' values. They are also used if the component is invoked but the active menu item does not correspond to the invoked component.

Imagine the link `index.php?option=com_foobar`. This link will invoke the `com_foobar` component, but because no menu item is specified the active menu item will be the first menu item in the main menu.

Now imagine the link `index.php?Itemid=53&option=com_foobar`. This link will invoke the `com_foobar` component, and because the menu item is specified, the active menu item will be menu item `53`. Assuming this menu item is for the corresponding component then the component parameters saved to the menu item will be used.

In order to access the page parameters there is a useful method in the application, `getPageParameters()`. We briefly mentioned this method in Chapter 4.

This method returns a JParameter object that is loaded with the Component and Menu Item Parameters. The Menu Item Parameters always take precedence over the component parameters. For example if the component defined a parameter `foobar` and so did the menu item, the value recorded by the menu item would be the value that would be used in the JParameter object.

It is common to use this method in the `display()` method of JView sub-classes and assign the resultant object to the view for use by the layout. This example demonstrates how we can do this:

```
$params =& $mainframe->getPageParameters();
$this->assignRef('params', $params);
```

We can then use `params` as an attribute in our template files. This example demonstrates how we can check the value of the `show_something` parameter before proceeding to 'show something':

```
<?php if ($this->params->get('show_something')) : ?>
<div id="something">
    <?php echo $this->something; ?>
</div>
<?php endif; ?>
```

It is generally easier when developing templates to include all possible elements. Once this is complete, it is generally easier to add the necessary parameters and make each element optional.

Modifying the Document

The document, as described in Chapter 2, is a buffer used to store the content of the document that will be returned when a request is complete. There are a number of different things that we can modify in the document that will customize the resultant page.

Whenever we want to modify the document, we use the JFactory class to get the global document object. This example demonstrates how:

```
$document =& JFactory::getDocument();
```

Notice that we use the `=&` assignment operator. If we do not, any modification we make to the document will not be applied.

All of the following examples in this section assume that `$document` is the global document object.

Page Title

The page title is the most commonly modified part of the page. The title is the contents of the `title` tag that is located in the XHTML `head` tag.

There are two methods related to the title: `getTitle()` and `setTitle()`. The `getTitle()` method retrieves the existing title; `setTitle()` sets the title to a new value.

This example demonstrates how we use `setTitle()` to make the title 'Some Exciting Title'.

```
$document->setTitle(JText::_('Some Exciting Title'));
```

Notice that we use JText to translate the title before passing it. This is because the `setTitle()` method does not translate new titles for us.

 We never have to set the document title. If we don't, the site name will be used.

It's not uncommon to use the two methods in conjunction. This way we can append title information. This is such an example:

```
$title = $document->getTitle().' - '.JText::_('Some Exciting Title')
$document->setTitle($title);
```

Pathway/Breadcrumb

The pathway, also known as the breadcrumb (trail), describes to the user their current navigational position in a website. This is an example of a pathway for a menu item named 'Joomla! Overview':

Home >> Joomla! Overview

Joomla! handles the pathway to the depth of the menu item. Beyond that we must manually add items to the breadcrumb. For example, a component that handles categories and multiple items will generally add to the pathway in order to display its internal hierarchy.

The pathway is handled by a global JPathway object. We can access the object using the application. This example demonstrates how we get the breadcrumb handler:

```
$pathway =& $mainframe->getPathway();
```

Notice that, as per usual, we must use the `=&` assignment operator. If we do not, any changes we make to `$pathway` will not be reflected.

We use the `addItem()` method to add new items to the pathway. Imagine we are viewing a category in a component and we want to add the category as an extra layer in the pathway trail:

```
$pathway->addItem($categoryName);
```

There is one glaringly obvious thing missing from this example. There is no URI. Since we are viewing the category, there is no need to specify the URI because it is the current URI.

The last item in the pathway is never a link. We only need to specify a URI when we add items that are not going to be the last item in the pathway. This example demonstrates how we might build the pathway for an item within the aforementioned category:

```
$pathway->addItem($categoryName, $categoryURI);
$pathway->addItem($itemName);
```

Notice this time we include a URI when adding the category item. It is normal to add to the pathway in the `display()` method of each JView class. It is important to realize that we must always add pathway items in order of appearance.

There is one pitfall to the currently explained way of adding items to the pathway. It is likely that in the described scenario, we would be able to create a menu item that links directly to a category or item in the component.

We can overcome this by interrogating the current menu item. This example shows how we get access to the current menu item:

```
$menus =& JMenu::getInstance();
$menuitem =& $menus->getActive();
```

The JMenu class is responsible for the handling of Joomla! menus. The `getActive()` method returns a reference to the currently selected menu item object. This object is a stdClass object that contains various attributes that relate to the menu item.

The attribute that we are interested in is `query`. This attribute is an associative array that describes the URI query associated with the menu item. So to enhance our category pathway we would do this:

```
if ($menuitem->query['view'] != 'category')
{
    $pathway =& $mainframe->getPathWay();
    $pathway->addItem($categoryName);
}
```

The `view` key is the layout that the menu item is set to view.

To improve our pathway when viewing an item we can build on this example by adding a `switch` statement:

```
if ($menuitem->query['view'] != 'item')
{
    $pathway =& $mainframe->getPathWay();

    switch ($menuitem->query['view'])
    {
        case 'categories':
            $pathway->addItem($categoryName, $categoryURI);
        default:
            $pathway->addItem($itemName);
    }
}
```

We now have the ability to build the pathway from the point at which the menu item enters the component.

By using a switch statement without any breaks we make the building of the pathway extremely versatile. It would be very easy for us to add an extra hierarchical layer to the pathway based on this.

JavaScript

In order to add JavaScript cleanly it should be added to the document header. We can use the following methods to add JavaScript in this way:

- The `addScript()` method is used to add a link to an external JavaScript file. This is an example of how to use the `addScript()` method:

```
$js = JURI::base().'components/com_foobar/assets/script.js';
$document->addScript($js);
```

- The `addScriptDeclaration()` method is similar; it allows us to add RAW JavaScript to the header. This is an example of how to use the `addScriptDeclaration()` method:

```
$js = 'function notify(text) { alert(text); }';
$document->addScriptDeclaration($js);
```

We can use these two methods for any type of script. If we want to use script other than JavaScript, we can supply a second parameter defining the script MIME type. For example, if we wanted to use Visual Basic Script we would specify the MIME type `text/vbscript`.

CSS

In order to add CSS styles cleanly they should be added to the document header. We can use the methods `addStyleSheet()` and `addStyleDeclaration()` to add CSS.

`addStyleSheet()` is used to add a link to an external CSS file. This is an example of how to use the `addStyleSheet()` method:

```
$css = JURI::base().'components/com_foobar/assets/style.css';
$document =& JFactory::getDocument();
$document->addStyleSheet($css);
```

The nice thing about using this method is we can also specify the media type to which the styles apply. Imagine we have a special CSS file that is intended to format a document when we come to print. To achieve this we can specify the media type `print`:

```
$document->addStyleSheet($css, 'text/css', 'print');
```

Notice that the second parameter is `text/css`; this parameter is used to identify the MIME type and is used in the same way as it is in the `addScript()` and `addScriptDeclaration()` methods.

The third parameter is the media type, in this case `print`. This is a list of the CSS2 recognized media types:

- all
- aural
- braille
- embossed
- handheld
- print
- projection
- screen
- tty

For more information about CSS media types please refer to the official documentation available at `http://www.w3.org/TR/1998/REC-CSS2-19980512/media.html`.

The `addStyleDeclaration()` method allows us to add RAW CSS styles to the header. This is an example of how to use the `addStyleDeclaration()` method:

```
$css = '.somestyle { padding: 10px; }';
$document->addStyleDeclaration($css);
```

Metadata

Metadata tags are used to help describe a document. There are two different types of metadata: `http-equiv` and non `http-equiv`. Metadata that is `http-equiv` is used to determine metadata to be used as HTTP header data.

There are two metadata methods in the document:

- `getMetaData()`: This is used to retrieve the document metadata.
- `setMetaData()`: This is used to add metadata to the document.

When we create extensions that handle information that we want search engines to index, it is important to add metadata to the document. This example adds some keywords metadata:

```
$keywords = 'monkey, ape, chimpanzee, gorilla, orang-utan';
$document->setMetaData('keywords', $keywords);
```

Adding `http-equiv` metadata is very similar. Imagine we want to turn off browser theme styling. We can use the `http-equiv` metadata type `MSTHEMECOMPATIBLE`:

```
$document->setMetaData('MSTHEMECOMPATIBLE', 'no', true);
```

It is that final parameter, when set to `true`, which tells the method that the metadata is `http-equiv`.

The `getMetaData()` method works in much the same way, except we retrieve values. Imagine we want to append some keywords to the document:

```
$keywords = explode(',', $document->getMetaData('keywords'));
$keywords[] = 'append me';
$keywords[] = 'and me';
$document->setMetaData('keywords', implode(',', $keywords));
```

This gets the existing keywords and explodes them into an array; this ensures we maintain the keyword comma separators. We proceed to add some new keywords to the array. Finally, we implode the array and reset the keywords metadata.

Custom Header Tags

If we want to add a different type of tag, not a script, CSS, or metadata, we can use the `addCustomTag()` method. This method allows us to inject code directly into a document header.

Imagine we want to add a comment to the document header:

```
$comment = '<!-- Oi, stop looking at my page source! :p -->';
$document->addCustomTag($comment);
```

Translating

A major strength of Joomla! is its built-in multilingual support. Joomla! has special language handling classes that translate strings. The default language is configured in the Language Manager. The language can be overridden by a logged-in user's preferences.

Translating Text

We use the static JText class to translate text. JText has three methods for translating text: `_()`, `sprintf()`, and `printf()`. The method that we use most is `_()`. This method is the most basic; it simply translates a string.

This example outputs the translation of Monday; if a translation cannot be found, the original text is returned:

```
echo JText::_('Monday');
```

The `JText::sprintf()` method is comparable to the PHP `sprintf()` function. We pass one string to translate, and any number of extra parameters to insert into the translated string.

The extra parameters are inserted into the translated string at the defined points. We define these points using **type specifiers**, this is the same as when using the PHP `sprintf()` function. This list describes the different type specifiers:

	Argument Type	Representation
%F	Floating point	Floating point
%f	Floating point	Floating point (locale aware)
%c	Integer	ASCII character (does not support UTF-8 multi-byte characters)
%b	Integer	Binary Number
%d	Integer	Decimal
%u	Integer	Decimal (Unsigned)
%x	Integer	Hexadecimal
%X	Integer	Hexadecimal
%o	Integer	Octal
%e	Scientific Expression	Decimal
%s	String	String

This example demonstrates how we use the `JText::sprintf()` method:

```
$value = JText::sprintf('SAVED_ITEMS', 3);
```

If the translation for SAVED_ITEMS were Saved %d items, the returned value would be Saved 3 items.

Alternatively, we can use the JText::printf() method. This method is comparable to the PHP function printf(). This method returns the length of the resultant string and outputs the translation.

As with JText::sprintf(), the extra parameters are inserted into the translated string at the defined points, which are defined using the type specifiers defined in the table given on the previous page.

This example returns the byte length (not UTF-8 aware) of Saved %d items and outputs the translated string:

```
$length = JText::printf('SAVED_ITEMS', 3);
```

 The extra parameters used by the JText sprintf() and sprint() methods are not translated. If we want to translate them, we must do so before passing them.

Defining Translations

Different languages are identified by tags defined by RFC 3066. Each language has its own separate folder and will have many translation files, all of which will be held in the same folder. This table identifies some of the more common language tags:

Language	Tag
English, Britain	en-GB
French, France	fr-FR
German, Germany	de-DE
Portuguese, Portugal	Pt-PT
Spanish, Spain	es-ES

Translations are stored in INI files in the root language and administrator language directories. When we create extensions we use the languages tag in the extension manifest file to define the language files that we want to add. A complete description of the languages tag is available in the *Appendix*.

A translation file will normally consist of a header, describing the contents of the file, and a number of translations. Translations comprise two parts: a name in uppercase, and the translated text. The name of the translated string is the value we use to identify the translation when using the three JText translation methods.

If we use lowercase characters when defining the name of a translation, we will not be able to retrieve the translation.

When we create new extension translation files we must follow the standard naming convention, `tag.extensionName.ini`.

Imagine we want to create a German translation for the component 'My Extension'. We would have to name the translation file `de-DE.com_myextension.ini`. This is an example of what our file contents might look like:

```
# myExtension German Translation
# Version 1.0

WELCOME=Willkommen
HOW ARE YOU=Wie geht's?
THANK_YOU=Danke schön
SEEYOULATER=Bis später
POLITEHELLO=Guten tag %s
```

The names of the translations, to the left of the equal signs, have no specific naming convention. This examples use a mixture of different conventions we can use to name translations. Whatever way we choose to name our translations, we should always be consistent.

When we translate long pieces of text it is sometimes easier to use abbreviations. For example the name for an incorrect login is `LOGIN_INCORRECT`, but the translated text is far longer.

When we create and edit translation files, it is essential to ensure that the file is UTF-8 encoded. There are lots of text editors available that support UTF-8 multi-byte character encoding. One such editor is SciTE, a freely available source-code editor (`http://www.scintilla.org/SciTE.html`):

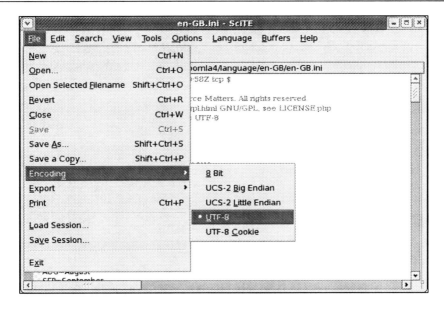

Debugging Translations

It can be useful when creating a new translation to enable language debugging. When language debugging is enabled, all the text that has passed through a translation mechanism will be highlighted and some additional information is displayed at the bottom of the page.

In order to enable language debugging, we must edit the global configuration. In the **System** tab we must set **Debug Language** to **Yes** (and the debug plugin must be enabled):

Successfully translated strings are encapsulated by bullet characters; strings translated from a constant are encapsulated in double exclamation marks; strings that are not translated are encapsulated in double question marks. Untranslated strings appear at the bottom of the page.

Using JavaScript Effects

Joomla! includes **mootools**—a powerful compact JavaScript framework. Mootools enables us to do many things, but it is used extensively in Joomla! to create client-side effects. Some of these, such as the accordion, are accessible via Joomla! classes. Others require special attention.

In some instances it may be necessary to manually add the mootools library to the document. We can do this using the JHTML `behavior.mootools` type:

```
JHTML::_('behavior.mootools');
```

JPane

A **pane** is an XHTML area that holds more than one set of information. There are two different types of panes:

- Tabs: Tabs provides a typical tabbed area with tabs to the top that are used to select different panes.
- Sliders: Sliders, based on the mootools accordion, are vertical selections of headings above panels that can be expanded and contracted.

We use the JPane class to implement panes. This example demonstrates a basic tabular pane with two panels:

```
$pane =& JPane::getInstance('Tabs');
echo $pane->startPane('myPane');
{
    echo $pane->startPanel('Panel 1', 'panel1');
    echo "This is Panel 1";
    echo $pane->endPanel();

    echo $pane->startPanel('Panel 2', 'panel2');
    echo "This is Panel 2";
    echo $pane->endPanel();
}
echo $pane->endPane();
```

There are essentially two elements to a pane: the pane itself and the panels within the pane. We use the methods `startPane()` and `endPane()` to signify the start and end of the pane. When we use `startPane()` we must provide one string parameter, which is a unique identifier used to identify the pane.

Panels are always created internally to a pane and use the methods `startPanel()` and `endPanel()`. We must provide the `startPanel()` method with two parameters, the name, which appears on the tab, and the panel ID.

This is a screenshot of the pane created from the given example code:

Had we wanted to create a slider pane instead of a tab pane when we used the `getInstance()` method, we would need to have supplied the parameter `Sliders` instead of `Tabs`. This is a screenshot of the same pane as a slider:

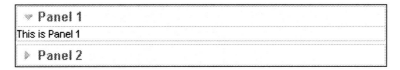

Panes are used extensively in Joomla!

 As a general rule, tabs are used for settings and sliders are used for parameters.

Tooltips

Tooltips are small boxes with useful information in them that appear in response to `onmouseover` events. They are used extensively in forms to provide more information about fields and their contents.

In the previous chapter, we discussed the use of JHTML. We use JHTML to render tips easily. There are two types that we use:

- `behavior.tooltip` is used to import the necessary JavaScript to enable tooltips to work and it does not return anything. We only ever need to call this type once in a page.

- `tooltip` is used to render a tooltip in relation to an image or a piece of text. There are six parameters associated with `tooltip`, of which five are optional. We will explore the more common uses of these parameters.

The most basic usage of `tooltip` returns a small information icon, which `onmouseover` displays a tooltip; as this example demonstrates:

```
echo JHTML::_('tooltip', $tooltip);
```

The next parameter allows us to define a title that is displayed at the top of the tooltip:

```
echo JHTML::_('tooltip', $tooltip, $title);
```

The next parameter allows us to select an image from the includes/js/ ThemeOffice directory. This example uses the warning.png image:

```
echo JHTML::_('tooltip', $tooltip, $title, 'warning.png');
```

The next obvious leap is to use text instead of an image and that is just what the next parameter allows us to do:

```
echo JHTML::_('tooltip', $tooltip, $title, null, $text);
```

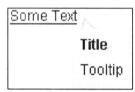

 There are some additional parameters all of which relate to using hypertext links. A full description of these is available in Chapter 8.

We can modify the appearance of tooltips using CSS. There are three style classes that we can use: .tool-tip, .tool-title, and .tool-text. The tooltip is encapsulated by the .tool-tip class, and the .tool-title and .tool-text styles relate to the title and the content.

This code demonstrates how we can add some CSS to the document to override the default tooltip CSS:

```
// prepare the cSS
$css = '/* Tooltips */
.tool-tip
{
    min-width: 100px;
    opacity: 0.8;
    filter: alpha(opacity=80);
    -moz-opacity: 0.8;
}

.tool-title
{
    text-align: center;
}

.tool-text {
    font-style: italic;
}';

// add the CSS to the document
$doc =& JFactory::getDocument();
$doc->addStyleDeclaration($css);
```

Fx.Slide

We will use the mootools `Fx.Slide` effect to demonstrate how we can build a PHP class to handle some mootools JavaScript. The `Fx.Slide` effect allows an XHTML element to seamlessly slide in and out of view horizontally or vertically.

We'll create a class named 'Slide', which will handle the `Fx.Slide` effect. The class will have five methods: `__construct()`, `startSlide()`, `endSlide()`, `button()`, and `addScript()`.

The way in which we use `Fx.Slide` requires us to add JavaScript to the window `domready` event. This event is fired once the **DOM (Document Object Model)** is ready. If we do not add the JavaScript in this way it is likely that we will incur problems. This is because if important parts of the DOM are missing, such as a slider, then the JavaScript will not be able to execute properly.

As the `domready` event can only trigger one event handler, we'll use the `addScript()` method as a static method to build up an event handler. This will allow us to use the Slider class to add multiple sliders without overwriting any previous `domready` event handlers.

This is the `Slide` class:

```
/**
 * Handles mootools Fx.Slide
 */
class Slide extends JObject
{
    /**
     * Slider mode: horizontal|vertical
     */
    var $_mode;

    /**
     * Constructor
     *
     * @param string Slide mode: horizontal|vertical
     */
    function __construct($mode = 'vertical')
    {
        $this->_mode = $mode;

        // import mootools library
        JHTML::_('behavior.mootools');
    }

    /**
     * Starts a new Slide
     *
     * @param string Slider ID
     * @param string Slider class
     * @return string Slider XHTML
     */
    function startSlider($id, $attributes = '')
    {
        // prepare slider JavaScript
        $js = "var ".$id." = new Fx.Slide('".$id."', {mode:
            '".$this->_mode."'});";
        Slide::addScript($js);

        // return the slider
        return '<div id="'.$id.'" '.$attributes.'>';
    }

    /**
     * Ends a slide
     *
```

```
 * @return string Slider XHTML
 */
function endSlide()
{
    // end the slide
    return '</div>';
}

/**
 * Creates a slide button
 *
 * @param string Button text
 * @param string Button Id
 * @param string Slider Id
 * @param string Button type: toggle|slideIn|slideOut|hide
 * @return string Slider XHTML action button
 */
function button($text, $buttonId, $slideId, $type = 'toggle')
{
    // prepare button JavaScript
    $js = "$('".$buttonId."').addEvent('click', function(e){"
        ."   e = new Event(e);"
        ."   ".$slideId.".".$type."();"
        ."   e.stop();"
        ."   });";
    Slide::addScript($js);

    // return the button
    return '<a id="'.$buttonId.'" href="#"
                name="'.$buttonId.'">'.$text.'</a>';
}

/**
 * Adds the JavaScript to the domready event and adds the event
        handler to the document
 *
 * @static
 * @param string JavaScript to add to domready event
 */
function addScript($script = null)
{
    // domready event handler
    static $js;

    if ($script)
    {
```

```
        // append script
        $js .= "\n".$script;
    }
    else
    {
        // prepare domready event handler
        $script="window.addEvent('domready',
                function(){".$js."});"

        // add event handler to document
        $document =& JFactory::getDocument();
        $document->addScriptDeclaration($script);
    }
    }
}
```

Notice that at no point do we tell the document that we need to include the mootools library. This is because mootools is always included when we render an HTML document.

So how do we use our newly created class? Well it's relatively simple. We use `startSlide()` and `endSlide()` to indicate a slider; anything that we output between these two calls will be within the slider. We use the `button()` method to output a button, which when pressed will perform a slider event on the slider. Once we have outputted all the sliders we intend to, we use the static `addScript()` method to add the necessary JavaScript to the document.

This example demonstrates how we can create two slides using our `Slide` class:

```
$slide = new Slide();

echo $slide->button('Toggle Slide 1', 'toggle1', 'slide1');
echo $slide->startSlider('slide1', 'class="greyBox"');
echo 'Slide 1';
echo $slide->endSlider();

echo $slide->button('Toggle Slide 2', 'toggle2', 'slide2');
echo $slide->startSlider('slide2', 'class="greyBox"');
echo 'Slide 2';
echo $slide->endSlider();

Slide::addScript();
```

Notice that we call the static `addScript()` method at the end with no parameters. This will add the necessary JavaScript to make our slides work. We should never call the `addScript()` method without parameters more than once.

The resultant slides look like this:

```
Toggle Slide 1
    Slide 1
Toggle Slide 2
    Slide 2
```

When we use the toggle buttons, the corresponding slides will vertically slide in and out. The buttons don't have to toggle the slides; when we create the buttons we can specify the button type as `toggle`, `slideIn`, `slideOut`, or `hide`. Buttons don't have to be placed above the slide that they control; we can place them anywhere.

Both of these particular slides are vertical, but there is nothing to prevent us from using horizontal and vertical slides on the same page. To do this we would require two `Slide` objects, one which when instantiated is passed the variable `horizontal`:

```
$slideHorizontal = new Slide('horizontal');
$slideVertical   = new Slide();
```

There are many different effects we can achieve using mootools, and we don't have to use a PHP class to implement them. If you want to take advantage of mootools then the best place to start is at the mootools website: `http://mootools.net/`.

Summary

In terms of extension design, we have explained how we can use redirects in conjunction with the application message queue to decrease the development work required and make the user experience friendlier. Use of both these elements should always be considered when we create component controller methods that modify data.

An important feature of component design is the overriding effect that menu parameters have on a page. This design can cause great consternation to administrators and developers alike who are unaware of the overriding effects. It's important, not only to understand this concept, but also to pass the necessary information on to your component administrators.

To help create clean and valid XHTML documents we are able to modify the document before it is sent to the browser. We do this using several different methods that allow us the ability to edit the document headers. We should never be tempted to 'whop in a tag', which should be in the document header!

Making our extensions multilingual is a very easy process, and doing so will greatly improve the quality of the extension. Even when an extension is intended solely for one language or we only have one translation we should still use the multilingual mechanisms. This will help to make the extension future proof.

We can use JavaScript to greatly enhance the appearance and user-friendly nature of our extensions. In addition to the existing implementations that allow us to harness the mootools JavaScript library, we can create our own PHP classes to handle other parts of the mootools library or, if we prefer, another JavaScript library. Exploring the mootools website is a good idea, if we want to create an original interface.

10
APIs and Web Services

The terms **API** (**Application Programming Interface**) and **web service** when used together describe how we access remote third-party services from an application. We can use web services and APIs in our Joomla! extensions.

This chapter explores some of the Joomla! API, specifically in relation to web services. We will also discuss some of the more common web services and take a more in-depth look at the Yahoo! Search API.

The final section of this chapter investigates how to implement web services of our own, using XML-RPC plugins. For more information about plugins please refer to Chapter 6.

XML

XML (Extensible Markup Language) is often used to send and receive web service data. It is important that we understand how XML is structured so that we can interact with such web services.

This example demonstrates how a typical XML document is constructed:

```
<?xml version="1.0" encoding="UTF-8" ?>
<rootNode>
    <subNode attr="Some Value">Some Data</subNode>
</rootNode>
```

The first line of code is known as the **XML declaration**. It declares that the document is XML, which version of XML it is, and what the character encoding is.

We then encounter the opening tag `rootNode`. XML documents have one root node that encapsulates the XML document.

Within `rootNode` is another node, `subNode`. This node contains some data and an attribute called `attr`. There is no limit to the depth of an XML document; this is one of the things that make XML so flexible.

When creating our own XML schemas, we can choose the names of all the tags and attributes that we are going to implement. Here are some quick pointers that should help when we come to define and write our own XML documents:

- Tag and attribute names are case sensitive.
- Tag and attribute names can only contain letters and numbers.
- Special characters within data must be encoded.
- Tags must be nested correctly.
- Attribute values must be encapsulated in double quotes.

Parsing

Joomla! provides us with three different XML parsers: DOMIT (DOM), JSimpleXML (Simple), and SimplePie (RSS/Atom). We will explore how to use the JSimpleXML parser because it is the most commonly used XML parser in Joomla!.

The first thing we need to do is obtain an instance of the parser. We do this using the JFactory method `getXMLParser()`. When we use this method we must tell it which XML parser we want to use:

```
$parser =& JFactory::getXMLParser('Simple');
```

The next step is to load and parse some XML. There are two ways in which we can do this; we can either load XML from a file or from a pre-existing string. This example demonstrates how we load XML from a file:

```
$parser->loadFile($pathToXML_File);
```

Loading XML from a string is a very similar process, as this example demonstrates:

```
$xml = '<?xml version="1.0" ?>
<catalogue name="Some Music Collection">
    <album>
        <title>Moving Pictures</title>
        <artist>Rush</artist>
        <year>1981</year>
        <tracks>
            <track length="4:33">Tom Sawyer</track>
            <track length="6:06">Red Barchetta</track>
            <track length="4:24">YYZ</track>
```

```
            <track length="4:19">Limelight</track>
            <track length="10:56">The Camera Eye</track>
            <track length="4:43">Witch Hunt</track>
            <track length="4:43">Vital Signs</track>
        </tracks>
    </album>
</catalogue>';

$parser->loadString($xml);
```

That is all we have to do in order to parse XML using the JSimpleXML parser!

 We can only use a JSimpleXML parser once; if we attempt to use the load methods more than once, we will encounter errors.

Once we have loaded some XML into the parser we can use the parser `document` attribute to interrogate the data. Before we rush into this, let's take a closer look at the XML we used in the previous example. The XML has been used to record the contents of a music catalogue, in this case 'Some Music Collection'.

The root node is `catalogue` and has one attribute, `name`, which is used to identify the catalogue in question. Next, there is an `album` node. This node encapsulates four other nodes: `name`, `artist`, `year`, and `tracks`. The `tracks` node identifies individual tracks in `track` nodes that identifies a name and the length of the track in a `length` attribute.

The parser `document` attribute is a JSimpleXMLElement object. JSimpleXMLElement objects are used to describe individual XML nodes. In the case of the `document` attribute, this is always the root node.

Having loaded the XML, we'll start interrogating the data by retrieving the name of the catalogue:

```
$document =& $parser->document;
$catalogue = $document->attributes('name');
```

Notice that the first thing we do is get a reference to the document attribute. Although we don't have to do this, it is generally easier than accessing the document directly using `$parser->document`.

Next we use the `attributes()` method. This method returns the value of an attribute from the current node. When we use this method we supply the name of the attribute we wish to retrieve, in this case `name`. If a requested attribute does not exist, `null` is returned.

If we want to retrieve all of the attributes associated with a node, we simply omit to pass the name of an attribute. This returns an associative array of the node's attributes.

What if, for some reason, there was a possibility that the root node wasn't of the expected type? We can use the `name()` method to get the name of the node type; in our case we are checking for a `catalogue` node:

```
if ($document->name() != 'catalogue')
{
    // handle invalid root node
}
```

Nodes can have child nodes; in the case of our example, the root node has one child node, `album`. The root node could well contain more `album` nodes. To retrieve child nodes we use the `children()` method. This method returns an array of nodes, each of which is a JSimpleXMLElement object:

```
$children = $document->children();
```

What if there was a mixture of `album` and `single` nodes? A `single` node would be essentially identical to the `album` node, except it would contain data specifically for music released as single.

We could use the `$children` array and determine the type of each node using the `name()` method. This is slightly cumbersome, and for larger XML files rather intensive.

Luckily for us, the child nodes are categorized into types. These are accessible through attributes that are named after the node type. So, in order to retrieve the `album` nodes from the root node we would do this:

```
$albums =& $document->album;
```

Our next task is to process the `$albums` array. As we iterate over the array, we will have to access the sub-nodes: `name`, `artist`, `year`, and `tracks`. We could use a similar method to that we used in the above example. However, there is another way.

We can use the `getElementByPath()` method to retrieve a node, provided that its path is unique. An album will only ever have one of each of these sub-nodes.

This example iterates over the `$albums` array and outputs `title`, `artist`, and `year` (we will deal with `tracks` shortly):

```
for ($i = 0, $c = count($albums); $i < $c; $i ++ )
{
    // get the album
    $album =& $albums[$i];
    echo '<div>';
```

```
    if ($name =& $album->getElementByPath('title'))
    {
        // display title
        echo '<strong>'.$name->data().'</strong><br/>';
    }
    if ($artist =& $album->getElementByPath('artist'))
    {
        // display the artist
        echo '<em>'.$artist->data().'</em>';
    }
    if ($year =& $album->getElementByPath('year'))
    {
        // display the year of release
        echo ' ('.$year->data().')';
    }
    echo '</div>';
}
```

Our use of the `getElementByPath()` method is clear. We simply pass the name of the child node. In more complex data structures we might want to use a deeper path. To do this we use forward slashes to separate the node names.

The other method that we use in the example is `data()`. This method returns any data that is contained within a node. Remember that the `getElementByPath()` method returns JSimpleXMLElement objects, and `title`, `artist`, and `year` are nodes in their own right.

We are now left with one last thing to do. We need to get the track listing for each album. To do this, we will iterate over the `tracks` node child nodes:

```
if ($tracks =& $album->getElementByPath('tracks'))
{
    // get the track listing
    $listing =& $tracks->track;

    // output listing table
    echo '<table><tr><th>Track</th><th>Length</th></tr>';
    for ($ti = 0, $tc = count($listing); $ti < $tc; $ti ++)
    {
        // output an individual track
        $track =& $listing[$ti];
        echo '<tr>';
        echo '<td>'.$track->data().'</td>';
        echo '<td>'.$track->attributes('length').'</td>';
        echo '</tr>';
    }
    echo '</table>';
}
```

We retrieve the `tracks` node using `getElementByPath()`. We get each track using the `track` attribute. We get the name of the track using the `data()` method. We get the track length attribute using the `attributes()` method.

We can use this example in conjunction with the previous example in order to output each album and its track listing. This example demonstrates what the resultant output could look like once some CSS has been applied:

Moving Pictures
Rush (1981)

Track	Length
Tom Sawyer	4:33
Red Barchetta	6:06
YYZ	4:24
Limelight	4:19
The Camera Eye	10:56
Witch Hunt	4:43
Vital Signs	4:43

Georgia Wonder 2006
Georgia Wonder (2006)

Track	Length
Genius	5:18
Two Weeks To Live	6:26
Falling Down	3:40
Hello Stranger	6:36
Carnival	4:06

Editing

In addition to interrogating XML data, we can modify data. Imagine we want to add a new album to the catalogue. We need to use the `addChild()` method; this method adds a new sub-node of a specified type and returns a reference to the new node:

```
$newAlbum =& $document->addChild('album');
```

Now that we have added the new `album` node, we need to add to the album the child nodes `title`, `artist`, `year`, and `tracks`:

```
$title  =& $newAlbum->addChild('title');
$artist =& $newAlbum->addChild('artist');
```

```
$year    =& $newAlbum->addChild('year');
$tracks =& $newAlbum->addChild('tracks');
```

The first three of these nodes require us to set the data values. Unfortunately, we can't do this when we create the node; we must do this afterwards using the `setData()` method:

```
$title->setData('Green Onions');
$artist->setData('Booker T. &amp; The MG\'s');
$year->setData('1962');
```

Those are the easy ones. It is toughest to deal with the `tracks` node. We need to add multiple `track` nodes to this node, each of which needs to include the track length as a parameter:

```
$track =& $tracks->addChild('track', array('length' => '1.45'));
$track->setData('Green Onions');
```

The second parameter that we pass to the `addChild()` method is an associative array of node parameters. In this case we specify the length of the track as 1.45. We then proceed to set the name of the track using the `setData()` method.

There is another way in which we could have added the `length` parameter to the `track` node. The `addAttribute()` method is used to add and modify attributes. Imagine we accidentally entered the wrong length value and we want to correct it:

```
$track->addAttribute('length', '2.45');
```

Saving

The last thing that we look at is how to save XML. Imagine we have parsed an existing XML file and we have made some alterations to the parsed XML. In order to apply these changes we need to convert the parsed document back into an XML string and save it to the original file.

The JSimpleXMLElement class includes a method called `toString()`. This method takes the parsed XML and converts it into an XML string:

```
// get the root node
$document =& $parser->document;
$xmlString = $document->toString();
```

The string returned from the `toString()` method is missing one vital part of an XML document, the XML declaration. We must manually add this to `$xmlString`:

```
$xmlString = '<?xml version="1.0" encoding="UTF-8" ?>'
             ."\n".$xmlString;
```

Now that we have prepared the new contents of the XML file, we need to save it. To do this, we use the JFile class that we import from the `joomla.filesystem` library:

```
if (!JFile::write($pathToXML_File, $xmlString))
{
    // handle failed file save
}
```

Yes, it really is as easy as that!

There are numerous methods in the JSimpleXMLElement class that allow us to manipulate and interrogate data. For a full description of all these methods please refer to the official documentation at: `http://api.joomla.org/`.

 It is vital when working with JSimpleXML and JSimpleXMLElement to pass objects by reference. Failing to do this can result in loss and corruption of data.

AJAX

AJAX (**Asynchronous JavaScript and XML**) is a JavaScript mechanism used to request data, normally in XML format, from which a page can be updated. We can use AJAX in our Joomla! extensions in a bid to improve the user experience.

Joomla! does not include any support specifically for AJAX. However, Joomla! does include the lightweight JavaScript framework, mootools. This framework includes useful client-side features for handling AJAX.

Before we ascend into the intricacies of JavaScript, we need to look at how we deal with an AJAX request. This might seem back to front, but it will make building the JavaScript far easier.

Response

To send a response we need to return an XML document. To do this we must use a component. Joomla! supports five core document response types:

- Error
- Feed
- HTML
- PDF
- RAW

XML is clearly missing from the list. This essentially leaves us with two options: we can either create another document type, or we can use a RAW document. We will use the RAW document type.

 The RAW format is used when a `format` value is provided in the request, and is not equal to Feed, HTML, PDF, or Error.

Before we start, we need to consider the data we are going to retrieve. We'll work with a basic table, `#__items`, with three fields, `id`, `name`, and `text`. When a request is made we return a single record from the table.

The first thing we need to do is create the RAW view. To do this we create a new PHP file called `view.raw.php` in the items view (the view in which we create this file is based on the entity).

Once we have created this, we need to add a view class to the file; this is the same as it would be for any other view in a component. Our next job is to build the `display()` method.

This method is essentially very similar to the `display()` method that would be located in the item's `view.html.php` file. The first thing we need to do in this method is retrieve the data:

```
// get the data
$data =& $this->get('Data');
```

No surprises here. This retrieves the data from the item model using the `getData()` method.

Now that we have the data we need to sort out the response. We'll use the JSimpleXMLElement class to build the XML response:

```
// import library
jimport('joomla.utilities.simplexml');

// create root node
$xml = new JSimpleXMLElement('item', array('id' => $data->id));
```

This creates a root node of type `item` with an attribute `id` populated with the value of the chosen item's ID. Now we can add some sub-nodes:

```
// add children
$name =& $xml->addChild('name');
$text =& $xml->addChild('text');

// set child data values
$name->setData($data->name);
$text->setData($data->text);
```

This adds two sub-nodes, `name` and `text`, and populates them with the item's corresponding values.

Now that we have built our XML response, our last task is to output the XML. We start with the XML declaration and then use the `toString()` method:

```
echo '<?xml version="1.0" encoding="UTF-8" ?>'."\n";
echo $xml->toString();
```

If we were to test this, we would experience a slight oddity; the response will be displayed as plain text. Although we have declared the content as XML, we have not declared the document header MIME type as `text/xml`. To do this we use the document `setMimeEncoding()` method:

```
$document =& JFactory::getDocument();
$document->setMimeEncoding('text/xml');
```

We're now ready to take a look at our XML response. We can do this by simply adding the string `&format=raw` to the end or our URI query string when viewing an item. This tells Joomla! that we want to use the RAW document and that we want to use the view class held in the `view.raw.php` file.

This is a screenshot of the resultant XML when we perform the request:

```
- <item id="10">
    <name>Example Item</name>
  - <text>
      <p> Lorem ipsum dolor sit amet, consectetuer adipiscing elit. Etiam eu odio ac nisi gravida vulputate.</p>
    </text>
  </item>
```

One important thing to notice here is the use of the XHTML paragraph tag within the text node. The paragraph tag is part of the text value within the database, but the XML doesn't treat it as an XML node. This is because when we use the JSimpleXMLElement `toString()` method, node data is automatically encoded.

Request

AJAX requests hinge on the JavaScript XMLHttpRequest class. This class is used to perform HTTP requests. In Joomla! we don't have to directly use this class because Joomla! comes with the mootools library.

There are a few different ways in which we can handle AJAX using mootools. We can use the Ajax class, the XHR class, or the `send()` method. We generally only use the Ajax and XHR classes directly if we are creating complex AJAX requests.

We will explore the `send()` method. This method is intended for use with form elements; it submits form data and allows us to handle the response when it is received. For more information about the Ajax and XHR classes please consult the official mootools documentation: `http://docs.mootools.net/`.

Before we delve into the JavaScript we need to create a form which can be used to initiate an AJAX request:

```
<form id="form1" method="post" action="<?php
        echo JRoute::_('index.php?option=com_mycomponent'); ?>">
    <input name="id" type="text" id="id" />
    <input name="format" type="hidden" id="format" value="raw" />
    <input name="view" type="hidden" id="view" value="wfaq" />
    <input name="Submit" type="submit" value="Submit" />
</form>
```

When we use this form we are rewarded with the XML document we described in the previous section.

OK, so this isn't the desired functionality; we don't want to be presenting users with XML documents. What we want to do now is add some JavaScript to handle the response.

It's important when we add the JavaScript that we encapsulate it within the window `domready` event. This ensures that the JavaScript isn't executed until the **DOM** (Document Object Model) is fully loaded:

```
// add mootools
JHTML::_('behavior.mootools');

$js = "window.addEvent('domready', function()
    {
        $('form1').addEvent('submit', function(e)
        {
            // Stop the form from submitting
            new Event(e).stop();

            // Update the page
            this.send({ update: $('update') });
        });
    });"
```

Before we add this JavaScript to the page, let's take the time to examine it in more detail.

The first thing we do is to invoke the mootools JHTML behavior. This ensures that the mootools library is loaded; without it the JavaScript we want to use will not work.

The first line of JavaScript adds a new event handler function to the window `domready` event. Within the event handler function we add a new `submit` event handler function to `form1`. This function will be executed when `form1` is submitted.

 We use the `$('someDOM_ID')` syntax to point the JavaScript at a specific DOM element identified by the supplied ID.

The first thing that this function does is prevent the form submission event from continuing. If we do not do this, the user will be redirected to the XML. The next thing we do is execute the `send()` method.

There are a number of settings that we can pass to the `send()` method. In this case we pass the DOM element we want to update, aptly named `update`. This brings us to our next task before we can use our JavaScript. We need to add an element to the document where the results from the AJAX request will be displayed:

```
<div id="update">Update Area</div>
```

We can now proceed and use the form button. This is a screenshot before the AJAX is put in action:

And, this is the screenshot after the AJAX is put in action:

| Submit |
| Example Item <p> Lorem ipsum dolor sit amet, consectetuer adipiscing elit. Etiam eu odio ac nisi gravida vulputate.</p> |

There is one rather obvious issue with this AJAX—the updated area has been populated with the RAW XML response. In some cases, this is useful because we don't have to return an XML response.

If we wanted to simply display some basic text, instead of responding with an XML document, we could respond with an XHTML snippet. However, we are trying to deal with an XML response. This means that we need to parse the XML and update the page accordingly.

This example builds on the JavaScript we used earlier. This time we have removed the `update` setting and added the `onComplete` setting. The `onComplete` setting is a function that is executed on completion of a request:

```
// Update the page
this.send({ onComplete: function(response, responseXML)
{
    alert('AJAX Response Received');
}});
```

The onComplete function is always passed two parameters, response and responseXML. response is the RAW response. responseXML is an XMLDocument object generated from the parsed response; this is the parameter in which we are interested.

Remembering what our XML response looked like, we need to access the root node, item. We then need to access the sub-nodes name and text. From these we can create an XHTML string with which to update the page.

This example shows how we do this using the responseXML object's documentElement property and the Element object getElementsByTagName() method and nodeValue property:

```
// Update the page
this.send({ onComplete: function(response, responseXML)
{
    // get the XML nodes
    var root = responseXML.documentElement;
    var name = root.getElementsByTagName('name').item(0);
    var text = root.getElementsByTagName('text').item(0);

    // prepare the XHTML
    var updateValue = '<div><strong>'
        + name.firstChild.nodeValue + '</strong></div><div>'
        + text.firstChild.nodeValue + '</div>';
}});
```

There is one last thing we need to do. We must update the page with the new value. We do this at the end of the onComplete function:

```
// Update the page
this.send({ onComplete: function(response, responseXML)
{
    // get the XML nodes
    var root = responseXML.documentElement;
    var name = root.getElementsByTagName('name').item(0);
    var text = root.getElementsByTagName('text').item(0);

    // prepare the XHTML
    var updateValue = '<div><strong>'
        + name.firstChild.nodeValue + '</strong></div><div>'
        + text.firstChild.nodeValue + '</div>';
```

```
    // update the page element 'update'
    $('update').empty().setHTML(updateValue);
}});
```

Now when we use the form, the update element content will be updated with an XHTML interpretation of the XML retrieved by the AJAX request. This screenshot depicts the resultant updated page with some CSS applied:

When we encounter difficulties creating JavaScript, it can be useful to use a JavaScript debugger. An example of such a debugger is the freely available Firebug, a utility for Firefox that provides us with a number of useful tools (http://www.getfirebug.com):

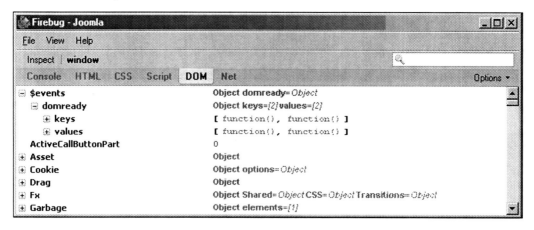

LDAP

LDAP (Lightweight Directory Application Protocol) is often associated with user authentication. While it is true that LDAP is used extensively for authentication, directory applications can be used for far more.

We'll stick with the user theme, but instead of authenticating, we'll use an LDAP connection to create a listing of users and their telephone numbers.

Joomla! provides us with the JLDAP class; this class allows us to connect to an LDAP server and browse the contents. To use the class we must import the corresponding library:

```
jimport('joomla.client.ldap');
```

Before we jump in head first, there is one more thing we need to take a look at. For the purpose of the following examples we will use an LDAP test server.

This screenshot depicts the LDAP tree we're interested in:

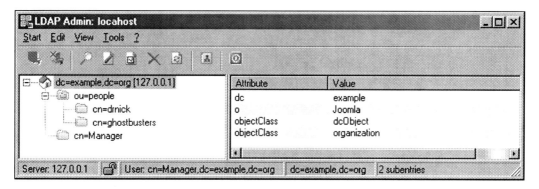

In order to interrogate the LDAP server we must connect to it. We'll assume the following settings are being used:

Setting	JLDAP Setting Name	Value
Host	host	192.168.0.2
Port	port	389
LDAP v3	use_ldapV3	True
TLS	negotiate_tls	False
No Referrals	no_referrals	True
Base DN	base_dn	dc=example,dc=org
User DN	users_dn	cn=[username],dc=example,dc=org

When we create a new JLDAP object we have the option to pass an object to it with the necessary settings. The easiest way to achieve this is normally via a JParameter object. This means that we can use the JParameter and JElement classes to allow an administrator to define the necessary LDAP settings:

```
$params = new JParameter($paramString);
$client = new JLDAP($params);
```

The next step is to connect to the LDAP server. This is relatively easy:

```
if (!$client->connect())
{
    // connection failed, handle it!
}
```

The `connect()` method instantiates a connection with the LDAP server. Once we are connected we need to bind to the server. There are two ways of doing this.

We can bind anonymously; this is generally less common because of security issues and privacy of data. To do this we use the `anonymous_bind()` method:

```
if (!$client->anonymous_bind())
{
    // bind failed, handle it!
}
```

Alternatively, we can bind as a user. In this example, we bind as the user `Manager` with the password `secret`, the default user and password in an OpenLDAP server:

```
if (!$client->bind('Manager', 'secret'))
{
    // bind failed, handle it!
}
```

You might be scratching your head because of the username. Should this should be a **DN (Distinguished Name)**? We don't have to provide the username as a DN because our settings include `users_dn`.

The value of this is `cn=[username],dc=example,dc=org`. When we bind to LDAP, we automatically use this string, substituting `[username]` with the bound username.

If we don't want to use this, when we connect, we can supply the full user DN and pass a third parameter. When this third parameter is `true`, no substitution based on the `users_dn` setting occurs:

```
if (!$client->bind('cn=Manager,dc=example,dc=org', 'secret', true))
{
    // bind failed, handle it!
}
```

Once we have successfully bound to the server we can start looking for LDAP objects. To do this we need to use the `search()` method. This method searches the base DN and all **OUs (Organization Units)** within it. When we perform a search we must define one or more filters.

The filter syntax is defined by RFC 2254. For more information please visit: `http://www.ietf.org/rfc/rfc2254.txt?number=2254`.

We are looking specifically for `Person` objects. The filter we use to describe this is `(objectClass=Person)`. This will filter out any LDAP objects that are not of the class `Person`:

```
$filters = array('(objectClass=Person)');
$results = $client->search($filters);
```

Notice that `$filters` is an array. This is because we are able to supply multiple searches at once. When we do this the results are combined into a single result set.

If we don't want to search the base DN, we can specify a different DN to search within. The screenshot we showed earlier describes users in the `people` OU. We can restrict the search to this OU:

```
$people = 'ou=people,dc=example,dc=org'
$results = $client->search($filters, $people);
```

Once the search has been performed, `$results` is populated with an array of results. Each result is represented as an associative array. Our next task is to present the results:

```
for ($i = 0, $c = count($results); $i < $c; $i ++)
{
    $result =& $results[$i];
    echo '<div>';
    echo '<strong>'.$result['givenName'][0].'</strong><br />';
    echo $result['description'][0].'<br />';
    echo '<em>'.$result['telephoneNumber'][0].'</em>';
    echo '</div>';
}
```

Notice that each result array element is an array in its own right. This is because LDAP allows multiple values for object attributes. The only exception to this is the DN; LDAP objects can only have one location.

Our example assumes that the object attributes `givenName`, `description`, and `telephoneNumber` are always present in the results. In a production environment, we would test the attributes to ensure they are present.

If we apply some suitable CSS when we output the results we may be presented with something like this:

Ghost Busters
Who you gonna call?
555-2368

Dr Nick
This will make the operation seem like a wonderful dream
555-NICK

There are many other things that we can achieve using the JLDAP class. For a complete description of all of the available methods please refer to the official JLDAP documentation: `http://api.joomla.org/Joomla-Framework/Client/JLDAP.html`.

Email

Email has revolutionized communication. Joomla! provides us with the JMail class, which allows us to send emails. JMail supports three different mechanisms for sending email: the PHP mail function, Sendmail, and SMTP.

There is a global JMail object that we can access using the JFactory method `getMailer()`. This object is configured with the global mail settings that administrators edit through the Global Configuration Server settings:

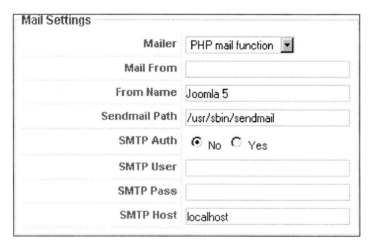

The first thing we need to do when we come to send an email is retrieve the JMail object and set the sender's email address:

```
$mailer =& JFactory::getMailer();
$mailer->setSender('example@example.org');
```

There are two ways in which we can specify the email address. We can either use a string, as in the given example, or we can use an array that defines the email address and name:

```
$sender = array('example@example.org', 'example')
$mailer =& JFactory::getMailer();
$mailer->setSender($sender);
```

If we want to, we can add reply-to addresses. Unlike setting the sender, the email addresses must either be an array of strings or an array of arrays:

```
$reply = array('example@example.org', 'Example');
$mailer->addReplyTo($reply);

$reply0 = array('example@example.org', 'Example');
$reply1 = array('example@example.org', 'Example');
$replies = array($reply0, $reply1);
$mailer->addReplyTo($replies);
```

We can add recipients in three ways:

- As a normal recipient: Using addRecipient()
- As a BCC (Blind Carbon Copy) recipient: Using addBCC()
- As a CC (Carbon Copy) recipient: Using addCC()

Unlike the sender and reply-to address we cannot define the recipient email address name. We either provide an email string or an array of email strings:

```
$mailer->addRecipient('foo@example.org');

$recipients = array('bar@example.org', ' baz@example.org ');
$mailer->addRecipient($recipients);
```

Out next task is to set the subject line and the body text of the email. We do this using the setSubject() and setBody() methods:

```
$mailer->setSubject('Some Email');
$mailer->setBody('Lorem ipsum dolor sit amet.');
```

By default email body content is always plain text. We can modify the body to support HTML using the IsHTML() method; this sets the body MIME type to text/html:

```
$mailer->IsHTML(true);
```

Our final task is to send the email. This is done using the Send() method. This will send the email using the preconfigured email options:

```
if ($mailer->Send() !== true)
{
    // an error has occurred
    // a notice will have been raised by $mailer
}
```

That's it, we're all done. We can now prepare and send emails! There are just a few more things that can be useful to know.

If we want to modify the way in which the email will be sent, we can use the useSendmail() and useSMTP() methods. These methods, when supplied with the proper parameters, are used to set the mechanism by which the mailer will send emails.

If you have recognized any of the methods so far, you have probably worked with the open-source PHPMailer library. The JMail class is an extension of the PHPMailer class. If you prefer, you can use the PHPMailer class. To do this you will first have to import the necessary library:

```
jimport('phpmailer.phpmailer');
$mailer = new PHPMailer();
```

Be aware that when doing this the object will not be automatically loaded with the global email settings.

There is one last method that we will discuss. In addition to the JMail class, there is a static JMailHelper class. This class mainly consists of methods designed to clean data before adding to an email (we don't have to use these, JMail takes care of it for us).

There is another method in the helper, isEmailAddress(). This method confirms that an email address is of a valid format. This is especially helpful if we ever ask users to input their email address:

```
if (!JMailHelper::isEmailAddress($someEmailAddress))
{
    $this->setError(JText::_('INVALID_EMAIL_ADDRESS'));
    return false;
}
```

If we haven't used the JMail class earlier in the script, we will need to import the JMail library before we use the JMailHelper class:

```
jimport('joomla.utilities.mail');
```

File Transfer Protocol

FTP has long been established as the standard way for administrators to transfer files to their web servers. Joomla! provides us with the JFTP class, which can be used to connect to FTP servers and perform common functions.

The main purpose of this class is to overcome problems with access rights when working with the local file system. When FTP access is enabled in the site configuration, Joomla! will attempt to use FTP instead of PHP file system functions.

Whenever we connect to an FTP server we require certain settings to be in place. If we want to use the FTP settings defined in the global configuration, we can use the JClientHelper class to easily access these settings.

This example demonstrates how we can use JClientHelper static `getCredentials()` method to get the FTP settings:

```
jimport('joomla.client.helper');
$FTP_Settings = JClientHelper::getCredentials('ftp');
```

The JClientHelper static `getCredentials()` method returns an associative array with the following keys: `enabled`, `host`, `port`, `user`, `pass`, and `root`. We briefly mentioned earlier that the global FTP access can be enabled and disabled; the `enabled` key provides us with the value of this option. We must never attempt to use the global FTP settings if this value is not equivalent to 1:

```
if ($FTP_Settings['enabled'] == 1)
{
    // It is OK, we can use the global FTP settings
}
```

Of course we don't have to use the global FTP settings. We can just as easily use some other settings, perhaps specified in a component configuration.

To use the JFTP class we must first import and create a new instance of the class. We use the static JTFP `getInstance()` method to create a new instance of the class. This example does just the same:

```
jimport('joomla.client.ftp');

$client =& JFTP::getInstance($FTP_Settings['host'],
    $FTP_Settings['port'],
```

```
    null,
    $FTP_Settings['user'],
    $FTP_Settings['pass']);
```

The third parameter, in the above example set to `null`, is an optional associative array of FTP options. This array can contain the `type` and `timeout` keys:

- `type` is used to determine the FTP connection mode, either of `FTP_AUTOASCII`, `FTP_BINARY`, or `FTP_ASCII`; the default mode is `FTP_BINARY`.

- `timeout` is used to set the maximum time, in seconds, which should lapse before the FTP connection timeouts. PHP versions prior to 4.3.0 do not support the `timeout` option.

The great thing about using the `getInstance()` method is that the returned object will already have created a connection to the FTP server and authenticated itself. Obviously there may be occasions when this fails. To ensure that the JFTP object has successfully connected we can use the `isConnected()` method:

```
if (!$client->isConnected())
{
    // handle failed FTP connection
}
```

Most of the available JFTP methods are self explanatory and are standard FTP type functions. This table describes some of the more common methods we can use with a JFTP object:

Method	Description
quit	Closes the FTP connection
pwd	Determines the current working directory. When using the global settings the root key value should indicate the location of the Joomla! installation.
chdir	Changes the current working directory
rename	Renames a file or folder
chmod	Changes a file or folder mode (permissions)
delete	Removes a file or folder
mkdir	Creates a new folder
create	Creates a new file
read	Reads the contents of a file
get	Retrieves a file
store	Stores a file on the server
listNames	List the names of files in the current working directory
listDetails	List the names of the files and folders in the current working directory

Web Services

There are many Web Service APIs that we can use in conjunction with Joomla!. This is a list of few of the more common Web Service APIs that we are likely to use:

- eBay
- Google (Calendar, Checkout, Maps, Search)
- Microsoft (Live, MSN, XBOX)
- Yahoo! (Mail, Maps, Search)

The API and service that we use determines the way in which we handle the API. We will take a look at the Yahoo! Search API. Before we start, we need to discuss the Yahoo! Application ID.

Yahoo! uses a unique ID to identify the applications that use its API. If you intend to use the Yahoo! API, it is important that you register your application before you start development. This will ensure that you are able to obtain the desired ID.

 Most Web Service APIs require us to use an ID of some description. This allows the owners of the API to analyze the usage of their services.

For the purposes of this example we will use the application ID YahooDemo — this is the default ID used when demonstrating the use of the Yahoo Search API.

The first thing that we need to do to create our Yahoo! Search is build the request query that we will use to obtain the results. This example assumes that we have used a search box named yahooSearch:

```
// get the search terms
$query = rawurlencode(JRequest::getString('yahooSearch',
                    'Joomla!', 'DEFAULT', JREQUEST_ALLOWRAW));
```

We use the PHP rawurlencode() method because $query will be used in a URI. We use the JREQUEST_ALLOWRAW mask so as not to lose any data from the request. There is a full explanation of the JRequest masks in Chapter 11.

We make the assumption that if no search terms are provided we want to search for Joomla!. In reality we would probably redirect the user.

Next we need to create the request URI from which we will obtain the
search results:

```
// Prepare the request URI
$request = 'http://search.yahooapis.com/WebSearchService/V1/
            webSearch?appid=YahooDemo&query='.$query.'&results=4';
```

Now that we have the URI we can proceed to interact with the Yahoo! API. We
use the PHP function `file_get_contents()` to perform the request and retrieve
the results:

```
// Perform search
if (!$xml = file_get_contents($request))
{
    // handle failed search request
}
```

The results of the request, if successful, are returned as an XML document. How we
choose to interpret these results is up to us. We explained how to use the JSimpleXML
parser earlier in the chapter. We can use it to interpret the Yahoo! results:

```
$parser =& JFactory::getXMLParser('Simple');
$parser->loadString($xml);
$results =& $parser->document->Result;
```

Now that we have a parsed XML document, we can process the search results.
The `$results` variable becomes an array of `result` nodes; these are the nodes that
Yahoo! uses to encapsulate each result.

We will keep the processing simple, and output the results directly to screen as an
ordered list. This example uses the result sub-nodes `ClickUrl`, `Title`, `Summary`,
and `DisplayUrl`. In each case, we always access the zero element; we can do this
because we know that only one node of each of these types will ever be present in a
`result` node:

```
echo '<ol>';
for ($i = 0, $c = count($results); $i < $c; $i ++)
{
    $result =& $results[$i];
    echo '<li>';
    echo '<strong><a href="'.$result->ClickUrl[0]->data().'"
                target="_blank">'.$result->Title[0]-
                >data().'</a></strong><br />';
    echo $result->Summary[0]->data().'<br />';
    echo $result->DisplayUrl[0]->data();
    echo '</li>';
}
echo '</ol>';
```

If we add some CSS to our document we can create a highly customizable search facility, which a user need not even know is based on the Yahoo! API:

I. **Joomla!**
    Joomla! - Content Management System and Web Application Framework ... If you have some Joomla! ... With today's release of Joomla! ...
    www.joomla.org/

II. **Joomla! - What is Joomla! ?**
    Joomla! - Content Management System and Web Application Framework ... Joomla! ... Once Joomla! ...
    www.joomla.org/content/view/12/26/

III. **Joomla! - Wikipedia, the free encyclopedia**
     Encyclopedia article about the Joomla! CMS system, including history and features. ... Joomla! ... In the project's roadmap, the core developers say Joomla! ...
     en.wikipedia.org/wiki/Joomla

IV. **Joomla! Help Site**
    Joomla! - Content Management System and Web Application Framework ... The Joomla! ... has successfully led the Documentation Team since before the birth of Joomla! ...
    help.joomla.org/

This example has demonstrated how easy it is to use web services. Although this example is not particularly advanced, it shows how quickly we can create very powerful tools for Joomla!.

Building a Web Service (XML-RPC Plugin)

XML-RPC is way in which systems can call procedures on remote systems via HTTP using XML to encode data. Joomla! includes an XML-RPC server that we can extend using plugins. For more information about plugins, please refer to Chapter 6.

 The XML-RPC server will only function if the 'Enable Web Services' option in the Global Configuration is enabled.

Before we begin, it is important to understand that Joomla! relies heavily on the phpxmlrpc library, which is available from: `http://phpxmlrpc.sourceforge.net`. Due to this, some of the conventions we will encounter when building XML-RPC plugins will differ from the rest of Joomla!.

When we briefly discussed XML-RPC in Chapter 6, we described an event that enables us to define XML-RPC web service calls. This is only one part of XML-RPC plugins; the second part is a static class or group of functions that handle an XML-RPC request.

Before we delve any further, we need to be familiar with the XML-RPC data types. There are six simple data types and two compound data types. This table describes the six simple data types:

Type	Variable	Description
base64	`$xmlrpcBase64`	Base64 binary encoded data
boolean	`$xmlrpcBoolean`	True or false: 0 = false, 1 = true
dateTime.iso8601	`$xmlrpcDateTime`	Date and time in iso8601 format, for example YYYYMMDDTHH:MM:SS
double	`$xmlrpcDouble`	Floating-point number
int/i4	`$xmlrpcInt or $xmlrpcI4`	Integer
string	`$xmlrpcString`	ASCII text

This table describes the two compound data types:

Type	Variable	Description
array	`$xmlrpcArray`	Array
struct	`$xmlrpcStruct`	Associative array (hash)

Compound data types are so called because they combine the other types. `array` and `struct` data types encapsulate multiple values, each of which can be of any data type.

If you are wondering exactly why we care about the different data types in XML-RPC, it is because we need them in order to create a signature for the different XML-RPC calls. A signature defines the data that is outputted and inputted by a web service call.

We will start by creating a plugin called 'foobar' that will perform some basic mathematical functions. The first thing we need to do is create a handler for the `onGetWebServices` event:

```
$mainframe->registerEvent('onGetWebServices', 'plgXMLRPCFoobar');

/**
 * Gets the available XML-RPC functions
 *
 * @return array Definition of the available XML-RPC functions
 */
function plgXMLRPCFoobar()
{
    // get the XMl-RPC types
    global $xmlrpcI4, $xmlrpcInt, $xmlrpcBoolean, $xmlrpcDouble,
```

```
        $xmlrpcString, $xmlrpcDateTime, $xmlrpcBase64,
        $xmlrpcArray, $xmlrpcStruct, $xmlrpcValue;

    // return the definitions
    return array
      (
        // addition service
        'foobar.add' => array
        (
            'function' => 'plgXMLRPCFoobarServices::add',
            'docstring' => 'Adds two numbers.',
            'signature' => array(array($xmlrpcStruct, $xmlrpcDouble,
                                       $xmlrpcDouble))
        ),
        // subtraction service
        'foobar.subtract' => array
        (
            'function' => 'plgXMLRPCFoobarServices::subtract',
            'docstring' => 'Multiplies two numbers.',
            'signature' => array(array($xmlrpcStruct, $xmlrpcDouble,
                                       $xmlrpcDouble))
        )
      );
}
```

This example is a little busy, and what it is doing is less than obvious! So let's break it down into its component parts. The first thing that we do in the `plgXMLRPCFoobar()` function is to declare a bunch of variables global.

We described these variables in the tables about XML-RPC data types. There is one addition to this list, `$xmlrpcValue`; this variable is used to encapsulate all other data types. This is an example of an integer in an XML-RPC document:

```
<value><int>666</int></value>
```

 Technically, we do not have to use the type variables because they are only strings. For example, the value of `$xmlrpcDouble` is `double`. However, using the variables helps ensure compatibility should the values of these variables change.

Once we have made these variables global, we build an associative array and return it. The keys in this associative array are the names that a client would use to invoke an XML-RPC service call. In our example, we define two keys: `foobar.add` and `foobar.subtract`.

The values for these keys are also associative arrays. This table describes the keys we use in these arrays:

Key	Description
docstring	A string describing the purpose of the XML-RPC call
function	The function that Joomla! will execute when an XML-RPC response of this nature is received
signature	Defines the return type and the input required from and XMLRPC request

To explain this further, we will use the `foobar.add` array as an example:

- The `function` is defined as `plgXMLRPCFoobarServices::add`. This means that when a `foobar.add` call is made we will execute the static `add()` method in the plgXMLRPCFoobarServices class.

 An XML-RPC function can be a static method in a class or a function.

- The `docstring` is nice and easy; it tells us that this web service call 'Adds two numbers'. This is only a human-readable string, and generally does not carry any meaning to the client machine itself.

- The `signature`, used to define the input and output of the call, is an array. The output value is always the first value in the array. The remaining elements describe the input values that a client must provide when calling the service.

In our example, the `signature` tells us that the call will return a struct, and requires two double input values. This is what the `foobar.add` signature value looks like:

```
array(array($xmlrpcStruct, $xmlrpcDouble, $xmlrpcDouble))
```

You may have noticed that the `signature` is an array of arrays. This is because service call can have multiple signatures. Imagine we want to allow the addition of two or three values; we would need to define two signatures, as this example demonstrates:

```
array(
    array($xmlrpcStruct, $xmlrpcDouble, $xmlrpcDouble),
    array($xmlrpcStruct, $xmlrpcDouble, $xmlrpcDouble,
        $xmlrpcDouble)
)
```

Now that we have defined the web service calls, we need to create the procedures that drive them. For our example, we need to create the static methods `add()` and `subtract()` in a class named plgXMLRPCFoobarServices. It is normal to implement these procedures within the same class as the event handler.

When we define the parameters for these methods, we must define the same number of parameters as we did in the signatures. This example shows how we might implement the `add()` and `subtract()` methods:

```
**
 * Foobar XML-RPC service handler
 *
 * @static
 */
class plgXMLRPCFoobarServices
{
    /**
     * Adds values together
     *
     * @static
     * @param float xmlrpcDouble
     * @param float xmlrpcDouble
     * @return xmlrpcresp xmlrpcDouble
     */
    function add($value1, $value2)
    {
        global $xmlrpcDouble, $xmlrpcStruct;

        // determine the sum of the two values
        $product = $value1 + $value2;

        // build the struct response
        $result = new xmlrpcval(array(
            'value1' => new xmlrpcval($value1, $xmlrpcDouble),
            'value2' => new xmlrpcval($value2, $xmlrpcDouble),
            'product' => new xmlrpcval($product, $xmlrpcDouble)
            ), $xmlrpcStruct);

        // encapsulate the response value and return it
        return new xmlrpcresp($result);

    }

    /**
     * Subtracts a value from another
     *
```

```
 * @static
 * @param float xmlrpcDouble
 * @param float xmlrpcDouble
 * @return xmlrpcresp xmlrpcDouble
 */
function subtract($value1, $value2)
{
    global $xmlrpcDouble, $xmlrpcStruct;

    // determine the difference of the two values
    $product = $value1 - $value2;

    // build the struct response
    $result = new xmlrpcval(array(
        'value1' => new xmlrpcval($value1, $xmlrpcDouble),
        'value2' => new xmlrpcval($value2, $xmlrpcDouble),
        'product' => new xmlrpcval($product, $xmlrpcDouble)
        ), $xmlrpcStruct);

    // encapsulate the response value and return it
    return new xmlrpcresp($result);
}
}
```

The example introduces two classes that are fundamental to creating a response.

The xmlrpcval class is used to define an XML-RPC value. When we construct a class of this type, we pass two parameters, the value itself and the value type.

The xmlrpcresp class is used to encapsulate an XML-RPC response. When we construct a class of this type, we pass one parameter, the return xmlrpcval object. If an error is encountered, there is a different set of parameters that we can pass. For more information about this, please refer to the official phpxmlrpc documentation: http://phpxmlrpc.sourceforge.net/doc/.

This means that our static example methods will both return a struct value. The returned struct value will be populated with three values—value1, value2, and product. We return value1 and value2 so that the client can verify that nothing has corrupted the input values during transport.

To test an XML-RPC plugin we can use the phpxmlrpc debugger, which is available at http://phpxmlrpc.sourceforge.net/.

The debugger enables us to make XML-RPC calls to remote systems and view the responses. The path to the Joomla! XML-RPC server is identical to that of the root of the installation plus the folder xmlrpc.

This is a screenshot of the debugger when used to list available methods on a Joomla! installation located at 192.168.0.6 (the exact output will depend upon which XML-RPC plugins that are enabled):

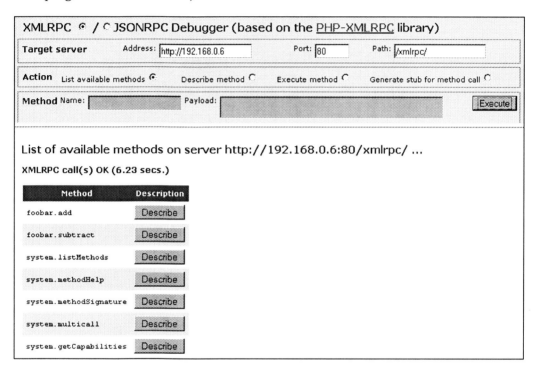

Next to each method is a **Describe** button. We can use this to find out more information about a method and to generate the payload necessary to execute the method. To execute an individual method we must change the action to **Execute method** and complete the payload field as necessary.

This screenshot depicts the debugger when used to execute the **foobar.add** method:

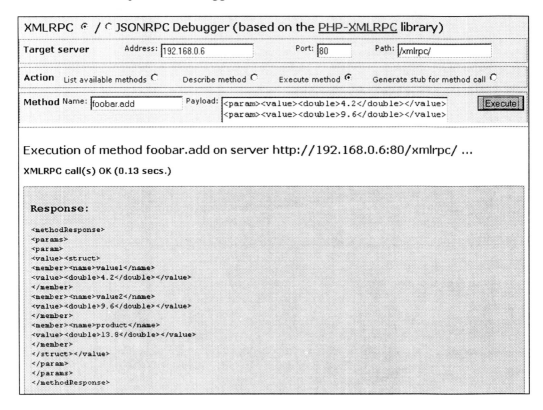

In this instance, we pass the double values 4.2 and 9.6. The response shows the output from the XML-RPC server. The response, as specified by the signature, is a struct. It contains three values—value1, value2, and product.

If you experience problems when building XML-RPC plugins, you should try setting the debugger **Show debug info** option to **More**. This will enable a more verbose output, including the RAW input and response.

Joomla! includes an XML-RPC client, located in xmlrpc/client.php. To use this client, debugging must be enabled in the Global Configuration. The client is relatively simple; the phpxmlrpc debugger provides us with a far more powerful mechanism with which to interrogate the XML-RPC server.

Summary

XML is integral to many web services. It is essential if we intend to use a web service that relies on XML that we understand how to parse and navigate a parsed XML document.

The provided XML parsers make Joomla! especially flexible when it comes to handling XML. In this chapter, we described how to use the JSimpleXML parser. Before we use this parser, we should always consider any possible benefits of using the other parsers that are easily available to us.

AJAX has become a bit of a 'buzz word' and as a result it is sometimes used inappropriately just because we can. Before we implement any AJAX we should always consider the impact and suitability of using it.

Two important things to consider are client support and search engine indexing. Client browsers that do not support AJAX should be provided with an alternative solution. Search engines cannot execute JavaScript so when they index a page they will fail to index any data returned by AJAX requests.

LDAP is a very powerful technology. Its main use as an authentication method and as a network management tool often means that we use it as a data source. However LDAP is bi-directional and we can write to LDAP servers provided we have sufficient access rights.

For networks that use LDAP directory applications, the use of easily accessible LDAP management and interrogation tools can be invaluable.

Using email is a common task. Joomla!'s JMail class provides us with the power to send emails. Administrators often want to enable notification within extensions so that they are not required to continually log in to a system.

The JFTP class provides us with an additional way of accessing a file system. In addition to using FTP with remote servers, we can use FTP locally, when enabled, to give us better control over our Joomla! installation. We normally use the classes located in the joomla.filesystem library when dealing with the local file system.

There are many other APIs and web services available on the Internet. Simple integration of these is often 'lapped up' by administrators. Beyond this, we can seamlessly use web services to improve the functionality of our extensions drastically.

11
Error Handling and Security

Security and graceful error handling is imperative to any good computer system. For systems like Joomla!, which are often available on the World Wide Web, poor security or incorrect error handling carries a high risk factor, and that risk is often higher when using third-party extensions.

This chapter focuses on four main subjects:

- Errors, Warnings, and Notices
- Dealing with CGI Request Data
- Access Control
- Attacks

Handling errors is a common task; we will explore the different error levels, which we use to classify our errors, and ways in which we can modify the error levels and how they are handled.

Many security flaws in Joomla! extensions originate from inadequate processing of input data. We will explore how we should access CGI request data and how we can process that data to ensure that it does not pose a security risk.

We use access control to restrict, and allow, the tasks that users can perform. We will investigate the Joomla! access control mechanisms and how we can implement them in our extensions.

The final subject that we will look at is attacks. Attacks are malicious attempts to break a system. There are many ways in which an attacker can go about this; we will stick to the most common methods.

Errors, Warnings, and Notices

When we encounter errors it is important that we take some counter action. Joomla! provides a common error handling mechanism, which we access using the static JError class. JError takes advantage of the `phpTemplate` library, in particular the `patError` and `patErrorManager` classes. A complete description of the JError class and all of its methods is available in the *Appendix*.

Error Level	Error Type	Class Method
1 (E_ERROR)	Error	JError::raiseError()
2 (E_WARNING)	Warning	JError::raiseWarning()
8 (E_NOTICE)	Notice	JError::raiseNotice()

Level E_ERROR errors get an error document (JDocumentError), set the error, and render the document, sending the response and terminating the application. When we invoke any of the raise methods we pass two parameters, an error code and an error message.

The error code is a string that is used to identify the error. Error codes are rendered using one of three templates `403.php`, `404.php`, and `500.php`. If the error code is `403` (Access Denied) or `404` (Page could not be found), we use the `403.php` and `404.php` templates respectively. These templates include some additional standard text that describes the normal reasons for receiving a `403` or a `404` error. All other error codes use the `500.php` (Internal Server Error) template:

```
JError::raiseError('403', JText::_('Access Forbidden'));
```

403 - Access denied

You may not be able to visit this page because of:

1. An **out-of-date bookmark/favourite**
2. A search engine that has an **out-of-date listing for this site**
3. A **mis-typed address**
4. You have **no access** to this page
5. The requested resource was **not found**

Please try one of the following pages:

* Home Page

Not Authorised

```
JError::raiseError('500', JText::_('An error has occurred.'));
```

Level `E_ERROR` errors (`JError::raiseError()`), are for fatal errors. When a non fatal error occurs we can use the weaker, warning and notice levels. These two levels are handled in the same way, but it is still useful to make the distinction between the two; it helps aid classification of errors and the process of debugging:

```
JError::raiseWarning('ERROR_CODE', JText::_('Look out! There is a
                                giant boxing kangaroo behind you!'));
```

This is perhaps not the most useful of messages and perhaps a little unlikely, but you get the idea. Exactly how you choose to classify your errors is up to you. Classification of errors tends to be relatively intuitive. An error that is not fatal, but should not have occurred, is a warning. An error that is not fatal, and is more or less expected to occur at some point is a notice.

The error code we used in the last example, `ERROR_CODE`, may seem a little odd. We can specify any error code we want; the exact intricacies of how Joomla! core error codes are going to be classified has not been fully decided. In the short-term Joomla! core errors are using scheme error codes and `SOME_ERROR_CODE`.

Return Values

Using the three methods we also get a return value, a JException object. The JException class contains all sorts of useful information about an error; including the error level, error code, and error message. When we raise an `E_ERROR` level error the object will also contain back-trace information, such as the file and line the error occurred on.

There are many methods in other classes that, if an error occurs, will return the result. We can test the return value of a method to see if it is an error using the `JError::isError()` method. As an example, the JController `execute()` method returns an error if no method is mapped to the task we try to execute:

```
$result = $SomeCOntroller->execute('someTask');
if(JError::isError($result))
{
    // handle invalid task
}
```

Customizing Error Handling

The handling of errors is not set in stone. We can modify the way each of the levels is handled and we can add new levels. We can choose any of the following modes (maximum of one mode per error level):

Mode	Description
Ignore	Error is ignored
Echo	Prints the JException message to screen
Verbose	Prints the JException message and back-trace information to screen
Die	Terminates the application and prints the JException message to screen
Message	Adds a message to the application queue
Log	Adds a log entry to the application error log
Trigger	Triggers a PHP error
Callback	Calls a static method in another class

To modify the error handling of an existing error level we can use the `JError::setErrorHandling()` method. This example redefines the notice error to use the Ignore mode. Some modes require a third parameter, an array of options specific to the mode:

```
JError::setErrorHandling(E_NOTICE, 'Ignore');
```

To define a new error level we can use the `JError::registerErrorLevel()` method. If the error level is already defined the method will return false:

```
define('MY_ERROR', 666);
if( !JError::registerErrorLevel(MY_ERROR, 'My Extension Error',
                                            'Message') )
{
    JError::raiseError('SOME_ERROR', JText::_('Error level already
                                    defined').' ['.MY_ERROR.']');
}
```

Once we have defined a new error level, to raise an error of that level we can use the `JError::raise()` method. The `raise()` method can be used with any of the defined error levels, including `E_ERROR`, `E_WARNING`, and `E_NOTICE`:

```
JError::raise(MYEXT_ERROR, 'SOME_ERROR', JText::_('Look out!
                    It\'s those boxing kangaroos again!'));
```

Dealing with CGI Request Data

It is essential that we sanitize incoming data (i.e. remove any unexpected data and ensure the data is of an expected type). Joomla! provides us with the static class JRequest, which eliminates the need to directly access the request hashes `$_GET`, `$_POST`, `$_FILES`, `$_COOKIE`, and `$_REQUEST`. Using JRequest to its full potential we can perform useful data preprocessing.

Preprocessing CGI Data

To access a request value we must use the static `JRequest::getVar()` method. In this example we get the value of the input `id`:

```
$id = JRequest::getVar('id');
```

If we want to, we can define a default value; this is the value that will be returned if the request value is not defined. In this example we use the value `0` if the request `id` is not set:

```
$id = JRequest::getVar('id', 0);
```

By default `JRequest::getVar()` obtains data from the `$_REQUEST` hash. We can specify the source hash of the data as any one of the following: `GET`, `POST`, `FILES`, `COOKIE`, and `DEFAULT`. If we specify `DEFAULT` or an unknown source hash, the data will be retrieved from the `$_REQUEST` hash. In this example we get the data from the `$_POST` hash:

```
$id = JRequest::getVar('id', 0, 'POST');
```

Casting is a mechanism we can use to guarantee that a variable is of a specific type. We have a choice of the following types:

Cast Type	Description	Alias Method
ALNUM	Alphanumeric string; can include A-Z, a-z, and 0-9.	——
ARRAY	Array.	——
BASE64	Base64 string; can include A-Z, a-z, 0-9, forward slashes, plus signs, and equal signs.	——
BOOL / BOOLEAN	Boolean value.	getBool()

Cast Type	Description	Alias Method
CMD	String syuitable for use as a command; can include A-Z, a-z, 0-9, underscores, fullstops, and dashes.	getCmd()
FLOAT / DOUBLE	Floating-point number.	getFloat()
INT / INTEGER	Whole number.	getInt()
PATH	File system path.	———
STRING	String; this will attempt to decode any special characters.	getString()
WORD	String with no spaces; can include A-Z, a-z, and underscores.	getWord()

In this example we cast the value to an integer:

```
$id = JRequest::getVar('id', 0, 'POST', 'INT');
```

The trouble with the cast type parameter is that we must specify a default value and the hash before we can specify the type. To overcome this we can use the alias methods described in the table. This example retrieves someValue as a floating-point number:

```
$value = JRequest::getFloat('someValue');
```

We can use the default value and source hash parameters with the alias methods in the same way as we do with the getVar() method.

We can apply different masks to reduce the data preprocessing. There are three masks: JREQUEST_NOTRIM, JREQUEST_ALLOWHTML, and JREQUEST_ALLOWRAW. By default no mask is applied. In this example we get name from the $_POST hash and apply the JREQUEST_NOTRIM mask:

```
$name = JRequest::getVar('name', null, 'POST', 'STRING',
                               JREQUEST_NOTRIM);
```

We can also use the mask when using the getString() alias method:

```
$name = JRequest::getString('name', null, 'POST', JREQUEST_NOTRIM);
```

To demonstrate the effects of the different masks, here is how four different inputs will be parsed:

#	Input Value
1	<p>Paragraph <a onClick="alert('foobar');">link</a></p>
2	CSS <link type="text/css", href="http://somewhere/nasty.css" />
3	space at front of input
4	&ltp&gtPara&lt/p&gt

#	Output value (No mask)
1	Paragraph link
2	CSS
3	space at front of input
4	&ltp&gtPara&lt/p&gt

#	Output value (mask JREQUEST_NOTRIM)
1	Paragraph link
2	CSS
3	space at front of input
4	&ltp&gtPara&lt/p&gt

#	Output value (mask JREQUEST_ALLOWHTML)
1	<p>Paragraph <a>link</a></p>
2	CSS
3	space at front of input
4	&ltp&gtPara&lt/p&gt

#	Output value (mask JREQUEST_ALLOWRAW)
1	<p>Paragraph <a onClick="alert('foobar');">link</a></p>
2	CSS <link type="text/css", href="http://somewhere/nasty.css" />
3	space at front of input
4	&ltp&gtPara&lt/p&gt

You may have noticed that using the mask JREQUEST_ALLOWHTML, the JavaScript and CSS is stripped from the data. JavaScript and CSS are removed from the data because they present a security risk. Attacks that exploit this type of security flaw are known as **XSS** (Cross Site Scripting) attacks; this is discussed in more detail later in the chapter. If we want to retrieve the data in its original form, we must use the JREQUEST_ALLOWRAW mask.

Escaping and Encoding Data

Escaping is the act of prefixing special characters with an escape character. In PHP there are two configuration settings, magic_quotes_gpc and magic_quotes_runtime that, if enabled, will automatically escape data. Joomla! always disables these.

Data that we retrieve is never automatically escaped; it is the responsibility of our extensions to escape data as necessary. Joomla! provides us with some useful ways of escaping data, namely the JDatabase `getEscaped()` and `Quote()` methods and the static JOutputFilter class.

 Common escape syntax includes prefixing a backslash to special characters and duplicating special characters. Ensure that you use the correct escape syntax for the system with which your data interacts.

Encoding data is the act of changing data from one format to another; this is always a lossless transition. The encoding that we examine is the encoding of special XHTML characters. This is of particular use when dealing with data that we want to display in a RAW state in an XHTML page and when storing data in XML.

Escaping and Quoting Database Data

If we use un-escaped data when interacting with a database, we can inadvertently alter the meaning of a query. Imagine we have a database table #__test containing two fields, id, a numeric ID field, and content, a text field. This is how we might choose to build our update query.

```
$db =& JFactory::getDBO();
$query = false;
if( $id = JRequest::getVar('id', 0, 'GET', 'INT') )
{
    $data = JRequest::getVar('content', 0, 'GET', 'STRING',
                                        JREQUEST_ALLOWRAW);
    $query =   " UPDATE ".$db->nameQuote('#__test').
               " SET ".$db->nameQuote('content')."=".
                 $db->Quote($data).
               " WHERE ". $db->nameQuote('id')."=".$id;
}
```

Assuming $id=123 and $data="Foo's bar", the value of $query will be:

```
UPDATE `#__test` SET `content`='Foo\'s bar' WHERE `id`=123
```

We use nameQuote() to encapsulate a named query element, for example a field, in quotes. MySQL does not require quotes around named query elements, but it is good practice to add them because other database servers may require them.

We use Quote() to encapsulate query string values in quotes. Quote() also performs the getEscaped() method on the data, before encapsulating it; this escapes the data.

In our example we didn't bother to escape data in $id; there are three reasons why we didn't need to do this. We cast the value of $id to an integer when we retrieved it from the $_GET hash. We set the default value to 0. We checked it was a positive value.

Encode XHTML Data

When we want data to appear exactly as it was entered in an XHTML page we need to encode the data. We do this using the PHP function htmlspecialchars(), which encodes HTML special characters into HTML entities. In Joomla! when we use htmlspecialchars(), we are encouraged to specify the quote style ENT_QUOTES. This ensures that we also encode single quote characters as the HTML entity &#039:

```
$value = "Foo's value is > Bar's value";
echo htmlspecialchars($value, ENT_QUOTES);
```

This will produce the following:

```
Foo&#039;s value is &gt; Bar&#039;s value
```

When we are outputting data like this, if the data is coming from an object, we can use the JOutputFilter::objectHTMLSafe() method. This method executes the htmlspecialchars() function on all of the public properties of the object:

```
$o = new JObject();
$o->set("name", "Foo's name");
$o->set("content", "Foo is > Bar");
JOutputFilter::objectHTMLSafe($o, ENT_QUOTES, 'content');
print_r($o);

JObject Object
(
   [name] => Foo&#039;s name
   [content] => Foo is > Bar
)
```

The last two parameters are optional. By default the second parameter, quote type, is ENT_QUOTES. The third parameter can be a string or an array of strings that identify properties within the object we don't want to encode.

There are other methods within JOutputFilter that we can use to encode data, including making URIs XHTML standards compliant and replacing ampersands with the HTML entity &amp.

Regular Expressions

REs (Regular Expressions) are revered by those who know how to use them, and considered a black art to those who don't. We can use Regular Expressions to sanitize data, to check the format of data, and to modify data. At the heart of REs are patterns; RE patterns are used to identify character patterns in data.

Patterns

Patterns are encapsulated with two identical characters, the **pattern delimiters**. Common pattern delimiters are the forward slash /, the hash #, and the tilde ~. You don't have to use the common pattern delimiters, but using them can make your code more readable for other developers.

Between the pattern delimiters is where we define what it is we are looking for. If we wanted to search for the occurrence of the term 'monkey' our pattern would look like this: /monkey/. This example will search for 'monkey' anywhere in our data; we can restrict this pattern further using the caret ^ and dollar $ characters. If we place the caret ^ character at the start of the pattern, it means that the 'data must start with' /^monkey/ (includes start of line and start of string). If we put a dollar sign at the end of the pattern it means that the 'data must end at' /monkey$/ (includes end of line and end of value).

We can, if we choose to, combine the caret character and the dollar character /^monkey$/; this is the same as asking, is the data equivalent to the string 'monkey'? In this context it is relatively useless, because we would use $data == 'monkey'.

A character class is a way of defining multiple characters that can be matched to just one actual character. If we wanted to search for 'monkey' or 'fonkey' we can define a character class that consists of the characters 'm' and 'f'. To do this we encapsulate the characters in square braces /[mf]onkey/.

There are a number of shortcuts we can use to make building character classes easier. The dash character can be used to specify a range from character to character. This example matches 'aonkey' through 'zonkey': /[a-z]onkey/.

So far we have dealt with simple consecutively matched items, but we can use **quantifiers** to duplicate a pattern. Quantifiers attach themselves to the pattern element directly to the left. If we wanted to match monkey, but with as many 'o's as we want we can do this: /mo+nkey/. The plus character '+' means we must have one to many 'o's.

Quantifier	Description	Example
+	One to many. Matches monkey through mo...onkey.	/mo+nkey/
*	Zero to many. Matches mnkey through mo...onkey.	/mo*nkey/
?	Optional. Matches mnkey and monkey.	/mo?nkey/
{x} or {x,}	x number. Matches mooonkey.	/mo{3}nkey/
{x,y}	x number to y number. Matches monkey through mooonkey.	/mo{1,3}nkey/

We can add to the usefulness of quantifiers by surrounding a block in a pattern with parentheses. This way we can quantify the number of times a block occurs; this example matches 'monkeymonkeymonkey': /(monkey){3}/.

Continuing the shortcuts theme, there are certain characters that, if escaped, take on a whole new role. If we want to search for a whole word, we can use \w+. By itself \w is a character class that will match any word character. Word characters are letters, digits and underscores; sometimes locale may make a difference to what constitutes a word, for example accented characters may or may not be included.

Shortcut	Description	Character Class
\w	Word characters	Letters, digits, and underscores
\W	Opposite of \w	- - - - - - - -
\d	Numbers	Digits 0-9
\D	Opposite of \d	- - - - - - - -
\s	Spaces	Whitespace (not including new line characters)
\S	Opposite of \s	- - - - - - - -

Our pattern is case sensitive, so to allow any case we could do this /[a-zA-Z][oO][nN][kK][eE][yY]/. That's rather messy; instead we can use pattern modifiers, which are characters that can be placed after the pattern delimiters: /[a-z]onkey/i. The i modifier makes the pattern case insensitive.

Modifier	Effect
i	Ignore case.
s	By default the period character, '.', matches anything except newline characters. This modifier makes the period character match newline characters as well.

Modifier	Effect
m	Makes the caret ^ and dollar characters match the start and end of line characters as well as string start and end.
x	Whitespace is ignored, unless it is in a character class. Allows comments in the pattern; comments are signified by the hash character #. *Do not use the pattern delimiters within comments.*
u	This modifier makes the pattern UTF-8 aware; this is only available with PHP 4.1.0 and above.

Matching

It's all very well knowing how to write RE patterns, but how do we use them? PHP provides us with a selection of different functions that use REs. We'll begin by looking at `preg_match()`; this function searches for matches in the subject and returns an the number of times the pattern was matched.

```
echo preg_match('/\d/','h0w many d1g1t5 ar3 th3r3');
```

This example will output 7. Nice and simple really; if there had been no numbers in the subject then it would have outputted 0.

Let's take another approach to `preg_match()`; we can return occurrences of blocks from a pattern. We define blocks by encapsulating them in parentheses. A good example of this is parsing a date.

```
$matches = array();
$pattern = '/^(\d{4})\D(\d{1,2})\D(\d{1,2})$/';
$value = '1791-12-26';
preg_match($pattern, $value, $matches);
print_r($matches);
```

Before you run away screaming, let's break this down into its component parts. The pattern says: start of string, 4 digits, 1 non-digit, 1 or 2 digits, 1 non-digit, 1 or 2 digits, end of string. It's not all that complex, it just looks it. This will output:

```
Array
(
    [0] => 1791-12-26
    [1] => 1791
    [2] => 12
    [3] => 26
)
```

The first element of the array is the text that matched the full pattern. The rest of the elements are the matching blocks.

Replacing

We can use `preg_replace()` to replace patterns with alternative text. This is often used for stripping out unwanted data. In this example we remove all digits.

```
$value = preg_replace('/\d/', '', $value);
```

The first parameter is the pattern, in this instance, digits. The second parameter is the replacement string, in this instance, a null string. The final parameter is the subject.

We can take advantage of blocks in the same way as we did with `preg_match()`. Each matched block encapsulated in parentheses is assigned to a variable `$1` through `$n`. These variables are only accessible in the replacement parameter.

```
$pattern = '/^(\d{4})\D(\d{1,2})\D(\d{1,2})$/';
$replacement = '$1/$2/$3';
$value = '1791-12-26';
echo preg_replace($pattern,$replacement,$value);
```

This example will output:

```
1791/12/26
```

Access Control

Joomla!'s access control mechanisms are not as clear cut as they could be; this is due to an ongoing development cycle that is moving away from a legacy access control system. In the future, Joomla! will use a complete **GACL** (Group Access Control Lists) access control mechanism.

The current access control mechanism uses an incomplete, abstracted implementation of phpGACL. There are eleven user groups; these groups are sometimes referred to as usertypes. Joomla! also maintains a set of three legacy access groups, Public, Registered, and Special.

The legacy groups are stored in the `#__groups` table; theoretically this makes the legacy access groups dynamic. There is no mechanism for administrators to amend the legacy access groups and even if we manually add a new legacy access group to the `#__groups` table, the effects are not globally reflected; we should regard the legacy access groups as static. It is advisable not to make extensions dependent on the legacy access groups because they will probably be removed from Joomla! at a later date.

We should be most interested in the phpGACL groups (simply called groups or user groups). Currently no mechanism is provided for administrators to amend these groups, we can, however, take advantage of the powerful JAuthorization class that extends the gacl_api class. If we are careful we can add groups to Joomla! without impacting the Joomla! core. In the GACL implementation we commonly use four terms:

Name		Description
ACL	Access Control List	Permissions list for an object
ACO	Access Control Object	Object to deny or allow access to
AXO	Access eXtension Object	Extended object to deny or allow access to
ARO	Access Request Object	Object requesting access

For a more complete description of GACL refer to the official phpGACL documentation `phpgacl.sourceforge.net`.

To demonstrate how the user groups are initially defined, this screenshot depicts the phpGACL administration interface with the Joomla! user groups defined:

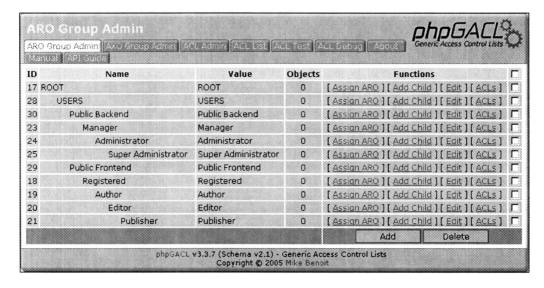

 Note that Joomla! does not include the phpGACL administration interface and that this screenshot is intended for demonstration purposes only.

In phpGACL, permissions are given to ARO groups and AROs, to access ACOs and AXOs. In Joomla! we only give permissions to ARO groups, and Joomla! users can only be a member of one group, whereas in phpGACL AROs can be members of multiple groups

These differences between Joomla! and phpGACL are due to one major factor. In phpGACL when we check permissions, we ask the question 'does ARO X have access to ACO Y?' In Joomla! we ask the question, 'Does ARO group X have access to ACO Y?'. The way in which we assign permissions in Joomla! will be altered in the future to use the same principals as phpGACL.

The three Access Object types, ACO, AXO, and ARO are all identified using two values, section and section value. To put this into context, the user group (ARO group) Super Administrator is identified as `users > super administrator`. The section name is `users`, and the section value is `super administrator`. A permission to manage contacts in the core contact component (ACO) is expressed as `com_contact > manage`. The section name is `com_contact`, and the section value is `manage`.

Menu Item Access Control

A misconception among some Joomla! administrators is that menu access (which uses the legacy access groups) constitutes security. Menu access is intended to define whether or not a specific menu item should be made visible to the current user.

Joomla! always attempts to transfer menu item permissions to the related menu item content; however, the solution is not infallible and must not be relied upon. The best way to deal with this is to add support for permissions in our extensions. The next section describes how to do this. We should also try to make administrators aware of the true meaning of the menu item access level.

In cases where Joomla! determines that something should not be accessible to a user, because of menu item access, Joomla! will return a `403` (Access Denied) error code.

Extension Access Control

Imagine we have a component called myExtension and we want to grant super administrator's access to 'manage'. This example gives permission to ARO group `users > super administrator` to ACO `com_myExtension > manage`.

```
$acl =& JFactory::getACL();
$acl->_mos_add_acl('com_myExtension', 'manage', 'users', 'super
                                               administrator');
```

Whenever we want to add permissions we have to use the above mechanism because currently only these ARO tables are implemented in Joomla!. The absent ARO tables are scheduled to be implemented in a later version of Joomla!.

In the short-term, when we create extensions that use Joomla!'s implementation of permissions, we should create a separate file with all the necessary calls to the ACL _mos_add_acl() method (as demonstrated in the preceding example). This way when Joomla! ultimately supports the ARO tables, we will be able to easily refactor our code to incorporate the new implementation.

> Calls to the _mos_add_acl() method must always be made prior to any permission checks. If they are not, the extra permissions will not have been applied in time. The best place to add the permissions is in the root extension file (this will depend upon the extension type).

Once we have added all of our permissions we will probably want to check if the current user has permissions. There are various ways of achieving this; we are encouraged to use the authorize() method in the JUser class:

```
$user =& JFactory->getUser();
if( ! $user-> authorize('com_myExtension', 'manage') )
{
    JError::raiseError(403, JText::_('Access Forbidden'));
}
```

If we are developing a component using the MVC architecture we use the JController object to automatically check permissions. The example below creates the component controller, sets the controller's ACO section, and executes the task:

```
$task = JRequest->getVar('task', 'view', 'GET', 'WORD');
$controller = new myExtensionController();
$controller->setAccessControl('com_myExtension');
$controller->execute($task);
```

When we run execute(), if the controller knows which ACO section to look at, it will check the permissions of the current user's group. The example above checks for permissions to ACO com_myExtension > $task.

We don't have to use the task as the section value; instead we can use the optional second parameter in the setAccessControl() method. This example checks for permissions to the ACO com_myExtension > manage irrespective of the task:

```
$task = JRequest->getVar('task', 'view', 'GET', 'WORD');
$controller = new myExtensionController();
$controller->setAccessControl('com_myExtension', 'manage');
$controller->execute($task);
```

When dealing with more complex permissions we can use AXOs to extend ACOs. Let's imagine we have a number of categories in our extension and we want to set manage permissions on each category. This example grants permissions to ACO group `users > super administrator` to ACO `com_myExtension > manage` AXO `category > some category`:

```
$acl =& JFactory::getACL();
$acl->_mos_add_acl('com_myExtension', 'manage', 'users', 'super
                    administrator', 'category', 'some category');
```

Unlike when we were dealing with just an ACO and ARO, we cannot use this in conjunction with a JController subclass. This is because the JController class is unable to deal with AXOs. Instead we should use the JUser object to check permissions:

```
$user =& JFactory->getUser();
if( ! $user-> authorize('com_myExtension', 'manage', 'category',
                                         'some category') )
{
    JError::raiseError('403', JText::_('Access Forbidden'));
}
```

When you define your ACOs you should always use the name of your extension as the ACO section. How you choose to define your ACO section value and your AXOs is entirely up to you. There is a great deal of emphasis put on the flexibility of Joomla!. As a third-party developer, you do not have to use the normal Joomla! access control. If you choose to use a custom access control system and the Joomla! MVC, you may want to consider overriding the `authorize()` method in your JController subclasses.

Attacks

Whether or not we like to think about it, there is always the potential threat of an attacker gaining access to our Joomla! websites. The most common way in which security is breached in Joomla! is through third-party extension security flaws.

Due to the number of extensions that have security defects, there is an official list of extensions that are considered insecure, available in the FAQ sections at `http://help.joomla.org`.

It is very important that, as third-party extension developers, we take great care in making our extensions as secure as we can. In this section we will investigate some of the more common forms of attack and how we can prevent them from affecting our extensions and we will take a look at how we can deal with users whom we believe to be attackers.

How to Avoid Common Attacks

The security flaws that we will investigate are some of the most likely to be exploited because they tend to be the easiest to initiate and there is plenty of literature explaining how to initiate them.

The attack types described here should not be considered a complete list. There are many ways in which an attacker can attempt to exploit a system. If you are concerned about attacks, you should consider hiring a security professional to help evaluate security vulnerabilities in your extensions.

Using the Session Token

A session is created for every client that makes a request. Joomla! uses its own implementation of sessions; integral to this is the JSession class. The session token, also refered to as the 'token', is a random alphanumeric string that we can use to validate requests made by a client. *The token can change during a session.*

Imagine that an attacker uses a utility to bombard a site with data; the data itself may not be suspicious. The attacker may just be attempting to fill your database with worthless information. If we include a hidden field in our forms with the name of the token, we can check if the user is submitting data via a form with a valid session.

We can get the token using `JUtility::getToken()`. In our template, where we render the form we want to secure, we add this:

```
<input type="hidden" name="<?php echo JUtility::getToken();
                                        ?>" value="1" />
```

When we call `JUtility::getToken()` we can optionally provide the Boolean `forceNew` parameter. This will force the generation of a new token. Before doing this we must consider the context in which we are calling the method. If there are any other forms present on the page that also use the token we may inadvertently prevent these from working. Components are always rendered first so are generally safer when forcing a new token.

Now all we need to do is verify the token when we receive a request from the form that we are trying to secure. In this example we specifically get the token from the `$_POST` hash, guaranteeing that the token came via the correct method. The error message is not very intuitive; this is purposeful, because it makes it harder for an attacker to determine the reason why they are receiving the error.

```
if(!JRequest::getVar(JUtility::getToken(), false, 'POST'))
{
    JError::raiseError('403', JText::_('Request Forbidden'));
}
```

Code Injection

Code injection occurs when code is included in input. The injected code, if not properly sanitized, may end up being executed on a server or on a client. There are a number of different ways in which injected code can compromise a Joomla! installation or a system with which we are interacting.

We will take a look at the two most common forms of code injection used to attack Joomla!: PHP and SQL code injection.

PHP Code Injection

We should use JRequest and, in some cases, REs to ensure that the input data that we are handling is valid. Most data validation is very simple and doesn't require much effort.

Even when data comes from an XHTML form control that is restricted to specific values, we must still validate the data.

There is one form of PHP code injection that we don't need to worry about. By default Joomla! always disables 'register globals'. In scripts where 'register globals' is enabled, all URI query values are automatically converted into variables, literally injecting variables into a script.

Imagine we are using an input value to determine which class to instantiate. If we do not sanitize the incoming data, we run the risk of instantiating a class that could be used to malicious effect. To overcome this we could use a predefined list of class names to ensure the data is valid:

```php
// define allowed classes
$allow = array('Monkey', 'Elephant', 'Lion');
// get the class name
$class = JRequest::getWord('class', 'Monkey', 'GET');
$class = ucfirst(strtolower($class));
```

Notice that we use the `getWord()` method to retrieve the value; this ensures that the value only includes letters and underscores. We also modify the case of the value so as to ensure it is in the same format as the expected value. Once we have defined the expectable class names and retrieved the value we can validate the value:

```php
if(!in_array($class, $allow))
{
    // unknown class, use default
    $class = 'Monkey';
}
```

Imagine we want to execute a shell command. This type of process is potentially very risky; some unwanted malicious commands such as `rm` or `del` could potentially reduce our server to a gibbering wreck. In this example we define an array of acceptable commands and use the PHP `escapeshellarg()` function to escape any arguments passed to the command.

```
$allowCmds = array('mysqld', 'apachectl');
$cmd = JRequest::getVar('cmd', false, 'GET', 'WORD');
$arg = JRequest::getVar('arg', false, 'GET', 'WORD');
if( $cmd !== false && !in_array($cmd, $allow) )
{
    $cmd .= ' '.escapeshellarg( $arg );
    system( $cmd );
}
```

Using the correct escape mechanism for the system we are accessing is imperative in preventing code injection attacks.

SQL Injection

Probably one of the most publicized vulnerabilities in PHP applications, SQL injection is potentially fatal. It is caused by inadequate processing of data before database queries are executed.

Joomla! provides us with the JDatabase methods `getEscaped()` and `Quote()` specifically for avoiding SQL injection. Consider the following value a' OR name IS NOT NULL OR name='b. If we used this value without escaping the value, we could inadvertently give an attacker access to all the records in a table:

```
SELECT * FROM `#__test` WHERE `name`='a' OR name IS NOT NULL OR
                                                         name='b'
```

We can overcome this using the `Quote()` method:

```
$db =& JFactory::getDBO();
$name = $db->QuotegetEscaped(JRequest('name'));
```

Using the `getEscaped()` method escapes any special characters in the passed string. In our example the inverted comas will be escaped by prefixing them with a backslash. Our query now becomes:

```
SELECT * FROM `#__test` WHERE `name`='a\' OR name IS NOT NULL OR
                                                      name=\'b'
```

The `Quote()` method is identical to the `getEscaped()` method except that it also adds quotation marks around the value. Generally we should use `Quote()` in preference to `getEscaped()`, because this method guarantees that we are using the correct quotation marks for the database server that is being used.

Something else we can verify is the number of results returned after we submit a query. For example, if we know that we should only get one record from a query, we can easily verify this.

```
$db->setQuery($query);
$row = $db->loadAssoc();
if( $db->getNumRows() !== 1 )
{
    // handle unexpected query result
}
```

XSS (Cross Site Scripting)

XSS is the use of scripts that are executed client side that take advantage of the user's local rights. These attacks normally take the form of JavaScript. Another, slightly less common, form of XSS attack uses specially crafted images that execute code on the client; a good example of this is a Microsoft security flaw that was reported in 2004 (http://www.microsoft.com/technet/security/bulletin/MS04-028.mspx).

When we use JRequest::getVar() we automatically strip out XSS code, unless we use the JREQUEST_ALLOWRAW mask. We generally use this mask when dealing with large text fields that use are rendered using an editor; if we do not, valuable XHTML formatting data will be lost.

When we use the JREQUEST_ALLOWRAW mask we need to think carefully about how we process the data. When rendering the data remember to use the PHP htmlspecialchars() function or the static JOutput class to make the data safe for rendering in an XHTML page. When using the data with the database, remember to escape the data using the database object's Quote() method.

If you want to allow your users to submit formatted data, you may want to consider using **BBCode** (Bulletin Board Code). BBCode is a simple markup language that uses a similar format to XHTML. Commonly used on forums, the language allows us to give the user the power to format their data without the worry of XSS. There are all sorts of BBCode tags; exactly how they are rendered may differ.

BBCode	XHTML	Example
[b]Bold text[/b]	Bold text	Bold text
[i]Italic text[/i]	<i>Italic text</i>	Italic text
[u]Underlined text[/u]	<u>Underlined text</u>	Underlined text
:)	<img src="/somewhere/smile.jpg" />	☺
[quote]Some quote[/quote]	<div class="quote">Some quote</div>	Some quote

Joomla! does not include any BBCode-parsing libraries. Instead we must either build our own parser or include an existing library. One such BBCode library is a class available from `http://www.phpclasses.org/browse/package/951.html` created by Leif K-Brooks and released under the PHP License. This class gives us lots of control; it allows us to define our own BBCode tags, use HTML entity encoded data, and import and export settings.

 When we use BBCode, or a similar parsing mechanism, it is important that if we intend to allow the data to be editable, we store the data in its RAW state.

File System Snooping

A common error when working with files is to allow traversal of the file system. Joomla! provides us with a number of classes for dealing with the file system. This example imports the `joomla.filesystem` library and builds a path based on the value of the CGI request `file` (the path must not be relative).

```
jimport('joomla.filesystem');
$path = JPATH_COMPONENT.DS.'files'.DS
        .JRequest('file', 'somefile.php', 'GET', 'WORD');
JPath::check($path);
```

When we use the `JPath::check()` method, if `$path` is considered to be snooping, an error will be raised and the application will be terminated. Snooping paths are identified as paths that do not start with `JPATH_BASE` and do not attempt to traverse the tree using the parent directory indicator `..` (two periods).

Other classes in the `joomla.filesystem` library include JFile, JFolder, and JArchive. It's important to realize that none of these classes validate path parameters to prevent snooping. This is because there are times when we expect a path to be classified as snooping.

Dealing with Attacks

Parsing input is only one part of security handling. Another part is the evasive action that an extension can automatically take if an attack is detected. Here are three good ways of dealing with detected attacks; they could be used separately or in conjunction with one another:

1. Log the user out, possibly blocking their account.

2. Maintain a log file of detected attacks.

3. Email the site administrator and inform them of the attack.

Log Out and Block

If the attack has come from a logged in user we can end the user's session and optionally block them from logging in until an administrator unblocks their account. Logging out a user and blocking them may not be appropriate. An instance appearing to be an attack could be a genuine mistake on the part of the user or a misclassification. We could use a 'three strikes and you're out' approach. This way we can reduce the chance of irritating genuine users but maintain a high level of security.

One way of implementing this would be to build a Plugin, an event handler class (extends JPlugin) registered to the application. This modular approach to dealing with attacks, would allow us to reuse the plugin throughout our extensions. The UML diagram shows one design we could use.

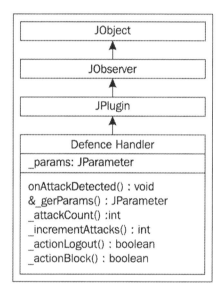

_params is a temporary store for the Plugin parameters (JParameter object). onAttackDetected() is the method that will be executed when an attack is detected. &_getParams() gets the Plugin parameters (uses _params). _attackCount() gets the number of detected attacks so far (stored in the session). _incrementAttacks() increments the number of attacks and returns the new number of attacks. When the user exceeds the maximum number of detected attacks _actionLogout() and _actionBlock() are run, if they are enabled in the Plugin parameters.

This is the definition of the parameters; this would be in the plugin XML file.

```xml
<params>
    <param name="sessionValue" type="text" size="20"
                default="detectedAttacks" label="sessionValue"
                description="Name of session value to store attack
                counter in." />
    <param name="maxAttacks" type="text" size="2" default="3"
                label="maxAttacks" description="Maximum number of
                detections per session." />
    <param name="@spacer" type="spacer" default="" label=""
                description="" />
    <param name="logout" type="radio" default="1" label="logout"
                description="Logout user.">
        <option value="0">Off</option>
        <option value="1">On</option>
    </param>
    <param name="block" type="radio" default="1" label="block"
                description="Block user.">
        <option value="0">Off</option>
        <option value="1">On</option>
    </param>
</params>
```

The example shows how we could implement the `_logout()` method. Notice we check if the user is logged in before attempting to log them out.

```php
/**
 * Logs the current user out.
 *
 * @access private
 * @return boolean true on success
 */
function _actionLogout()
{
    global $mainframe;
    $user =& JFactory::getUser();
    if($user->get('id') &&  $mainframe->logout() )
    {
        return true;
    }
    return false;
}
```

The next example shows how we could implement the `_block()` method. Notice we check if the user is logged in before attempting to block them.

```
/**
 * If they are logged in, blocks the current user's account.
 *
 * @access private
 * @return boolean true on success
 */
function _block()
{
    $user =& JFactory::getUser();
    print_r($user);
    if($user->get('id'))
    {
        $user->set('block', '1');
        return $user->save(true);
    }
    return false;
}
```

To be able to use the DefenceHandler class we need to register the event with the application. This creates a new instance of DefenceHandler and attaches it to the application event handler.

```
$mainframe->registerEvent('onAttackDetected',
                          'DefenceHandler');
```

If we detected an attack we would use the handler by triggering the event `onAttackDetected` in the application (`$mainframe`):

```
$mainframe->triggerEvent('onAttackDetected');
```

Attack Logging

Detecting attacks can prevent individual attacks but, when we encounter a persistent attacker, having a history of attacks can provide us with vital information. This information can be used to determine the nature of each attack and to try to identify the perpetrator.

Building on our previous example we can use the JLog class to build up a history of attacks. Here's an example of how we might implement the `_actionLog()` method in our DefenceHandler class.

```
/**
 * Logs an Attack.
 *
 * @access private
 * @return boolean true on success
 */
function _actionLog()
{
    $user =& JFactory::getUser();
    $uri  =& JFactory::getURI();
    $options = array('format'=>"{DATE}\t{TIME}\t{CIP}
                    \t{USER}\t{STRIKE}\t{REQUEST}");
    $log =& JLog::getInstance($extension.'.Defences.log',
                                            $options);
    $entry = array(
                    'REQUEST'    => $uri->toString(),
                    'USER'       => $user->get('id'),
                    'STRIKE'     => $this->strikeCount()
                );
    $log->addEntry($entry);
}
```

To use this we would need to modify the plugin XML file to include the option to log attacks and we would need to update the `onAttackDetected()` method to deal with logging.

Notify the Site Administrator

We may also want to notify the site administrator when a user exceeds the maximum number of attacks. This time we need to add a `_actionNotify()` method to our DefenceHandler class and a text field for an email address in our plugin's XML file parameters.

```
/**
 * Logs an Attack.
 *
 * @access private
 * @param string email address
 * @return boolean true on success
 */
function _actionNotify( $email )
{
    global $mainframe;
    $mailer =& $mainframe->getMailer();
    $mailer->setSender($email);
```

```
$mailer->setRecipient($email);
$mailer->setSubject(JText::_('Excessive Attacks Detected'));
$mailer->setBody(JText::_"A user has exceeded the number of
                         allowed attacks. Please consult your
                         error log for more details."));

$mailer->Send();
}
```

This example is relatively simple. We could develop the method further by adding a more comprehensive subject line and body. If logging is enabled we could also include a copy of the log as an attachment (we would have to be careful if the log file was very large).

Summary

Although we may perhaps never receive an error message from our extensions, the JError class gives us all of the necessary tools to ensure that any errors that are encountered can be cleanly dealt with. Using the PHP `die()` and `exit()` functions can potentially 'break' the current users session; we should always exit cleanly. If JError isn't up to this task, we should use `$mainframe->close()`.

Handling input from a URI query is very easy in Joomla! and the data type casting alone provides us with a massive form of protection against security flaws. We should remember that we can use the JRequest alias methods to easily cast an input value.

Taking input value preprocessing one step further, we can use REs to ensure that data is the expected format. Remember that we can also use REs to retrieve certain parts from a data pattern. This is especially useful if one input value contains multiple pieces of data.

When we deal with sensitive data we can restrict user access using the Joomla! GACL access control implementation. When we are creating components using the MVC architecture, we can use the controller to check for authorization.

Attackers are very resourceful and will go to great lengths to discover and exploit security flaws. Remember to always sanitize incoming data and escape outgoing data. Joomla! and PHP provide us with a plethora of utilities that, if used correctly, can ensure that our extensions are as secure as possible.

12
Utilities and Useful Classes

Joomla! includes a number of useful utilities and classes that are used to perform specific tasks. In this chapter, we will discuss the use of the most commonly used utilities and classes.

Joomla! extensions that require date and time handling can use the JDate class to handle date and time parsing, formatting, and time zones. In this chapter, we discuss how to use JDate to handle all of these aspects of date and time values.

Many extensions use the file system to store important data. In addition to the PHP file-system handling functions, we can use the `joomla.filesystem` library. This library has a number of advantages over the PHP functions, including the use of FTP, where appropriate, to overcome file-system permission problems.

We use arrays constantly in PHP, and Joomla! is no exception. The static JArrayHelper class includes a number of very useful methods that we can use to process arrays.

PHP only provides us with a few data structures. Joomla! adds the tree data structure to this list. In this chapter, we investigate how we can use and extend the Joomla! tree data structure.

Logging events can be a very useful function. We discuss the use of the JLog class to create log files and append log entries to log files.

This list names the classes discussed in this chapter:

- JArchive
- JArrayHelper
- JDate
- JFile
- JFolder

- JLog
- JMail
- JNode
- JPath
- JTree

Dates

The hardest part of handling dates is coping with different time zones and formats. Luckily, Joomla! provides us with the JDate class that handles date formatting. Before we start using the JDate class we need to import the relevant library:

```
jimport('joomla.utilities.date');
```

A JDate object is designed to handle a single date. This means that we must create a new JDate object for every date. When we create a new JDate object, in its most basic form, the object automatically attempts to determine the current date and time.

This example demonstrates how we create a new JDate object for the current date and time:

```
$dateNow = new JDate();
```

When we create a new JDate object we can pass two optional parameters:

- Date and time, which the object will parse
- Time zone

The first parameter can be passed in a number of different formats.

Supported date and time formats include Unix timestamps, RFC 2822, ISO 8601, and any format that the PHP `strtotime()` function is capable of parsing.

For more information about RFC 2822, ISO 8601, and `strtotime()` refer to these sites respectively:

```
http://tools.ietf.org/html/rfc2822
```

```
http://www.iso.org/iso/en/prods-services/popstds/
datesandtime.html
```

```
http://php.net/strtotime
```

These examples demonstrate the use of some of the date and time formats that are supported by JDate when creating a new JDate object:

```
// Unix timestamp
$date1 = new JDate(-1417564800);

// ISO 8601
$date2 = new JDate('1925-01-30T00:00:00');

// RFC 2822
$date3 = new JDate('Fri, 30 Jan 1925 00:00:00');

// User string
$date4 = new JDate('January 30th 1925');
```

The time zone parameter is defined as the number of hours offset from **UTC** (Coordinated Universal Time), also referred to as **GMT** (Greenwich Mean Time) and **Z** (Zulu Time).

A UTC offset is expressed as UTC+/- the number of hours. For example: UTC+1.

In Joomla! we always handle dates and times in UTC+0 and apply time-zone offsets when we come to display them.

This example uses the same time as the previous examples but in the UTC+1 time zone. Adding the offset parameter corrects the time by removing 1 hour:

```
// ISO 8601 (UTC+1)
$date5 = new JDate('1925-01-30T01:00:00', 1);
```

Both RFC 2822 and ISO 8601 define a way in which we can include the offset within a date and time string. If we pass a date and time that defines the offset and we pass the second parameter, the second parameter will be ignored.

This RFC 2822 example is in **CET** (Central European Time), which has an offset of plus 1 hour (if the optional time zone parameter were used, it would be ignored):

```
// RFC 2822 (CET)
$date5 = new JDate('Fri, 30 Jan 1925 01:00:00 CET');
```

This ISO 8601 example uses a numeric time zone designator of plus 1 hour (if the optional time zone parameter were used, it would be ignored):

```
// ISO 8601
$date2 = new JDate('1925-01-30T00:00:00 +0100');
```

The JDate methods that we tend to use most commonly return the date and time in a specific format. These examples detail the four predefined formats that we can easily convert dates into:

```
// get date formatted in RFC 2822
$rfc822 = $date->toRFC822();

// get date formatted in ISO 8601
$iso8601 = $date->toISO8601();

// get date formatted for a MySQL datetime field
$mySQL = $date->toMySQL();

// get date as unix timestamp
$timestamp = $date->toUnix();
```

You may have noticed that the RFC 2822 method is called `toRFC822()`. No, it is not a typo! RFC 2822 replaced RFC 822. The two terms are often used interchangeably and, unfortunately, it is not unusual to encounter dates and times that use elements from RFC 822 and RFC 2822. The `toRFC822()` method actually returns an RFC 2822 date and time string.

The `toMySQL()` method is of particular interest if we are using dates and times with the database. The string that this method returns is suitable for use with a MySQL database. For more information, please refer to Chapter 3.

If we want to format the date differently, we can use the `toFormat()` method. To specify the format we use the same format designators as the PHP `strftime()` function. This table details some of the more common format designators:

Format Designator	Description
a	Weekday name (abbreviated)
A	Weekday name
b	Month name (abbreviated)
B	Month name
d	Day of the month (zero padded)
e	Day of the month
H	Hour (24 hour and zero padded)
I	Hour (12 hour and zero padded)
m	Month (zero padded)
M	Minute (zero padded)
p	12 hour 'am' or 'pm'.
S	Second (zero padded)
y	Year (two digits)
Y	Year (four digits)

This example outputs a date in a custom format:

```
// custom date format
$custom = $date->toFormat('%A, %Y/%m/%d');
```

We don't have to supply a custom format string to the `toFormat()` method. If we choose not to, the default format is `%Y-%m-%d %H:%M:%S`.

In most cases, we should not directly use a string to specify the format. Instead, we should use a translated string. This guarantees that we use a format that is valid for the current locale.

The table below describes the date and time format names and their English (British) value:

Format Name	en-GB value	Example
DATE_FORMAT_LC	%A, %d %B %Y	Thursday, 01 January 1970
DATE_FORMAT_LC1	%A, %d %B %Y	Thursday, 01 January 1970
DATE_FORMAT_LC2	%A, %d %B %Y %H:%M	Thursday, 01 January 1970 00:00
DATE_FORMAT_LC3	%d %B %Y	01 January 1970
DATE_FORMAT_LC4	%d.%m.%y	01.01.70
DATE_FORMAT_JS1	y-m-d	1970-01-01

The DATE_FORMAT_JS1 format is slightly different from the other formats. It is to be used with JavaScript, not JDate or PHP date functions.

This example demonstrates how we use DATE_FORMAT_LC2:

```
// LC2
$lc2 = $date->toFormat(JText::_('DATE_FORMAT_LC2'));
```

Notice that we use JText to translate the date format before passing it to the JDate `toFormat()` method. This is what translates the format string to the current locale format. Remember that, although the syntax suggests it, the date format names are not PHP constants.

If we want to use a format that is not described by any of the above formats, we should consider adding the format to the language file that our extension uses.

The last method we will discuss is the `setOffset()` method. This method is used to apply an offset to the date when it is passed through the `toFormat()` method. To apply the offset UTC+2 to a date and time before we display it, we would do the following:

```
$date->setOffset(2);
```

Notice that the offset is specified in hours. *An offset applied in this way only affects the resultant date and time when using the* toFormat() *method.*

One useful thing to be aware of, when working with dates and time, is the application requestTime. The requestTime is a date and time that is recorded by the application when a request is made.

This example demonstrates how we can access the requestTime and output it using the DATE_FORMAT_LC2 format:

```
$rDate = new JDate($mainframe->get('requestTime'));
echo $rDate->toFormat(JText::_('DATE_FORMAT_LC2'));
```

The final aspect that we will touch on is the use of JHTML, discussed in Chapter 8, to output a date. If all we are trying to do is parse a date so that we can apply a format and an offset, we can use the basic JHTML date type.

This example outputs the requestTime time using the DATE_FORMAT_LC2 format:

```
// get the date and time of the request
$date = $mainframe->get('requestTime');

// output the date and time
echo JHTML::_('date', $date, JText::_('DATE_FORMAT_LC2'));
```

The nice thing about using this is that it automatically applies the site time zone offset to the date if we do not specify the offset ourselves.

Since users can specify the time zone in which they are located, using their timezone parameter, we can easily apply this or the site offset. When we use the getParam() method to get the value of a user's parameter, if the parameter is not set, null is returned.

The date type works in such a way that if a null value is given as the offset the site offset is used. This example demonstrates how we can apply the user's offset or the default site offset when using the date type:

```
// get the date and time of the request
$date = $mainframe->get('requestTime');

// get the user's time zone
$user =& JFactory::getUser();
$usersTZ = $user->getParam('timezone');

// output the date and time
echo JHTML::_('date', $date, JText::_('DATE_FORMAT_LC2'), $usersTZ);
```

File System

We normally store data in the database; however, we can also store data within the file system. Joomla! provides us with the `joomla.filesystem` library. This library enables us to work easily with the file system. There are four main parts of this library:

- JPath
- JFolder
- JFile
- JArchive

Paths

The static JPath class is integral to the library. Before we jump in, we must import the relevant library in order to use the JPath class:

```
jimport('joomla.filesystem.path');
```

We'll start by looking at the `clean()` method. This method is used to tidy up a path by removing any unnecessary directory separators and ensuring all remaining directory separators are of the correct type for the current system.

This example demonstrates how we use the `clean()` method:

```
$path = JPATH_BASE.'\foo//bar\\baz';
$cleanPath = JPath::clean($path);
```

The values displayed demonstrate the values associated with `$path` and `$cleanPath` respectively (assuming `JPATH_BASE` is equal to `/var/www/html/joomla`):

- `$path`: /var/www/html/joomla\foo//bar\\baz
- `ScleanPath`: /var/www/html/joomla/foo/bar/baz

A similar method in the JPath class is the `check()` method. This method is used to prevent snooping. For more information about this method refer to Chapter 11.

The next method we will look at is the `find()` method. We use this method to search for a specific file that might be located in a number of different paths. Imagine we want to locate the file `somefile.txt` and we know that it will be located in the root of either the frontend or backend of the current component:

```
$paths = array(JPATH_COMPONENT, JPATH_COMPONENT_ADMINISTRATOR);
$filePath = JPath::find($paths, 'somefile.txt');
```

The first parameter that we pass to the method is an array of paths. The second parameter is the name of the file that we are attempting to locate.

The `$paths` array is ordered by priority. This is because the file we are searching for may exist in more than one of the defined paths. So in our example, if the file were present in both locations, the frontend path would be returned because it has priority.

If the file is successfully found, then the path to that file is returned. If the file is not found in any of the locations, then `false` is returned.

 The find() method is not recursive; it does not search subfolders.

The remaining methods are all designed for handling permissions. We'll begin by looking at the `getPermissions()` method.

This method is used to determine the permissions of a file or folder. When passed a path, the method returns a string that describes the permissions in terms of Read, Write, and Execute:

```
echo JPath::getPermissions($cleanPath);
```

This is an example of the value that might be returned:

```
rwxrwxr-x
```

If the supplied path does not exist then a string suggesting no permissions will be returned:

```
---------
```

In addition to getting permissions, we can set permissions. We do this using the `setPermissions()` method. By default the permissions are modified to `0644` for files and `0755` for folders. If supplied with the path to a folder, this method acts recursively, updating the file and folder permissions for all sub-files and folders:

```
JPath::setPermissions($cleanPath);
```

In order to set different permissions to the default permissions, we can supply two additional parameters, the first being the permissions to apply to the files, the second being the permissions to apply to the folders.

This example uses the permissions `0664` for files and `0775` for folders:

```
JPath::setPermissions($cleanPath, '0664', '0775');
```

The `setPermissions()` method returns a Boolean response. If the method fails to update any of the permissions successfully `false` is returned.

Before we use the `setPermissions()` method, we can use the `canChmod()` method to ensure that we have the ability to modify the mode of a path:

```
if (JPath::canChmod($cleanPath))
{
    JPath::setPermissions($cleanPath);
}
```

There is one last method that we will look at. The `isOwner()` method is used to determine if the process user is the owner of a specific file:

```
if (JPath::isOwner($cleanPath))
{
    // Process user is the owner
}
```

 It is important to understand that the permissions-based methods relate to the system user that is used to execute the script. They do not relate to the Joomla! users.

Folders

We can handle folders using the static JFolder class. Before we explore how to use JFolder we need to import the relevant library:

```
jimport('joomla.filesystem.folder');
```

The JFolder class has a `makeSafe()` method that works in much the same way as the JFile `makeSafe()` method. The JFolder version of this method removes unsafe characters from a folder path. This example cleans the `$folder` path:

```
$folder = JPATH_COMPONENT.DS.'Foo&Bar';
$cleanFolder = JFolder::makeSafe($path);
```

The resultant value of `$cleanFolder` will be the same as `$folder` except the ampersand will have been removed because it is deemed an unsafe character.

JFolder contains a number of common file-system commands. We are provided with five methods that deal explicitly with folder management. The first of these is the `exists()` method. This method is used to check if a folder exists and returns a Boolean value:

```
if (!JFolder::exists($cleanFolder))
{
    // handle folder does not exist
}
```

We can use the following methods to manage a folder: `copy()`, `move()`, `delete()`, and `create()`. It's better to use these methods than to use the normal PHP file management functions because, if FTP is enabled, these methods will attempt to use an FTP connection. This decreases the chance of errors due to lack of user rights.

The `copy()` method copies a folder to a new location. The method accepts four parameters: path to the source folder, path to the destination folder, an optional base path, and an optional force flag.

If a base path is provided, it will be prepended to the source and destination paths. When the force flag is `true`, overwrite is enabled; by default the force flag is `false`.

This example force copies the `foo` folder to the `bar` folder in the frontend root of the current component:

```
if (!JFolder::copy('foo', 'bar', JPATH_COMPONENT, true))
{
    // handle failed folder copy
}
```

The `move()` method relocates a folder. This method returns a Boolean value. This example moves the folder `foo` to the folder `bar` in the frontend root of the current component:

```
if (!JFolder::move('foo', 'bar', JPATH_COMPONENT))
{
    // handle failed folder move
}
```

The `delete()` method removes folders from the file system. This method returns a Boolean value. This example deletes the folder 'foo' from the frontend root of the current component:

```
if (!JFolder::delete(JPATH_COMPONENT.DS.'foo'))
{
    // handle failed folder delete
}
```

The last of these management-type methods is the `create()` method. This method creates a new folder in the file system. This example creates the folder `baz` in the frontend root of the current component:

```
if (!JFolder::create(JPATH_COMPONENT.DS.'baz'))
{
    // handle failed folder creation
}
```

There is a second parameter that we can optionally provide when using the `create()` method. This parameter determines the access rights of the newly created folder; by default this is `0777`. This example creates a folder with the access rights `0775`:

```
if (!JFolder::create(JPATH_COMPONENT.DS.'baz', 0775))
{
    // handle failed folder creation
}
```

Notice that the second parameter is prefixed with a `0`; this ensures that the value is treated as an octal integer. If we don't do this, we run the risk of the access rights mode being misinterpreted. For a full description of file access rights mode in PHP please consult the official PHP documentation: `http://php.net/manual/function.chmod.php`.

The last three methods we will explore are all used to read the contents of a folder and they are: `folders()` and `files()`.

The `folders()` method is used to list the folders within a folder. In its most basic usage this method returns an array of all of the direct sub-folders. This example gets the names of all of the folders in the core Poll component:

```
$folder = JPATH_ADMINISTRATOR.DS.'components'.DS.'com_poll';
$folders = JFolder::folders($folder);
```

The resultant array will look like this:

```
Array
(
    [0] => elements
    [1] => tables
    [2] => views
)
```

The second parameter is an optional filter. This filter is an RE filter (see Chapter 11 for more information on REs). By default the filter is `'.'` (A period signifies any character).

The third parameter, also optional, is a Boolean parameter that determines if we want a recursive listing of folders. A recursive listing means that we will be provided with all sub-folders even if they are not direct descendants. By default this is `false`. This example demonstrates the use of the method when used recursively:

```
$folder = JPATH_ADMINISTRATOR.DS.'components'.DS.'com_poll';
$folders = JFolder::folders($folder, '.', true);
```

The resultant array will look like this:

```
Array
(
        [0] => elements
        [3] => poll
        [1] => tables
        [2] => views
)
```

The main problem with this method is that there are no indications as to which folders are direct descendants. We can use the final parameter to over come this.

The final parameter is a Boolean value that determines if the returned array is a list of folder names or a list of folder paths. This example demonstrates the use of the method when used to get the full paths of the folders:

```
$folder = JPATH_ADMINISTRATOR.DS.'components'.DS.'com_poll';
$folders = JFolder::folders($folder, '.', true);
```

The resultant array will look like this:

```
Array
(
        [0] => /joomla/administrator/components/com_poll/elements
        [1] => /joomla/administrator/components/com_poll/tables
        [2] => /joomla/administrator/components/com_poll/views
        [3] => /joomla/administrator/components/com_poll/views/poll
)
```

The `files()` method is used to list the files within a folder. This method works in precisely the same way as the `folders()` method described above.

The last method that we will investigate is the `listFolderTree()` method. This method returns an array of associative arrays that model the structure of an area in the file system. This example gets an array that describes the frontend root folder of the current component:

```
$structure = JFolder::listFolderTree(JPATH_COMPONENT, '.');
```

The first parameter is the folder in which to start, the second parameter is the RE filter that the name of the folders must match.

The returned array, for the component com_mycomponent, may look like this:

```
Array
(
        [0] => Array
```

```
(
    [id] => 1
    [parent] => 0
    [name] => files
    [fullname] => /var/www/html/joomla/components/
                             com_mycomponent/views
    [relname] => /components/com_mycomponent/views
)
)
```

Additional parameters include the maximum recursive depth, which by default is 3, the current depth, and the parent ID. We don't normally use the last two parameters; these are intended for internal use when the method calls itself recursively.

Files

We can handle files using the static JFile class. Before we explore how to use JFile, we need to import the relevant library:

```
jimport('joomla.filesystem.file');
```

We'll start with four of the more basic JFile methods, each of which is used to handle the name of a file. The first of these is called makeSafe(). This method takes a string and removes any unsafe characters for use as a filename. This is especially useful when we allow users to enter a filename of their choice:

```
$filename = JRequest::getVar('filename');
$cleanFilename = JFile::makeSafe($filename);
```

The resultant value of $cleanFilename will be the same as $filename, except that any unsafe characters will have been removed.

 The parameter that we pass to the makeSafe() method must not be a path to a file. If we do pass a path, the directory separators will be stripped.

If we are dealing with a path to a file we can use the getName() method to determine the filename. Once we have done this, we can use the makeSafe() method to ensure the filename is safe to use:

```
$fileName = JFile::getName($pathToFile);
$cleanFilename = JFile::makeSafe($filename);
```

If we want to determine the extension of a file, we can use the getExt() method; this method works with a filename and with a path to a file. Along the same lines, we can remove the extension from a filename; this also works with filenames and a path to a file.

This example demonstrates how we can use these methods in conjunction with one another:

```
if (JFile::getExt($filename) == 'txt')
{
    echo JText::sprintf('%s is a text file',
                        JFile::stripExt($filename));
}
```

We will now venture into common file-system commands. We are provided with four methods that deal explicitly with file management. The first of these is the `exists()` method. This method returns a Boolean response and is used to check if a file exists:

```
if (!JFile::exists($pathToFile))
{
    // handle file does not exist
}
```

If a file exists then we can use any of the following methods to manage that file: `copy()`, `move()`, and `delete()`. It's better to use these methods than to use the normal PHP file-management functions because, if FTP is enabled, these methods will attempt to use an FTP connection in priority to PHP functions. This decreases the chance of error due to lack of user rights.

The `copy()` method copies a file to a new location. The method accepts three parameters: the path to the source file, the path to the destination file, and an optional base path. If a base path is provided, it will be prepended to the source and destination paths.

The `copy()` method returns a Boolean response. This example copies the `foo.php` file to the `bar.php` file in the frontend root of the current component:

```
if (!JFile::copy('foo.php', 'bar.php', JPATH_COMPONENT))
{
    // handle failed file copy
}
```

The `move()` method works in the same way, except that it relocates the file rather than creating a copy of the file. This method returns a Boolean response. This example moves the file `foo.php` to the file `bar.php` in the frontend root of the current component:

```
if (!JFile::move('foo.php', 'bar.php', JPATH_COMPONENT))
{
    // handle failed file move
}
```

The last of these management-type methods we'll look at is the `delete()` method. This method removes one or more files from the file system. This method returns a Boolean response. This example deletes the file `foo.php` from the frontend root of the current component:

```
if (!JFile::delete(JPATH_COMPONENT.DS.'foo.php'))
{
    // handle failed delete
}
```

If we want to delete multiple files at once, we can pass an array of file paths to the `delete()` method. This example deletes the files `foo.php` and `bar.php` from the frontend root of the current component:

```
$files = array(JPATH_COMPONENT.DS.'foo.php',
               JPATH_COMPONENT.DS.'bar.php');
if (!JFile::delete($files))
{
    // handle failed delete
}
```

The next two methods we will look at are used to read and write data to and from files. These methods are aptly named `read()` and `write()`. We'll start by using the `read()` method to access the contents of a file:

```
$file = JPATH_COMPONENT.DS.'foo.php';
$contents = JFile::read($file);
```

The contents of the file is read into the `$contents` variable as a string. If the `read()` method is unsuccessful, the method returns `false`. It is not uncommon, once a file is successfully read, to use the `explode()` function to split the contents into an array of lines:

```
$lines = explode("\n", $contents);
```

To write to a file we use a similar approach. When we call the `write()` method we must provide the path to the file that we intend to write and the data that we want to write to the file. This example appends some data to the end of the file:

```
$lines[] = "\n<?php echo 'This file has been updated!'; ?>"
if (!JFile::write($file, implode("\n", $lines)))
{
    // handle failed file write
}
```

The last method that we will look at is the `upload()` method. This method is intended to move files that have been uploaded. The method is similar to the `move()` method except it handles the creation of the destination path and it sets the permissions of the uploaded file.

This example takes the `uploadFile` array from the `FILES` request hash and copies it to its new location:

```
$file = JRequest::getVar('uploadFile', '', 'FILES', 'array');
if (!JFile::upload($file, JPATH_COMPONENT.DS.'files'))
{
    // handle failed upload
}
```

Archives

The `joomla.filesystem.archive` library provides us with two important things, the static JArchive class and a number of archive adapters. JArchive allows us to easily unpack archive files using the archive adapters. An adapter handles a specific type of archive. This list details the core archive adapters:

- BZIP2
- GZIP
- TAR
- ZIP

Before we start using this library we must always import it:

```
jimport('joomla.filesystem.archive');
```

We will start by exploring the use of JArchive to unpack archives. To do this we need to use the `extract()` method. We pass two parameters to this method: the path to the archive file and the path to directory to which we want to extract the contents.

This example extracts an archive to the 'temp' directory in the current component:

```
if (!JArchive::extract($pathToArchive, $destination))
{
    // handle failed archive extraction
}
```

When we use the `extract()` method we are invoking an archive adapter that is automatically selected based upon the file extension. This list describes the supported archive format extensions:

- `.bz2`
- `.bzip2`
- `.gz`
- `.gzip`

- .tar
- .tbz2
- .tgz
- .zip

Note that if the archive is a **tarball**, a compressed file that contains a `tar` archive, the inner TAR file will automatically be extracted.

 If we attempt to extract an unsupported archive type, a warning will be thrown.

Arrays

Arrays are an integral part of PHP and we constantly use them when building Joomla! extensions. PHP provides us with a number of very useful functions for working with arrays. We can use the static JArrayHelper class to simplify other common tasks when working with arrays.

The JArrayHelper class is located in the `joomla.utilities.array` library. Before we can use the JArrayHelper class we must import the relevant library:

```
jimport('joomla.utilities.array');
```

Imagine we have a CSV file, which holds records with mathematical data:

```
2, 4.6
0, 0.0
1, 2.5
4, 8.2
```

Now imagine we want to order the data by ID (the first field) and we want the values (second field) to be displayed as integers.

The first thing we need to do is retrieve the contents of the CSV file; we do this using the JFile class, discussed earlier in this chapter:

```
jimport('joomla.filesystem.file');
if (false === ($data = JFile::read($CSV_FilePath)))
{
    // handle failed to read CSV file
}
```

Once we have retrieved the data we need to split it into an array of lines. We then need to convert each line into an object. If we do not use objects, we will be unable to use the JArrayHelper sorting method.

To create the objects, we use the toObject() method. This method creates a new object and adds properties to the object based on the array keys. In this example, when we use the toObject() method, the resultant objects will be of type stdClass and have two keys—id and value:

```
// convert CSV data into an array of lines
$data = explode("\n", $data);

// iterate over each line
for($i = 0, $c = count($data); $i < $c; $i ++)
{
    // split the values
    $temp = explode(',', $data[$i]);

    // cast all the values to integers (always rounds down)
    JArrayHelper::toInteger($temp);

    // set the named values
    $temp['id'] = $temp[0];
    $temp ['value'] = $temp[1];

    // remove keys 0 and 1
    unset($temp[0], $temp[1]);

    // convert the array to an object
    $data[$i] = JArrayHelper::toObject($temp);
}
```

The first JArrayHelper method that we use in this example is toInteger(). This method casts all of the values in the $temp array into integers.

The objects created in the above example are of type stdClass. If we want to, we can specify a different class. This example demonstrates how we would create objects of type JObject:

```
$data[$i] = JArrayHelper::toObject($temp, 'JObject');
```

The class that we specify must not have any constructor parameters, or all the constructor parameters must be optional.

If we ever need to convert an object back to an array, we can use the fromObject() method:

```
$array = JArrayHelper::fromObject($object);
```

Now that we have an array of objects we can start to play around with that array. The first thing we'll do is sort the array by the ID of each record. We do this using the `sortObjects()` method:

```
JArrayHelper::sortObjects($data, 'id');
```

By default this method sorts the data in ascending order; if we want to sort the data in descending order, we must supply the third optional parameter set to `-1`:

```
JArrayHelper::sortObjects($data, 'id', -1);
```

This describes the resultant array when using all of the previous code with the example CSV file; notice that each element is a `stdClass` object, all attributes of the objects are integers, and the objects are in order of ID:

```
Array
(
    [0] => stdClass Object
        (
            [id] => 0
            [value] => 0
        )

    [1] => stdClass Object
        (
            [id] => 1
            [value] => 2
        )

    [2] => stdClass Object
        (
            [id] => 2
            [value] => 4
        )

    [3] => stdClass Object
        (
            [id] => 4
            [value] => 8
        )

)
```

The next thing that we will do is determine the total of the values. We could do this by iterating over the array and adding each value to the total. Another way of achieving this is by using the `getColumn()` method and the `array_sum()` function together:

```
$total = array_sum(JArrayHelper::getColumn($data, 'value'));
```

The getColumn() method is used to retrieve a column of data from an array structure. In order for this method to work as expected, the array must be populated with either objects or arrays.

Imagine we have an array of values of mixed types and we want to retrieve different values from that array casting the values to the appropriate type as we do so. To do this we can use the getValue() method:

```
$array = array(12, '1.3');
$value = JArrayHelper::getValue($array, 0, '', 'ALNUM')
```

The first parameter is the array from which we want to retrieve the value; the array will be passed by reference. The second parameter is the name of the array element key the value of which we want to get.

The third and fourth parameters are both optional. The first of these is the default value, and the last of these is the type to which we want to cast the retrieved value. This table describes the different types that are supported:

Name	Description
INT, INTEGER	Whole number
FLOAT, DOUBLE	Floating-point number
BOOL, BOOLEAN	true or false
WORD	String consisting of the letters A-Z (this is not case sensitive)
STRING	String
ARRAY	Array of mixed values

For a more comprehensive range of type-casting options, we can use the JInputFilter class that supports ten different data types. For a complete description of JInputFilter refer to the official API documentation: http://api.joomla.org/Joomla-Framework/Filter/JInputFilter.html.

The last method that we will explore is the toString() method. The most common way in which we use this method is to produce a string that can be used to describe attributes in an XHTML tag.

In this example, we create an image tag, which uses an array to populate its attributes:

```
$attributes = array();
$attributes['src'] = 'http://example.org/image.gif';
$attributes['class'] = 'image';
echo '<img '.JArrayHelper::toString($attributes).' />';
```

The resultant output will appear like this:

```
<img src="http://example.org/image.gif" class="image" />
```

There are additional parameters that we can use with the `toString()` method to modify the output. The method uses inner and outer glue. The inner glue is used between a key and a value; the outer glue is used between key-value pairs:

```
echo JArrayHelper::toString($attributes, ' : ', ";\n");
```

This time we use a colon for the inner glue and a semicolon and a new line character for the outer glue. The resultant output will appear like this:

```
src : "http://example.org/image.gif";
class : "image"
```

Trees

Trees are used to model hierarchical data. Joomla! provides us with the JTree and JNode classes; we can use these to build tree data structures. Before we start using these classes we must import the relevant library:

```
jimport('joomla.base.tree');
```

The first thing we do when creating a new tree is to build a new JTree object. Although we don't technically require a JTree object in order to create a tree, it ensures we can always easily access the root of the tree. There are no parameters that we need to pass when creating a new tree:

```
$tree = new JTree();
```

When a new tree is created, we automatically create a new JNode object, which is known as the root node. The **root node** is the node to which all other nodes in the tree can trace their roots.

The first thing we normally do once we have created a tree is add some child nodes. To do this we will use the JTree `addChild()` method:

```
$tree->addChild(new JNode());
```

When we use the JTree `addChild()` method, the child isn't necessarily added as a direct descendant to the root node. Trees use a pointer to determine the current/working node. When we add a new child node it is added to the present working node's children. By default the working node is the root node.

The next diagram depicts a tree using the JNode and JTree classes. The root node is node A—the root node never changes during the life of the tree. The working node is node B—the working node is likely to change repeatedly during the life of the tree.

If we were to use the `addChild()` method, the new node would be added as child to working node, in this case node B. When we create a new JTree, the root node is also initially the working node.

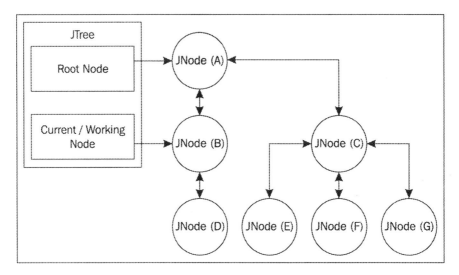

Notice that the arrows between child nodes and parent nodes are bi-directional. This is because we can navigate between nodes in both directions. The JTree pointers are unidirectional; this means that the nodes are unaware of the encapsulating JTree object.

If we want to create a branch of nodes, when we add a new node we can pass another parameter. When this parameter is `true`, the newly added node will become the working node.

To traverse the tree we can use the `reset()` and `getParent()` methods. The `reset()` method is used to set the working node to the root node. The `getParent()` method is used to set the working node to the parent node of the present working node.

So far we have only added blank nodes. How do we store data in nodes? The JNode class is a subclass of JObject; this means that we have access to the `get()` and `set()` methods:

```
$node = new JNode();
$node->set('name', 'Child Node 1');
$tree->addChild($node);
```

Although this makes the JNode class more useful, we can make nodes that are designed especially for our needs. The best way for us to make use of the JTree is to define a new JNode subclass that has additional properties:

```
// subclass of JNode
class myNode extends JNode
{
    // name property
    var $name = '';

    // constructor
    function __construct($name='')
    {
        $this->set('name', $name);
        parent::__construct();
    }
}
```

Now we can create a far more bespoke tree:

```
$tree->addChild(new myNode('Node 1'));
$tree->addChild(new myNode('Node 2'));
```

A prime example to this sort of use of the JTree class is the iLink and iLinkNode classes. These two classes extend the JTree and JNode classes respectively. They are used to build the menu trees that are commonly used in Joomla!.

Log Files

We are provided with the JLog class that is specifically for handling log files. In order to use this class we must first import it:

```
jimport('joomla.utilities.log');
```

We'll start by exploring the use of JLog to handle the global error log file. The global error log file is a PHP file normally located in the logs. A common use of this file is to log failed login attempts.

To get a JLog object to handle the global error log file we use the getInstance() method:

```
$errorLog =& JLog::getInstance();
```

Next we will add a new entry to the log file. New entries are appended to the end of the log file and they are derived from associative arrays. The keys required in the array differ dependent on the log file we are handling. For the global error log file we can use the following keys:

- DATE
- TIME
- LEVEL
- C-IP
- STATUS
- COMMENT

If we do not provide values for the DATE, TIME, or C-IP keys, they are automatically populated. We are not required to provide any key-value pairs; however, this would make the log file relatively useless.

To add a new entry we use the addEntry() method. This example adds an example entry to the log file:

```
$entry = array('status' => 'OK', 'comment' => 'Example');
$errorLog->addEntry($entry);
```

The great thing about this method is that if the log file doesn't exist it will be created at this stage. When a log file is created a set of standard headers are added to the log file. This is an example of what the headers may look like:

```
#<?php die('Direct Access To Log Files Not Permitted'); ?>

#Version: 1.0

#Date: 1954-06-07 12:00:00

#Fields: date    time    level   c-ip    status comment

#Software: Joomla! 1.5.0 Beta 2 [ Khepri ] 04-May-2007 00:00 GMT
```

Notice that the first line includes that common bit of PHP we use in all Joomla! PHP files. This ensures that the log file isn't directly accessible. In order for it to work, the log file must be a PHP file.

Entries are added beneath the header and each field is separated by a tab character. This is an example of the entry that would be added as a result of our previous example:

```
1906-12-09    12:00:00    -    192.168.0.2    OK    Example
```

Notice that the fields are in the order identified by the header and the level value is a dash. The level value is a dash because we did not provide a value when we added the entry.

The `addEntry()` method returns a Boolean response. This is because we cannot guarantee that the entry will be added successfully. We might be unable to create the log file or unable to write to the log file.

This is an example of how we might choose to deal with the potential problem:

```
if (!$errorLog->addEntry($entry))
{
    // handle a failed entry
    JError::raiseNotice('SOME_ERROR', JText::sprintf('LOGFAIL',
                                        $entry['comment']);
}
```

To test this example, modify the access rights to your error log file. If we wanted to make the failed entry handling even more robust, we could use the JMail class to send an email to the site administrator.

In addition to the global error log file we can use the JLog class to handle bespoke log files. To do this we still use the `getInstance()` method but we must provide some additional parameters.

The first of these is the name of the log file not including the path. If we do not provide any more parameters the log file will be located in the same directory as the global error file.

The second parameter is an associative array of options. JLog currently only supports one option, `format`. The `format` option is used to determine the format in which the log entries are stored. By default this is:

```
{DATE}\t{TIME}\t{LEVEL}\t{C-IP}\t{STATUS}\t{COMMENT}
```

When we define a custom format string we use curly braces to encapsulate entry field names. These fields relate directly to the keys that we described earlier when adding an entry to a log file.

The third and final parameter is the path to the log file. This defaults to the global log file path defined in the config (`config.log_path`).

This example gets an instance of a JLog that will handle the `mylog.php` log file located in the root of the frontend of the current component. Each entry log entry will have three fields, DATE, TIME, and DESCRIPTION in that order:

```
$options = array('format' => '{DATE}\t{TIME}\t{DESCRIPTION}');
$log =& JLog::getInstance('mylog.php', $options, JPATH_COMPONENT);
```

We add entries to this log file using the JLog object in the same way as we did with the previous example:

```
$entry = array('description' => 'Example Log Entry');
$log->addEntry($entry);
```

Summary

Joomla!'s powerful library is an extremely useful resource. Not only does it provide us with common Joomla! classes, but it also provides us with some invaluable utilities and useful classes.

Working with the file system is a common activity. Migrating to the `joomla.filesystem` library is extremely easy and it provides us with far more power and consistency than the basic PHP file-system functions.

Arrays have long been a key data type. PHP provides us with many useful functions for handling arrays; Joomla! extends this functionality through the JArrayHelper class.

Data structures are often used to model information. The tree structure is a very common data structure and Joomla! provides us with a way of easily building such a structure.

We should always bear in mind that if there isn't something appropriate within the Joomla! library to handle a specific task, we can always turn to the other libraries with which we are provided.

If we are still unable to find a solution we can always turn to other libraries outside of the Joomla! sphere. A good resource for such libraries is PHP classes (http://www.phpclasses.org/), a repository of freely available PHP classes.

Appendix

The appendix consists of three main sections:

- Classes
- Parameters
- Configuration

There is also some official documentation available from the Joomla! help site (`http://help.joomla.org`), developers site (`http://dev.joomla.org`), and API site (`http://api.joomla.org`).

Classes

This section details a number of the core classes. Additional documentation can be found at the official API site: `http://api.joomla.org`.

 This reference uses standard UML notation:

```
methodOrFunctionName(paramsList) : returnType
```

The following example describes a method called `someMethod` with two parameters, `anArray` and `xyz`, which returns a string. The parameters are of type array and Boolean respectively. The `array` type includes associative arrays; more information about array parameters and return types is given in the description of each method. The ampersand denotes that `anArray` will be passed by reference:

```
someMethod( &anArray : array, xyz : boolean ) : string
```

The next example returns a reference (denoted by the ampersand before the method name) to an instance of a JObject class. Methods and functions that return a reference must use the `=&` assignment operator to prevent copying of the returned value.

The returned object can be a subclass of JObject. The string parameter message is optional, and if it is not specified, it will contain the default value `foobar`:

```
&anotherMethod( message : string='foobar' ) : JObject
```

This last example doesn't return a value; this is signified by the return type void. The `someParameter` parameter is of type mixed. A mixed type means that the value can be any type:

```
andAnotherMethod( someParameter : mixed ) : void
```

It is important to remember that all method and property names that begin with an underscore are to be treated as private/protected. There is one exception to this. Methods that are named solely with an underscore, _(), are not to be considered private. This method name is used when a class has a method that we use frequently, for example `JText::_('translate some text')`.

JObject

JObject is a common base class. It provides constructor compatibility between PHP 4 and 5, and provides some common methods. For information about using JObject as a parent class, refer to Chapter 2.

Properties

_errors : array	Object error history

Constructors

JObject( ) : JObject

This constructor removes the need for subclasses to use the `className()` style constructor. Subclasses need only define the `__construct()` constructor, which, if PHP 5 is not being used, is called by this method. Although this constructor does not define any parameters, this does not restrict the subclasses. Multiple parameters can still be used, all of which will be passed to the highest level `__construct()` method.

__construct( ) : JObject

This constructor is designed to be overridden in subclasses. Overriding methods should always call `parent::__construct()`.

Methods

get(property : string, default : mixed=null) : mixed

Accessor; gets the value of the requested property. If the property is not set, then the optional default value will be returned. This method will not return a reference; in subclasses it can be beneficial to add specific methods where a reference to a property is more suitable. Private properties, identified by an underscore at the start of the name, can be returned using this method.		
Parameters	property	Name of the property to return
	[default]	The default value to return if the property has not been initialized
Returns	Value of property	

getError(i : int=null, toString : boolean=true) : mixed

Returns an error that occurred during the execution of one of the object's methods. The error can be an object or a string. See JError for more information about errors.		
Parameters	[i]	Error number; by default the last error is retrieved
	[toString]	Return a string even if the error is an object
Returns	Error object or string associated with the object	

getErrors( ) : array

Returns a copy of the _error property.	
Returns	Array of errors associated with the object

getPublicProperties(assoc : boolean=false) : array

Gets the names of all the public properties of the object; this includes run-time properties, not just class properties. Names of private properties will not be returned; private properties are identified by an underscore at the start of the name. If assoc is true, gets an associative array including the property values.	
Parameters	[assoc]	Get associative array with values; default is false
Returns	Array of public property names or associative array of object property values

set(property : string, value : mixed=null) : void

Mutator; sets the value of the property in the object.		
Parameters	property	Name of the property
	[value]	Value of the property

setError(error : mixed) : void

Adds an error to the object's error history.		
Parameters	[error]	String or error object

toString( ) : string

Gets a string representation of the object. This method gets the name of the class.	
Returns	String representation of the object

JUser

extends JObject
Handles a site user. If the user is not logged in, id and gid will be zero and usergroup will be null. For more information about dealing with users refer to Chapter 7.

Properties

_errorMsg : string	Log of errors, separated by new lines
_params : JParameter	Parameters from #__users.params field. Metadata available from administrator/components/com_users/user.xml.
activation : string	Activation string, used to verify account registration
aid : int	Access group ID
block : int	Access blocked. 0=not blocked, 1=blocked.
clearPW : string	Clear text password, only present when changing password
email : string	Email address
gid : int	Group ID, relates to the legacy #__groups table
id: int	User ID, relates to the #__users.id field
lastvisitDate : string	Date on which the user last visited the site
name : string	User's name, their actual name/nickname, not username
params : string	INI parameter string, used when updating and creating users
password : string	MD5-hashed password
registerDate : string	Date on which the account was registered
sendEmail : int	Receive system emails. 0=no, 1=yes.
username : string	Username
usertype : string	User group that the user is a member of (ARO group). If the user is not logged in this will be null.

Constructors

__construct(identifier : int=0) : JUser

Builds a new JUser object and loads the user's details from the database.		
Parameters	[identifier]	User's ID

Methods

authorize(acoSection : string, aco : string, axoSection : string=null, axo : string=null) : boolean

Determines if the user is authorized to perform an action. Acts as a pass-through for JAuthorization. This is only for GACL authorization.		
Parameters	acoSection	ACO Section (the term 'section' does not relate to content sections)
	aco	ACO value
	[axoSection]	AXO Section (the term 'section' does not relate to content sections)
	[axo]	AXO value
Returns	`true` if authorized	

bind(&array : array) : boolean

Binds an associative array to the object. There are two ways to use this: updating an existing user and creating a new user. Create is assumed if the object property `id` is empty (zero is considered empty).		
When updating an existing user, `array` can contain any of the public properties associated with a JUser object. If user parameters are going to be bound they must be passed in a key named `params` and be in INI string format. The values are then bound to the object.		
When creating a new user the `username` property must already be set. If `password` is omitted from `array` a random password will be generated.		
Parameters	array	Associative array with which to bind
Returns	`true` on success	

defParam(key : string, value : mixed) : mixed

If the user's parameter is not defined, this defines the parameter and sets the value.		
Parameters	key	Name of the parameter
	value	Value of the parameter
Returns	Previous value of the user's parameter	

delete( ) : boolean

Removes user from the Joomla! database.	
Returns	`true` on success

getError( ) : string

Gets the object's error log.	
Returns	Error log

static &getInstance(id : mixed=0) : JUser

Gets a reference to a global instance of a JUser object. If the object does not exist, it will be created. `id` can be a string or an integer. If it is a string it will be assumed that it is a username, and if it is an integer it will be assumed that it is a user's ID. To get a reference to the current user object, use `JFactory::getUser()`.		
Parameters	[id]	User's ID or username
Returns	Reference to a JUser object	

getParam(key : string, default : mixed=null) : mixed

Gets a user's parameter from the `_params` property. If the parameter does not exist, the value of `default` will be returned.		
Parameters	key	Name of the parameter
	[default]	Default value
Returns	Value of the parameter, or default value if the parameter does not exist	

&getParameters( ) : JParameter

Gets a refernce to the user's parameters (`_params` property).	
Returns	Reference to the user's parameters

&getTable( ) : JTableUser

Gets a reference to a new JTableUser object loaded with the current user's details.	
Returns	Reference to a new JTableUser object

load(id : int) : boolean

Loads a user based on their ID. On failure, a warning will be raised.		
Parameters	id	User ID
Returns	`true` on success	

save(updateOnly : boolean=false) : boolean

Saves the user to the database. If `updateOnly` is `true`, then the creation of a new user will not be permitted. If this is the case, and an attempt is made to save a new user, the method will still return `true`. Before saving the user a number of sanity checks are made, including data validation and authorization verification. If any of these fail then the method will return `false`.		
Parameters	[updateOnly]	Only save if it is an existing user
Returns	`true` on success	

setLastVisit(timestamp : string) : boolean

Updates the user's database record last visit date; note that this does not update the `lastvisitDate` property of the object.		
Parameters	timestamp	Timestamp for the last visit
Returns	`true` on success	

setParam(key : string, value : mixed) : mixed

Sets the value of a user's parameter.		
Parameters	key	Name of the parameter
	value	Value of the parameter
Returns	Previous value of the parameter	

setParameters(data : string, path : string=null) : void

Loads an INI parameter string. `path`, if specified, is the path to an XML file defining the parameters; if not specified, the default user XML file is used.		
Parameters	data	INI parameter string
	[path]	XML parameter definition file path

_bind(from : mixed, ignore : string="") : boolean

Used by the `bind()` and `load()` methods to bind data to the object. `from` must be an object or associative array. `ignore` defines a list of key/property names that should not be bound to the object.		
Parameters	from	Object or associative array to bind
	[ignore]	Properties and keys to ignore
Returns	`true` on success	

_setError(msg : string) : void

Appends `msg` to the object's error log.		
Parameters	msg	Error message

JModel

abstract, extends JObject
Base class for model classes that use the MVC implementation. For more information about JModel refer to Chapter 4.

Properties

_db : JDatabase	Reference to the database connection
_name: string	Model name
_state : JObject	State of the object

Constructors

__construct(config : array=array()) : JModel

Builds a new JModel object. `config`, an associative array, can contain the keys `'name'` and `'table_path'`. `'name'` is transposed to the model name; if `'name'` is not specified the name will be extracted from the name of the class. This will only work if the name of the class is in the format `optionalPrefixModelSomeName`. `'table_path'` will be added to the JTable include paths. If `table_path` is not specified, but `JPATH_COMPONENT_ADMINISTRATOR` is defined, then the path `JPATH_COMPONENT_ADMINISTRATOR.DS.'tables'` will be added.		
Parameters	[config]	Associative array of configuration options

Methods

static addIncludePath(path : string=") : array

Adds a new path to the array of paths used to find JModel classes.		
Parameters	[path]	Path to add
Returns	Paths to search for JModel subclasses	

static addTablePath(path : mixed=") : void

Adds a new path to the array of paths used to find JTable classes. `path` can be a string, or an array of strings. Pass through method for `JTable::addIncludePath()`.		
Parameters	[path]	Path or array of paths to add

&getDBO( ) : JDatabase

Gets a reference to a database connection.	
Returns	Reference to a database connection

static &getInstance(type : string, prefix : string=") : JModel

Gets a reference to a new instance of a JModel subclass object. If the class cannot be found, returns `false`.		
Parameters	type	Name of the JTable
	[prefix]	Prefix of the class name, normally `Model`
Returns	Reference to a new instance of a JModel-derived object	

getName( ) : string

Gets the model name.	
Returns	Model name

getState(property : string=null) : mixed

Gets a model state property. If `property` is not specified, a complete copy of the model's state object is returned.	
Parameters	[property]	Name of state property
Returns	State property or a complete copy of the model's state object

&getTable(name : string=", prefix : string='Table') : JTable

Gets an instance of a JTable subclass object. If `name` is not specified, then the model name will be used. The parameters are concatenated to create the class name, in the form `$prefix.$name`. If the class is not present, the paths defined in JTable will be searched for a file named `$prefix.$name.'.php'` where the class should reside.		
Parameters	[name]	Name of the JTable
	[prefix]	Class prefix
Returns	Reference to a new instance of a JTable subclass object	

setDBO(&db : JDatabase) : void

Sets the reference to the database connection.	
Parameters	Database connection

setState(property : string, value : mixed=null) : mixed

Sets a user state property.		
Parameters	property	Name of state property
	[value]	Value of state property
Returns	Previous value of state property	

_createFileName(type : string, parts : array=array()) : string

Gets the name of the file that a class should be located in. `parts` must include the key name. `type` should always be `'table'`.		
Parameters	type	The type of resources; only accepts `'table'`
	[parts]	Associative array of name parts
Returns	Name of the file that a class should be located in	

&_createTable(name : string, prefix : string='Table') : mixed

Used by `getTable()` to create a new instance of a JTable subclass object. Returns null or an error on failure.		
Parameters	name	Name of JTable
	[prefix]	Class prefix, normally `Table` or `JTable`
Returns	Reference to a new instance of a JTable subclass object	

&_getList(query : string, limitstart : int =0, limit : int=0) : array

Executes a query and gets a reference to an array of resultant objects.		
Parameters	query	Query to execute
	[limitstart]	Start record
	[limit]	Maximum number of records
Returns	Reference to an array of objects as a result of the query	

_getListCount(query : string) : int

Gets the number of results obtained from `query`. Should be used cautiously; causes the query to be executed. If possible, consider using `$db->getNumRows()` directly after `&_getList()`; this prevents the query being executed twice.		
Parameters	[query]	Query to count number of results from
Returns	Number of results	

JView

abstract, extends JObject
Base class for view classes that use the MVC implementation. For more information about JModel refer to Chapter 4.

Properties

_basePath : string	Path to view base
_defaultModel : string	Name of the default model
_escape : array	Array of names of functions used to escape output. Can also contain arrays with two elements, a class name and method name. For more information see `http://php.net/manual/function.call-user-func.php`.
_layout : string	Template layout, normally `default`
_layoutExt : string	Template extension, normally `php`
_models : array	Array of models
_name: string	Name of view
_output : string	Output from the template
_path : array	Associative array of arrays of paths for resources
_template : string	Path to template

Constructors

__construct(config : array=array()) : JView

Builds a new JView object. `config` is an associative array that might contain the keys `name`, `base_path`, `template_path`, `helper_path`, and `layout`. `name` will be transposed to the view name, unless the view name has already been defined. `template_path` adds a path to the template paths. `layout` is the name of the template layout (template filename prefix), normally HTML.		
Parameters	[config]	Associative array of options.

Methods

addEscape( ) : void

If provided with parameters, the parameters will be used as the function and methods to use with the `escape()` method. Parameters must be strings or arrays with two elements, a class and method name.

addHelperPath(path : mixed) : void

Adds paths to search for template files. `path` can be a string or an array of strings.	
Parameters	path	A path or array of paths

addTemplatePath(path : mixed) : void

Adds paths to search for template files. `path` can be a string or an array of strings.	
Parameters	path	A path or array of paths

assign(arg0 : mixed, arg1 : mixed=null) : boolean

Dynamically adds properties to the object. If `arg0` is an object/array, each of the properties/keys will be added to the object. If `arg0` is a string, it will be used as the name of the property, and `arg1` will be assigned to the value. Properties will be ignored if they start with an underscore.		
Parameters	arg0	Object/Array to add or a property name
	[arg1]	Value if `arg0` is a string
Returns	`true` on success	

assignRef(key : string, &val : mixed) : boolean

Dynamically adds the property, identified by `key`, to the object with a reference to `val`. If `key` starts with an underscore it will be rejected.		
Parameters	key	Name of the property to add
	val	Value to add a reference to
Returns	`true` on success	

display(tpl : string=null) : mixed

Calls the `loadTemplate()` method and gets the rendered result. If an error occurs a JException object will be returned. If `tpl` is specified, then it will be used as a suffix to the layout with an underscore separator.	
Parameters	[tpl]	The template suffix
Returns	Rendered template on success. Error on failure.

escape(value : mixed) : mixed

Performs escape functions on `value`. This method can be used dynamically, by calling it with extra parameters; extra parameters will be treated as the escape functions. For more information see `http://php.net/manual/function.call-user-func.php`.	
Parameters	value	Value to escape
Returns	Escaped value

&get(method : string, model : string=null) : mixed

Gets the result of a get method, from a registered model. If the model is not defined then the default model will be used. The method is identified as `'get'.$method`. If the specified model does not exist then the request will passed to the parent (JObject) class `JObject::get($method, $model)`.		
Parameters	method	Method or property to return
	[model]	Model to run the method on, or default value
Returns	`get` accessor result. `false` on failure (can be ambiguous depending upon the method being called, or the property being returned).	

getLayout( ) : string

Gets the view layout.	
Returns	View layout

&getModel(name : string=null) : JModel

Gets a JModel subclass object from the view. name is the name of the JModel class. If name is not provided, the default model is retrieved. JView supports a one-to-many relationship with JModels, but only one object per class.		
Parameters	[name]	Name of model class
Returns	Reference to a registered model	

getName( ) : string

Gets the name of the view.	
Returns	View name

loadHelper(hlp : string=null) : string

Searches known helper paths for the specified helper.		
Parameters	[tpl]	Template suffix
Returns	Rendered template	

loadTemplate(tpl : string=null) : string

Loads and renders a template. The rendered result is returned and stored in the object output buffer. If tpl is specified, it is appended to the layout name with an underscore separator, for example if tpl was 'item' and the template layout was 'default', the template name would be 'default_item'.		
Parameters	[tpl]	Template suffix
Returns	Rendered template	

setEscape( ) : void

Resets the escape callback functions and methods to use with the escape() method. If provided with parameters, the parameters will be used as the function and methods to use with the escape() method. Parameters must be strings or arrays with two elements, a class and method name. For more information see http://php.net/manual/function.call-user-func.php.

setLayout(layout : string) : string

Sets the view layout, normally default.		
Parameters	layout	View layout
Returns	Previous layout	

setLayoutExt(value : string) : string

Sets the layout extension to use.		
Parameters	Value	JModel to associate
Returns	Previous value	

&setModel(&model : JModel, default : boolean=false) : JModel

Registers a JModel subclass object with the view. If default is true, the registered model will become the default model. JView supports a one-to-many relationship with JModels, but only one object per model class.		
Parameters	model	JModel to associate
	[default]	Set as the default model
Returns	Reference to the newly registered model (returns $model)	

_addPath(type : string, path : mixed) : void

Adds paths to search for subclass files, normally templates. type is the type of path. To add a template path type would need to be 'template'. path can be a string or an array of strings.		
Parameters	type	Type of path
	path	A path or array of paths

_createFileName (type : string, parts : array) : string

Gets a filename based on type and parts. type can be 'template'. parts must contain the key 'name'.		
Parameters	type	Type of filename
	parts	Filename parts
Returns	Name of a file	

_setPath(type : string, path : mixed) : void

Adds paths to search for files, normally templates. type is the type of path. To add a template path type would need to be 'template'. path can be a string or an array of strings. Using this method will prepend JPATH_COMPONENT.DS.'views'. DS.'nameOfView'.DS.'tmpl' to template paths.		
Parameters	type	Type of path
	path	A path or array of paths

JController

abstract, extends JObject
Base class for controller classes that use the MVC implementation. For more information about JModel refer to Chapter 4.

Properties

_acoSection : string	ACO Section (relates to GACL)
_acoSectionValue : string	ACO Section Value (relates to GACL)
_basePath : string	Path to controller base
_doTask : string	Task method that is being executed
_message : string	Message to include in redirect
_messageType : string	Type of message to include in redirect
_methods : array	Class method names
_name: string	Name of the controller
_path : array	Directories in which to search for views and models
_redirect : string	Redirect URI
_task : string	Current or last task to be executed
_taskMap : array	Task-to-method map

Constructors

__construct(config : array=array()) : JController

Builds a new JController object. `config`, an associative array, can contain the keys `name`, `base_path`, `default_task`, `model_path`, and `view_path`. `name` becomes the controller name, unless the controller name is already defined by the subclass. `default_task` is the task that will be executed by default (this is not the same as the method). `model_path` and `view_path` are the paths in which to search for JModel and JView subclasses (`JPATH_COMPONENT` is prepended to the paths).		
Parameters	[config]	An associative array of configuration options

Methods

addModelPath(path : mixed) : void

Adds paths to search for JModel subclass files. `path` can be a string or an array of strings.		
Parameters	path	Path or array of paths to JModel subclass files

addViewPath(path : mixed) : void

Adds paths to search for JView subclass files. `path` can be a string or an array of strings.		
Parameters	path	Paths to JView subclass files

authorize(task : string) : boolean

If the object ACO Section is not defined authorization is automatically granted. If the object ACO Section has been defined, it determines if the current user has the rights to complete the specified task. If the ACO section value is not specified, task is used as the ACO section value.		
Parameters	task	The task to execute
Returns	Returns true on authorized, false on not authorized	

display(cachable : boolean=false) : void

Attempts to display. Uses JRequest (view and layout) to determine the view name and which template layout to use. If view is not known then the controller name is used. layout determines which template to use, normally default. If cachable is true then the global cache object is used to get and populate the display cache.		
Parameters	[cachable]	Use cached response

execute(task : string) : mixed

Executes the method mapped to task. If a mapped method for task does not exist, it attempts to execute the default task. If a mapped method for the default task does not exist, a 404 error is raised. When a mapped method is found, access rights are checked using the authorize() method. If access is denied, a 403 error is raised.		
Parameters	task	The task to execute
Returns	Result of the executed method. Returns error if no mapped method exists.	

&getModel(name : string, prefix : string="") : JModel

Gets a new instance of a JModel subclass object. If prefix is not specified, the name of the controller concatenated with the word 'Model' is used. name is the model class name suffix. If the class does not exist, Joomla! will attempt to load it from the model paths. If the file where the class is expected to reside is found but the class is missing, an error will be thrown.		
Parameters	name	Name of model (normally the entity name)
	[prefix]	Class prefix
Returns	A new instance of a JModel subclass object; null on failure	

getName( ) : string

Gets the name of the controller.	
Returns	Controller name

getTask( ) : string

Gets the current task or the last task that was executed.	
Returns	Current task or the last task that was executed

getTasks( ) : array

Gets the different task methods that are available for this controller.	
Returns	Array of task methods

&getView(name : string='', type : string='', prefix : string='', config : array=array()) : JView

Gets a JView subclass object. If name is not specified, the controller name is used. If `prefix` is not specified, the prefix will be `$controllerName.'View'`. `type` is the view layout, normally HTML. This method is normally called only specifying `name`.

`$view = $SomeController->getView('Item');`

This would attempt to instantiate the class SomeViewItem.

Parameters	[name]	View name
	[type]	View type; relates to the document type
	[prefix]	View prefix, default is `View`
	[config]	Configuration array to pass to the view
Returns	JView subclass object	

redirect( ) : boolean

If a redirect has been set, it redirects the browser and closes the application.	
Returns	Returns false on failure

registerDefaultTask(method : string) : void

Registers the default task method. The default task is the task that is executed when an attempt is made to execute a task that is not mapped to a method.	
Parameters	method	Default task method

registerTask(task : string, method : string) : void

Registers a task, with a method.	
Parameters	task	Task name
	method	Method name

setAccessControl(section : string, value : string=null) : void

Sets the object authorization ACO and ACO value. This is used by the authorize method.	
Parameters	section	ACO section
	[value]	ACO value

setMessage(text : string) : void

Sets the object redirect message. This is only used if the redirect method is called.		
Parameters	text	Redirect message

setRedirect(url : string, msg : string=null, type : string='message') : void

Sets the object redirect options. This is only used if the redirect method is called.		
Parameters	url	Redirect URI
	[msg]	Redirect message
	[type]	Message type

_addPath(type : string, path : mixed) : void

Adds paths to search for JModel or JView subclass files. type can be 'view' or 'model'. path can be a string or an array of strings.		
Parameters	type	Type of path
	path	Path or array of paths

_createFileName (type : string, parts : array=array()) : string

Gets a filename based on type and parts. type can be 'view' or 'model'. parts must contain the key 'name' and if type is 'view' it can optionally contain the key 'type', which relates to the layout.		
Parameters	type	Type of filename
	[parts]	Filename parts
Returns	Name of a file	

&_createModel(name : string, prefix : string='') : JModel

Builds a new JModel subclass object. name is the class name suffix, normally the entity name. prefix is the class name prefix, normally $controllerName.'View'.		
Parameters	name	Model name (normally the entity name)
	[prefix]	Model class name prefix
Returns	A new JModel subclass object	

&_createView(name : string, prefix : string=", type : string=", config : array=array()) : JView

Builds a new JView subclass object. name is the class name suffix, normally the entity name. prefix is the class name prefix, normally $controllerName. 'View'. type is the layout, normally HTML.		
Parameters	name	View name, normally the entity name
	[prefix]	View class name prefix
	[type]	View output type
	[config]	Configuration array to pass to the view
Returns	A new JView subclass object	

_setPath(type : string, path : mixed) : void

Adds paths to search for JModel or JView subclass files. type can be view or model. path can be a string or an array of strings. Using this method will prepend JPATH_COMPONENT. DS. $type to each path.		
Parameters	type	Type of path
	path	Path or array of paths

JTable

abstract, extends JObject
Class that handles individual database tables. JTable uses a buffering mechanism, which allows it to handle records on an individual basis. For more information about JTable refer to Chapter 3.

Properties

_tbl: string	Table name
_tbl_key : array	Primary key
_errorNum : int	Error Number
_db : JDatabase	Database connection

Constructors

__construct(table : string, key : string, &db : JDatabase) : JTable

Builds a new JTable object.		
Parameters	table	Table name
	key	Primary Key
	db	Database connection

Methods

static addIncludePath(path : mixed='') : array

Adds paths to search for JTable subclasses. `path` can be a string or an array of strings.	
Parameters	[paths]	Path or array of paths to add
Returns	Array of paths	

bind(from : mixed, ignore : mixed=array()) : boolean

Binds a subject (normally a record) to the object. For all the public object properties, this finds a corresponding key or property in `from`, and binds them to the object.	
Parameters	from	Bind subject, object or associative array
	[ignore]	Fields to ignore, string or array
Returns	`true` on success	

canDelete(oid : string=null, joins : array=null) : boolean

Determines if there are any records linked to the buffered record or, if `oid` is specified, the record identified by `oid`. `joins` identifies linked tables. `joins` is an optional two-dimensional array; the inner arrays are associative, and must contain the keys `name`, `idfield`, and `joinfield`. `name` is the linked table name, `idfield` is the linked table's primary key, and `joinfield` is the foreign key in the linked table.	
Parameters	[oid]	Record ID
	[joins]	Associative array of table join constraints
Returns	`true` if there are no dependent records	

check( ) : boolean

This method is used to validate the contents of the record buffer. This should be overridden in subclasses.	
Returns	`true` on success

checkin(oid : string=null) : boolean

Checks-in the buffered record or, if `oid` is specified, checks-in the record identified by `oid`. This sets the record's `checked_out` field to zero and `checked_out_time` to a null date-time.	
Parameters	[oid]	Record ID
Returns	`true` on success	

checkout(who : id, oid : string=null) : boolean

Checks out the buffered record or, if `oid` is specified, checks out the record identified by `oid`. This sets the record's `checked_out` field to who and `checked_out_time` to the current date-time.		
Parameters	who	User's ID
	[oid]	Record ID
Returns	`true` on success	

delete(oid : string=null) : boolean

Deletes the buffered record or, if `oid` is specified, deletes the record identified by `oid`.	
Parameters	[oid]	Record ID
Returns	`true` on success	

&getDBO( ) : JDatabase

Gets the database connection object.	
Returns	Database connection object

getErrorNum( ) : int

Gets the object error number. `0` (zero) means no error.	
Returns	Error number

static &getInstance(type : string, prefix : string='JTable') : mixed

Gets a new JTable subclass object. `type` is the name of the file the class resides in and the class name suffix, normally the entity name. `prefix` is the class name prefix. Core JTable subclasses use the prefix `'JTable'`; third-party JTable classes tend to use the prefix `'Table'`.		
Parameters	type	Class name suffix and file name
	[prefix]	Class name prefix
Returns	New JTable subclass object	

getKeyName( ) : string

Gets the name of the primary key field.	
Returns	Name of the primary key

getNextOrder(where : string="") : int

Gets the next place available in the current ordering. Using `reorder()` before using this method will ensure there are no gaps in the ordering.		
Parameters	[where]	WHERE clause
Returns	Next place available in the current ordering	

getTableName( ) : string

Gets the name of the table.	
Returns	Name of the table

hit(oid : string=null, log : boolean=false) : void

Increases the hit counter of the buffered record or, if `oid` is specified, the record identified by `oid`.		
Parameters	[oid]	Record ID
	[log]	Has no effect

[static] isCheckedOut(with : int=0, against : int=null) : boolean

Determines if the buffered record is checked out by any user other than the current user. If used statically (both `with` and `against` must be specified) compares `with` to `against`.		
Parameters	[with]	Current user's ID
	[against]	Record's `checked_out` value (checked-out user's ID)
Returns	`true` if the record is checked out by any user other than the current user	

load(oid : string=null) : boolean

Resets the record buffer and loads a single record into the buffer. `oid` is the value of the record's primary key.		
Parameters	[oid]	Record ID
Returns	`true` on success	

move(dirn : int, where : string="") : void

Moves a record up or down the ordering (table must have an ordering field). -1 = move up, 1 = move down.		
Parameters	dirn	Direction to move
	[where]	WHERE clause

publish(cid : array=null, publish : int=1, user_id : int=0) : boolean

Sets the publish value of records identified by cid, an array of record IDs (this only works when the table's primary key is numeric). Although cid is optional, if it is not specified the method will fail. If the table has a checked_out field, any records that are checked out by other users will not be affected.		
Parameters	[cid]	Array of record IDs
	[publish]	Publish value, 1 or 0
	[user_id]	Current user's ID
Returns	true on success	

reorder(where : string="") : boolean

Removes gaps in ordering.		
Parameters	[where]	WHERE clause
Returns	true on success	

reset( ) : void

Resets the object to the initial class option values.

save(source : mixed, order_filter : string="") : boolean

Binds source to the object; source must be an object or an associative array. Checks the buffer, stores the buffer, checks-in the record, and if order_filter is specified uses it to determine which field must be common during the execution of the reorder() method.		
Parameters	source	Record to save
	[order_filter]	Name of field by which records are ordered
Returns	true on success	

setDBO(&db : JDatabase) : void

Sets the JDatabase connection object.		
Parameters	db	Database connection object

store(updateNulls : boolean=false) : boolean

Saves the record buffer to the database. If the record buffer primary key property is set, an UPDATE will be executed, otherwise an INSERT will be executed.		
Parameters	[updateNulls]	Update null values
Returns	true on success	

setErrorNum(value : int) : void

Sets the object error number. 0 (zero) means no error.		
Parameters	value	Error number

toXML(mapKeysToText : boolean=false) : string

Gets an XML representation of the buffered record.		
Parameters	[mapKeysToText]	Maps foreign keys to text
Returns	XML string	

JError

static
Error handler. For more information about JError refer to Chapter 11.

Methods

static customErrorPage(&error : JException) : void

Gets the global instance of JDocumentError and passes it the error, then renders the page. This removes any previous output, and terminates the script.	
Parameters	error	JException error object
Return	$error	

static &getError(unset : boolean=false) : mixed

Gets the last error in the global error stack, or false if there are no errors. If unset is true, then the error will be removed from the stack.	
Parameters	[unset]	Remove last error from the global error stack
Returns	First error in the global error stack, or false if there are no errors	

static getErrorHandling(level : int) : array

Gets a copy of the associative array used to determine the handling of the specified error level. The array contains the key mode and, optionally, the key options. If an unknown level is passed, then null will be returned.	
Parameters	level	Error level
Return	Associative array used to determine error handling mechanism of level	

static &getErrors( ) : array

Gets a reference to the global error stack.	
Returns	Reference to the global error stack

static &handleCallback(&error : JException, options : array) : mixed

Calls a method in another class, passes `error` to it, and returns the result. `options` must have two string elements, the class name and method name to be called. This is essentially a pass-through method for the PHP `call_user_func()` function.		
Parameters	error	JException error object
	options	`array('classname', 'methodname')`
Return	Result of the executed method	

static &handleDie(&error : JException, options : array) : JException

Terminates the script and outputs the JException message to screen in HTML. If `$_SERVER['HTTP_HOST']` is not set, the message will either be echoed in plain text, or if `STDERR` is defined, written to `STDERR`.		
Parameters	error	JException error object
	options	Array of options (ignored)
Return	`$error`	

static &handleEcho(&error : JException, options : array) : JException

Outputs JException message to screen in HTML. If `$_SERVER['HTTP_HOST']` is not set, the message will either be echoed in plain text, or if `STDERR` is defined, written to `STDERR`.		
Parameters	error	JException error object
	options	Array of options (ignored)
Return	`$error`	

static &handleIgnore(&error : JException, options : array) : JException

Handle ignore error. No actions taken, returns `error`.		
Parameters	error	JException error object
	options	Array of options (ignored)
Return	`$error`	

static &handleLog(&error : JException, options : array) : JException

Adds a log entry to the error log. A new error log is created every day in the format `Y-m-d.error.log`. The entry includes the date, time, level, code, and message.		
Parameters	error	JException error object
	options	Array of options (passed to JLog)
Return	`$error`	

static &handleMessage(&error : JException, options : array) : JException

Adds the JExcpetion message to the application message queue.		
Parameters	error	JException error object
	options	Array of options (ignored)
Return	$error	

static &handleTrigger(&error : JException, options : array) : JException

Triggers a PHP user-level error, warning, or notice.		
Parameters	error	JException error object
	options	Array of options (ignored)
Return	error	

static &handleVerbose(&error : JException, options : array) : JException

Outputs JException message, info, and backtrace to screen in HTML. If $_SERVER['HTTP_HOST'] is not set, the message will either be echoed in plain text, or if STDERR is defined, written to STDERR.		
Parameters	error	JException error object
	options	Array of options (ignored)
Return	$error	
Return	$error	

static isError(&object : mixed) : boolean

Checks if object is an error (is of class JException or Exception).	
Parameters	object	Object to check
Returns	true if object is an error

static &raise(level : int, code : string, msg : string, info : mixed=null, backtrace : boolean=false) : mixed

Raises a new error of `level` and executes the associated error handling mechanisms. `level` relates to the PHP error levels, E_NOTICE, E_WARNING, and E_ERROR. Error handling levels and mechanisms can be altered.		
Parameters	level	Error level
	code	Error code
	msg	Error message
	[info]	Additional error information
	[backtrace]	Include `debug_backtrace()` information
Returns	Depends on error handling mechanism; normally a JException object	

static &raiseError(code : string, msg : string, info : mixed=null) : mixed

Raises a new error (E_ERROR) and executes the associated error handling mechanisms (by default `JError::handleCallback()`, which in turn calls, `JError::customErrorPage()`).		
Parameters	code	Error code
	msg	Error message
	[info]	Additional information
Return	Depends on error handling mechanism; normally a JException object	

static &raiseNotice(code : string, msg : string, info : mixed=null) : mixed

Raises a new notice (E_NOTICE) and executes the associated error handling mechanisms (by default this is `JError::handleMessage`). Normally this method will display a notice message on the resultant page		
Parameters	code	Error code
	msg	Error message
	[info]	Additional information
Return	Depends on error handling mechanism; normally a JException object	

static &raiseWarning(code : string, msg : string, info : mixed=null) : mixed

Raises a new warning (E_WARNING) and executes the associated error handling mechanisms (by default JError::handleMessage()). Normally this method will display a warning message on the resultant page.		
Parameters	code	Error code
	msg	Error message
	[info]	Additional information
Return	Depends on error handling mechanism; normally a JException object	

static registerErrorLevel(level : int, name : string, handler : string='ignore') : boolean

Defines a new error level. If the level already exists it will be rejected. name describes to the error type. handler defines the mode to use when an error of the new level is encountered (ignore, echo, verbose, die, messages, or log). To use callback, use JError::setErrorHandling() after registering the new level.		
Parameters	level	New error level
	name	Name
	[handler]	Handler (mode)
Return	true on success	

static setErrorHandling(level : int, mode : string, options : array='null') : mixed

Sets the error handling mechanism for level. Only levels that have already been defined can be modified. mode specifies what will occur when an error of the specified level is encountered (ignore, echo, verbose, die, messages, log, or callback). options, if set, is passed to the handler method. For example, if mode was 'message', then the JError::handleMessage() method would be called with two parameters — the JException object and options. If 'mode' is callback, the options array must be specified, and it must contain two string elements, a class name and a method to execute. callback is special, because it is the only mode in which a method outside of the JError class can be used to handle an error.		
Parameters	level	Error level
	mode	Error handler
	[options]	Options to pass to the handler method
Return	true on success; error on failure	

static translateErrorLevel(level : int) : mixed

Gets the name of the error level. If the error level is not defined, false will be returned.		
Parameters	level	Error level
Return	Name of error level; false if error level is not defined	

JDocument

abstract, extends JObject
Encapsulates and caches a response during the execution of an application. This enables us to make modifications to any part of the document irrespective of where we are in the output process. For more information about the document please refer to Chapter 2.

Properties

_buffer : string	Document rendered content buffer
_charset : string	Character encoding; default encoding is UTF-8
_engine : object	Rendering engine, used by core subclass JDocumentPDF
_generator : string	Generator metadata
_lineEnd : string	EOL character/string
_mdate : string	Document modified date
_metaTags : array	Metadata tags
_mime : string	MIME type
_namespace : string	Namespace, not used by core JDocument subclasses
_profile : string	Document profile, not used by core JDocument subclasses
_script : array	Embedded scripts
_scripts : array	URIs to linked scripts
_style : array	Embedded styles
_styleSheets : array	URIs to linked Cascading Style Sheets
_tab : string	Tab character/string
_type : string	Document type
description : string	Document description
direction : string	Text direction (ltr or rtl); default is left-to-right
language : string	Language setting, default is en (English)
link : string	Base URI of the document
title : string	Document title

Constructors

__construct(options : array=array()) : JDocument

Builds a new JDocument. Subclasses call parent::_construct($options). options can contain the keys, lineend, charset, language, direction, tab, and link.		
Parameters	[options]	Associative array of configuration options

Methods

addLink(url : string) : void

Sets base URI of the document.		
Parameters	url	Base URI

addScript(url : string, type : string='text/javascript') : void

Adds a link to a script to the document.		
Parameters	url	Script URI
	[type]	MIME type

addScriptDeclaration(content : string, type : string='text/javascript') : void

Embeds a script in the document.		
Parameters	content	Script
	[type]	MIME type

addStyleSheet(url : string, type : string='text/css', media : string=null, attribs : array=array()) : void

Links a stylesheet to the document. media is the link tag's media attribute. Common media types include screen, handheld, print, and aural. attribs is an associative array of link tag attributes.		
Parameters	url	Script URI
	[type]	MIME type
	[media]	Link tag media attribute type
	[attribs]	Associative array of tag attributes

addStyleDeclaration(content : string, type : string='text/css') : void

Embeds styles in the document.		
Parameters	content	Style content
	[type]	MIME type

getBuffer( ) : string

Gets the buffered contents of the document.	
Returns	Document contents

getCharset( ) : string

Gets the character set encoding.	
Returns	Character set encoding

getDescription( ) : string

Gets the document description.	
Returns	Document description

getDirection( ) : string

Gets the text direction of the document, `ltr` (left-to-right) or `rtl` (right-to-left).	
Returns	Text direction

getGenerator( ) : string

Gets the document generator.	
Returns	Document generator

getHeadData( ) : array

Gets an associative array of header data. Must be implemented in child classes.	
Returns	Associative array of header data

static &getInstance (type : string='html', attributes : array=array()) : JDocument

Gets a global instance of a JDocument subclass object, based on `type` (error, feed, HTML, PDF, or RAW) and `attributes`. Use `JFactory::getDocument()` to get the application document.		
Parameters	[type]	JDocument type
	[attributes]	Associative array of options
Returns	Global instance of a JDocument subclass object	

getLanguage( ) : string

Gets the language of the document.	
Returns	Document language

getLink( ) : string

Gets the document base URI.	
Returns	Document base URI

getMetaData(name : string, http_equiv : boolean=false) : string

Gets the document metadata. If the metadata is http-equiv (equivalent to an HTTP header) then specify `http_equiv` as `true`.		
Parameters	name	Metadata name
	[http_equiv]	Get HTTP header equivalent metadata
Returns	Metadata	

getModifiedDate( ) : string

Gets the document modified date.	
Returns	Document modified date

getTitle( ) : string

Gets the document title.	
Returns	Document title

getType( ) : string

Gets the document type.	
Returns	String representation of document type

&loadRenderer(type : string) : JDocumentRenderer

Gets a new instance of a JDocumentRenderer subclass object. `type` can be `Atom`, `RSS`, `Component`, `Head`, `Message`, `Module`, or `Modules`. If you define your own JDocumentRenderer class, you must include the class, before using this method.	
Parameters	type	Renderer type
Returns	Instance of a JDocumentRenderer-derived object

render(cache : boolean=false, params : array=array()) : string

Gets the rendered document. This method varies depending upon the subclass.		
Parameters	cache	Cache document
	params	Associative array of options
Returns	Rendered document	

setBuffer(content : string) : void

Sets the buffered contents of the document.		
Parameters	content	Document contents

setCharset(type : string='utf-8') : void

Sets the character set encoding. This does not convert content to the new character set.		
Parameters	[type]	Character set

setDescription(description : string) : void

Sets the document description.		
Parameters	description	Document description

setDirection(dir : string='ltr') : void

Sets the text direction of the document, ltr (left-to-right) or rtl (right-to-left).		
Parameters	[dir]	Text direction

setGenerator(generator : string) : void

Sets the document generator; default is Joomla! 1.5 - Open Source Content Management.		
Parameters	generator	Generator name

setLanguage(lang : string='en') : void

Sets the language of the document.		
Parameters	[lang]	Language

setLineEnd(style : string) : void

Sets the document EOL character string. style can be win, unix, mac, or a custom EOL character string.		
Parameters	style	System type or EOL string

setMetaData(name : string, content : string, http_equiv : boolean=false) : void

Sets metadata. If the metadata is http-equiv (equivalent to an HTTP header) then specify http_equiv as true.		
Parameters	name	Metadata name
	content	Metadata content
	[http_equiv]	Header equivalent

setMimeEncoding(type : string='text/html') : void

Sets the document MIME encoding.		
Parameters	[type]	MIME encoding

setModifiedDate(date : string) : void

Sets the document modified date.		
Parameters	date	Modified date

setTab(string : string) : void

Sets the document indentation string, e.g "\t".		
Parameters	string	Indentation string

setTitle(title : string) : void

Sets the document title.		
Parameters	[title]	Document title

setType(type : string) : void

Sets the document type.		
Parameters	type	JDocument type

_getLineEnd( ) : string

Gets the EOL character/string.	
Returns	EOL character string

_getTab( ) : string

Gets the indentation character string.	
Returns	Indentation character string

JApplication

abstract, extends JObject
Base application class. The frontend and backend application classes both extend this class. This class encapsulates the process from request to response. For more information about the application refer to Chapter 2.

Properties

_clientId : int	Client type; 0 = site, 1 = admin, 2 = installation
_router : JRouter	Application router
_messageQueue : array	Queued messages

Constructors

__construct(clientId : int=0) : JApplication

Builds a new JApplication object with the specified `clientId`. Subclasses generally do not require the `clientId` parameter.		
Parameters	[clientId]	0 = site, 1 = admin, 2 = installation

Methods

addCustomHeadTag(html : string) : void

Deprecated; use of this method is no longer advised.		

Adds a custom HTML tag to the head if the document type is HTML. Instead use:
 	
 ```$document =& JFactory::getDocument();```
```if($document->getType() == 'html')```
```{```
``` $document->addCustomTag('<!—a custom tag-->');```
```}```		

Parameters	HTML	HTML to add to the head

addMetaTag(name : string, content : string, prepend : string=", append : string=") : void

Deprecated; use of this method is no longer advised.		

Adds metadata to the document. Instead use:
 	
 ```$document =& JFactory::getDocument();```
```$document->setMetadata('metaName', 'metaValue');```		

Parameters	name	Metadata name
	content	Metadata value
	[prepend]	*Deprecated, no effect*
	[append]	*Deprecated, no effect*

appendMetaTag(name : string, content : string) : void

Deprecated; use of this method is no longer advised.		

Adds metadata to the document. Instead use:
 	
 ```$document=& JFactory::getDocument();```
```$document->setMetadata('metaName', 'metaValue');```		

Parameters	name	Metadata name
	content	Metadata value

appendPathway(name : string, link : string=null) : boolean

Deprecated and created during the development of Joomla! 1.5.		
Appends an item to the pathway. Instead use JPathWay:		
`$pathway = mainframe->getPathWay();` `$pathway->addItem($name, $link);`		
Parameters	name	Item name
	[link]	Item link
Returns	`true` on success	

close(code : int=0) : void

Closes the application gracefully.		
Parameters	[code]	`exit()` code

dispatch(component :string) : void

Dispatches the request and executes the relevant component, storing the rendered result in the global JDocument object.		
Parameters	[component]	Component being invoked

enqueueMessage(msg : string='', msgType : string='message') : void

Adds a new message to the application message queue. Clears the session message queue.		
Parameters	msg	Message
	[msgType]	Type of message

getBasePath(client : int=0, addTrailingSlash : boolean=true) : string

Deprecated; use of this method is no longer advised.		
Gets the base path to application entry point, not including the file name. Instead use:		
`$basePath = JURI::base();`		
Parameters	[client]	*Deprecated, no effect*
	[addTrailingSlash]	*Deprecated, no effect*
Returns	Path to application entry point, not including the file name	

getBlogCategoryCount( ) : int

Deprecated; use of this method is no longer advised.	

Counts the number of menu items that are blog categories (`content_blog_category`). Instead use:
 	
    `$menus  = &JMenu::getInstance();`
    `$count  = count($menus->getItems('type', 'content_blog_category'));`	

Returns	Number of menu items that are blog categories

getBlogSectionCount( ) : int

Deprecated; use of this method is no longer advised.	

Counts the number of menu items that are blog sections (`content_blog_section`). Instead use:
 	
    `$menus  = &JMenu::getInstance();`
    `$count  = count($menus->getItems('type', 'content_blog_section'));`	

Returns	Number of menu items that are blog sections

getCfg(varname : string) : mixed

Gets a configuration value.		
Parameters	varname	Name of config value
Returns	Configuration value	

getClientId( ) : int

Gets the client id. 0 = site, 1 = administrator, 2 = installer.	
Returns	Client ID

getContentItemLinkCount( ) : int

Deprecated; use of this method is no longer advised.	

Counts the number of menu items that are content item links (`content_item_link`). Instead use:
 	
    `$menus  = &JMenu::getInstance();`
    `$count  = count($menus->getItems('type', 'content_item_link'));`	

Returns	Number of menu items that are content item links

getCustomPathway( ) : array

Deprecated and created during the development of Joomla! 1.5.	
Instead use JPathWay:	
`$pathway = mainframe->getPathWay();`	
`$customPathway = $pathway->getPathWayNames();`	
Returns	Array of breadcrumbs

getGlobalBlogSectionCount( ) : int

Deprecated; use of this method is no longer advised.	
Counts the number of menu items that are blog sections (`content_blog_section`). Instead use:	
`    $menus = &JMenu::getInstance();`	
`    $count = count($menus->getItems('type', 'content_blog_section'));`	
Returns	Number of menu items that are blog sections

getHead( ) : string

Deprecated; use of this method is no longer advised.	
Gets the document head. Instead use:	
`    $document =& JFactory::getDocument();`	
`    $head = $document->get('head');`	
Returns	Document head

getItemId(id : int) : int

Deprecated; use of this method is no longer advised.		
Gets the menu `ItemId` for the specified content item. Instead use:		
`    ContentHelper::getItemid($id, $categoryId, $sectionId);`		
Parameters	id	Content item ID
Returns	Menu `ItemId` for the specified content item	

getMessageQueue( ) : array

Gets a copy of the application message queue. If no application messages exist and there are session messages, the session message queue will be moved to the application message queue.	
Returns	Array of application messages

getPageTitle( ) : string

Deprecated; use of this method is no longer advised.	

Gets the title of the document. Instead use:
 	
`    $document=& JFactory::getDocument();`
`    $title = $document->getTitle();`	

Returns	Menu `ItemId` for the specified content item

getPath(varname : string, user_option : string=null) : string

Deprecated; use of this method is no longer advised.		
Determines path to a resource. `varname` (resource type) can be `front`, `html`, `front_html`, `toolbar`, `toolbar_html`, `toolbar_default`, `toolbar_front`, `admin`, `admin_html`, `admin_functions`, `class`, `helper`, `com_xml`, `mod0_xml`, `mod1_xml`, `plg_xml`, or `menu_xml`. `user_option` refers to a user-related option, for example `com_content`. Instead use: `    $path = JApplicationHelper::getPath($varname, $user_option);`		
Parameters	varname	User_option type
	[user_option]	User option
Returns	Path	

&getRouter( ) : JRouter

Gets the application router object.	
Returns	Application router object

getStaticContentCount( ) : int

Deprecated; use of this method is no longer advised.	

Counts the number of menu items that are static content (`content_typed`). Instead use:
 	
`    $menus = &JMenu::getInstance();`
`    $count = count($menus->getItems('type', 'content_typed'));`	

Returns	Number of menu items that are static content

getTemplate( ) : string

Gets the name of the application template.	
Returns	Application template name

getUser( ) : JUser

Deprecated; use of this method is no longer advised.	
Gets the current user object. Instead use:	
`$user =& JFactory::getUser();`	
Returns	User object

getUserState(key : string) : mixed

Gets a value from the user session registry.		
Parameters	key	Name of the user session registry value
Returns	Value from the user session registry	

getUserStateFromRequest(key : string, request : string, default : mixed=null, type : string='none') : string

Gets a value from the user session registry, updating with a request value if a request value exists.		
Parameters	key	Name of the session registry value
	request	Name of the request value
	[default]	Default value
	[type]	Name of the hash from which the request value should be retrieved
Returns	Up-to-date value from the user session registry	

initialise(options : array=array()) : void

Initializes the application. Prepares application language, defines date formats, and builds the application router.		
Parameters	[options]	Associative array of options

isAdmin( ) : boolean

Checks if application is administrator (client ID is 1).	
Returns	`true` if application is backend

isSite( ) : boolean

Checks if application is frontend (client ID is 0).	
Returns	`true` if application is frontend

loadConfiguration(file : string) : void

Loads the application configuration and sets the database debug mode.	
Parameters	file	Path to configuration file

loadSession(name : string) : void

Loads the session. Creates a new session, if the session does not already exist.	
Parameters	name	Session name

login(credentials : array, options : array=array()) : mixed

Checks Joomla! credentials. `credentials` must include the keys `username` and `password`. If the login fails a warning will be raised. If any `onLoginUser` event handlers return false, login will be unsuccessful.		
Parameters	credentials	Associative array of user credentials
	[options]	Options to pass to the authentication plugins
Returns	`true` on success	

logout( ) : boolean

If a user is logged-in, logs them out	
Returns	`true` on success

prependMetaTag(name : string, content : string) : void

Deprecated; use of this method is no longer advised.	
Adds metadata to the document. Instead use: `$document=& JFactory::getDocument(); $document->setMetadata('metaName', 'metaValue');`	
Parameters	name	Metadata name
	content	Metadata value

registerEvent(event : string, handler : string) : void

Registers an event handler with the global event dispatcher. `handler` must be the name of a function or the name of a class that has a method of the same name as `event`.		
Parameters	event	Name of event
	handler	Function or class name

render( ) : void

Renders the response and adds it to the static JResponse body.

redirect(url : string, msg : string='', msgType : string='message') : void

Redirects to the specified url and, if specified, enqueues msg, ready to be served in the next request. This method closes the application. If the headers have not been sent an HTTP 301 (Moved Permanently) response will be made, otherwise a JavaScript redirect will be used.		
Parameters	url	Redirect URI
	[msg]	Optional message to enqueue
	[msgType]	Type of message

route( ) : void

Route the applictaion. Chooses the route through the application to take, based on the request URI.

setPageTitle(title : string=null) : void

Deprecated; use of this method is no longer advised.		

Sets the title of the document. Instead use:
 	
`    $document =& JFactory::getDocument();`
`    $document->setTitle($title);`		

Parameters	[title]	Document title

setUserState(key : string, value : mixed) : mixed

Sets a value in the user session registry.		
Parameters	key	Name of the user session registry value
	value	Key value
Returns	Value from the user session registry	

triggerEvent(event : string, args : array=null) : array

Triggers an event. This will notify any registered event handlers associated with the event that the event has occurred. args is exploded and each element is passed as individual argument to the handler.		
Parameters	event	Event to trigger
	[args]	Array of arguments to pass to the handlers
Returns	Array of the resultant returns from the event handlers	

&_createConfiguration(file : string) : JConfig

Loads the global configuration. The configuration file must define the class JConfig.		
Parameters	file	Path to configuration file
Returns	JConfig configuration object	

&_createRouter( ) : JRouter

Gets the application router. If the application router does not exist, it is created.	
Returns	Application router

&_createSession(name : string) : JTableSession

If a session does not exist, creates a session and adds it to the #__session table. If a session already exists, updates the session expiry time.		
Parameters	name	Session name
Returns	Session JTable object	

JURI

extends JObject
Handles URIs

Properties

_fragment : string	URI fragment (internal document location)
_host : string	Host
_pass : string	URI Password (not the Joomla! user's password)
_path : string	Path
_port : int	Port number
_query : string	GET query
_scheme : string	URI scheme (e.g. http)
_uri : string	URI
_user : string	URI Username (not the Joomla! user's username)
_vars : array	GET query, associative array

Constructors

__construct(uri : string=null) : JURI

Builds a new JURI object. If uri is specified, it will be parsed.	
Parameters	[uri]	URI to parse

Methods

static base( ) : string

Gets the base URI for the entry point, not including the filename.	
Returns	Base URI

current( ) : string

Gets the URI of the current location including the scheme, host, port, and path.	
Returns	Current URI

delVar(name : string) : void

Deletes a value from the URI query.		
Parameters	name	Name of query value

getFragment( ) : string

Gets the URI fragment identifier (denoted by a hash, #).	
Returns	URI fragment identifier

getHost( ) : string

Gets the URI host name. This does not include the path to the resource.	
Returns	Host name or IP address

static &getInstance(uri : string='SERVER') : JURI

Gets a global instance of a JURI object. If `uri` is not specified, `uri` will be constructed based on the current request.		
Parameters	[uri]	URI object to get
Returns	Global instance of a JURI object	

getPass( ) : string

Gets the URI password. This is part of the scheme authorization; it is not the same as Joomla! authorization.	
Returns	Scheme password

getPath( ) : string

Gets the URI path. This does not include the host name.	
Returns	URI path

getPort( ) : int

Gets the URI port. If it is the default port for the scheme, this may not return anything.	
Returns	Port number

getQuery(toArray : boolean=false) : mixed

Gets the URI query. If `toArray` is false, it will return a string, otherwise it will return an associative array.		
Parameters	[toArray]	Get in array format
Returns	URI query string	

getScheme( ) : string

Gets the URI scheme, normally `http` or `https`.	
Returns	URI scheme

getUser( ) : string

Gets the URI username. This is part of HTTP authorization; it is not the same as Joomla! authorization, or Joomla! user's username.	
Returns	Scheme username

getVar(name : string=null, default : mixed=null) : string

Gets a value from the URI query. Returns `default` if not set.		
Parameters	[name]	Name of query value
	[default]	Default value
Returns	Value from the URI query	

isSSL( ) : boolean

Determines if the URI scheme is `https`.	
Returns	`true` if scheme is `https`

parse(uri : string) : boolean

Attempts to parse a URI, the results of which are stored in the object.		
Parameters	uri	URI to parse
Returns	`true` on success	

setFragment(anchor : string) : void

Sets the URI fragment identifier.		
Parameters	anchor	Fragment identifier

setHost(host : string) : void

Sets the URI host name. This does not include the path to the resource.		
Parameters	host	Host name or IP address

setPass(pass : string) : void

Sets the URI password. This is part of the scheme authorization; it is not the same as Joomla! authorization.		
Parameters	pass	Scheme password

setPath(path : string) : void

Sets the URI path.		
Parameters	path	URI path

setPort(port : int) : void

Sets the URI port.		
Parameters	port	Port number

setQuery(query : mixed) : void

Sets the URI query. This can be done using a query string or an associative array.		
Parameters	query	Query string or associative array

setScheme(scheme : string) : string

Sets the URI scheme, normally `http` or `https`.		
Parameters	scheme	Scheme to set to

setUser(user : string) : void

Sets the URI username. This is part of the scheme authorization; it is not the same as Joomla! authorization.		
Parameters	user	Scheme username

setVar(name : string, value : string) : string

Sets a value in the URI query. Returns the previous value.		
Parameters	name	Name of query value
	value	New value
Returns	Previous value	

toString(parts : array=array('scheme', 'user', 'pass', 'host', 'port', 'path', 'query', 'fragment')) : string

Returns the URI in string format, including the defined parts. The default value for `parts` includes all of the possible parts of the URI. Order of elements in `parts` is not important.		
Parameters	[parts]	Parts to include in the URI
Returns	String representation of the JURI object	

_buildQuery(params : array, akey : string=null) : string

Builds a URI query from the `params` associative array. `akey` is used internally as part of a callback routine for array query values.		
Parameters	path	Path to clean
	[akey]	Array name
Returns	Cleaned path	

_cleanPath(path : string) : string

Cleans the passed URI. Removes any unnecessary clutter from the path.		
Parameters	path	URI to clean
Returns	Cleaned path	

JLanguage

extends JObject
Handles languages and translation.

Properties

_debug : boolean	Debug mode
_default : string	Default language (en-GB)
_lang : string	Language name
_metadata : array	Language metadata
_orphans : array	Strings that failed translation (only maintained during debug)
_paths : array	Array of loaded language file paths
_strings : array	Associative array of translations
_used : array	Array of used strings (only maintained during debug)

Constructors

__construct(lang : string=null) : JLanguage

Builds a new JLanguage object. Loads the specified language; if `lang` is not specified the default language, `en-GB`, will be loaded.		
Parameters	[lang]	Language to load

Methods

exists(lang : string, basePath : string=JPATH_BASE) : boolean

Checks if a language exists in the default language folder. basePath is one level above where the languages reside.		
Parameters	lang	Language to look for
	[basePath]	Basis for building language path
Returns	true if the language exists	

get(property : string, default : mixed=null) : mixed

Gets metadata about the language. Common properties include name and tag.		
Parameters	property	Property to retrieve
	[default]	Default if the property is not set
Returns	Value of the property	

getBackwardLang( ) : string

Gets the backward-compatible language name. Used for legacy support.	
Returns	Backward-compatible language name

getDebug( ) : boolean

Checks if the language object is in debug mode.	
Returns	true if the language object is in debug mode

getDefault( ) : string

Gets the default language.	
Returns	Default language

&getInstance(lang : string) : JLanguage

Gets a global instance of JLanguage. If an instance for the specified lang does not exist, it will be created.	
Parameters	lang	Language to load
Returns	A global instance of JLanguage

getKnownLanguages(basePath : string=JPATH_BASE) : array

Gets a two-dimensional associative array of all the known languages. The array contains keys named the same as the languages, which contain associative arrays of the corresponding language metadata.		
Parameters	[basePath]	Path on which to look for the languages folder
Returns	Two-dimensional associative array languages and metadata	

getLanguagePath(basePath : string=JPATH_BASE, language : string=null) : string

Gets the path to a language. If language is not specified, the path will point to all languages.		
Parameters	[basePath]	Basis for building language path
	[language]	Language name
Returns	Path to a language, or all languages	

getLocale( ) : array

Gets an array of the language locales, for example en-GB, en, english.	
Returns	Array of the different language locales

getMetaData(lang : string) : array

Returns an associative array containing the metadata about the specified language.		
Parameters	lang	Language to get metadata for
Returns	Associative array of metadata; returns null on failure	

getName( ) : string

Gets the name of the language.	
Returns	Language Name

getOrphans( ) : array

Gets the orphan strings. This is an array of strings that could not be translated. This information is only collated if the language object is in debug mode.	
Returns	Array of orphan (not translated) strings

getPaths(extension : string=null) : array

Gets an array of loaded language file paths. If extension is defined, only information about language files that are specific to that extension will be returned.		
Parameters	[extension]	Name of the extension
Returns	Array of loaded language file paths	

getPdfFontName( ) : string

Gets the PDF font name.	
Returns	PDF font name

getTag( ) : string

Gets the language tag, for example en-GB.	
Returns	Language tag

getUsed( ) : array

Gets an array of strings that were successfully translated.	
Returns	Array of successfully translated strings

getWinCP( ) : string

Gets the Windows Code Page name.	
Returns	Windows Code Page name

hasKey(key : string) : boolean

Checks if a translation exists.		
Parameters	key	Translation to look for
Returns	true if translation exists	

isRTL( ) : boolean

Checks if the language is written right-to-left.	
Returns	true if Language is written right-to-left

load(extension : string='joomla', basePath : string=JPATH_BASE) : boolean

Loads a language file. extension is used to identify the extension for which we are loading the language file, this determines where the file is located. basePath is one level above where the languages reside. If a language fails to load, normally because the file does not exist, or is inaccessible, the equivalent default language will be loaded. Note that the new translations are merged with previously loaded translations.		
Parameters	[extension]	Name of the extension
	[basePath]	Basis for building language path
Returns	true on success	

setDebug(debug : boolean) : boolean

Turns debug on or off.		
Parameters	debug	Turn debug on or off
Returns	Previous debug value	

setDefault(lang : string) : string

Sets the default language.		
Parameters	lang	Default language
Returns	Previous default language value	

setLanguage(lang : string) : string

Sets the language and loads the metadata. This does not load the translations; use the `load()` method to load the translations.		
Parameters	lang	Language identifier
Returns	Returns previous language	

_(string : string, jsSafe : boolean=false) : string

Attempts to translate `string`. `jsSafe`, if `true`, will add slashes to the translated string. If a translation cannot be found the original string will be returned. If debug is enabled, translated strings will be encapsulated by bullet characters, strings translated from a constant will be encapsulated in double exclamation marks, and strings that are not translated will be encapsulated in double question marks.		
Parameters	string	String to translate
	[jsSafe]	Add slashes to translated string
Returns	Translated string	

_load(filename : string, extension : string='unknown') : mixed

Loads a language file and returns an associative array of translations.		
Parameters	filename	Language path and filename to load
	[extension]	Name of the extension
Returns	Associative array of translations; `false` on failure	

_getCallerInfo( ) : array

Gets back-trace information that can be used to determine where a method call originated.	
Returns	Back-trace information

_parseLanguageFiles(dir : string=null) : array

Gets a two-dimensional associative array of all the languages in the path specified by `dir`. The returned associative array contains keys named the same as the languages, which contain associative arrays of the corresponding metadata.	
Parameters	[dir]	Path to look for languages in
Returns	Two-dimensional associative array of languages and metadata	

_parseXMLLanguageFile(path : string) : array

Parses an individual XML language information file and returns an array of metadata.	
Parameters	path	Path to XML language information file
Returns	Associative array of metadata	

_parseXMLLanguageFiles(dir : string=null) : array

Gets a two-dimensional associative array of all the XML language information files in `dir`. The array contains keys named the same as the languages, which contain arrays of metadata. Normally there will only be one XML language information file per language.	
Parameters	[dir]	Path to XML language information files
Returns	Two-dimensional associative array of languages and metadata	

JLanguageHelper

static
Performs language functions that are not specific to an individual language

Methods

static detectLanguage( ) : string

Attempts to detect the language using the HTTP headers. If unable to detect, assumes `en-GB`.
Returns	Detected language

static createLanguageList(actualLanguage : string, basePath : string=JPATH_BASE, caching : boolean=true) : array

Gets an array of language options. Each element is an associative array with three keys, `name`, `value`, and `selected`. This can be used to build a selection list of languages.	
Parameters	actualLanguage	Current language
	[basePath]	Path in which to find known languages
	[caching]	Use cached response
Returns	Two-dimensional array of language options	

JText

static
Translates strings to the correct language using the JLanguage class.

Methods

static printf(string : string) : int

Works like the PHP `printf()` function, except that `string` is translated. This method accepts a variable number of parameters. The additional arguments will not be translated. The result is outputted, and the method returns the length of the outputted string. If no additional parameters are specified, a null string will be returned. Refer to the PHP manual for more information: `http://php.net/manual/function.printf.php`.		
Parameters	string	String to translate
	(extra arguments)	Multiple arguments to insert into `string`
Returns	Length of translated string	

static sprintf(string : string) : string

Works like the PHP `sprintf()` function, except that `string` is translated. This method accepts a variable number of parameters. The additional parameters will not be translated. If no additional parameters are specified, a null string will be returned. Refer to the PHP manual for more information: `http://php.net/manual/function.sprintf.php`.		
Parameters	string	String to translate
	(extra arguments)	Multiple arguments to insert into `string`
Returns	Translated string	

static _(string : string, jsSafe : boolean=false) : string

Attempts to translate `string`. `jsSafe`, if `true`, will add slashes to the translated string. See the JLanguage `_()` method for more information.		
Parameters	string	String to translate
	[jsSafe]	Add slashes
Returns	Translated string	

JElement

abstract, extends JObject
This class is used to aid integration of extensions into Joomla!. A core use of this class enables the selection of bespoke parameters options when creating new menu items. The class is used in conjunction with an XML definition of an element, and used extensively by the JParameter class. For more information about JElement refer to the *Parameters (Core JElements)* section in this *Appendix*.

Properties

_name : string	Element name
_parent : object	Parent object that created the instance

Constructors

__construct(parent : object=null) : JElement

Builds a new JElement object and sets the parent object.		
Parameters	[parent]	Parent object

Methods

fetchElement(name : string, value : string, &xmlElement : JSimpleXMLElement, control_name : string) : string

Gets the rendered element. This method must be overridden in subclasses. For example, the output could be:		
<pre><input type="text" name="controlName[name]" id="controlNamename" value="value" class="text_area" size="20" /></pre>		
Parameters	name	Name and ID suffix
	value	Value
	xmlElement	JSimpleXMLElement element definition
	control_name	Name and ID prefix
Returns	Rendered element	

fetchTooltip(label : string, description : string, &xmlElement : JSimpleXMLElement, control_name : string=", name : string=") : string

Gets a tooltip, encapsulated in HTML label tags.		
Parameters	label	Content and title
	description	Title suffix
	xmlElement	JSimpleXMLElement element definition
	[control_name]	ID prefix
	[name]	ID suffix
Returns	HTML tooltip	

getName( ) : string

Gets the name of the element.	
Returns	Element name

render(&xmlElement : JSimpleXMLElement, value : string, control_ name : string='params') : array

Gets an array containing the rendered parts and attributes of the element. The array contains six items in order, tooltip `[0]`, rendered input element `[1]`, description `[2]`, label `[3]`, value `[4]`, and name `[5]`.		
Parameters	xmlElement	JSimpleXMLElement element definition
	value	Element value
	[control_name]	Name of the control
Returns	An array containing rendered parts and attributes of the element	

JParameter

extends JRegistry
Handles INI string parameters. This class is used in conjunction with JElement subclasses and XML files that define the nature of parameters. INI strings are used in database tables for values that do not have a specific field. An instance of the class can be used to handle multiple INI strings (with different XML definitions), using groups to separate each one. When dealing with one INI string, omitting the group will always use the default group, '`_default`'. For more information about JParameter refer to the *Parameters* (*Core JElements*) section in this *Appendix*.

Properties

_elementPath : array	Array of paths in which to find JElement subclasses (not restricted to groups)
_elements : array	Associative array of JElement objects (not restricted to groups)
_raw : string	INI string
_xml : array	Associative array of JSimpleXMLElement objects that define parameters (one object per group)

Constructors

__construct(data : string, path : string='') : JParameter

Builds a new JParameter object and loads `data` and, if specified, the XML file.		
Parameters	data	INI string
	[path]	Path to XML file

Methods

addElemenrPath(path : mixed) : void

Adds a path, or array of paths, to search for JElement subclass files.	
Parameters	path	Path or array of paths

bind(data : mixed, group : string=' _default') : boolean

Binds data with parameters in the specified group. data can be an associative array, an object, or an INI string.		
Parameters	data	Data to bind
	[group]	Parameter group
Returns	true on success	

def(key : string, value : string='', group : string= '_default') : string

If the parameter is not defined, sets the value of the parameter in the specified group.		
Parameters	key	Parameter to get
	[value]	Value if not defined
	[group]	Parameter group
Returns	Up-to-date value of the parameter	

get(key : string, default : string='', group : string='_default') : string

Gets the value of a parameter in the specified group. Returns the default value if the parameter is not set.		
Parameters	key	Parameter to retrieve
	[default]	Default value to return
	[group]	Parameter group
Returns	Value of the parameter	

getGroups( ) : mixed

Gets an associative array of the group names and the number of parameters in each, defined by the corresponding JSimpleXMLElement object. Groups that do not have a JSimpleXMLElement object will not be included.	
Returns	Associative array of group names and number of parameters in each. Returns false if no XML has been successfully loaded.

getNumParams(group : string=' _default') : mixed

Gets the number of parameters defined by the associated JSimpleXMLElement object, in the specified group.		
Parameters	[group]	Parameter group
Returns	Number of parameters; false if no JSimpleXMLElement object exists	

getParam(&node : JSimpleXMLElement, control_name : string='params', group : string=' _default') : mixed

Gets an array of parameter details from a group. The array contains six items in order: tooltip [0], HTML rendered string [1], description [2], label [3], value [4], and name [5].		
Parameters	Node	JSimpleXMLElement parameter to render
	[control_name]	Input names
	[group]	Parameter group
Returns	Array of parameter details from a group	

getParams(name : string='params', group : string=' _default') : mixed

Gets a two-dimensional array of all the parameters in a group. The inner arrays contain six items in order: tooltip [0], HTML rendered string [1], description [2], label [3], value [4], and name [5].		
Parameters	[name]	Input names and ID prefix
	[group]	Parameter group
Returns	Two-dimensional array of all the parameters in a group; false on failure	

&loadElement(type : string, new : boolean=false) : mixed

Gets an instance of a JElement subclass object based on type. If an instance of the specified type does not exist, it will be created. If new is true, a new instance will be created even if there is an existing instance. JElements subclass objects are not restricted to groups.		
Parameters	path	Path to XML file
	[new]	Force create new instance
Returns	Instance of a JElement object; false on failure	

loadSetupFile(path : string) : boolean

Builds a JSimpleXMLElement object from an XML file. The XML file can include the group name; if it does not, the group ' _default' will be assumed.		
Parameters	path	Path to XML file
Returns	true on success	

render(name : string='params', group : string=' _default') : mixed

Renders a group within the parameters and returns an HTML string.		
Parameters	[name]	Input names and ID prefix
	[group]	Parameter group
Returns	HTML rendered string; `false` on failure	

renderToArray(name : string='params', group : string=' _default') : mixed

Renders a group within the parameters and returns an array of HTML strings.		
Parameters	[name]	Input names and ID prefix
	[group]	Parameter group
Returns	Array of HTML rendered parameters; `false` on failure	

set(key : string, value : string='', group : string='_default') : string

Sets the value of a parameter in the specified group.		
Parameters	key	Parameter to set
	[value]	New value
	[group]	Parameter group
Returns	Previous value of the parameter	

setXML(&xml : JSimpleXMLElement) : void

Sets an XML definition; the group is extracted from the group attribute of the object.	
Parameters	[xml]	JSimpleXMLElement object to add

JCache

abstract, extends JObject
Handles caching. Several subclasses exist for caching different items; subclasses are sometimes referred to as JCache types. JCache uses JCacheStorage subclass objects to store and retrieve cache data.

Properties

_handler : JCacheStorage	Storage handler
_options : array	Cache handling options

Constructors

__construct(options : array) : JCache

Builds a new JCache object. The `options` associative array can contain the keys `language`, `cachebase`, `defaultgroup`, `caching`, and `storage`. `language` is used to create separate caches for different languages. `cachebase` is used as the path to the base cache folder. `defaultgroup` is the group name used when no group is specified in other methods. `caching` is a Boolean value; if `true` caching is enabled. Cached data is identified by an ID and a group. The way the cache is stored differs, depending on the chosen storage handler. `storage` is a string that defines the default storage handler type.		
Parameters	options	Associative array of options

Methods

clean(group : string=null, mode : string='group') : boolean

Removes all cached items in `group`. If `mode` is `'group'`, removes all cached data in `group`, if `mode` is `'notgroup'`, removes all cached data in other groups.		
Parameters	[group]	Selected group
	[mode]	Cleaning mode
Returns	`true` on success	

gc( ) : boolean

Removes any redundant cached data (data that has expired).	
Returns	`true` on success

get(id : string, group : string=null) : mixed

Gets cached data. Cached data is identified by an ID and a group. Returns `false` if no cached data is available.		
Parameters	id	Cached data ID
	[group]	Cached data group
Returns	Cached data; `false` if no cached data is found	

static &getInstance(type : string='output', options : array=array()) : JCache

Gets a new instance of a JCache subclass object based on `type`. `options` is passed to the constructor.		
Parameters	[type]	JRegistry instance identifier
	[options]	Options to pass to the constructor
Returns	A new instance of a JCache derived object	

static getStores( ) : array

Gets an array of storage handler names that will operate correctly in the current environment.	
Returns	Array of storage handler names

remove(id : string, group : string=null) : boolean

Removes cached data, identified by id and group.		
Parameters	id	Cached data ID
	[group]	Cached data group
Returns	true if the data is removed	

setCacheValidation( ) : void

Deprecated; this method no longer performs any action, and there is no replacement function or method.

setCaching(enabled : boolean) : void

Enables and disables caching.		
Parameters	enabled	Turn caching on or off

setLifeTime(lt : int) : void

Sets the maximum lifetime of cached items in seconds.		
Parameters	lt	Lifetime of cached items in seconds

store(data : string, id : string, group : string=null) : boolean

Adds data to the cache, identified by id and group.		
Parameters	data	Data to chache
	id	Cached data ID
	[group]	Cached data group
Returns	true if the item is stored	

&_getStorageHandler( ) : JCacheStorage

Gets the cache storage handler. If the handler does not exist it will be created.	
Returns	Cache storage object

JMail

extends PHPMailer
Sends emails.

Constructors

JMail( ) : JMail

Builds a new JMail object.

Methods

addAtachment(attachment : mixed) : void

Adds one attachment if `attachment` is a string (filename). Adds multiple attachments if `attachment` is an array (filenames).		
Parameters	attachment	Attachment file path or array of attachment file paths

addBCC(bcc : mixed) : void

Adds one blind carbon copy recipient if `bcc` is a string. Adds multiple blind carbon copy recipients if `bcc` is an array.		
Parameters	bcc	Email address string or array of email addresses

addCC(cc : mixed) : void

Adds one carbon copy recipient if `cc` is a string. Adds multiple carbon copy recipients if `cc` is an array.		
Parameters	cc	Email address string or array of email addresses

addRecipient(recipient : mixed) : void

Adds one recipient if `recipient` is a string. Adds multiple recipients if `recipient` is an array.		
Parameters	recipient	Email address string or array of email addresses

addReplyTo(replyto : array) : void

Sets the reply-to email address and name. `replyto` can be an array of two elements `array('email@address', 'name')` or an array of arrays in this format.		
Parameters	from	Email address array

static &getInstance(id : string='Joomla') : JMail

Gets a reference to a global instance of a JMail object. If the object does not exist it will be created. id identifies the JMail object to return.		
Parameters	[id]	JMail ID
Returns	Reference to a global JMail object	

&Send( ) : mixed

Sends the email.	
Returns	true on success, error on failure

setBody(content : string) : void

Sets the email body.		
Parameters	content	Email body

setSender(from : mixed) : void

Sets the sender's email address and name. from can either be an array of two elements — array ('email@address', 'name') — or a string consisting of one email address		
Parameters	from	Email address string or array of email address and email name

setSubject(subject : string) : void

Sets the email subject line.		
Parameters	subject	Email subject line

useSendmail(sendmail : string=null) : boolean

If sendmail is specified, sets the object to use the sendmail path. If sendmail is not specified, sets the object to use the PHP mail() function.		
Parameters	[sendmail]	Path to sendmail
Returns	true if sendmail is enabled	

useSMTP(auth : boolean=null, host : string=null, user : string=null, pass : string=null) : boolean

If all parameters are specified, sets the object to use SMTP. If any of the parameters are not specified, sets the object to use the PHP mail() function.		
Parameters	[auth]	Use SMTP authorization
	[host]	SMTP host
	[user]	Username
	[pass]	Password
Returns	true if SMTP is enabled	

JMailHelper

static
Performs mail functions that are not specific to an individual JMail object.

Methods

static cleanAddress(address : string) : mixed

Determines if an email address is clean. An unclean email address may include spaces, semicolons, and commas.		
Parameters	address	Address to clean
Returns	Email address or `false` if the address is deemed to be unclean	

static cleanBody(body : string) : string

Cleans a multi-line string for use in an email body. Removes unsafe characters and potentially confusing MIME header strings.		
Parameters	body	String to clean
Returns	Cleaned string	

static cleanLine(value : string) : string

Cleans a line for use in an email. Removes unsafe characters.		
Parameters	value	String to clean
Returns	Cleaned string	

static cleanSubject(subject : string) : string

Cleans an email subject line. Removes unsafe characters and potentially confusing MIME header strings.		
Parameters	subject	String to clean
Returns	Cleaned string	

static cleanText(value : string) : string

Cleans a multi-line string for use in an email. Removes unsafe characters and potentially confusing MIME header strings.		
Parameters	value	String to clean
Returns	Cleaned string	

static isEmailAddress(email : string) : boolean

Checks if email is a valid email address.		
Parameters	email	Email to validate
Returns	true if email is in a valid format	

JFactory

static
Joomla! static factory class for accessing global objects and building new objects.

Methods

static &getACL( ) : JAuthorization

Gets the global authorization object. If the authorization object does not exist it will be created.	
Returns	Global authorization object

static &getCache(group : string='', handler : string='callback', storage : string=null) : JCache

Gets the global cache object. If the cache object does not exist it will be created. group is the group to which the cache belongs. handler is the handler to use; this can be callback, output, page, or view. storage is the storage mechanism to use; this can be apc, eaccelerator, file, memcache, or xcache. In most instances, it will not be necessary to define handler or storage.		
Parameters	[group]	Cache group
	[handler]	Handler type
	[storage]	Storage type
Returns	Global cache object	

static &getConfig(file : string=null, type : string='PHP') : JRegistry

Gets the global configuration object. If the object does not exist, it will be created. file is the path, including the name, of the configuration file. type is the format of configuration file; this currently has no effect. The parameters need only be specified the first time this method is run.		
Parameters	file	Path and name of the configuration file
	[type]	Type of configuration file
Returns	Global configuration object	

static &getDBO( ) : JDatabase

Gets the global database object. If the database object does not exist it will be created.	
Returns	Global database object

static &getDocument( ) : JDocument

Gets the global document object. If the document object does not exist it will be created.	
Returns	Global document object

static &getEditor(editor : string=null) : JEditor

Gets a new instance of the specified editor. If `editor` is not specified, the default editor will be used.	
Parameters	[editor]	Type of editor
Returns	A new editor object	

static &getLanguage( ) : JLanguage

Gets the global language object. If the language object does not exist it will be created.	
Returns	Global language object

static &getMailer( ) : JMail

Gets the global mail object loaded with the site mail settings. If the mail object does not exist it will be created.	
Returns	Global mail object

static &getSession(options : array=array()) : JSession

Gets the global session object. If the session does not exist it will be created. The `options` associative array is the options to pass on to the session storage handler; this only needs to be specified the first time the method is executed.	
Parameters	[options]	Options to pass to the session storage handler
Returns	Global session object	

static &getTemaplate( ) : JTemplate

Gets the global template object. If the template object does not exist it will be created.	
Returns	Global template object

static &getURI(uri : string='SERVER') : JURI

Gets a global instance of the specified JURI object. If `uri` is not specified, the requested URI will be used.	
Parameters	[uri]	URI
Returns	A global JURI object.	

static &getUser( ) : JUser

Gets the current user object.	
Returns	Global user object

static &getXMLParser(type : string='DOM', options : array=array()) : object

Creates a new XML Parser object. Supported types are RSS, Atom, Simple, and DOM; if an unrecognized type is provided, a DOM XML parser will be created. The options associative array can contain the key rssUrl if the type is Atom or RSS. The options associative array can contain the key lite if the type is DOM. The XML parser classes include SimplePie, JSimpleXML, DOMIT_Document, and DOMIT_Lite_Document.		
Parameters	[type]	Type of Parser
	[options]	Parser options
Returns	A new XML parser object	

static &_createACL( ) : JAuthorization

Creates the global authorization object.	
Returns	New global authorization object

static &_createConfig(file : string, type : string='PHP') : JRegistry

Creates the global configuration object. file is the path to the configuration file. type is the format of the configuration file.		
Parameters	file	Path to the configuration file
	[type]	Type of configuration file
Returns	New global configuration object	

static &_createDBO( ) : JDatabase

Creates the database object.	
Returns	New global database object

static &_createDocument( ) : JDocument

Creates the global document object. The document type is determined by the value of the format request. If no format is included, HTML is assumed.	
Returns	New global document object

static &_createLanguage( ) : JLanguage

Creates the language object.	
Returns	New global language object

static &_createMailer( ) : JMail

Creates the global mail object.	
Returns	New global mail object

static &_createSession(options : array=array()) : JSession

Creates the global session object. If the session has expired, it will be restarted.		
Parameters	[options]	Session storage handler options
Returns	New global session object	

static &_createTemplate( ) : JTemplate

Creates the template object.	
Returns	New global template object

JRegistry

extends JObject
Handles configuration details in a hierarchy using namespaces.

Properties

_defaultNameSpace : string	Namespace to use by default
_registry : array	Registry data

Constructors

__construct(namespace : string='default') : JRegistry

Builds a new JRegistry object and adds the namespace, setting it as the default.		
Parameters	[namespace]	Default namespace

Methods

static &getInstance(id : string, namespace : string='default') : JRegistry

Gets a global instance of JRegistry, identified by id. If the instance does not exist it will be created.		
Parameters	id	JRegistry instance ID
	[namespace]	Default namespace, only used if the instance does not exist
Returns	A global instance of JRegistry	

getNameSpaces( ) : array

Gets the names of all the namespaces in the registry.	
Returns	Array of namespace names

getValue(regpath : string, default : mixed=null) : mixed

Gets a value from the registry. regpath can include multiple levels separated by periods. If the path includes no periods, the value will be retrieved from the default namespace. If the value is not set, the default value will be returned.		
Parameters	regpath	Path to value
	[default]	Default value
Returns	Value of the item identified by regpath	

loadArray(array : array, namespace : string=null) : boolean

Loads an associative array into the registry namespace. The array keys must not contain periods. If the namespace is not specified, the default namespace will be used.		
Parameters	array	Associative array to load
	[namespace]	The namespace to load the array into
Returns	true	

loadFile(file : string, format : string='INI', namespace : string=null) : boolean

Loads a configuration file into the registry namespace. The file parameter keys must not contain periods. Possible formats are INI, PHP, and XML. If the namespace is not specified, the default namespace will be used.		
Parameters	file	File path
	[format]	File format
	[namespace]	Namespace to load the file into
Returns	true	

loadINI(data : string, namespace : string=null) : boolean

Loads an INI string into the registry namespace. The INI parameter keys must not contain periods. If the namespace is not specified, the default namespace will be used.		
Parameters	data	INI string
	[namespace]	The namespace to load the INI into
Returns	true	

loadObject(&object : object, namespace : string=null) : boolean

Loads public properties of an object into the registry namespace. If the namespace is not specified, the default namespace will be used.		
Parameters	object	Object to load
	[namespace]	The namespace to load the object into
Returns	`true`	

loadXML(data : string, namespace : string=null) : boolean

Loads an XML string into the registry namespace. The XML parameter keys must not contain periods. If the namespace is not specified, the default namespace will be used.		
Parameters	data	XML string
	[namespace]	Namespace to load the XML into
Returns	`true`	

makeNameSpace(namespace : string) : boolean

Creates a new namespace in the registry. If the namespace already exists, it will be overwritten.	
Parameters	namespace	Namespace to create
Returns	`true`	

merge(&source : JRegistry) : boolean

Merges the registry data with `source` registry data. The source values take precedence over existing values.	
Parameters	source	JRegistry to merge from
Returns	`true` on success	

setValue(regpath : string, value : mixed) : mixed

Sets a value in the registry. The `regpath` can include multiple levels separated by periods. If the path includes no periods, the value will be set in the default namespace. If the `regpath` does not exist, it will be created.		
Parameters	regpath	Path to value
	value	Value
Returns	Previous value	

toArray(namespace : string=null) : array

Gets an associative array representation of the registry namespace. If `namespace` is not specified, the default namespace will be used.	
Parameters	namespace	The namespace to get
Returns	Array representation of the registry	

toObject(namespace : string=null) : array

Gets an object (stdClass) representation of the registry namespace. If namespace is not specified, the default namespace will be used.		
Parameters	[namespace]	The namespace to load the array into
Returns	Object representation of the registry	

toString(format : string='INI', namespace : string=null, params : mixed) : string

Gets a string representation of the registry namespace in the specified format. Possible formats are INI, PHP, and XML. If the namespace is not specified, the default namespace will be used. params is passed to the format handler objectToString() method; use of params depends upon format. Some format handlers are restricted to a maximum depth.		
Parameters	[format]	Registry format handler name
	[namespace]	The namespace to get
	[params]	Options to pass to the format handler
Returns	String representation of the registry	

JSession

extends JObject
Handles a user session and stores session data in namespaces. For more information about sessions refer to Chapter 7.

Properties

_expire : int	Length of inactive time before session expires.
_security : array	Security session validation options. Can include the keys fix_browser and fix_adress (note that fix_adress is not a typo).
_state : string	State of the session (active, expired, destroyed, or error)
_store : JSessionStorage	Session storage handler

Constructors

__construct(store : string='none', options : array=array()) : JSession

Builds a new JSession object. store is the storage handler type, normally database.		
Parameters	[store]	Storage handler type
	[options]	Options to pass to the storage handler

Methods

clear(name : string, namespace : string='default') : mixed

Removes a value from the session.		
Parameters	name	Name of value to remove
	[namespace]	Namespace to remove the value from
Returns	Cleared value	

close( ) : void

Closes the session gracefully.

destroy( ) : boolean

Resets the session removing any existing session data. This does not remove the session cookie or session id. Equivalent to the PHP `session_destroy()` function.	
Returns	true

fork( ) : boolean

Creates a new session, and copies the exiting session data to the new session.	
Returns	true

&get(name : string, default : mixed='null', namespace : string='default') : mixed

Gets a value from the session. If the value is not set, `default` is returned.		
Parameters	name	Name of the value to retrieve
	[default]	Default value
	[namespace]	Namespace to retrieve the value from
Returns	Value from the session	

getExpire( ) : int

Gets the number of inactive minutes to wait before the session expires.	
Returns	Session lifetime in minutes

getId( ) : string

Gets the ID of the session. Returns null if the session has been destroyed.	
Returns	Session ID

static &getInstance(handler : string, options : array) : JSession

Gets the global instance of JSession. If it doesn't already exist it will be created.		
Parameters	handler	Storage handler type
	options	Options to pass to the storage handler
Returns	Global session object	

getName( ) : string

Gets the name of the session. Returns null if the session has been destroyed.	
Returns	Session name

getState( ) : string

Gets the state of the session (`active`, `expired`, `destroyed`, or `error`).	
Returns	State of the session

getStores( ) : array

Gets the names of session storage handlers that work in the current environment.	
Returns	Array of session storage handler names

getToken(forceNew : boolean=false) : string

Gets the session token. The token is a random alphanumeric string that can be used to increase security of requests.	
Parameters	[forceNew]	Create a new token
Returns	Token string	

has(name : string, namespace : string='default') : boolean

Checks if a value is set in the session.		
Parameters	name	Name of value to check
	[namespace]	Namespace to check the value in
Returns	`true` if the value is set in the session	

hasToken(tCheck : string, forceExpire : boolean=true) : boolean

Compares the session token with `tCheck`. If the tokens do not match and `forceExpire` is `true`, the session will be expired.		
Parameters	tCheck	Token to check session against
	forceExpire	Expire session if invalid token
Returns	`true` if tokens match	

isNew( ) : boolean

Dtermines if the session was created during this request.	
Returns	`true` if the session was created during this request

restart( ) : boolean

Restarts the session. This will remove any existing session data.	
Returns	`true`

set(name : string, value : mixed, namespace : string='default') : mixed

Sets a value in the session.		
Parameters	name	Name of value to set
	value	Value
	[namespace]	Namespace to set the value in
Returns	Previous value	

_createId( ) : string

Creates a new session ID.	
Returns	A new session ID

_createToken( ) : string

Creates a new token.	
Returns	New token string

_setCounter( ) : boolean

Increments the session counter. Must only be invoked once per request.	
Returns	`true`

_setOptions(&options : array) : boolean

Sets session options. The `options` associative array can include the keys `name`, `id`, `expire`, and `security`.		
Parameters	options	Session options
Returns	`true`	

_setTimers( ) : boolean

Sets the session timers. Includes the session start time, the last request time, and the current request time.	
Returns	`true`

_start( ) : boolean

Starts the session. Continues a previous session or creates a new session. Equivalent to the PHP session_start() function.	
Returns	`true`

_validate(restart : boolean=false) : boolean

Validates the session. If the session has exceeded the maximum expiry time, the session state will be changed to `expired`. Checks the client address and client browser match the security array, if they are defined in the security array.	
Parameters	[restart]	Restart the session if the session state is not active
Returns	`true` if the session is valid	

JRoute

static, extends JObject
Handles internal URIs.

Methods

static _(url : string, xhtml : boolean=true , ssl : int=0) : string

Converts a URI into a Search Engine-Friendly (**SEF**) URI. This method should be used for all internal URIs. No processing will be performed if we are in the administrative area. `xhtml` determines if ampersands should be encoded as HTML special character &.		
Parameters	url	URI to convert
	xhtml	Make URI XHTML standard
	ssl	URI is SSL
Returns	Converted URI	

JMenu

extends JObject
Handles menus and menu items.

Properties

_active : int	ID of the current menu item
_default : int	ID of the default homepage menu item
_items : array	Array of menu items (stdClass objects)

Constructors

__construct( ) : JMenu

Builds a new JMenu object and loads all of the published menu items for every menu.

Methods

authorize(id : int, accessid : int=0) : boolean

Checks the user group has rights to view the menu item.		
Parameters	id	Menu item ID
	[accessed]	Legacy group ID
Returns	`true` if authorized to view the menu item	

&getActive( ) : boolean

Gets the current menu item. Gets the default menu item if the current item is not set.	
Returns	Active menu item; returns null on failure

&getDefault( ) : object

Gets the default menu item (homepage).	
Returns	Default menu item object

static &getInstance( ) : JMenu

Gets the global instance of JMenu, creating it if it does not exist.	
Returns	Global instance of JMenu

&getItem(id : int) : object

Gets a menu item based on `id`. If the menu item does not exist, returns null.	
Parameters	id	Menu item ID
Returns	Menu item object

getItems(attribute : string, value : string, firstonly : boolean=false) : mixed

Gets an active menu item or an array of menu items. Returned active menu item attributes must match the specified attribute and value. If firstonly is true, only gets the first matching menu item.		
Parameters	attribute	Attribute to check
	value	Value to check attribute against
	[firstonly]	Only get the first matching menu item
Returns	A menu item or an array of menu items	

getMenu( ) : JParameter

Gets a copy of all the menu items.	
Returns	Array of menu items

&getParams(id : int) : JParameter

Gets the parameters of the specified menu item. If the menu item does not exist, or is not published, returns an empty JParameter object.	
Parameters	id	Menu item ID
Returns	JParameter object populated with the parameters from the specified menu item

&setActive(id : int) : boolean

Sets the active menu item.	
Parameters	id	Menu item ID
Returns	true on success

setDefault(id : int) : boolean

Sets the default menu item (homepage).	
Returns	true on success

_load( ) : mixed

Loads published menu items from the #__menu table and returns them as an array of stdClass objects in published order. This method uses caching; if changes are made to the #__menu table records after this method has been called once, the changes will not be reflected if the method is used a second time.	
Returns	Array of published menu items; false on failure

JPathway

extends JObject
Handles breadcrumbs. This class is used to model the breadcrumb trail, which is used in most templates as a way of describing a user's current position within a Joomla! site. For more information about the breadcrumb trail refer to Chapter 9.

Properties

_count : int	Number of breadcrumbs
_pathway : array	Array of breadcrumbs

Methods

addItem(name : string, link : string='') : boolean

Adds a breadcrumb to the end of the trail.		
Parameters	name	Name of breadcrumb
	[link]	Breadcrumb URI
Returns	`true` on success	

getPathWay( ) : array

Gets an array of the breadcrumbs. Breadcrumbs are represented as stdClass objects with two properties, `name` and `link`.	
Returns	Array of breadcrumbs in order of display

getPathWayNames( ) : array

Gets an array of breadcrumb names.	
Returns	Array of breadcrumb names in order

setItemName(id : int, name : string) : boolean

Sets the name of a breadcrumb. `id` refers to the breadcrumb number; breadcrumbs are numbered from zero.		
Parameters	id	Breadcrumb number
	name	Breadcrumb name
Returns	`true` on success	

_makeItem(name : string, link : string) : object

Builds a new menu item and returns it.		
Parameters	name	Name of new breadcrumb
	link	Breadcrumb URI
Returns	New breadcrumb object (stdClass)	

JDatabase

abstract, extends JObject
Handles a database connection. There are two core subclasses (sometimes called drivers or adapters), JDatabaseMySQL and JDatabaseMySQLi. Additional subclasses, enabling support of other database servers, are intended to be added later. For more information about JDatabase refer to Chapter 3.

Properties

_cursor : mixed	Result of last `mysql_query()` call
_debug : int	Debug mode; 0 = disabled, 1 = enabled
_errorMsg : string	Error message from last query
_errorNum : int	Error number from last query
_hasQuoted : boolean	There are specific fieldnames to be quoted
_limit : int	Maximum number of records to return from a query
_log : array	Query history (only maintained if debug is enabled)
_nameQuote : string	Named SQL element quotes (tables, fields, databases)
_nullDate : string	Null date string
_offset : int	Record offset
_quoted : array	Array of values that should be quoted
_resource : mixed	Database resource
_sql : string	Current query
_table_prefix : string	Database table prefix, normally `'jos_'`
_ticker : int	Number of queries executed (only maintained if debug is enabled)
_utf : boolean	Supports UTF-8
name : string	Database driver name

Constructors

__construct(options: array) : JDatabase

Builds a new JDatabase object and prepares the internal properties. Subclasses also connect to the specified database. `options` normally includes the keys: `host`, `user`, `password`, `database`, `prefix`, and `select`.		
Parameters	options	Database options

Destructors

__destruct( ) : boolean

Runs when the object is destroyed. Ensures the database connection is closed cleanly.	
Returns	`true` on success

Methods

addQuoted(quoted : mixed) : void

Adds a new value that should always be encapsulated in quotes. `quoted` can be a string or an array of strings.		
Parameters	quoted	String or array of values to quote

BeginTrans( ) : void

Emulates ADOdb functionality.
This method must be overridden in subclasses. If you intend to use this, please ensure the database driver supports it.

CommitTrans( ) : string

Emulates ADOdb functionality.
This method must be overridden in subclasses. If you intend to use this, please ensure the database driver supports it.

connected( ) : boolean

Determines if the database connection is alive.	
Returns	`true` if currently connected to the database

debug(debug : int) : void

Sets debug mode; 0 = disabled, 1 = enabled.		
Parameters	debug	Debug mode

ErrorMsg( ) : string

Emulates ADOdb functionality.	
Gets the error message from the last query. If no error was encountered, the error message will be an empty string.	
Returns	Error message from the last query

ErrorNo( ) : int

Emulates ADOdb functionality.	
Error number from the last query. If no error was encountered, the error number will be zero.	
Returns	Error number from the last query

Execute(query : string) : mixed

Emulates ADOdb functionality.		
Executes query. If the query is a SELECT query, the results will be returned in a JRecordSet object. If the query is not a SELECT query, an empty JRecordSet will be returned on success. If the query fails, false will be returned.		
Parameters	query	Query to execute.
Returns	JRecordSet object; false on failure	

explain( ) : string

Explains the current query.	
Returns	XHTML string describing the active query.

GenID(foo1 : string=null, foo2 : int=null) : mixed

Emulates ADOdb functionality.		
Gets a sequence ID for databases that are sequence aware (sequences are used with databases that allow multiple connections, to reduce the chance of errors). If you are creating an application that relies on sequences, ensure that the JDatabase subclass object supports GenID() fully. Subclasses must implement this method to enable GenID() support. JDatabaseMySQL and JDatabaseMySQLi do not support GenID(); using GenID() with these databases will always return 0.		
Parameters	foo1	Sequence name
	foo2	Start ID
Returns	Sequence ID; normally an integer, but sometimes a string	

getAffectedRows( ) : int

Gets the total number of records that were affected by the last query.	
Returns	Number of records that were affected by the last query

GetCol(query : string) : array

Emulates ADOdb functionality.		
Executes query and returns an array of the first column from the resultant records.		
Parameters	query	Query to execute
Returns	Array of first column from records	

getCollation( ) : string

Gets the database collation. This method is not infallible for MySQL databases; MySQL allows the collation to be set at four different levels, server, database, table, and column. This method returns the collation used by `#__content.fulltext`; it is possible that the collation may differ elsewhere in the database. This method only works if the database supports UTF-8.	
Returns	Collation name

static getConnectors( ) : array

Gets an array of the names of database drivers supported in the current environment.	
Returns	Array of available driver names

getEscaped(text : string) : string

Escapes a string for use as a value in a query.		
Parameters	text	String to escape
Returns	Escaped string	

getErrorMsg(escaped : boolean=false) : string

Gets the error message from the last query. If no error was encountered returns an empty string.		
Parameters	[escaped]	Escape the message with slashes
Returns	Error message from the last query	

getErrorNum( ) : int

Gets the error number from the last query. If no error was encountered, returns 0 (zero).	
Returns	Error number from the last query

static &getInstance(options : array=array()) : JDatabase

Gets a global instance of JDatabase, creating it if it does not already exist. An instance exists for every different set of `options`. The options array normally contains the keys defined in the constructor options array and the key `driver`. `driver` determines the subclass that is instantiated, available core drivers are `MySQL` and `MySQLi`.		
Parameters	options	Database options
Returns	A global instance of JDatabase	

getNullDate( ) : string

Gets a null date string specific to the current database driver.	
Returns	Null date-time string

getNumRows(cur : resource=null) : mixed

Gets the number of records that were returned in the last query. If cur is specified, it will determine the number of rows that were returned for the corresponding query. This only works if the query was a SELECT, SHOW, DESCRIBE, or EXPLAIN query.		
Parameters	[cur]	Database resource
Returns	Number of records that were returned in the last query; false on failure	

GetOne(query : string) : string

Emulates ADOdb functionality. Executes query and returns the value in the first field in the first record.		
Parameters	query	Query to execute
Returns	Value in the first field in the first record of the results	

getPrefix( ) : string

Gets the database table prefix, normally jos_.	
Returns	Database table prefix

getQuery( ) : mixed

Gets the active query.	
Returns	Active query

GetRow(query : string) : array

Emulates ADOdb functionality. Executes query and gets the first record as an array.		
Parameters	query	Query to execute
Returns	First record as an array	

getTableCreate(tables : array) : array

Gets an associative array of table creation queries for the tables named in tables.		
Parameters	tables	Array of table names
Returns	Associative array of table creation queries	

getTableFields(tables : array) : array

Gets an associative array of table fields and types. For example, a table called `jos_test` with two fields might return this:

```
Array
(
    [jos_test] => Array
        (
            [id] => int
            [name] => varchar
        )
)
```

Parameters	tables	Array of table names
Returns	Associative array of tables and table fields	

getTableList( ) : array

Gets the names of the tables in the database.

Returns	Array of table names

getUTFSupport( ) : boolean

Determines if the database supports UTF-8.

Returns	`true` if the database supports UTF-8

getVersion( ) : string

Gets the database server version.

Returns	Database server version

hasUTF( ) : boolean

Determines if the database supports UTF-8. You should use `getUTFSupport()` in preference to this method, which returns a cached value of `hasUTF()`.

Returns	`true` if the database supports UTF-8

insertid( ) : int

If the last query was an `INSERT` query on a table with an auto-increment primary key, this method gets the ID inserted as a result of the last query. If it was not an `INSERT` query, zero will be returned.

Returns	Inserted ID from the last query

insertObject(table : string, &object : object, keyName : string=null) : boolean

Treats `object` as a new record and attempts to insert it into the specified table. If `keyName` (primary key fieldname) is specified, the object will be updated with the record primary key value; this is for use with tables with auto-increment primary keys only.		
Parameters	table	Table name
	object	Record object
	[keyName]	Primary key
Returns	`true` on success	

isQuoted(fieldname : string) : boolean

Determines if `fieldname` is amongst the fieldnames to be encapsulated in quotes. If no values have been specified to be quoted, returns `true`.	
Parameters	fieldname	Fieldname to check
Returns	`true` if the fieldname should be encapsulated in quotes	

loadAssoc( ) : array

Executes the current query and gets the first record as an associative array.
Returns	First record from query as an associative array

loadAssocList(key : string=") : array

Executes the current query and gets a two-dimensional array of records. Each inner array represents a record as an associative array. If `key` is specified (primary key fieldname) the returned array will be associative, using the record primary key as array key.	
Parameters	[key]	Primary key
Returns	Two-dimensional array of records	

loadObject( ) : object

Executes the current query and returns the first record as an object (stdClass).
Returns	First record from query as an object

loadObjectList(key : string=") : array

Executes the current query and returns an array of record objects. Each object represents a record. If `key` is specified (primary key fieldname) the returned array will be associative, using the record primary key as array key.	
Parameters	[key]	Primary key
Returns	Array or associative array of record objects	

loadResult( ) : string

Executes the current query and gets the value in the first field of the first record.	
Returns	Value in the first field of the first record

loadResultArray(numinarray : int= 0) : array

Executes the current query and gets an array of the specified column/field number from the resultant records.		
Parameters	[numinarray]	Column/Field number
Returns	Array of column from records	

loadRow( ) : array

Executes the current query and returns the first record as an array.	
Returns	First record from query as an array

loadRowList(key : int=") : array

Executes the current query and returns a two-dimensional array of records. Each inner array represents a record as an array. If key is specified (primary key field number), the returned array will be associative, using the record primary key as array key.		
Parameters	[key]	Primary key
Returns	Two-dimensional array of records	

nameQuote(s : string) : string

Encapsulates a string in quotes. This is for strings that are named SQL elements (tables, fields, databases), not values.		
Parameters	s	String to encapsulate
Returns	Quote encapsulated string	

PageExecute(sql : string, nrows : int, page : int, inputarr : boolean=false, sec2cache : int=0) : JRecordSet

Emulates ADOdb functionality.		
Executes query and returns the results in a JRecordSet object. nrows and page are used to determine the offset and limit.		
Parameters	sql	Query to execute
	nrows	Number of records per page
	page	Results page (pagination)
	[inputarr]	Ignored; emulation purposes only
	[secs2cache]	Ignored; emulation purposes only
Returns	JRecordSet object	

query( ) : mixed

Executes the current query. If the query is successful and is a SELECT, SHOW, DESCRIBE, or EXPLAIN query, a resource will be returned. If the query is successful, and is not one of the above query types, true will be returned. If the query fails, false will be returned.	
Returns	Database resource or true on success; false on failure

queryBatch(abort_on_error : boolean=true, p_transaction_safe : boolean=false) : mixed

Executes a batch of queries. If abort_on_error is true the batch process will stop if an error occurs. If p_transaction_safe is true then all the queries will only be applied if they are all successful.		
Parameters	[abort_on_error]	Stop batch process on error
	[p_transaction_safe]	Perform as transaction
Returns	true on success; false or the failed resource on failure	

Quote(text : string) : string

Emulates ADOdb functionality.		
Encapsulates text in quotes and escapes text. Use this to make query values safe.		
Parameters	text	String to encapsulate in quotes and escape
Returns	Quoted string	

replacePrefix(sql : string, prefix : string='#__') : string

Substitutes occurrences of prefix in sql with the database table prefix.		
Parameters	sql	Query
	prefix	Database table prefix to replace
Returns	Query with correct table prefixes	

RollbackTrans( ) : string

Emulates ADOdb functionality.
This method must be overridden in subclasses. If you intend to use this, please ensure the database driver supports it.

stderr(showSQL : boolean=false) : string

Gets an error report of the last error. If showSQL is true, the SQL is included in the report.		
Parameters	[showSQL]	Display query
Returns	Error report	

SelectLimit(query : string, count : int, offset : int=0) : JRecordSet

Emulates ADOdb functionality.		
Executes query and returns the results in a JRecordSet object. offset and limit are used for pagination; in MySQL databases, this relates directly to the LIMIT clause.		
Parameters	query	Query to execute
	count	Maximum number of records
	[offset]	Start record
Returns	JRecordSet object	

setUTF( ) : void

Prepares the database connection for UTF-8 strings.

setQuery(sql : string, offset : int=0, limit : int=0, prefix : string='#__') : void

Sets the next query to execute. offset and limit are used for pagination; in MySQL this relates directly to the LIMIT clause. If you use offset or limit, then your SQL must not contain a LIMIT clause. prefix is the string that is replaced in the SQL by the database table prefix; it would be unusual to change this from the default #__.		
Parameters	sql	Query
	[offset]	Start record
	[limit]	Maximum number of records
	[prefix]	Table prefix to substitue

static test( ) : boolean

Determines if the driver (subclass) is compatible with the current environment.	
Returns	true of the driver is compatible with the current environment

updateObject(table : string, &object : object, keyName : string, updateNulls : boolean=true) : boolean

Treats object as an updated record and attempts to update the specified table from the record. If updateNulls is true, object properties that are null will still be used to update the record in the table.		
Parameters	table	Table name
	object	Record object
	keyName	Primary key
	[updateNulls]	Update values even if they are null
Returns	true on success	

Parameters (Core JElements)

We can use the XML tag `param` to define different parameters. Every `param` tag must include the following attributes:

Attribute	Description
description	Description of the parameter
label	Human-readable name of the input; this will always be translated by JText
name	Name of the input
type	Type of parameter; this relates to JElement subclasses
default	The default value (this does not work for all elements)

This is an example of a `param` tag:

```
<param name="title" type="text" default="My Title" label="Title"
description="Title of page" size="30" />
```

When we define the type we are informing Joomla! which JElement subclass to use to render the parameter. There are a number of core JElement subclasses available to us, each of which has its own set of attributes that modify the rendered output.

The following tables describe the parameter types from the core that we can use. Any attributes that are optional are encapsulated in square braces. Remember that when we use the `param` tag we also need to include the attributes defined in the previous table.

category		
Displays a drop-down selection box of published categories. The first option in the selection box is always – `Select Category` -; this option has a value of `0`.		
Parameters	class	CSS Style
	[section]	Section ID or component name if using component-specific categories. If not specified, all content categories are displayed.

editors	
Displays a drop-down selection box of all the published editors. The first option in the selection box is always – `Select Editor` -; this option has a value of `0`.	

filelist		
Displays a drop-down selection box of files in a specified directory. Can optionally include the options – Do not use – and – Use default –; these options have the values -1 and null respectively.		
Parameters	[directory]	Directory where the files are located, relative to the root of Joomla!
	[exclude]	RE file exclusion, applied after filter
	[filter]	RE filter to apply to file names
	[hide_default]	Hide the 'use default' option; Boolean
	[hide_none]	Hide the 'do not use' option; Boolean
	[stripExt]	Remove extensions from the file list; Boolean

folderlist		
Displays a drop-down selection box of folders in a specified directory. Can optionally include the options – Do not use – and – Use default –; these options have the values -1 and null respectively.		
Parameters	[directory]	Directory where the folders are located, relative to the root of Joomla!
	[exclude]	RE folder exclusion, applied after filter
	[filter]	RE filter to apply to folder names
	[hide_default]	Hide the 'use default' option; Boolean
	[hide_none]	Hide the 'do not use' option; Boolean
	[stripExt]	Remove extensions from the folder list; Boolean

helpsites
Displays a drop-down selection box of the different Joomla! help sites. The help sites are defined in the core administrator/help/helpsites-15.xml file.

hidden		
A hidden field. We cannot define a value here; this type is used in conjunction with an INI string in which the value will be defined.		
Parameters	[class]	CSS Style

imagelist		
Displays a drop-down selection box of image files in a specified directory. Can optionally include the options – Do not use – and – Use default –; these options have the values -1 and null respectively.		
Parameters	[directory]	Directory where the folders are located, relative to the root of Joomla!
	[exclude]	RE file exclusion, applied after filter
	[hide_default]	Hide the 'use default' option; Boolean
	[hide_none]	Hide the 'do not use' option; Boolean
	[stripExt]	Remove extensions from the file list; Boolean

languages		
Displays a drop-down selection box of known languages from a specific client.		
Parameters	client	JPATH_ suffix where a language folder is located. Normally BASE or ADMINISTRATOR.

list		
Displays a drop-down selection box of specified options. Options are defined by sub-tags called option. Each option tag includes a value attribute and the encapsulated content is the name.		
Parameters	[class]	CSS Style

menu
Displays a drop-down selection box of the different menus. The first option is always – Select Menu – with a value of null.

menuitem		
Displays a drop-down selection box of the different menu items grouped by menu. The first option is always – Select Item – with a value of null.		
Parameters	[state]	Published state of the menu items

password		
Displays a password text box.		
Parameters	[class]	CSS Style.
	[size]	Character width of the password box; this is not the same as the maximum number of characters.

radio		

Displays a selection of radio buttons. Options are defined by sub-tags called option. Each option tag includes a value attribute and the encapsulated content is the name. The first option is selected by default. We normally use radio buttons for show and hide options:
 	
 `<param name="show" type="radio" label="Hide/Show" description="Hide or Show">`
 `    <option value="0">Hide</option>`
 `    <option value="1">Show</option>`
 `</param>`		

Parameters	[class]	CSS Style

section
Displays a drop-down selection box of published sections. The first option in the selection box is always – Select Section –; this option has a value of 0.

spacer
Adds a horizontal rule.

sql		
Displays a drop-down selection box of items. The items are determined by executing the query attribute against the database. The query must return two fields, one called `id` and one called `value`. Use the AS alias clause in your SQL to set names of returned fields.		
Parameters	query	Query to execute

text		
Displays a text box.		
Parameters	[class]	CSS Style
	[size]	Character width of the text box; this is not the same as the maximum number of characters

textarea		
Displays a text box.		
Parameters	[class]	CSS Style
	cols	Number of columns
	rows	Number of rows

timezones
Displays a drop-down selection box of different time zones. Values are identified as plus or minus hours from **UTC** (Universal Time Code); UTC is the same as **GMT** (Greenwich Mean Time), and **Z** (Zulu Time).

Configuration

The site settings are located in the `config` namespace within the registry. Most of these settings originate from the `configuration.php` file. This table details the values we expect to be present in the `config` namespace:

Name	Description
absolute_path	Full path to the Joomla! installation, for example `/www/joomla`
cache_handler	Mechanism with which to handle caching; Joomla! supports APC, EAccelerator, Memcache, and File
cachetime	Cache life expectancy in seconds
caching	Caching enabled; `1` = enabled, `0` = disabled
db	Database name
dbprefix	Database table prefix

Name	Description
dbtype	Database driver
debug	Site debug status; 1 = enabled, 0 = disabled
debug_db	Database debug status; 1 = enabled, 0 = disabled
debug_lang	Language debug status; 1 = enabled, 0 = disabled
editor	Default editor
error_reporting	Error reporting level; -1 = system default, 0 = none, 7 = simple, 2047 = maximum
feed_limit	Number of content feed items to display
feed_summary	Display full text in feeds; 1 = true, 0 = false
fromname	Mail email address alias, see mailfrom
ftp_enable	FTP access enabled; 1 = true, 0 = false
ftp_host	FTP host, normally 127.0.0.1
ftp_pass	FTP account password
ftp_port	FTP port, normally 21
ftp_root	FTP path to Joomla! installation
ftp_user	FTP account username
gzip	GZIP compression enabled; 1 = true, 0 = false
helpurl	Joomla! help site
host	Host name
lang	Default language name
lang_administrator	Default backend language tag
lang_site	Default frontend language tag
language	Default language tag
lifetime	Session lifetime in minutes
list_limit	Default length of lists (pagination) in the backend
live_site	URI to the site
log_path	Path to the site LOG files
mailer	Email sending mechanism; Joomla! supports: PHP mail, sendmail, and SMTP
mailfrom	Default email sender address
memcache_settings	Settings for Memcache (serialized PHP data); Memcache is a PHP caching system
MetaAuthor	Global option to show the author's meta tag when viewing a content item; 1 = true, 0 = false
MetaDesc	Site metadata-description-tag content
MetaKeys	Site metadata keys tag content
MetaTitle	Display the site metadata title tag; 1 = show, 0 = hide

Name	Description
offline	Site offline; `1` = true, `0` = false
offline_message	This site is down for maintenance. Please check back again soon.
offset	Time zone hours offset from UTC (also known as GMT and Z)
password	Database account password
secret	Secret site word (random alphanumeric string)
sef	SEF enabled; `1` = true, `0` = false
sef_rewrite	Apache SEF mod_rewrite enabled; `1` = true, `0` = false
sendmail	`/usr/sbin/sendmail`
session_handler	Session storage handling mechanism; Joomla! supports: APC, database EAccelerator, and Memcache
sitename	Name of the Joomla! installation
smtpauth	SMTP requires authorization; `1` = true, `0` = false
smtphost	SMTP host, normally localhost
smtppass	SMTP account password
smtpuser	SMTP account username
tmp_path	Temporary directory; used for archive extraction
user	Database account username
xmlrpc_server	XMLRPC support; `1` = enabled, `0` = disabled

Index

A

access control
  about 323
  extension access control 325
  GACL access control mechanism 323
  GACL implementing, terms used 324
  menu item access control 325
AJAX
  about 284
  request 286 - 289
  response 284
  response, document types 284
API 277
application, Joomla!
  application object, accessing 18
  JAdministrator 17
  JSite 17
application message queue 243
Application Programming Interface. *See* API
arrays
  about 355
  different types 358
assets
  files 189
  files, dealing with 189
  folder, creating 190
Asynchronous JavaScript and XML. *See*
        AJAX
attacks
  about 327
  block() method, implementing 335
  code injection 329
  common attacks, avoiding 328
  dealing with 332
  file system snooping 332
  logging 335, 336
  logout() method, implementing 334, 335
  parameters, defining 334
  site administrator, notifying 336, 337
  user, blocking 333
  user, logging out 333
  XSS 331
authentication plugins
  about 142
  onAuthenticate event 142, 143
  properties 142
  status property, constants 143

B

backend component
  location 66
  structure 67
backend module 116
  display position 119
behavior, grouped types 196
  calendar 199
  caption 199
  combobox 199
  formvalidation 199
  keepalive 200
  modal 198
  mootools 199
  switcher 199
  tooltip 198
  uploader 199
browser
  browser list, known to Joomla! 187
  features 186
  features, checking using hasFeature()
        method 185

JBrowser method 188
quirks 186
quirks, list 187

C

CGI request data
database data, escaping 318
database data, quoting 318
dealing with 315
encoding 318
escaping 317
preprocessing 315 - 317
preprocessing, JRequest class used 315
Regular Expressions 320
XHTML data, encoding 319

classes
JApplication class 398
JArchive class 354
JArrayHelper class 355
JCache class 422
JController class 378
JDatabase class 442
JDate class 340
JDocument class 393
JElement class 95, 417
JError class 312, 388
JException class 313
JFactory class 428
JFiles class 351
JFolder class 347
JLanguage class 411
JLanguageHelper class 416
JLDAP class 290
Jloader class 157
JLog class 361
JMail class 294, 424
JMailHelper class 296, 427
JMenu class 438
JModel class 372
JNode class 359
JObject class 366
JObject class, inheriting from 28, 29
JObservable class 136
JOutputFilter class 318
JPagination class 224
JParameter class 96, 161, 419

JPath class 345
JPathway class 441
JPlugin class, extending 137
JRegistry class 174, 431
JRequest class 315
JRoute class 438
JSession class 434
JTable 52
JTable class 383
JText class 417
JTree class 359
JURI class 407
JUser class 368
JView class 374
naming conventions 27

code injection
about 329
PHP code injection, types 329
SQL code injection, types 330
types 329

common attacks, avoiding
session token, using 328

component backend
about 214
admin form 215, 216
submenu 222, 223
submenu, modifying 222
toolbar 216

components
about 65
backend component 65
building 82
configuration, dealing with 93
designing 65
elements 65, 95
frontend component 65
help files 99, 100
identifying 66
MVC 65
MVC structure 67
packaging 102
parameters 95

components, designing
component configuration, dealing with 93
components, packaging 102
document types, rendering 87
help files, using 99

routing 100 - 102
sandbox, setting up 65
components, packaging
install files 111
installing 111
queries 111
SQL install files 110
SQL uninstall files 110
uninstall files 112
uninstalling 112
XML manifest file 103
XML manifest file, tags 105
XML manifest file elements 103, 104
content plugins
$row object 144
$row object, attributes 144
about 144
implementing 144
onAfterDisplayContent event 145
onAfterDisplayTitle event 145
onBeforeDisplayContent event 145
onPrepareContent event 144
onPreparecontent event 145
controller
building 78
 multiple controllers, dealing with 83
task methods 80
cross site scripting. *See* **XSS**
CRUD
existing record, updating 56
record, creating 54
record, deleting 57
record, loading 55
table buffer, updating 54

D

database
about 41
accessing, JDatabase object, using 41
extending 42
database, extending
fields 42
multilingual requirements, dealing with 45
schema conventions 42
schema example 44
table prefix 42

database, querying
ADObd, using 51
query writing rules 46
results, processing methods 47
development tools
J!Code 14
J!Dump 14
directory structure   24
Distinguished Name 292
DN. *See* **Distinguished Name**
document
about 17
breadcrumb 259
CSS 262
CSS, adding methods 262
custom header tags 263
document object, accessing 18
JavaScript 261
JavaScript, adding methods 261
metadata 263
metadata methods 263
modifying 258
page title 259
pathway 259, 260
types 17
document types
feed 87
feed, building 88
feed view, creating 87
feed view, linking 89
pdf 90
pdf, modifying 90
raw 91
rendering 87

E

editors-xtd plugins
about 148
button, adding to editor content 148, 149
OnCustomEditorButton event 148
onCustomEditorButton event 150
editors plugins
about 146
onDisplay event 147
onGetContent event 147
onGetInsertMethod event 147

onInit event 147
onSave event 148
onSetContent event 148
email
about 294
recipients,ways of adding 295
sending 295
error handling
about 311
customizing 314
modes 314
notices 313
return values 313
warnings 313
errors
about 312
identifying, error code used 312
events
about 136
dispatching 136
handling 138 - 140
handling, functions used 138
handling, observer pattern used 136
JEventDispatcher object 136
results, handling 141
triggering 137
uses 137
extension access control 325 - 327
extension design
assets 189
browser 185
getInstance() methods, building 169
getInstance() methods, using 169
helpers 168
registry, using 174
session 184, 185
supporting classes 167
user 177
user parameters 178
extensions, types
components 10
languages 11
modules 10
plugins 10
plugins, types 11
templates 11
tools 11

F

factory patterns
about 30
implementing, JFactory class used 31
fields
checked_out_time checked_out field 43
checked out field 43
date field 44
hits field 43
ordering field 43
parameter field 43
published field 43
fields, manipulating
checking out records, checkout() method
used 59
handling parameter, JParameter class
used 61, 62
incrementing hits, hits() method used 59
ordering items, reorder() method used 60
publishing data, publish() method used 59
storing dates, JDate class used 62
file system
archive format extensions 354
archives 354
files 351
folders 347
folders, copying 348
folders, creating 348
folders, managing 348
folders, relocating 348
folders, removing 348
paths 345
paths, cleaning 345
paths, searching file 345
File Transfer Protocol *See* **FTP**
frontend component
location 66
structure 67
frontend module 116
display position 119
FTP
about 297
JFTP methods 297, 298

G

getInstance() methods
about 169
declaring 170
implementing 170 - 172
reasons for implementing 173
uses 169, 170
grid, grouped types 200
grouped types, joomla.html library
behavior 196 - 198
email 200
grid 200
grid, uses 200
image 203
list 204
list, uses 205
menu 208
select 209
groups, plugins. *See also* **plugins**
about 142
authentication plugins 142
content plugins 144
editors-xtd plugins 148
editors plugins 146
search plugins 151
system plugins 152
user plugins 152
XML-RPC plugins 155

H

helpers
about 121, 168
class, defining 122
getItem() method, creating 122
getItem() method,implementing 123
uses 124

I

itemized data
about 224
category filter, applying 236
category filter dropdown selection box,
adding 234
custom dropdown section filter,
constructing 237

filtering 231
filtering options 231
filters, uses 237
ordering 228 - 231
pagination 224
published state filter, applying 233
published state filter, implementing
232 - 234
retrieving, getData() method used 227
search filter, implementing 238
searching 231
iterative templates
about 213, 214

J

JApplication class
constructors 399
methods 399
properties 398
JArchive class
about 354
extract() method 354
JArrayHelper class
about 355
getColumn() method 358
getValue() method 358
sortObjects() method 357
toInteger() method 356
toObject() method 356
toString() method 358
JavaScript effect
mootools 268
JCache class
constructors 423
methods 423
properties 422
JController class
constructors 379
methods 379
properties 379
JDatabase class
constructors 443
destructors 443
methods 443
properties 442

JDate class
about 340
date format, handling 340 - 344
JDate object 340
JDate object, creating 340
methods, handling 342, 343
JDocument class
constructors 393
methods 394
properties 393
JElement class
about 95
constructors 418
extending 96
JElementMenus class 96
JElementMenus class, building 97
JElementMenus class, implementing 97, 98
JElementMenus class, using 98, 99
methods 418
properties 418
using 98
JError class
methods 388
JFactory class
methods 428
JFile class
about 351
copy() method 352
delete() method 353
exists() method 352
getExt() method 351
getName() method 351
makeSafe() method 351
move() method 352
read() method 353
upload() method 353
write() method 353
JFolder class
about 347
copy() method 348
create() method 348
delete() method 348
exists() method 347
files() method 350
folders() method 349
listFolderTree() method 350
makeSafe() method 347

move() method 348
JLanguage class
constructors 411
methods 412
properties 411
JLanguageHelper class
methods 416
JLog class
about 361
addEntry() method 362, 363
exploring, to handle global error log file 361
getInstance() method 361
JMail class
about 294
constructors 425
JMail object, accessing 294
methods 425
JMailHelper class
methods 427
JMenu class
constructors 439
methods 439
properties 438
JModel
search, implementing 239, 240
JModel class
constructors 372
methods 372
properties 372
JObject class
constructors 366
methods 367
properties 366
Joomla!
access control 323
Access Objects types 325
ADOdb emulating 51
API 277
application 17
attacks 327
browser list 187
CGI request data, dealing with 315
classes 27, 339, 365
coding standards, phpDocumentor 36 - 38
component backend 214
component HTML layouts, building 212
components 65

components XML metadata files 248
configuration 455
core database 41
database 41
database, extending 42
database, querying 46
development tools 13
directory structure 24
document 17
document, modifying 258
document types 17
error handling 311
errors 312
extension manager 12
extensions, common functions 7
extension types 9
factory patterns 30
file system 345
history 8
itemized data 224
JavaScript effects, using 268
JDate class 340
JED 12
JError class 312
JLDAP class 290
JLog class 361
JMail class 294
JMailHelper class 296
JNode class 360
joomla.filesystem library 345
joomla.html library 193
JoomlaCode.org 13
JPagination class 224
JRegistry class 174
JRequest class 315
JTable class 52
JTree class 359
libraries 26
menu item parameters, using 257
module design 115
modules 115
mootools 268
MVC 68
output, rendering 193
overview 7
parameters 452
parameters, types 252

patterns 30
PEAR coding standards, used 36
plugins 133
predefined constants 32
redirects 245 - 248
request 18
requirements 9
security 311
sessions 31
templates 212, 213
translating 264
URI structure 22
utilities 339
web service, building 301
XML parsers 278

Joomla!, multilingual support
Unicode character set, using 34
UTF-8 encoding, using 34
UTF-8 string handling 34

Joomla!, requirements
JSAS 9
XAMPP 9

joomla.filesystem library
parts 345

joomla.html library
about 193
basic types 193
basic types, description 195
behavior, grouped types 196
calender, types 196
date, types 195
email, grouped types 200
grid, grouped types 200
grouped types 194
iframe, types 195
image, grouped types 203
image, types 195
importing 194
link, types 195
list, grouped types 204
menu, grouped types 208
select, grouped types 209
tooltip, types 196

JoomlaCode.org
tools 13

JPagination class
attribute, using 225

attributes 224
getState() method 226
getTotal() method 225

JPane
about 268

JParameter class
about 96
constructors 419
def() method 161
get() method 161
methods 161, 420
properties 419
set() method 161

JPath class
about 345
canChmod() method 347
check() method 345
clean() method 345
find() method 345
getPermissions() method 346
isOwner() method 347
setPermissions() method 346

JPathway class
methods 441
properties 441

JPlugin class
parameters, accessing 161

JRegistry class
about 174
constructors 431
INI file, loading 175
methods 431
PHP class, exporting settings to 176
properties 431
registry tree 176
registry values, saving and loading 175

JRoute class
methods 438

JSession class
constructors 434
methods 435
properties 434

JTable
about 52
check() method, overriding 52
constructor, defining 52
CRUD 54

fields, manipulating 58
public properties, defining 52
subclasses, creating 52, 53

JTable class
constructors 383
methods 384
properties 383

JText class
methods 417

JTree class
about 359
addChild() method 359
getParent() method 360
reset() method 360

JURI class
constructors 407
methods 407
properties 407

JUser class
constructors 369
methods 369
properties 368

JView class
constructors 375
methods 375
properties 375

L

LDAP
about 290
Distinguished Name 292
JLDAP class 290
LDAP objects, searching 293
LDAP server, binding 292
LDAP server, connecting 291
LDAP server, interrogating 291
Organization Units 292

libraries
about 26
base libraries 26
importing 26

LightWeight Directory Application
     Protocol. *See* **LDAP**

listeners
about 138
class, building 139

registering 138
log files 361

M

menu item access control 325
menu parameters, categories
  advanced parameters 255, 256
  component parameters 253
  state parameters 253
  system parameters 252
  system parameters, list 257
  URL parameters 254, 255
Model View Controller. *See* **MVC**
module
  about 115
  components, working with 118
  designing 115
  helpers 121
  packaging 127
  parameters 120
  standalone modules 117
  templates 124
module, packaging
  XML manifest file 127
  XML manifest file, tags 128
module design
  backend module, installing process 116
  backend module display positions 119
  blank module, creating 115
  frontend module, installing process 115, 116
  frontend module display positions 119
  module, packaging 127
  modules, executing 116
  module settings 120
  sandbox, setting up 115
  standalone modules 117
  translating 126
module layouts. *See* **templates**
mootools
  about 268
  Fx.Slide effect 271 - 275
  pane 268
  pane, elements 268
  pane, implementing 268
  pane, types 268
  tooltips 269

tooltips, modifying 270
tooltips, types 269, 270
multilingual support
  strings, translating 34
MVC
  about 68
  backend structure 67
  component building 82 - 86
  component root file, altering 85
  controller 69
  controller, building 78 - 81
  controller, implementing 83
  design pattern 68
  design pattern, parts 68
  frontend structure 67
  getInstance() method, implementing 84, 85
  getmethods, implementing 72
  model 69
  model, building 70 - 74
   multiple controllers, dealing with 83
  structure 67
  view 69
  view, building 75 - 77
  view, implementing for html document
      type 75

O

Organization Units 292
OUs. *See* **Organization Units**

P

page, customizing
  about 243
  application message queue 243, 244
  document, modifying 258
  JavaScript effects, using 268
  translating 264
pagination
  about 224
  footer 224
parameters
  about 95, 120
  accessing 121
  groups 120
  menu item, creating 253
  menu item parameters, using 257, 258

menu parameters 252
menu parameters, categories 252
predefined types 95
simple parameters, adding 120
types 252
parsing 278 - 282
pathway, handling
JPathway object, used 259 - 261
patterns, Joomla!
Design patterns 30
iterator patterns 30
PHP
arrays 355
phpDocumentor, coding standards 36 - 38
plugins. *See also* **group, plugins**
about 133
designing 133
element 135
element names 135
events 136
events, handling 138 - 140
events handling, observer pattern used 133
groups 134, 141
language files, loading 159
listeners 138
listeners, registering 138
loading 155, 156
loading from group foobar 155
myimport() function, creating 157
myimport() function, using 157
packaging 161
parameters 160
sandbox, setting up 134
settings, dealing with 160
simple parameters, adding 160
translating 159
translation files, creating 159
using, as libraries 156
plugins, packaging
file naming conflicts 165
XML manifest file 162
XML manifest file, tags 162
predefined constants
about 32
date constants 33
path constants 32

Q

query value
format 22
Itemid 22
option 22
task 22

R

redirects
about 245
common uses 247
component XML metadata files 248
layout XML metadata files 250
need for 245
Regular Expressions
about 320
matching 322
pattern delimiters 320
pattern duplicating, quantifiers used 320,
321
pattern modifiers 321
patterns 320
patterns, shorcuts 321
replacing 323
request
backend request 18
frontend request 18
methods 29
process 18
working with 29
results, processing methods
loadAssoc( ) method 48
loadAssocList( ) method 49
loadObject( ) method 49
loadObjectList( ) method 50
loadResult( ) method 48
loadResultArray( ) method 48
loadRow( ) method 50
loadRowList( ) method 51

S

schema example
table 44
search plugins
about 151

onSearchAreas event 151
onSearchAreas event, triggering 151
onSearch event 151
security 311
sessions 31, 32
string handling
  PHP string functions 35
strings, translating
  JText class, methods 34
  JText class, used 34
system plugins
  about 152
  events 152
  onAfterDispatch event 152
  onAfterInitialise event 152
  onAfterRender event 152
  onAfterRoute event 152

T

templates
  about 124, 212
  handling 125
  iterative templates 213
  media 126
  rules 212
translating
  translating text 264
  translations, debugging 267
  translations, defining 265, 266
tree
  about 359
  creating 359
  root node 359

U

URI
  JRoute method, advantages 23
  outputting, JRoute method,using 23
  query element 22
  query value 22
  structure 22
user
  about 177
  attributes 177
  JUser object, accessing 178
  parameter attributes 178

user parameters
  about 178
  accessing 178
  common design issue, dealing with 179
  exploring 180 - 183
  user time zone, determining 178
  user timezone value, modifying 178
  ways of implementing 179
user plugins
  about 152
  onAfterDeleteUser event 154
  onAfterStoreUser event 153
  onBeforeDeleteUser event 154
  onBeforeStoreUser event 153
  onLoginFailure event 154
  onLoginUser event 154
  onLogoutUser event 154

W

web services
  about 277
  email 294
web sevices APIs
  about 299
  list 299
  Yahoo! Search, creating 299
  Yahoo! Search API 299

X

XML
  about 277
  data, interrogating 279
  document, constucting 277
  editing 282
  loading from a file 278
  parsing 278
  parsing, JSimpleXML parser used 279
  saving 283
  XML declaration 277
XML-RPC plugins
  about 155, 301
  add() method, implementing 305
  array, building and returning 303
  array,keys used 304
  compound data types 302
  foobar, creating 302, 303

onGetWebServices event 155
parts, event handler 155
parts, static class 155
simple data types 302
subtract() method, implementing 305
variables global, declaring 303

XML manifest file, tags
administration 105
author 105, 128, 162
authorEmail 105, 128, 162
authorUrl 105, 128, 163
copyright 105
copyright) 128, 163
description 106, 128, 163
filename 106, 129, 163
files 106, 129, 163
folder 106, 129, 163
install 106
install (root tag) 105, 128, 162
installfile 107
language 107, 129, 163

languages 107, 129, 164
license 107
lincense 129, 164
media 107, 130, 164
menu 108
name 108, 130, 164
param 108, 130, 164
params 108, 130, 164
queries 108
query 109
sql 109
submenu 109
uninstall 109
uninstallfile 109
version 109, 164
versionVersion 130

XML parsers
about 278
JSimpleXML parser 278
types 278

XSS 331

Thank you for buying
Mastering Joomla! 1.5 Extension and Framework Development

Packt Open Source Project Royalties

When we sell a book written on an Open Source project, we pay a royalty directly to that project. Therefore by purchasing Mastering Joomla! 1.5 Extension and Framework Development, Packt will have given some of the money received to the Joomla! project.

In the long term, we see ourselves and you—customers and readers of our books—as part of the Open Source ecosystem, providing sustainable revenue for the projects we publish on. Our aim at Packt is to establish publishing royalties as an essential part of the service and support a business model that sustains Open Source.

If you're working with an Open Source project that you would like us to publish on, and subsequently pay royalties to, please get in touch with us.

Writing for Packt

We welcome all inquiries from people who are interested in authoring. Book proposals should be sent to authors@packtpub.com. If your book idea is still at an early stage and you would like to discuss it first before writing a formal book proposal, contact us; one of our commissioning editors will get in touch with you.

We're not just looking for published authors; if you have strong technical skills but no writing experience, our experienced editors can help you develop a writing career, or simply get some additional reward for your expertise.

About Packt Publishing

Packt, pronounced 'packed', published its first book "Mastering phpMyAdmin for Effective MySQL Management" in April 2004 and subsequently continued to specialize in publishing highly focused books on specific technologies and solutions.

Our books and publications share the experiences of your fellow IT professionals in adapting and customizing today's systems, applications, and frameworks. Our solution-based books give you the knowledge and power to customize the software and technologies you're using to get the job done. Packt books are more specific and less general than the IT books you have seen in the past. Our unique business model allows us to bring you more focused information, giving you more of what you need to know, and less of what you don't.

Packt is a modern, yet unique publishing company, which focuses on producing quality, cutting-edge books for communities of developers, administrators, and newbies alike. For more information, please visit our website: www.PacktPub.com.

PUBLISHING

Learning Joomla! 1.5

Learning Joomla! 1.5 Extension Development

ISBN: 978-1-847191-30-4   Paperback: 200 pages

A practical tutorial for creating your first Joomla! 1.5 extensions with PHP

1. Program your own extensions to Joomla!

2. Create new, self-contained components with both back-end and front-end functionality

3. Create configurable site modules to show information on every page

4. Distribute your extensions to other Joomla! users

Joomla! Cash

Joomla! Cash

ISBN: 978-1-847191-40-3   Paperback: 160 pages

Money-making weapons for your Joomla! website

1. Learn to set up a cash-generating Joomla! website

2. Learn to implement a shopping cart on Joomla!

3. How to run an affiliate program from your site

4. Set up streams of income using Joomla!

5. Gain valuable search-engine ranking knowledge

Please check **www.PacktPub.com** for information on our titles

Printed in the United States
201327BV00020B/11/A